Visual QuickStart Guide

Mac OS X 10.1

Maria Langer

Peachpit Press

Visual QuickStart Guide

Mac OS X 10.1

Maria Langer

Peachpit Press
1249 Eighth Street
Berkeley, CA 94710
510-524-2178 • 800-283-9444
510-524-2221 (fax)

Find us on the World Wide Web at: http://www.peachpit.com/

Peachpit Press is a division of Pearson Education

Editor: Clifford Colby
Technical Editor: Victor Gavenda
Indexer: Emily Glossbrenner
Cover Design: The Visual Group
Production: Maria Langer, Connie Jeung-Mills

Colophon

This book was produced with Adobe inDesign 2.0 and Adobe PhotoShop 5.5 on a Power Macintosh G4. The fonts used were Utopia, Meta Plus, and PIXymbols Command. Screenshots were created using Snapz Pro X on a Strawberry iMac and Power Macintosh G4.

ISBN 0-321-11631-3

9 8 7 6 5 4 3 2 1

Printed and bound in the United States of America.

Dedication

To John Jones,

one of the nicest people I have the pleasure to call a friend.

Thanks!

To Cliff Colby, for his guidance during the preparation of this seventh edition of my Mac OS VQS. Cliff helped me decide what topics should be added to beef up this book after many topics were removed for inclusion in *Mac OS X Advanced: Visual QuickPro Guide*. And many congratulations to Cliff and his wife on the birth of their second son just as this book project was wrapping up.

To Nancy Ruenzel, Marjorie Baer, and the other powers-that-be at Peachpit Press, for giving me the opportunity to revise and expand *Mac OS X: Visual QuickStart Guide* for the new features in Mac OS X 10.1.

To Connie Jeung-Mills, for yet another smooth project.

To the rest of the folks at Peachpit Press, for doing what they do so well.

To Apple Computer, Inc., for continuing to refine the world's best operating system.

And to Mike, for the usual reasons.

www.marialanger.com

Table of Contents

Introduction to Mac OS X

Figure 1 The About This Mac window for Mac OS X 10.1.3.

Introduction

Mac OS X 10.1 (**Figure 1**) is the latest version of the computer operating system that put the phrase *graphic user interface* in everyone's vocabulary. With Mac OS, you can point, click, and drag to work with files, applications, and utilities. Because the same intuitive interface is utilized throughout the system, you'll find that a procedure that works in one program works in virtually all the others.

This Visual QuickStart Guide will help you learn Mac OS X 10.1 by providing step-by-step instructions, plenty of illustrations, and a generous helping of tips. On these pages, you'll find everything you need to know to get up and running quickly with Mac OS X—and more!

This book was designed for page flipping. Use the thumb tabs, index, or table of contents to find the topics for which you need help. If you're brand new to Mac OS, however, I recommend that you begin by reading at least the first two chapters. In them, you'll find basic information about techniques you'll use every day with your computer.

If you're interested in information about new Mac OS X features, be sure to browse through this **Introduction**. It'll give you a good idea of what you can expect to see on your computer.

✔ Tips

- The "X" in "Mac OS X" is pronounced "ten."
- When you're finished with the basics covered in this book and are ready for some more advanced information about Mac OS X, check out *Mac OS X Advanced: Visual QuickPro Guide*.

New Features in Mac OS X

Mac OS X is a major revision to the Macintosh operating system. Not only does it add and update features, but in many cases, it completely changes the way tasks are done. With a slick new look called "Aqua" (**Figure 2**) and with preemptive multitasking and protected memory that make the computer work more quickly and reliably, Mac OS X is like a breath of fresh air for Macintosh users.

Here's a look at some of the new and revised features you can expect to find in Mac OS X.

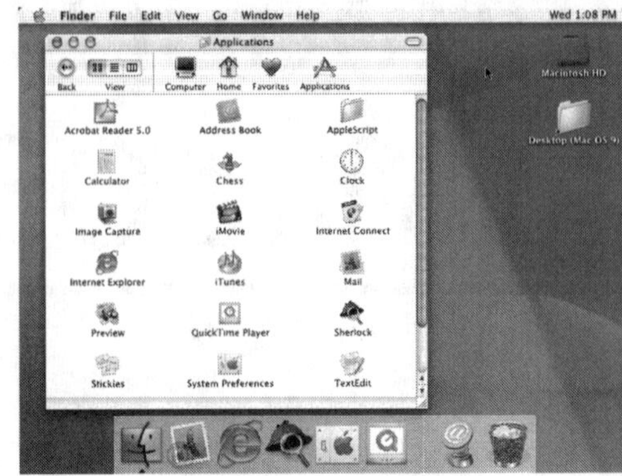

Figure 2 A look at the Aqua interface.

✔ Tips

- Many of these features are covered in this book. Others are covered in *Mac OS X Advanced: Visual QuickPro Guide*.
- *Preemptive multitasking* and *protected memory* are defined and discussed in **Chapter 5**.
- This section discusses the new features in the original release of Mac OS X. New features in Mac OS X 10.1 are covered later in this **Introduction**.

Installer Changes

- The Mac OS X installer automatically launches when you start from the Mac OS X install CD.
- The installer offers fewer customization features for installation.
- The Mac OS X Setup Assistant, which runs automatically after the installer restarts the computer, has a new look and offers several new options.

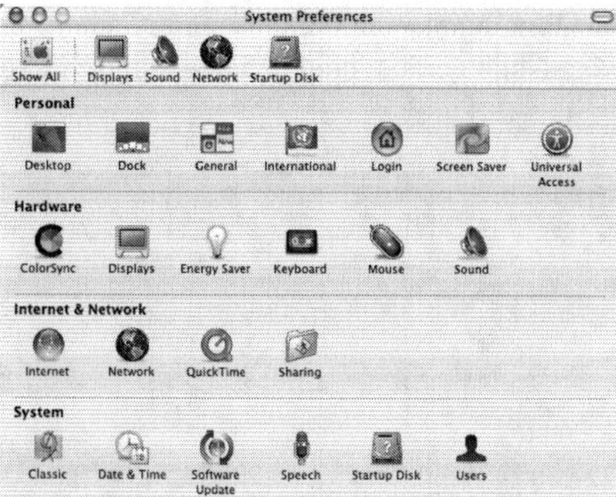

Figure 3 The System Preferences application. In Mac OS X 10.1, preferences are organized logically by function, as shown here.

System Changes

- System extensions and control panels no longer exist.
- By default, Mac OS X is set up for multiple users, making it possible for several people to set up personalized work environments on the same computer without the danger of accessing, changing, or deleting another user's files.
- A new Log Out command enables you to end your work session without shutting down the computer.
- A new System Preferences application (**Figure 3**) enables you to set options for the way the computer works.
- The default system font has been changed to Lucida Grande.
- Finder icons have a new "photo-illustrative" look (**Figure 2**).
- A new, customizable Dock (**Figure 2**) enables you to launch and switch applications.

Window Changes

- Finder windows offer a new column view (**Figure 4**). Button view is no longer available.
- Pop-up windows and spring-loaded folders are no longer supported.
- Window controls have been changed (**Figure 4**). The left end of a window's title bar now includes Close, Minimize, and Zoom buttons.
- *Drawers* (**Figure 5**) are subwindows that slide out the side of a window to offer more options.
- Document windows for different applications each reside on their own layer, making it possible for them to be intermingled. (This differs from previous versions of Mac OS which required all document windows for an application to be grouped together.)
- You can often activate items on an inactive window or dialog with a single click rather than clicking first to activate the window, then clicking again to activate the item.

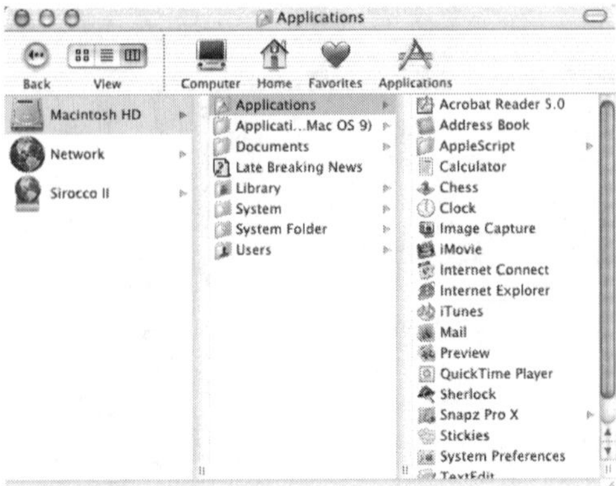

Figure 4 A window in column view.

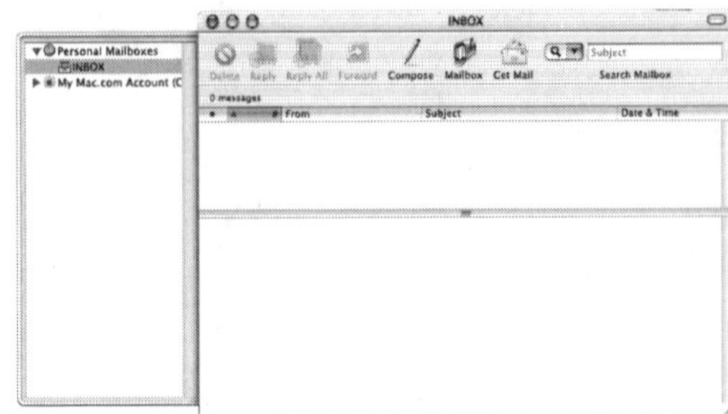

Figure 5 The Mail application utilizes the drawer interface.

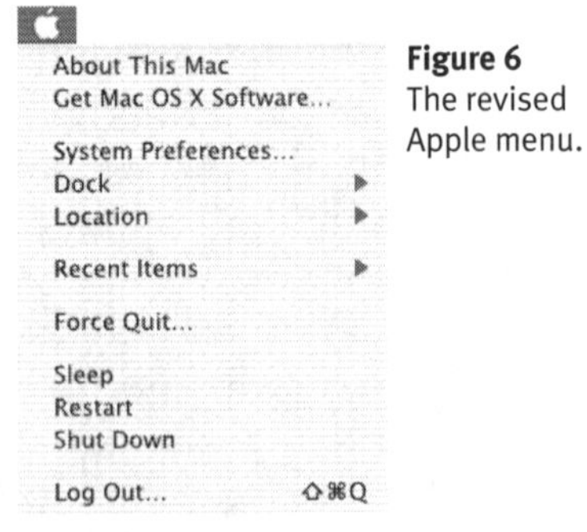

Figure 6 The revised Apple menu.

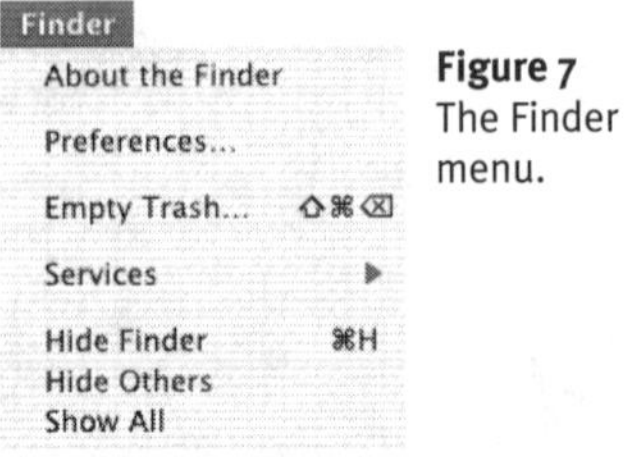

Figure 7 The Finder menu.

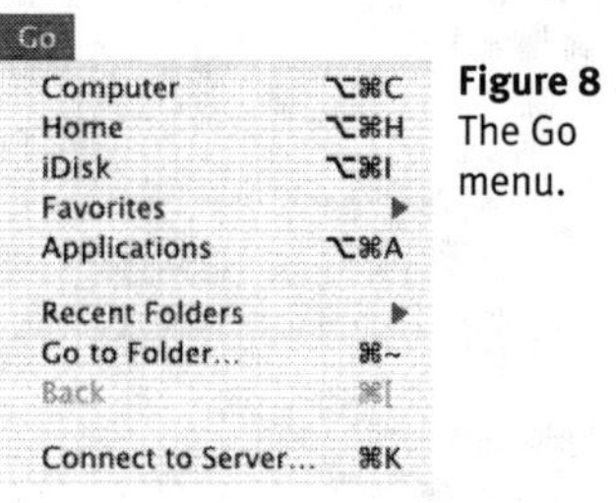

Figure 8 The Go menu.

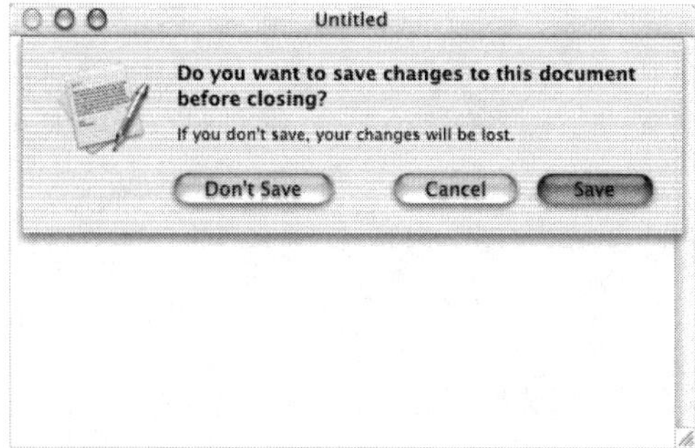

Figure 9 A dialog sheet is attached to a window.

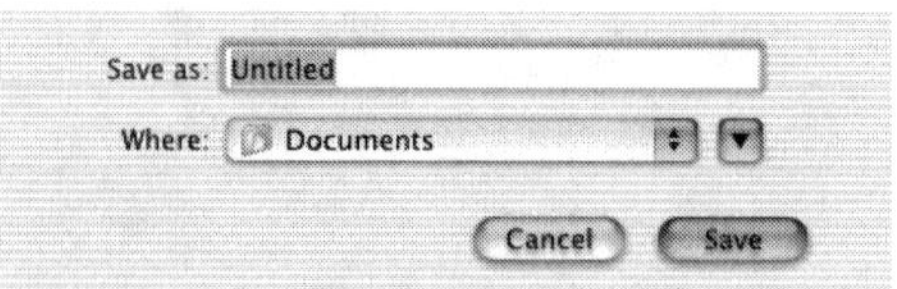

Figure 10 The Save Location dialog box collapsed to show only the bare essentials...

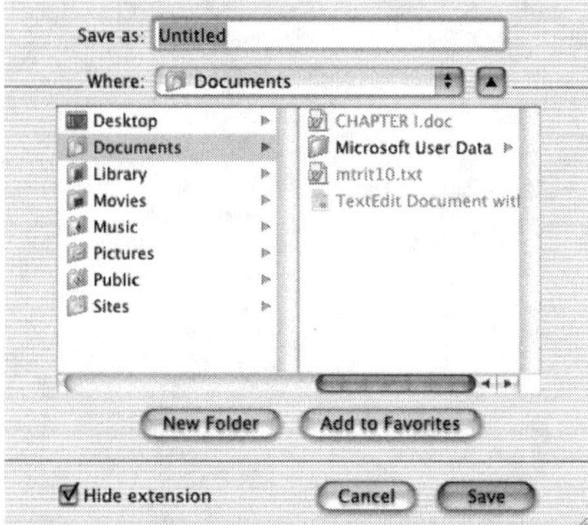

Figure 11 ...and expanded to show everything you need to save a file.

Menu Changes

- Menus are now translucent so you can see underlying windows right through them.
- Sticky menus no longer disappear after a certain amount of time. When you click a menu's title, the menu appears and stays visible until you either click a command or click elsewhere onscreen.
- The Apple menu, which is no longer customizable, includes commands that work in all applications (**Figure 6**).
- A number of commands have been moved to the revised Apple menu (**Figure 6**) and new Finder menu (**Figure 7**). There are also new commands and new keyboard equivalents throughout the Finder.
- A new Go menu (**Figure 8**) makes it quick and easy to open windows for specific locations, including favorite and recent folders.

Dialog Changes

- Dialogs can now appear as *sheets* that slide down from a window's title bar and remain part of the window (**Figure 9**). You can switch to another document or application when a dialog sheet is displayed.
- The Open and Save Location dialogs have been revised.
- The Save Location dialog can appear either collapsed (**Figure 10**) or expanded (**Figure 11**).

Application Changes

- Applications that are not Mac OS X compatible run in the *Classic environment,* which utilizes Mac OS 9.1
- The list of applications and utilities that come with Mac OS has undergone extensive changes to add and remove many programs.

Help Changes

- Balloon Help has been replaced with Help Tags (**Figure 12**).
- The Help Viewer offers more options for searching and following links.
- Guide Help is no longer available.

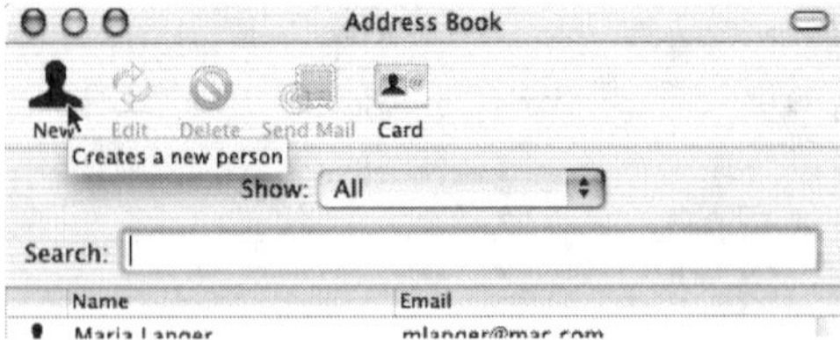

Figure 12 Help Tags replace Balloon Help.

New Features in Mac OS X 10.1

Mac OS X 10.1, the first major Mac OS X revision, which was released in Autumn of 2001, improves performance and features. Here's a quick summary of some of the changes.

✔ Tip

- Subsequent "maintenance" updates to Mac OS X 10.1 have been released. (Mac OS X 10.1.2 and 10.1.3 were used when writing this book.) These updates improve the performance, reliability, and compatibility of Mac OS, but generally do not change the way Mac OS looks or works. If you have a connection to the Internet, you can install these updates using Software Update; I explain how in **Chapter 1**.

Performance improvements

- Apple programmers tweaked Mac OS X to make it faster and more responsive. Improved performance is most noticeable when launching applications, resizing or moving windows, displaying menus, and choosing menu commands.
- OpenGL, which is responsible for 3D graphics, is 20 percent faster. It also has full support for the nViDIA GeForce 3 graphics card.

Finder & Aqua enhancements

- The columns in the Finder's list views can be resized by dragging the column border (**Figure 13**).
- Long file names in the Finder's icon view wrap to a second line (**Figure 14**).
- Arrows now appears to the right of folder names in the Finder's column view (**Figure 4**). This makes it easy to distinguish between folders and files in column view.
- File name extensions are turned off by default. You can display the extension for a file by setting an option in its Info window (**Figure 15**) or in the Finder Preferences window (**Figure 16**).
- You can now customizethe Dock to display it on the left, right, or bottom of the screen.
- The new Burn Disc command makes it quick and easy to create data CDs from within the Finder (**Figure 17**).

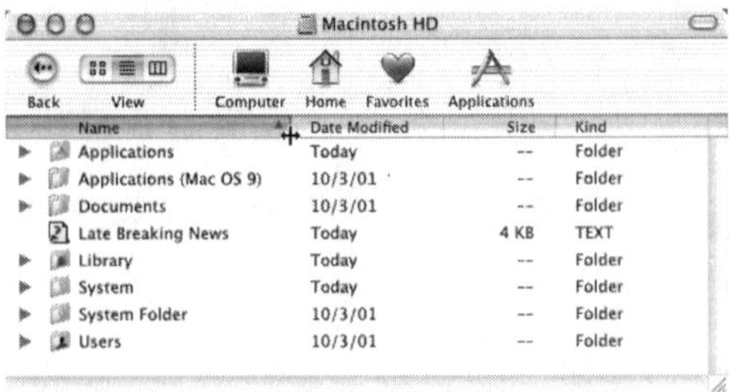

Figure 13 You can now change a column's width by dragging its border.

Figure 14 In icon view, long document names wrap to a second line.

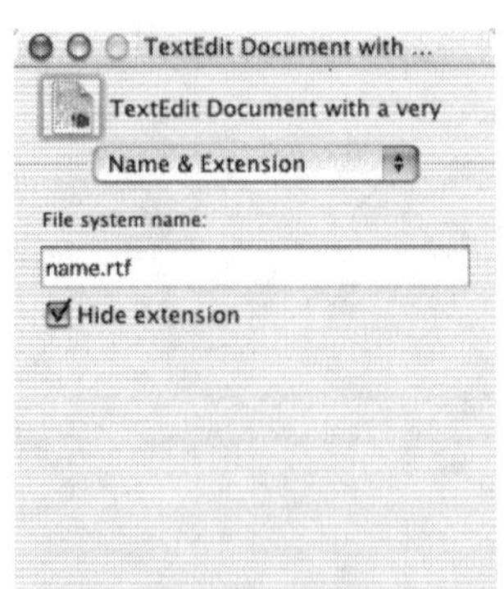

Figure 15 The Name & Extension options in a document's Info window.

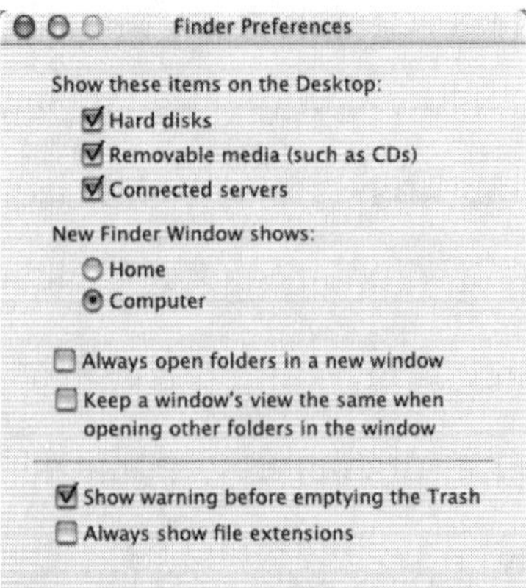

Figure 16 You can use Finder Preferences to specify whether extensions should show.

NEW FEATURES IN MAC OS X 10.1

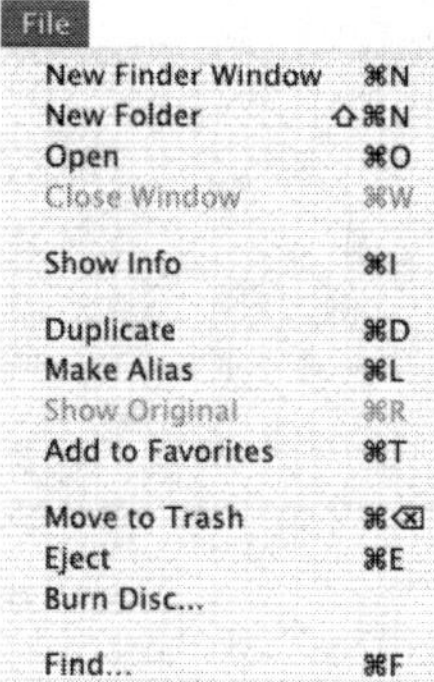

Figure 17 The Finder's File menu now includes a Burn Disc command.

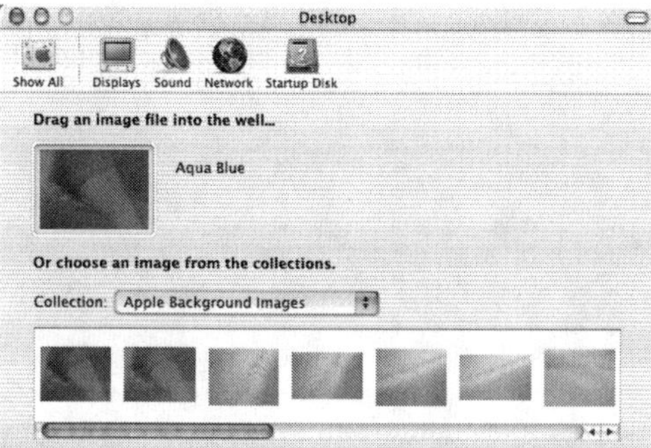

Figure 18 you can use the new Desktop preferences pane to choose a background image.

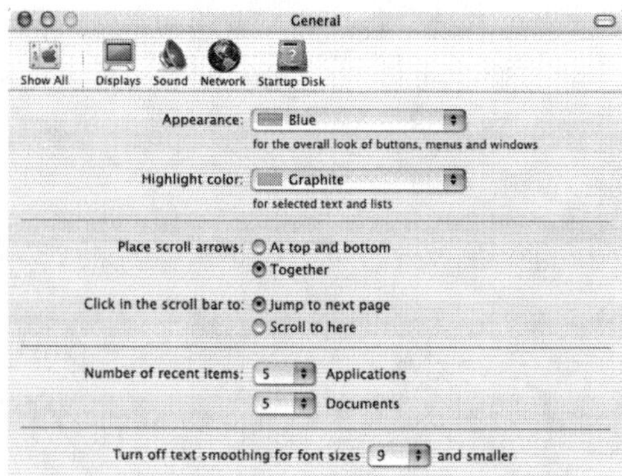

Figure 19 The General preferences pane now enables you to specify how many recent items should appear on the Apple menu.

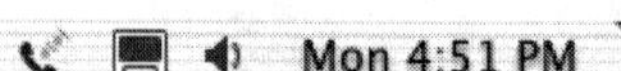

Figure 20 You can add menus for controlling various preferences. This example shows Modem, Displays, Sound, and Date & Time (the menu bar clock) options.

System Preferences improvements

- The System Preferences pane's icons are now organized logically by use (**Figure 3**).
- The Desktop preferences pane, which is brand new in Mac OS X 10.1, enables you to set a desktop picture (**Figure 18**). (This functionality was moved from Finder Preferences.)
- The General preferences pane now enables you to set how many recent items should appear on the Apple menu. It also enables you to set a font size threshold for the font smoothing feature (**Figure 19**).
- The Sound preferences pane enables you to select different settings for each output device.
- The Date & Time preferences pane enables you to display the menu bar clock as an analog clock.
- You can now display controls for a variety of System Preferences right in the menu bar (**Figure 20**). You specify whether you want to show or hide the controls in the applicable preferences pane.

Printing improvements

- Mac OS X 10.1 ships with over 200 PostScript printer description files, including files from Hewlett-Packard, Lexmark, and Xerox.
- In most cases, the driver for a USB printer will automatically be selected when the printer is added to the Print Center.

Networking improvements

- Mac OS X is now more compatible with network systems, including AppleShare, Windows NT, Windows 2000, and SAMBA.
- Mac OS X 10.1 now fully supports AirPort, with the AirPort Admin Utility and the AirPort Setup Assistant.

Application improvements

- Mac OS X 10.1 includes Java 2 for up-to-date Java compatibility.
- Internet Explorer 5.1 fully supports Java within the Web browser.
- iTunes now includes CD burning capabilities so you can create music CDs from your iTunes libraries.
- The new DVD Player application enables you to watch DVD movies on computers with DVD-ROM drives or SuperDrives.
- iDVD 2 includes many enhancements for creating your own DVD discs on SuperDrive-equipped Macs, including background encoding.
- AppleScript is now fully supported by Mac OS X. In fact, the Mac OS X 10.1 Finder is more scriptable than ever.

Setting Up Mac OS X 10.1

1

Setting Up Mac OS X 10.1

Before you can use Mac OS X, you must install it on your computer and configure it to work the way you need it to. The steps you need to complete to do this depend on the software currently installed in your computer.

1. If Mac OS 9.0.4 or earlier is installed on your computer, use the Mac OS 9.1 installer to update to Mac OS 9.1. Then restart your computer and use the Mac OS Setup Assistant to configure Mac OS 9.1. You can skip this step if Mac OS 9.1 or 9.2 is already installed and configured on your computer.
2. Use the Mac OS X installer to install Mac OS X. Then restart your computer and use the Mac OS Setup Assistant to configure Mac OS X. You can skip this step if Mac OS X or Mac OS X 10.1 is already installed and configured on your computer.
3. Use the Mac OS X 10.1 updater to update to Mac OS X 10.1. You can skip this step if Mac OS 10.1 is already installed on your computer.
4. Use the Mac OS 9.2 updater to update the Classic environment. You can skip this step if Mac OS 9.2 is already installed on your computer.

This chapter explains how to complete all of these steps, so you can properly install and configure Mac OS X and the Classic environment on your computer.

✔ Tips

- I explain how to determine which versions of Mac OS are installed on your computer on the next page.
- The Classic environment, which enables you to run Mac OS 9.x applications, is discussed in **Chapter 5**.

Determining Which Mac OS Versions Are Installed

In order to know what installation and configuration steps you need to perform, you must first learn which versions of Mac OS are installed. There are several ways to do this; the easiest is to consult the Startup Disk control panel (on Mac OS 9.2 or earlier) or the Startup Disk pane of System Preferences (on Mac OS X or later).

✔ Tips

- If your computer is brand new and you haven't started it yet, chances are you have Mac OS X 10.1 and Mac OS 9.2 (or later versions of each) installed. When you start your computer, it'll display the Mac OS Setup assistant. Skip ahead to the section titled "Configuring Mac OS X 10.1" later in this chapter.
- A quick way to tell whether your computer is currently running Mac OS 9.2 or earlier or Mac OS X or later is to consult the Apple menu icon on the far left end of the menu bar. A six-color apple appears on Mac OS 9.2 or earlier; a blue 3-D looking apple appears on Mac OS X or later.

To check the Startup Disk control panel on Mac OS 9.2 or earlier

1. Choose Apple > Control Panels > Startup Disk (**Figure 1**) to display the Startup disk control panel.
2. If necessary, click the triangle beside the name of your hard disk to display the System folders installed on your computer (**Figures 2** and **3**). The Version column indicates which versions of Mac OS are installed.
3. Click the Startup Disk control panel's close box to dismiss it.

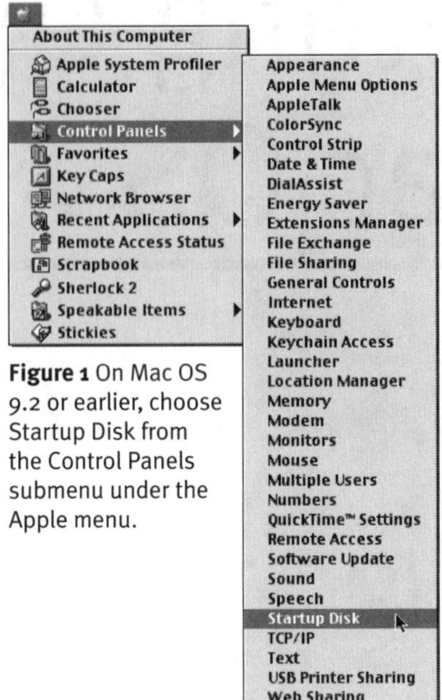

Figure 1 On Mac OS 9.2 or earlier, choose Startup Disk from the Control Panels submenu under the Apple menu.

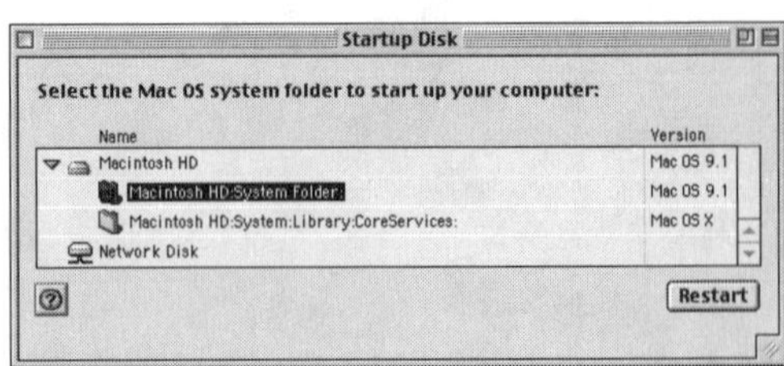

Figure 2 Here's what the Startup Disk control panel might look like with Mac OS 9.1 and Mac OS X installed...

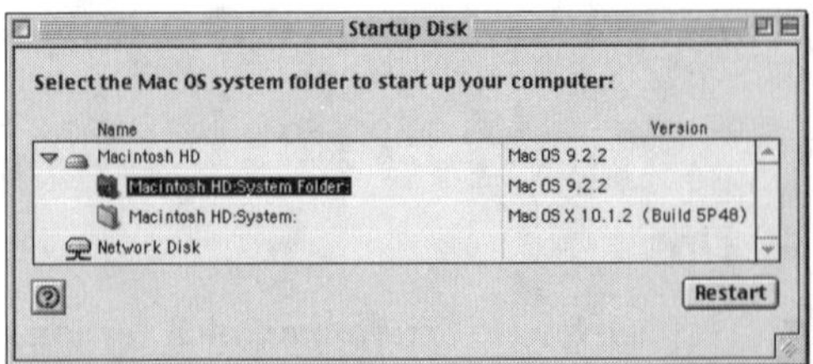

Figure 3 ... and here's what the Startup Disk control panel might look like with Mac OS 9.2.2 and Mac OS X 10.1.2 installed.

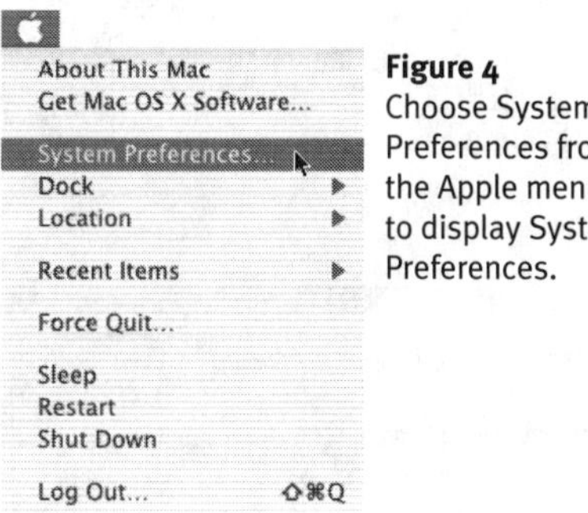

Figure 4 Choose System Preferences from the Apple menu to display System Preferences.

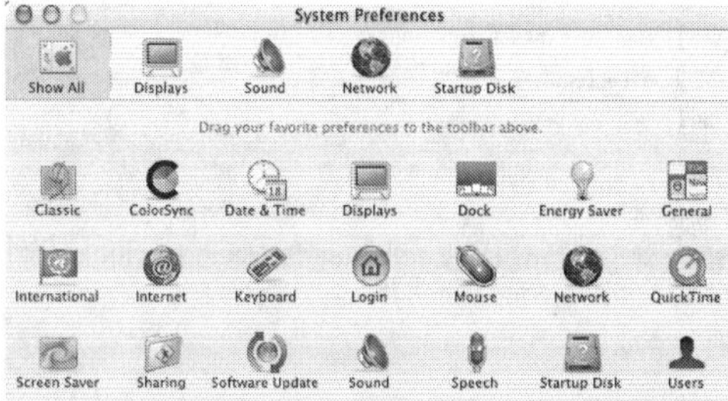

Figure 5 The System Preferences window looks like this in Mac OS X....

Figure 6 ... and like this in Mac OS X 10.1.

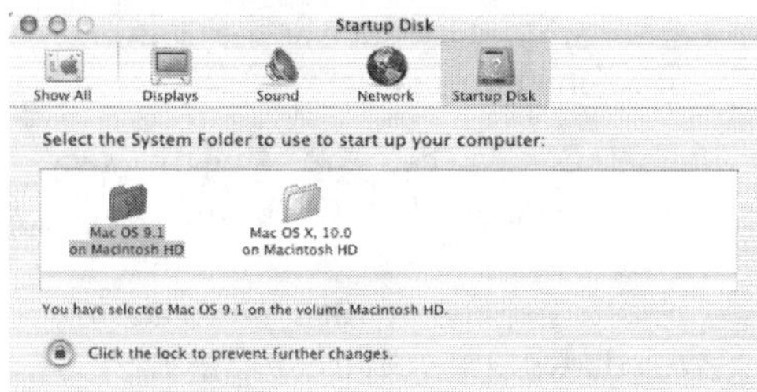

Figure 7 Here's what the Startup Disk pane might look like with Mac OS 9.1 and Mac OS X installed ...

To check the Startup Disk preferences pane on Mac OS X or later

1. Choose Apple > System Preferences (**Figure 4**) to display the System Preferences window (**Figures 5** and **6**).
2. Click the Startup Disk icon to display the Startup Disk pane (**Figures 7** and **8**). The installed versions of Mac OS appear beneath each System folder icon.
3. Choose System Prefs > Quit System Prefs (**Figure 9**) or press ⌘Q to dismiss System Preferences.

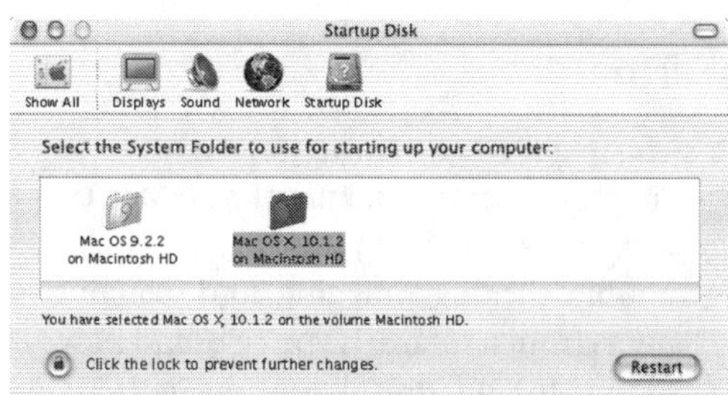

Figure 8 ... and here's what it might look like with Mac OS 9.2.2 and Mac OS X 10.1.2 installed.

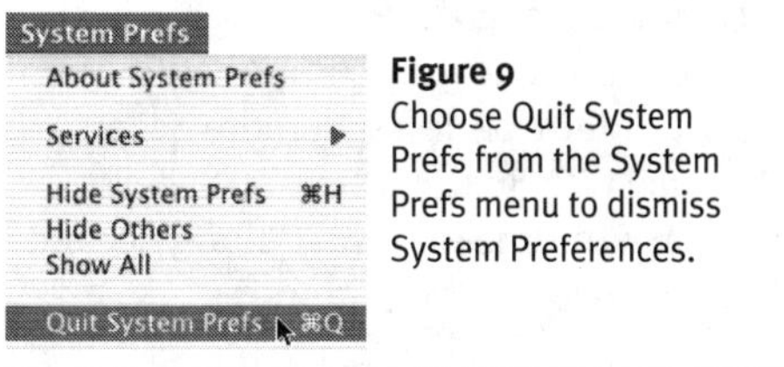

Figure 9 Choose Quit System Prefs from the System Prefs menu to dismiss System Preferences.

The Mac OS 9.1 Installer

Mac OS 9.1 comes with an installer application that makes software installation easy. Simply launch the installer and follow the instructions that appear on screen to select a destination disk, learn more about the software, agree to a license agreement, and select the Mac OS 9.1 components you want installed. The installer builds the System and Finder files for your computer and copies the software you specified to your hard disk.

The Mac OS 9.1 installer can perform two types of installations:

- **Standard Installation** lets you select the Mac OS 9.1 components you want installed. The installer copies all standard parts of each selected component to your hard disk.
- **Customized Installation** lets you select the Mac OS 9.1 components you want installed and then lets you select the parts of each component to be installed.

The first part of this chapter explains how to use the Mac OS 9.1 installer to perform both a standard and a customized installation.

Figure 10 To launch the Mac OS 9.1 installer, double-click this icon.

Figure 11 The Mac OS 9.1 installer's Welcome window appears when you launch it.

✔ Tips

- The installation instructions in this chapter assume you know basic Mac OS techniques, such as pointing, clicking, double-clicking, dragging, and selecting items from a menu. If you're brand new to the Mac and don't know any of these techniques, skip ahead to **Chapter 2**, which discusses Mac OS basics.
- A standard installation of Mac OS 9.1 includes the following components: Mac OS 9.1, Internet Access, Remote Access, Personal Web Sharing, Text-to-Speech, Mac OS Runtime for Java, ColorSync, and English Speech Recognition.
- You can click the Go Back button at any time during installation to change options in a previous window.
- You can press Return or Enter to "click" a default button—a button with a dark border around it—such as the Continue button in **Figure 11**.
- Remember, you can skip using the Mac OS 9.1 installer if Mac OS 9.1 or later is already installed on your computer. Consult the section titled "Determining Which Mac OS Versions Are Installed" earlier in this chapter to see what is installed on your computer.

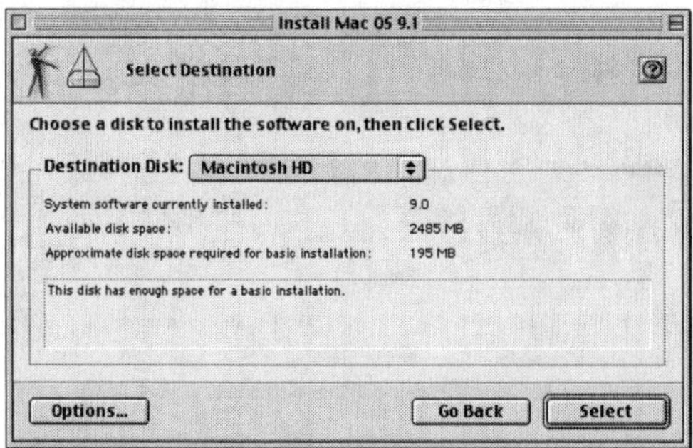

Figure 12 Use the Select Destination window to select the disk on which to install Mac OS 9.1.

Figure 13 Choose a disk from the Destination Disk pop-up menu.

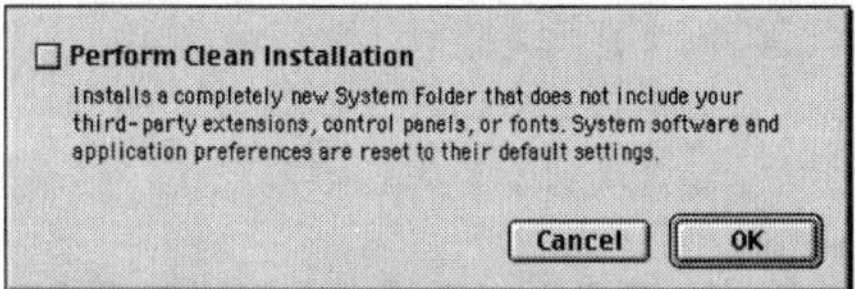

Figure 14 Turn on the Perform Clean Installation check box to create a brand new System Folder for Mac OS 9.1.

To launch the installer

1. Start your computer from the Mac OS 9.1 CD-ROM disc.

   or

   Start your computer the usual way and insert the Mac OS 9.1 CD-ROM disc.
2. Locate and double-click the Mac OS Install icon (**Figure 10**).
3. After a moment, the installer's Welcome window appears (**Figure 11**). Click Continue.

✔ Tip

- To start your computer from the Mac OS 9.1 CD-ROM disc, insert the disc, choose Special > Restart, and hold down C until the "Welcome to Mac OS" message appears. This is the recommended way to start your computer when installing OS software.

To select a destination disk

1. In the installer's Select Destination window (**Figure 12**), use the Destination Disk pop-up menu (**Figure 13**) to select the disk on which you want to install Mac OS 9.1.
2. Click Select.

✔ Tips

- Only those hard disks and removable high-capacity media (such as Zip and Jaz disks) that appear on your Desktop are listed in the Destination Disk pop-up menu (**Figure 13**).
- A status area beneath the Destination Disk pop-up menu indicates the version of Mac OS that is installed on the disk, as well as the available disk space and the amount of disk space required for a basic installation (**Figure 12**).
- To create a brand new System Folder for Mac OS 9.1, click the Options button. Turn on the Perform Clean Installation check box in the dialog that appears (**Figure 14**). The old System Folder is renamed "Previous System Folder," and you should delete it after you move non-Apple control panels, extensions, and preferences files to their proper locations in the new System Folder.

To read important information about Mac OS 9.1

1. Read the contents of the installer's Important Information window (**Figure 15**). Click the down arrow on the vertical scroll bar to scroll through the entire document.
2. When you have finished reading the information, click Continue.

✔ Tip

- Read the information in this window carefully! It provides important, late-breaking news about installing Mac OS, including compatibility information and special instructions not included in this book.

To read and agree to the Software License Agreement

1. If desired, choose a language from the pop-up menu at the top-right of the Software License Agreement window (**Figure 16**).
2. Read the contents of the window. Click the down arrow on the vertical scroll bar to scroll through the entire document.
3. When you have finished reading the agreement, click Continue.
4. A dialog appears, informing you that you must agree to the terms of the agreement you just read to continue (**Figure 17**). Click Agree.

✔ Tip

- If you click Disagree in step 4, the installer returns you to its Welcome window (**Figure 11**).

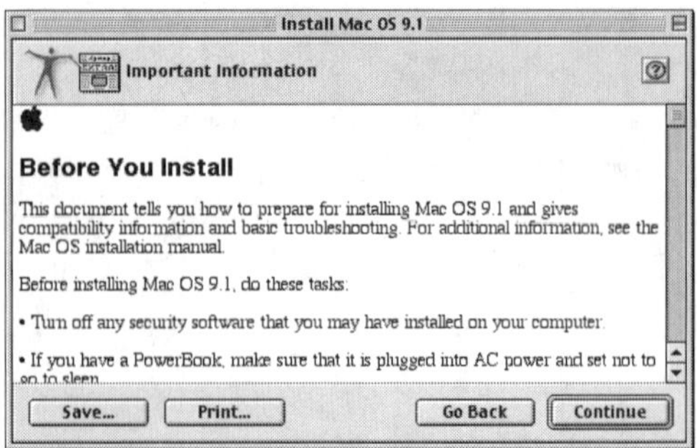

Figure 15 The Important Information window contains late-breaking news about installing Mac OS 9.1.

Figure 16 The Software License Agreement tells you exactly what you're allowed to do with Mac OS 9.1 software.

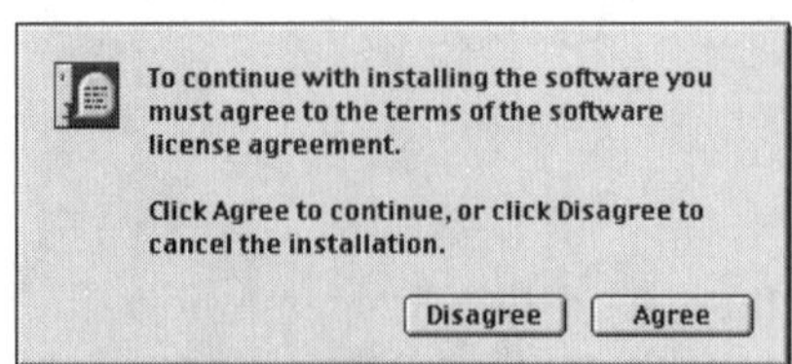

Figure 17 To complete the installation of Mac OS 9.1, you must click Agree in this dialog.

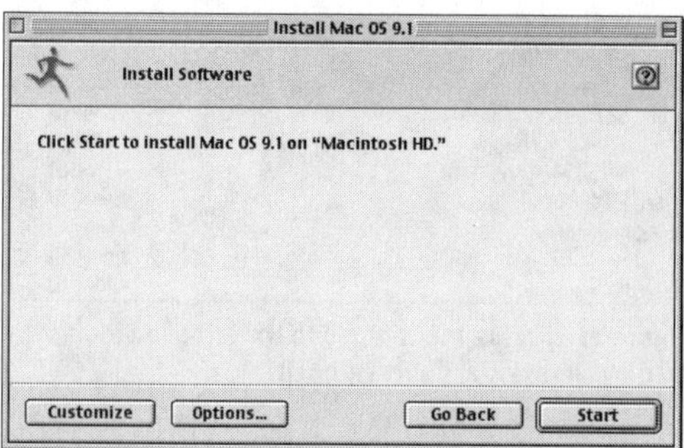

Figure 18 Use the Install Software window to select the Mac OS components you want to install.

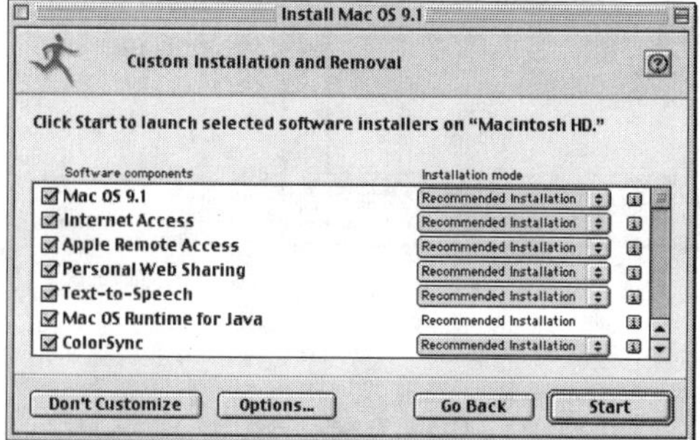

Figure 19 Use the Custom Installation and Removal window to select Mac OS 9.1 components for a custom installation.

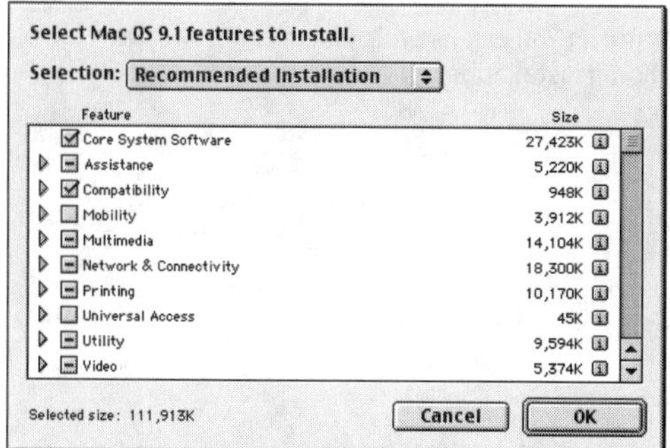

Figure 20 Windows like these enable you to select the parts of a specific component that you want to install.

To customize an installation

1. In the Install Software window (**Figure 18**), click the Customize button. The window changes to the Custom Installation and Removal window (**Figure 19**), which displays a list of software components.
2. Toggle the check box settings to turn on only those for the components you want to install. Be sure to click the down arrow at the bottom of the vertical scroll bar to view all the options.
3. If desired, choose an installation mode from the pop-up menu beside each checked component.
   - **Recommended Installation** installs the recommended parts of the component for your computer.
   - **Customized Installation** displays a dialog similar to the one in **Figure 20**. Use this option to specify which parts of the component should be installed, and click OK.

✔ Tips

- If you change your mind about making a custom installation, click the Don't Customize button (**Figure 19**) to go back to the Install Software window (**Figure 18**).
- To successfully use the Customized Installation option, you must be familiar with all parts of each component you want installed. This is a feature designed for Mac OS experts. If used improperly, it can cause erratic system behavior.
- You can click the triangle to the left of an item (**Figure 20**) to display individual items within it (**Figure 21**).
- You can click the info icon (or "i" button) to the right of an item to learn more about it (**Figure 22**). Click OK to dismiss the information dialog.

To set other installation options

1. Click the Options button in the Install Software or Custom Installation and Removal window to display a dialog like the one in **Figure 23**.
2. To prevent the installer from attempting to update the hard disk driver of the destination disk, turn off the Update Apple Hard Disk Driver check box.
3. To prevent the installer from creating an installation log file, turn off the Create Installation Report check box.
4. Click OK.

✔ Tips

- As shown in **Figure 23**, both of these options are enabled by default. If you're not sure how to set these options, leave them both turned on.
- If you're not sure what to do in step 3, leave the check box turned on. The Mac OS 9.1 installer can only update the driver on an Apple-branded hard disk—one that comes with a Macintosh computer. It cannot affect a hard disk made by another manufacturer. If the installer cannot update your disk's driver, it will display a message saying so and provide additional information about updating your driver.

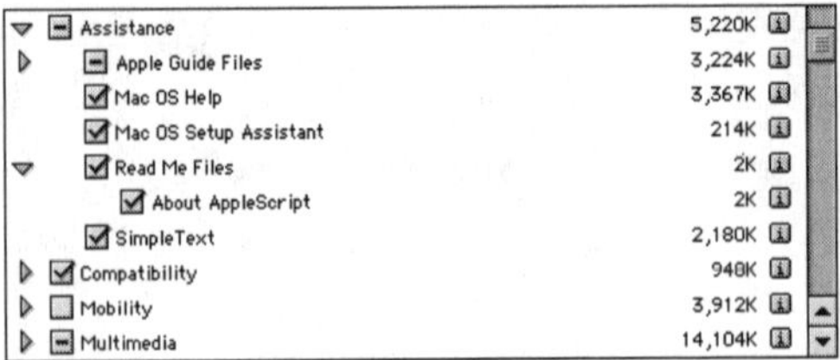

Figure 21 Clicking the triangle to the left of an item displays individual items within it.

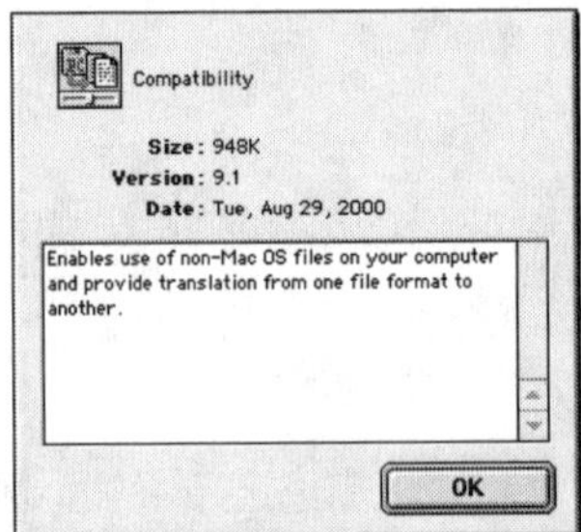

Figure 22 When you click an item's "i" button, a window full of information about the item appears.

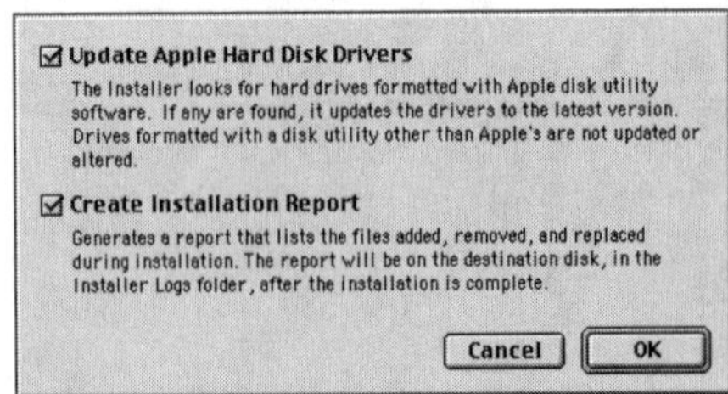

Figure 23 You can use this dialog to set two additional installation options.

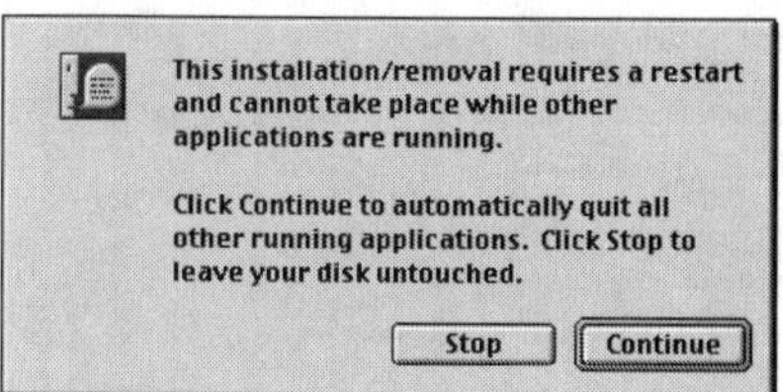

Figure 24 A dialog like this may appear after you click the Start button.

Figure 25 The Mac OS 9.1 installer displays a progress window as it works.

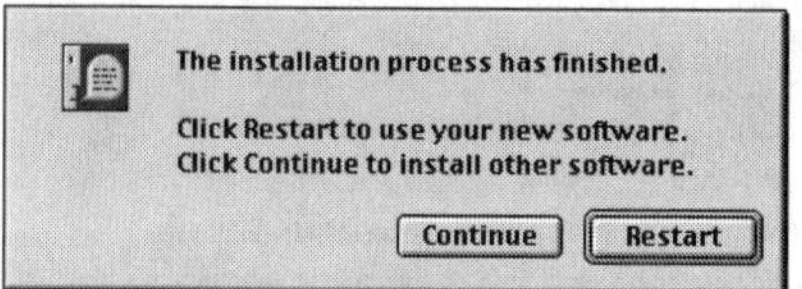

Figure 26 A dialog like this appears when the installation is complete.

Figure 27 To restart your computer, choose Restart from the Special menu.

To complete the installation

1. In the Install Software window (**Figure 18**) or Custom Installation and Removal window (**Figure 19**), click the Start button.
2. A dialog like the one in **Figure 24** may appear, informing you that other applications cannot be running during the install process and that you will have to restart your computer when it's finished. Click Continue.
3. The installer performs some maintenance tasks, then begins installing the software you selected. A progress window like the one in **Figure 25** appears to show you how it's doing.
4. When the installation is complete, a dialog like the one in **Figure 26** appears. Click Restart.

To restart your computer

If you are not prompted to restart your computer at the conclusion of the installation process (**Figure 26**), choose Special > Restart (**Figure 27**).

✔ Tips

- To configure and use your newly installed Mac OS 9.1 software, you must restart your computer. This loads the new software into the computer's RAM and, if necessary, launches the Mac OS Setup Assistant.
- Do not restart your computer by turning off power and then turning it back on! This can cause file corruption.

The Mac OS Setup Assistant

When you restart your computer after installing Mac OS 9.1, the Mac OS Setup Assistant automatically appears (**Figure 28**). This program uses a simple question and answer process to get information about you and the way you use your computer. The information you provide is automatically entered into the appropriate control panels to configure Mac OS 9.1.

✔ Tips

- Your computer may automatically rebuild the desktop file for attached disks when you restart after installing Mac OS 9.1. If so, a dialog like the one in **Figure 29** appears. Do not stop this process. When it is finished, the dialog will automatically disappear.
- If the Mac OS Setup Assistant does not automatically appear at startup, you can launch it by opening the Mac OS Setup Assistant icon in the Assistants folder on your hard disk.

Figure 28 The Mac OS Setup Assistant offers an easy way to configure Mac OS 9.1.

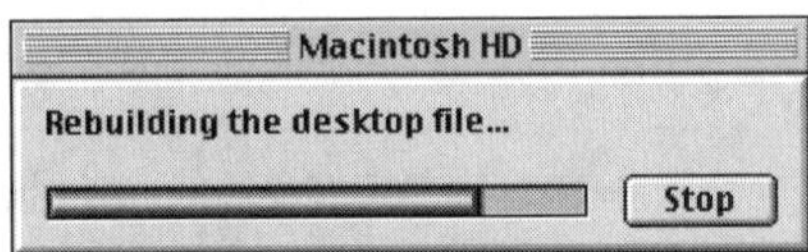

Figure 29 When you first start your computer after installing Mac OS 9.1, it may automatically rebuild the invisible desktop files on attached disks.

To use the Mac OS Setup Assistant

1. Read the information in each Mac OS Setup Assistant window. Enter information or make selections when prompted.
2. Click the right arrow button to continue.

   or

   Click the left arrow button to go back and make changes in previous windows.

✔ Tip

- The next few pages explain exactly how to enter information in each window that appears.

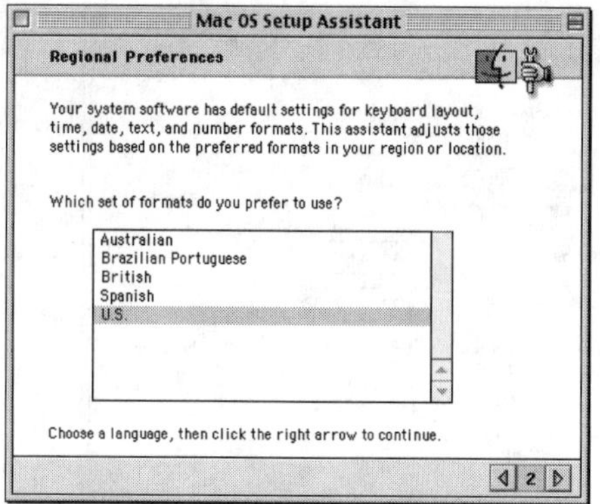

Figure 30 Use the Regional Preferences window to select your language version.

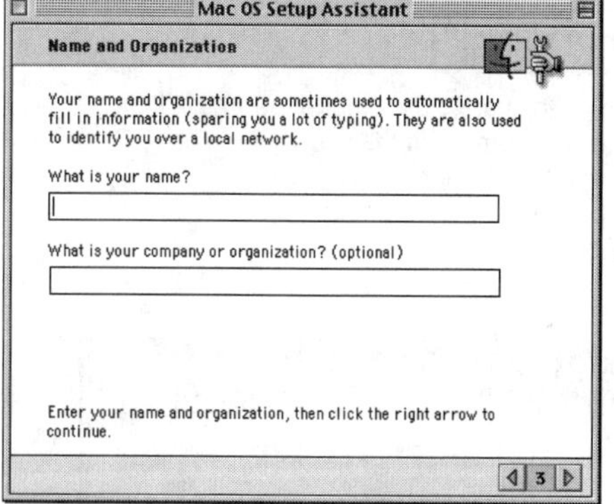

Figure 31 Enter your name and organization in these edit boxes.

To select regional preferences

1. If you haven't already done so, click the right arrow button in the Introduction window of the Mac OS Setup Assistant (**Figure 28**).
2. Read the information in the Regional Preferences window (**Figure 30**) to learn how Mac OS 9.1 uses your language version.
3. Click the language you prefer to select it.
4. Click the right arrow button.

✔ Tip

- The languages that appear in this window will vary depending on the language supported by your copy of Mac OS 9.1.

To enter your name & organization

1. Read the information in the Name and Organization window (**Figure 31**) to learn how Mac OS 9.1 uses your name and company.
2. Enter your name in the What is your name? edit box.
3. Press Tab or click in the What is your company or organization? edit box to position the blinking insertion point.
4. Enter the name of your company or organization.
5. Click the right arrow button.

✔ Tip

- You must enter a name in the What is your name? box. You may, however, leave the What is your company or organization? box empty if desired.

To set the time & date

1. Read the information in the Time and Date window of the Mac OS Setup Assistant (**Figure 32**) to learn how Mac OS 9.1 uses the time and date.
2. If daylight savings time is currently in effect, click the Yes radio button to select it.
3. If the time in the What time is it? box is not correct, change it. To do this, click an incorrect number in the time sequence to select it (**Figure 33**) and either type the correct number or click the up or down arrow button beside the time until the correct number appears.
4. If the date in the What is today's date? box is not correct, change it. To do this, click an incorrect number in the date sequence to select it and either type the correct number or click the up or down arrow button beside the date until the correct number appears.
5. Click the right arrow button.

✔ Tip

- The time and date, which are tracked by your computer's internal clock, may already be correct. If so, no changes will be necessary.

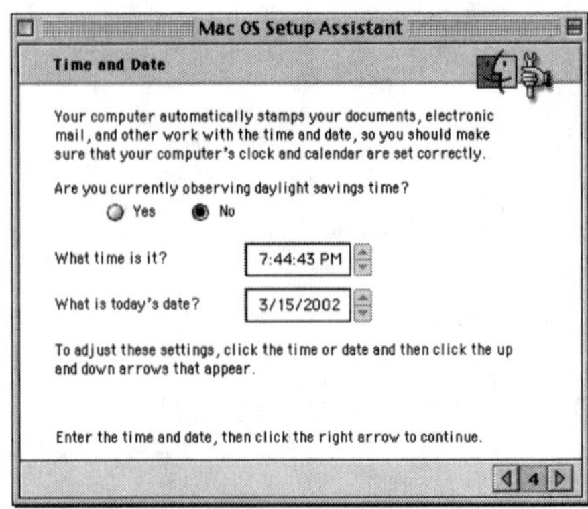

Figure 32 Use the Time and Date window to check and, if necessary, change the time or date.

Figure 33 To change the time (or date), click an incorrect number in the sequence to select it and then click the up or down arrow until the right number appears.

To select your geographic location

1. Read the information in the Geographic Location window of the Mac OS Setup Assistant (**Figure 34**) to learn how Mac OS 9.1 uses your location.
2. Click the up or down arrow on the scroll bar until the name of a city in your time zone (preferably near you) appears. Click it once to select it.
3. Click the right arrow button.

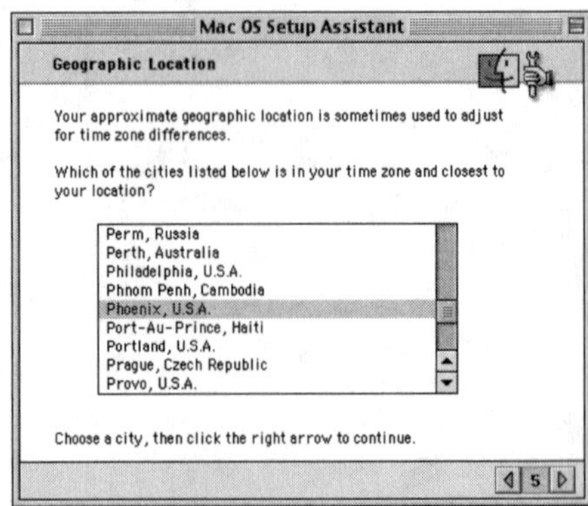

Figure 34 The Geographic Location window lists cities all over the world—including one near you.

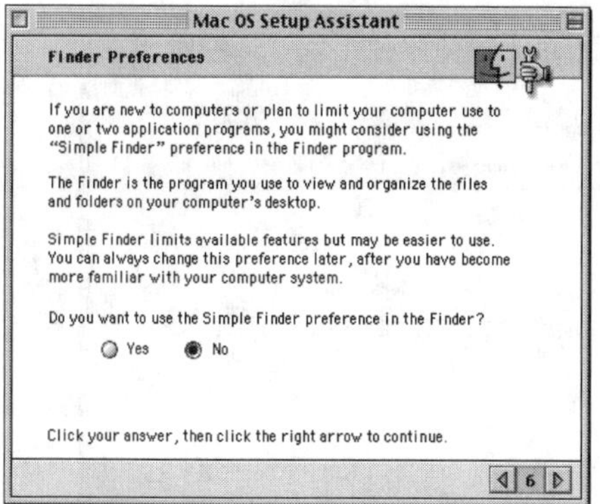

Figure 35 Use the Finder Preferences window to turn Simple Finder on or off.

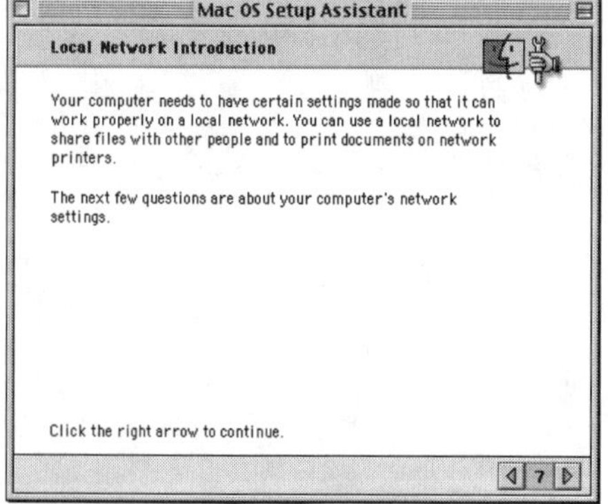

Figure 36 The Local Network Introduction window tells you a little about networks.

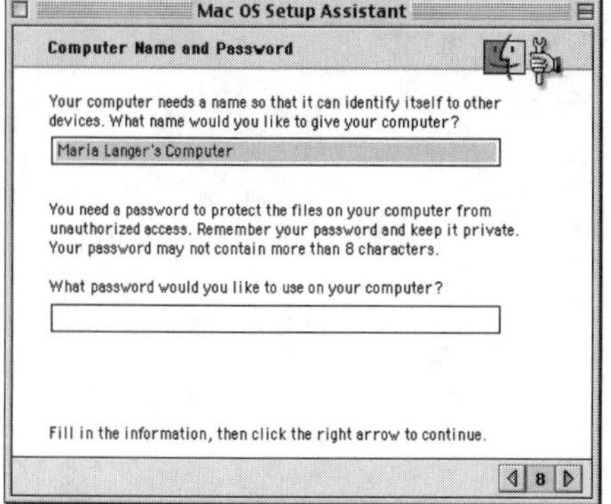

Figure 37 Use this window to enter a name for your computer and a password to protect your files from unauthorized network users.

To set Finder preferences

1. Read the information in the Finder Preferences window of the Mac OS Setup Assistant (**Figure 35**) to learn about the difference between the standard Finder and Simple Finder.
2. If you want fewer menu commands in the Finder, click the Yes radio button to select it.
3. Click the right arrow button.

To set network options

1. Read the information in the Local Network Introduction window of the Mac OS Setup Assistant (**Figure 36**) to learn more about networks.
2. Click the right arrow button.
3. Read the information in the Computer Name and Password window (**Figure 37**) to learn how Mac OS uses your computer's name and password.
4. To change the default name that the Mac OS Setup Assistant has assigned to your computer, type it in the top edit box. (The name should be selected as shown in **Figure 37**, so it is not necessary to click in the box first; simply type to overwrite the contents of the edit box.) Then press Tab or click in the bottom edit box to position the insertion point there.

   or

   To accept the default name that the Mac OS Setup Assistant has assigned to your computer, just press Tab or click in the bottom edit box to position the insertion point there.

Continued on next page...

Continued from previous page.

5. In the bottom edit box, enter a password you want to use to protect your computer from unauthorized access by other network users.
6. Click the right arrow button.
7. Wait while the Mac OS Setup Assistant validates the computer name and password.
8. Read the information in the Shared Folder window (**Figure 38**) to learn what a shared folder is and how it is used.
9. If you do not want a shared folder on the network, select the No radio button by clicking it. Then skip to step 11.
10. To change the default name that the Mac OS Setup Assistant has assigned to your shared folder, type it in the edit box. (The name should be selected as shown in **Figure 38**, so it is not necessary to click in the box first; simply type to overwrite the contents of the box.)
11. Click the right arrow button.

✔ Tips

- You must go through these steps even if your computer is not connected to a network.
- You must provide both a name and password for your computer.

Figure 38 Use this window to set up a shared folder—if you want one.

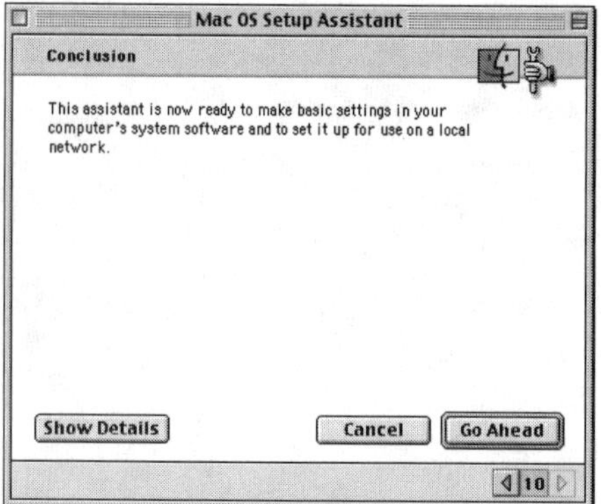

Figure 39 When the Mac OS Setup Assistant is finished asking for information, it displays this window.

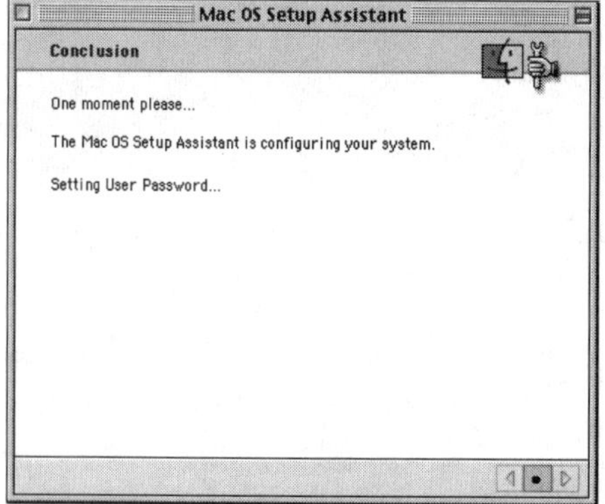

Figure 40 The Conclusion window also indicates the configuration progress.

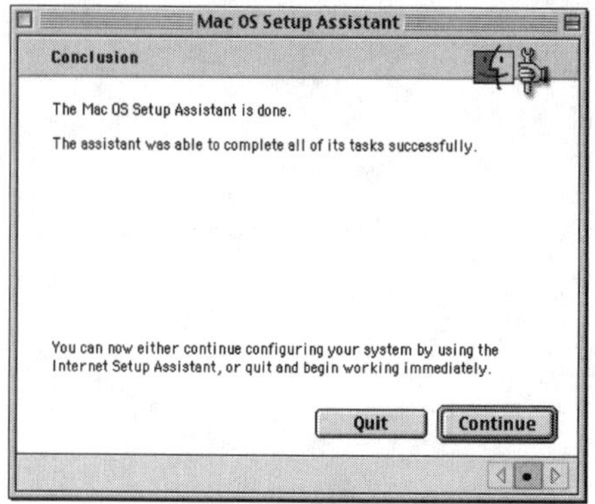

Figure 41 Finally, the Conclusion window tells you when the configuration is done.

To complete the setup process

1. Click the Go Ahead button in the Conclusion window of the Mac OS Setup Assistant (**Figure 39**).
2. Wait while the Mac OS Setup Assistant configures your system. The Conclusion window changes to indicate the configuration progress (**Figure 40**). When the configuration is complete, the Conclusion window tells you that the Mac OS Setup Assistant is done (**Figure 41**).
3. To stop configuring your computer, click the Quit button.

   or

   To go on to the Internet Setup Assistant, click the Continue button.

✔ Tips

- To check your settings one last time before they're written to your computer's configuration files, click the Show Details button (**Figure 39**). The Conclusion window changes to list all configuration options you entered or selected.
- If you have not installed the Internet Access component of Mac OS 9.1, the Continue button in the Conclusion window (**Figure 41**) will not appear.
- The Internet Setup Assistant is not covered in this book. You can find complete instructions for using it, excerpted from *Mac OS 9.1: Visual QuickStart Guide*, on the companion Web site to this book: `http://www.marialanger.com/booksites/macosxvs.html/`.

The Mac OS X Installer

Mac OS X's installer application handles all aspects of a Mac OS X installation. Simply start your computer from the Mac OS Installer CD-ROM and follow the instructions that appear on screen to install Mac OS X, restart your computer, and configure Mac OS X for your use.

This part of the chapter explains how to install and configure Mac OS X. Unfortunately, since there does not appear to be a way to take screen shots of the Mac OS X install procedure, this part of the chapter won't be very "visual." Follow along closely and you'll get all the information you need to complete the installation and configuration process without any problems.

✔ Tips

- The installation instructions in this chapter assume you know basic Mac OS techniques, such as pointing, clicking, double-clicking, dragging, and selecting items from a menu. If you're brand new to the Mac and don't know any of these techniques, skip ahead to **Chapter 2**, which discusses Mac OS basics.
- You can click the Go Back button at any time during installation to change options in a previous window.
- Remember, you can skip using the Mac OS X installer if Mac OS X or later is already installed on your computer. Consult the section titled "Determining Which Mac OS Versions Are Installed" earlier in this chapter to see what is installed on your computer.

To launch the Mac OS X installer

1. Start your computer from the Mac OS X CD-ROM disc.
2. Wait while Mac OS X and the installer load. (This could take several minutes.)
3. In the Select Language window that appears, select the radio button for the primary language you want to use with the installer and Mac OS X.
4. Click Continue.

✔ Tip

- To start your computer from the Mac OS X CD-ROM disc, insert the disc, choose Special > Restart, and hold down [C] until the "Welcome to Mac OS" message appears. This is the recommended way to start your computer when installing OS software.

To read important information about the installer & Mac OS X

1. Read the information in the Introduction ("Welcome to the Mac OS X Installer") window.
2. Click Continue.
3. Read the information in the Read Me ("Important Information") window.
4. Click Continue.
5. Read the information in the License ("Software License Agreement") window.
6. Click Continue.
7. Click the Agree button in the dialog sheet that appears.

✔ Tips

- Read the information in the "Important Information" window carefully! It provides important, late-breaking news about installing Mac OS, including compatibility information and special instructions not included in this book.
- If necessary, in step 5 you can use the pop-up menu to select a different language for the license agreement.
- In step 7, if you click the Disagree button, you will not be able to install Mac OS X.

To select a destination disk

1. In the Select Destination ("Select a Destination") window, click to select the icon for the disk on which you want to install Mac OS X. A green arrow appears on the disk icon.
2. Click Continue.

✔ Tips

- A note beneath the disk icons indicates how much space is available on each disk. You can see how much space a Mac OS X installation takes by looking at the bottom of the window. Make sure the disk you select has enough space for the installation.
- Although the Mac OS X Install CD will appear as an icon in the window, you cannot select it.
- If you turn on the Erase destination check box, you will erase all data on the destination disk.

To complete the installation

1. In the Installation Type ("Easy Install") window, click Install.
2. Wait while Mac OS X installs. A status window tells you what the installer is doing and may indicate how much longer the installation will take.
3. When the installer is finished, it restarts the computer and displays the first screen of the setup application.

✔ Tip

- The Customize button in the Installation Type window enables you to customize your Mac OS X installation. This option is provided for "Power Users" and should only be utilized if you have a complete understanding of Mac OS X components and features.

Configuring Mac OS X

When you start your computer after installing Mac OS X, the Mac OS X Setup Assistant automatically appears. This program uses a simple question and answer process to get information about you and the way you use your computer. The information you provide is automatically entered in the various System Preferences panes of Mac OS X to configure your computer for Mac OS X.

✔ Tips

- If you just bought your Macintosh and Mac OS X is installed, the first time you start your computer, you'll see the Mac OS X setup assistant described here. Follow these instructions to configure your computer.
- Remember, you can skip the Mac OS X configuration process if Mac OS X or later has already been installed and configured on your computer. Consult the section titled "Determining Which Mac OS Versions Are Installed" earlier in this chapter to see what is installed on your computer.

To set basic configuration options

1. In the Welcome window that appears after installing Mac OS X and restarting, select the name of the country you're in.
2. Click Continue.
3. In the Personalize Your Settings window, select a keyboard layout.
4. Click Continue.
5. In the Registration Information window, fill in the form. You can press Tab to move from one field to another.
6. Click Continue.
7. In the A Few More Questions window, use the pop-up menus and radio buttons to answer a few marketing questions.
8. Click Continue.
9. Read the information in the Thank You window.
10. Click Continue.
11. In the Create Your Account window, fill in the form to enter account information.
12. Click Continue.
13. Continue following instructions on the next page.

✔ Tips

- If your country is not listed in step 1, turn on the Show All check box to display more options.
- In step 3, you can turn on the Show All check box to show additional keyboard layouts.
- In step 5, you can learn about Apple's privacy policy by clicking the Privacy button. When you're finished reading the information in the dialog sheet that appears, click OK to dismiss it and return to the Registration Information window.
- When you enter your password in step 11, it displays as bullet characters. That's why you enter it twice: so you're sure you entered what you thought you did the first time.
- Remember the password you enter in step 11! If you forget your password, you may not be able to use your computer. It's a good idea to use the Password Hint field to enter a hint that makes your password impossible to forget.

To set up Mac OS X to use your existing Internet service

1. In the Get Internet Ready window, select the radio button for I'll use my existing Internet service.
2. Click Continue.
3. In the How Do You Connect window, select the radio button for your connection method. Your options are Telephone modem, Local area network (LAN), Cable modem, DSL (Digital Subscriber Line).
4. Click Continue.
5. Follow the instructions in one of the next three sections for your connection method.

✔ Tip

- You can get all of the information you need for setup from your ISP or network administrator.

To set up a telephone modem connection

1. In the Set up existing service window enter information about your ISP connection.
2. Click Continue.
3. In the Setting up your modem window, select your modem connection port and make and model.
4. Click Continue.
5. Skip ahead to the section titled "To set up iTools."

To set up a local area network connection

1. The Your Local Area Network window may appear to tell you that your network configuration has been obtained from a DHCP server.
   - ▲ If you want to use this information, select Yes and click Continue. You can then skip ahead to the section titled "To set up iTools."
   - ▲ If this window does not appear or you don't want to use this information, select No, change the configuration, and click Continue.
2. In the Your Internet Connection window, select an option from the TCP/IP Connection Type pop-up menu. The option you select will determine what fields appear beneath it.
3. Enter IP address, subnet mask, router address, DNS hosts, domain name, and proxy server information as required.
4. Click Continue.
5. Skip ahead to the section titled "To set up iTools."

To set up a cable modem or DSL connection

1. In the Your Internet Connection window, select an option from the TCP/IP Connection Type pop-up menu. The option you select will determine what fields appear beneath it.
2. Enter IP address, subnet mask, router address, DNS hosts, domain name, and proxy server information as required.
3. Click Continue.
4. Skip ahead to the section titled "To set up iTools."

To skip Internet setup

1. In the Get Internet Ready window, select the radio button for I'm not ready to connect to the Internet.
2. Click Continue.
3. In the dialog sheet that appears, click Yes to confirm that you don't want to setup an Internet connection.
4. In the Register With Apple window, select one of the options:
   - ▲ **Register Now** enables you to use your Internet connection to send registration information to Apple. Click Continue.
   - ▲ **Register Later** enables you to skip registration for now. Click Continue and skip ahead to the section titled "To set the time zone."
5. In the Your Phone Service window, enter your telephone number and provide other information as requested.
6. Click Continue.
7. In the Setting up your modem window, select your modem connection port and make and model.
8. Click Continue.
9. Continue following instructions in the section titled "To set up iTools."

✔ Tip

- ■ If you are connected to the Internet via a LAN, you can skip steps 5 through 8.

To set up iTools

1. In the Get iTools window, select one of the options:
   - ▲ **I'd like to create my iTools account** enables you to create a new iTools account. Click continue and follow step 2.
   - ▲ **I'm already using iTools** enables you to enter your iTools user name and password. After entering this information, click Continue and skip ahead to the section titled "To send registration information."
   - ▲ **I'm not ready for iTools** enables you to skip the iTools setup. Click Continue and skip ahead to the section titled "To send registration information."
2. In the Your iTools Account window, fill in the form with the requested information, including a user name, password, and birthday.
3. Click Continue.
4. Continue following instructions in the next section (if they apply).

✔ Tip

- **Appendix B** provides more information about iTools.

To send registration information

1. If the Now you're ready to connect window appears, click Continue to send your registration to Apple via modem or network connection.
2. Continue following instructions in the next section (if they apply).

To set up an e-mail account

1. If the Set Up Mail window appears, use it to enter information about your e-mail account.
2. Click Continue.

✔ Tip

- If the Set Up Mail window identifies your iTools mac.com e-mail account and you want to add another account, select the Add my existing e-mail account radio button. Then enter information for your account.

To set the time zone, date, & time

1. If the Select Time Zone window appears, click the map to indicate your time zone.
2. If necessary, choose an option from the pop-up menu to specify the exact time zone by name.
3. Click Continue.
4. If the Set Your Date and Time window appears, use it to set your computer's date and time:
   - ▲ To set the date, click today's date on the calendar. (You may have to use the arrow keys beside the name of the month and the year number to set the appropriate month and year first.)
   - ▲ To set the time, click the time digits you want to change and type a new entry. Repeat this process to enter the current time, then click Save.
5. Click Continue.
6. In the final window that appears click Go.

✔ Tips

- The Set Your Date and Time window will only appear if Mac OS X cannot connect to the Internet to retrieve date and time information from a time server.
- In step 4, you can also change the time by dragging the clock's hands and clicking Save when the time is correct.

Updating to Mac OS X 10.1 & Mac OS 9.2.1

The Mac OS X 10.1 upgrade package enables you to update Mac OS X and Mac OS 9.1 to Mac OS X 10.1 and Mac OS 9.2.1. The package comes with two updater CD-ROM discs, each with its own installer.

To complete the update, you begin by using the Mac OS X 10.1 Upgrade CD to update Mac OS X to Mac OS X 10.1. Then, if you expect to use the Classic environment and do not already have Mac OS 9.2.1 installed, you can use the Mac OS 9.2.1 Updater CD to update Mac OS 9.1 to Mac OS 9.2.1.

This part of the chapter explains how to use the Mac OS X 10.1 upgrade package to update Mac OS X and 9.1 to Mac OS X 10.1 and 9.2.1.

✔ Tips

- To use the Mac OS X 10.1 upgrade package, Mac OS X must already be installed on your computer.
- If Mac OS X 10.1 and 9.2.1 are already installed on your computer, you can skip this section.
- Unfortunately, it is does not appear possible to take screen shots of the Mac OS X 10.1 installation process. Follow along closely and you should be able to complete the update procedure without any problems.

To launch the Mac OS X 10.1 update installer

1. Insert the Mac OS X 10.1 Upgrade CD in your CD-ROM drive.
2. Double-click the Install Mac OS X icon (**Figure 42**).
3. If a dialog like the one in **Figure 43** appears, enter an administrator name and password and click OK.
4. In the Install Mac OS X dialog that appears (**Figure 44**), click Restart.
5. Wait while your computer restarts from the Upgrade CD.
6. In the Select Language window that appears, select the radio button for the main language you want to use with the installer and Mac OS X.
7. Click Continue.
8. Continue following instructions on the next page.

✔ Tip

- The administrator name and password is the short name and password you provided when you configured Mac OS X.

Figure 42 The contents of the Mac OS X 10.1 Upgrade CD.

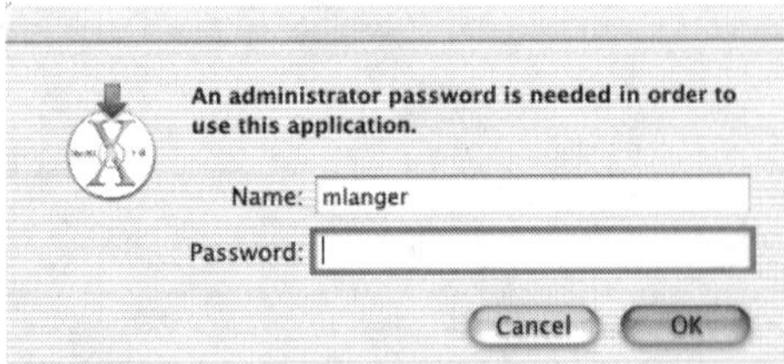

Figure 43 If this dialog appears, enter a valid administrator name and password.

Figure 44 Click Restart to restart your computer from the upgrade CD.

To complete the Mac OS X 10.1 update

1. Read the information in the Introduction ("Welcome to the Mac OS X Installer") window and click Continue.
2. Read the information in the Read Me ("Important Information") window and click Continue.
3. Read the information in the License ("Software License Agreement") window and click Continue.
4. Click Agree in the dialog sheet that appears.
5. In the Select Destination ("Select a Destination") window, click to select the icon for the disk on which you want to install Mac OS X 10.1. A green arrow appears on the disk icon. Click Continue.
6. In the Installation Type ("Easy Install") window, click Install.
7. Wait while Mac OS X 10.1 installs. When the installer is finished, it restarts the computer.

✔ Tips

- If Mac OS X is not installed on your computer, you will not be able to select your disk in the Select Destination window.
- The Customize button in the Installation Type window enables you to customize your Mac OS X upgrade installation. You can minimize the amount of disk space required by the update by turning off check boxes for the localized files you will not need.
- The configuration options you set when you first installed Mac OS X are automatically copied to the Mac OS X 10.1 installation. I tell you more about configuring Mac OS X earlier in this chapter.

To launch the Mac OS 9.2.1 update installer

1. Restart your computer with Mac OS 9.1. To do this, choose Apple > System Preferences (**Figure 4**), click the Startup Disk icon in the System Preferences window that appears (**Figure 6**), click to select the Mac OS 9.1 folder (**Figure 45**), click Restart, and click Save and Restart in the dialog sheet that appears.
2. Insert the Mac OS 9.2.1 Update CD in your CD-ROM drive. If necessary, double-click the CD-ROM icon to display its contents (**Figure 46**).
3. Double-click the folder icon for the language you prefer.
4. Double-click the Mac OS 9.2.1 Update icon (**Figure 47**). (The icon name will be different if you are using a language other than English.)
5. A progress window appears as the disk image for the Mac OS 9.2.1 Update file is verified. Wait until it finishes or click Skip.
6. A Mac OS 9.2.1 Update icon appears on the desktop and opens to display its contents (**Figure 48**).
7. Double-click the Mac OS Install icon.
8. After a moment, the installer's Welcome window appears (**Figure 49**).
9. Continue following the instructions on the next page.

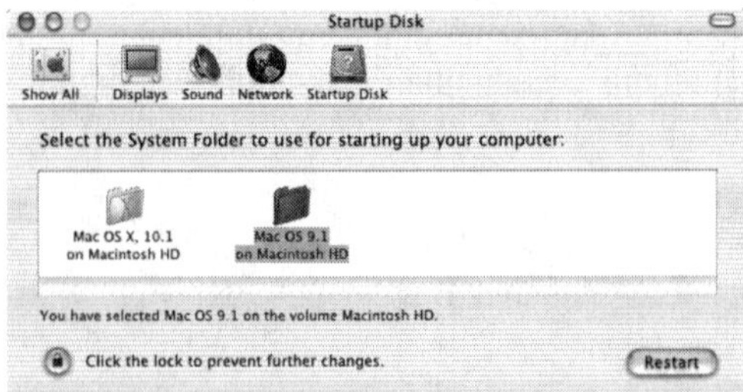

Figure 45 To restart with Mac OS 9.1, select the Mac OS 9.1 folder and click Restart.

Figure 46 The contents of the Mac OS 9.2.1 Update CD.

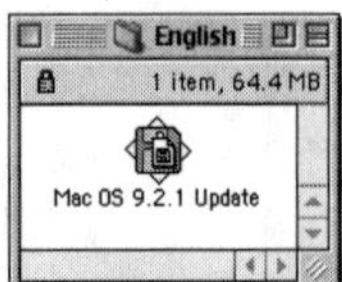

Figure 47 The Mac OS 9.2.1 Update icon in the English folder.

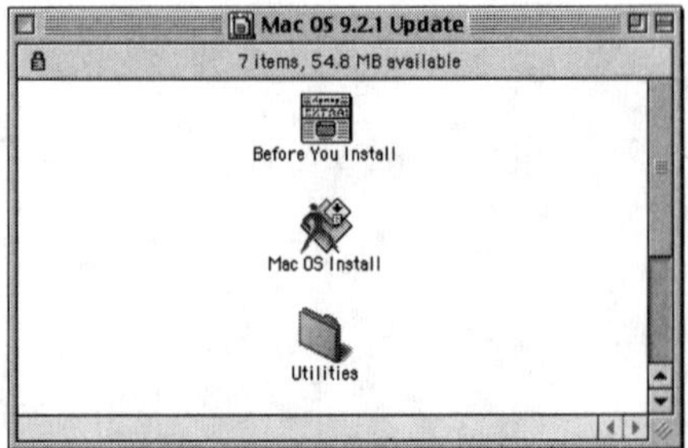

Figure 48 The contents of the Mac OS 9.2.1 Update disk image.

Launching the Mac OS 9.2.1 Updater

Figure 49 The Welcome window appears when you launch the Mac OS 9.2.1 update installer.

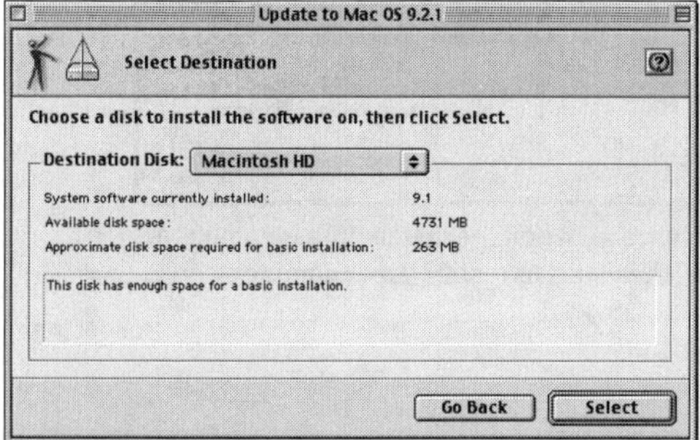

Figure 50 Use this window to select the disk on which Mac OS 9.1 is installed.

To complete the Mac OS 9.2.1 update installation

1. In the Welcome window that appears when you launch the installer (**Figure 49**), click Continue.
2. In the Select Destination window (**Figure 50**), make sure the disk containing Mac OS 9.1 is selected. Then click Select.
3. Read the contents of the Important Information window (**Figure 51**), and click Continue.
4. Read the contents of the Software License Agreement window (**Figure 52**), and click Continue.
5. In the dialog that appears, click Agree.
6. In the Install Software window (**Figure 53**), click Start.
7. A dialog appears, telling you that the installation requires a restart. Click Continue.

Continued on next page...

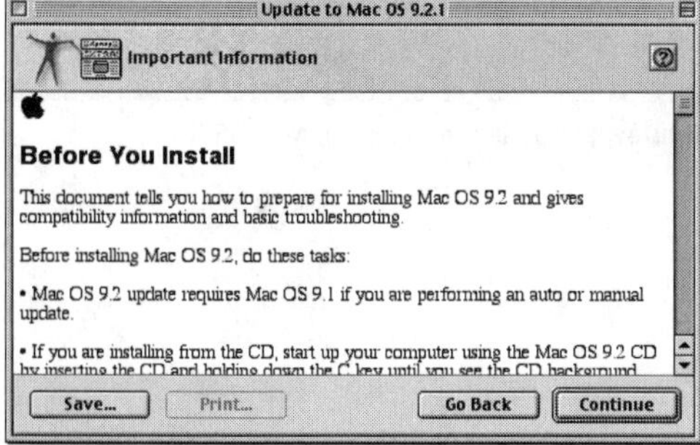

Figure 51 Read this to get late-breaking news about Mac OS 9.2.1.

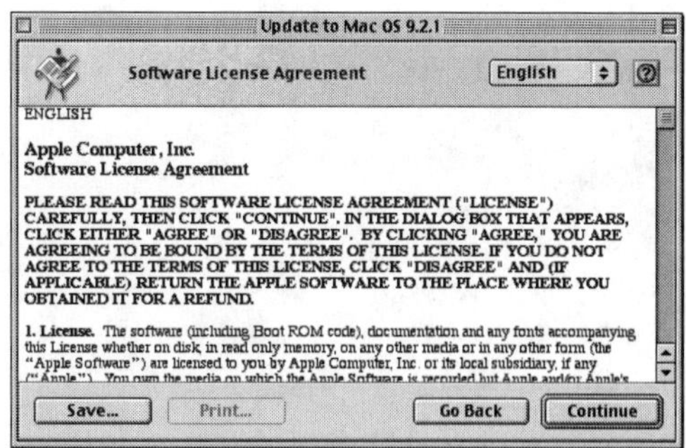

Figure 52 The Software License Agreement window in the Mac OS 9.2.1 update installer.

Continued from previous page.

8. Wait while the installer updates the system software.

9. Click Restart in the dialog that appears (**Figure 54**).

✔ Tip

- When the installation is complete and your computer has restarted, it may launch the Mac OS Setup Assistant. If so, follow the instructions earlier in this chapter to confirm or set options for Mac OS 9.2.1.

To restart with Mac OS X 10.1

1. Choose Apple > Control Panels > Startup Disk (**Figure 1**) to display the Startup disk control panel.

2. If necessary, click the triangle beside the name of your hard disk to display the System folders installed on your computer (**Figure 3**).

3. Select the folder for Mac OS X 10.1 (**Figure 55**).

4. Click Restart. Your computer restarts with Mac OS X 10.1.

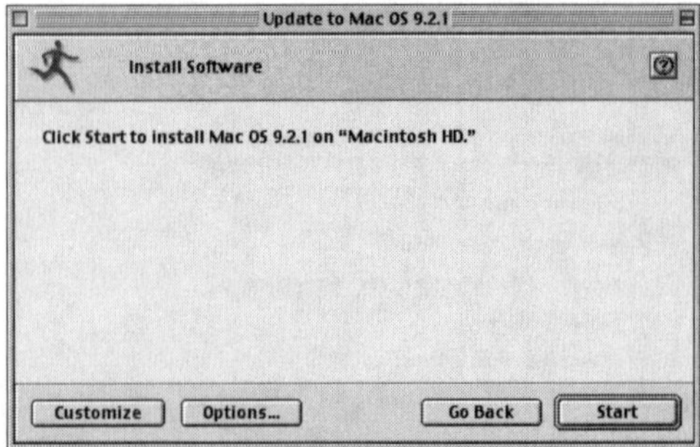

Figure 53 Click the Start button in the Install Software window to start the update.

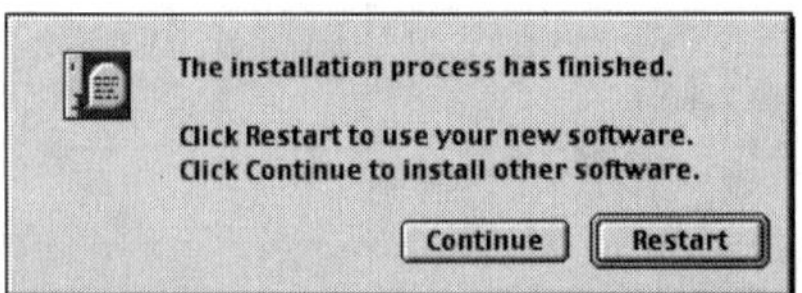

Figure 54 When the installation is complete, click Restart to restart your computer with Mac OS 9.2.1.

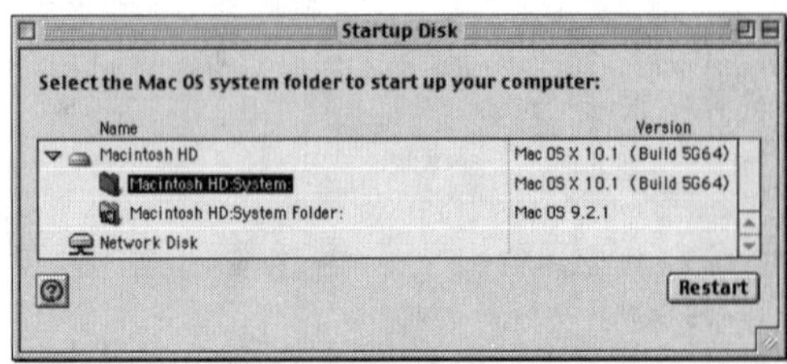

Figure 55 Choose the folder for Mac OS X 10.1.

Obtaining Other Mac OS Updates

If you have a connection to the Internet, you can use software that's part of Mac OS to check for and obtain Mac OS updates:

- The Software Update preferences pane enables you to check for updates to Mac OS X software.
- The Software Update control panel enables you to check for updates to Mac OS 9.x software.

This section explains how to use these tools to keep Mac OS up to date.

✔ Tips

- It's a good idea to check for updates to the system software on a regular basis—at least once a month.
- I used Software Update to update the System software to Mac OS X 10.1.2 (and later, 10.1.3) and Mac OS 9.2.2 when writing this book.
- This section provides basic information for using the two versions of Software Update. For more detailed information on using these utilities, consult these books:
  - The sequel to this book, *Mac OS X Advanced: Visual QuickPro Guide*, covers the Software Update preferences pane of Mac OS X.
  - *Mac OS 9.1: Visual QuickStart Guide* covers the Software Update control panel in Mac OS 9.1 and 9.2.

To update Mac OS X

1. Choose Apple > System Preferences (**Figure 4**) to display the System Preferences window (**Figure 6**).
2. Click the Software Update icon to display the Software Update pane (**Figure 56**).
3. Click Update Now. Your computer connects to the Internet and queries Apple's servers for information about updates. If an update is available, it displays it in a list in the Software Update window (**Figure 57**).
4. Turn on the check box beside each update item you want to download and install.
5. Click Install.
6. An Authenticate dialog like the one in **Figure 58** may appear. Enter an administrator name and password, and click OK.
7. If a Software License Agreement dialog sheet appears, click Agree.
8. Wait while your computer downloads and installs the updates.
9. If prompted to restart your computer, click Restart.

Tips

In step 4, if you select an item, a description of it appears in the bottom half of the window (**Figure 57**).

You don't have to install all items that appear in the Software Update window (**Figure 57**). If you skip an item, you will be offered another chance to download and install it the next time you check for updates with Software Update.

Figure 56 The Software Update pane.

Figure 57 A list of updates appears in the Software Update window.

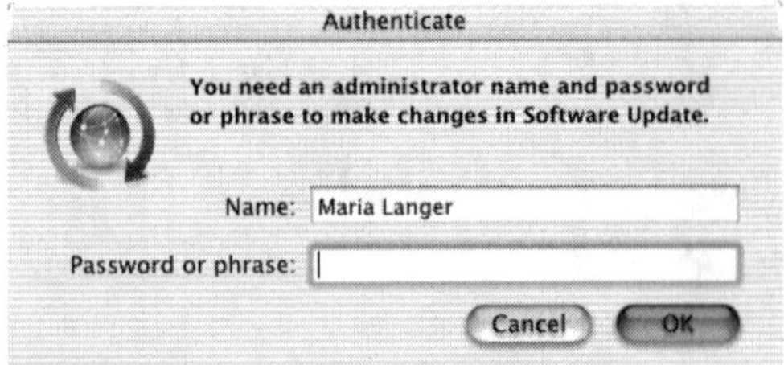

Figure 58 Enter an administrator name and password in the Authenticate dialog to update system software.

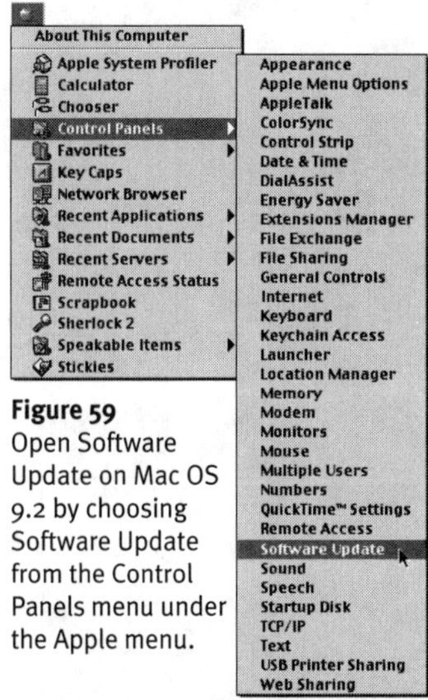

Figure 59 Open Software Update on Mac OS 9.2 by choosing Software Update from the Control Panels menu under the Apple menu.

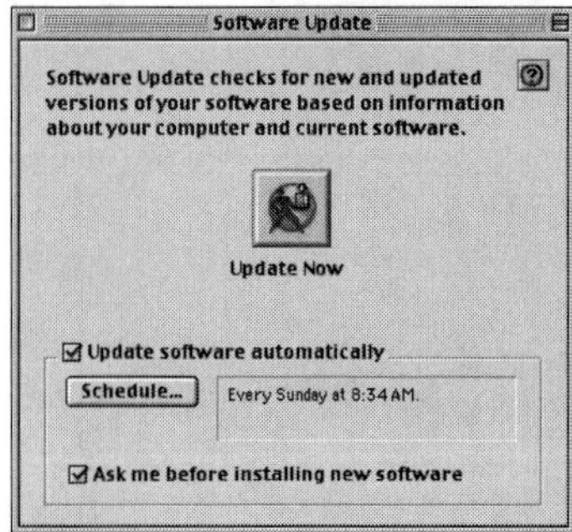

Figure 60 The Software Update control panel.

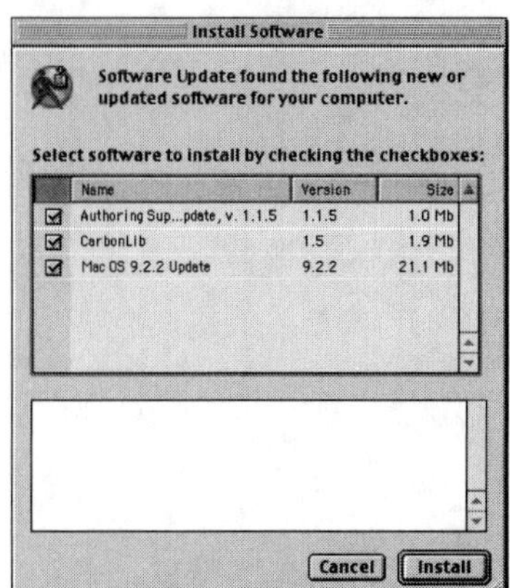

Figure 61 A list of available updates appears in the Install Software window.

To update Mac OS 9.x

1. Restart your computer with Mac OS 9.2. To do this, choose Apple > System Preferences (**Figure 4**), click the Startup Disk icon in the System Preferences window that appears (**Figure 6**), click to select the Mac OS 9.2 folder, click Restart, and click Save and Restart in the dialog sheet that appears.
2. Choose Apple > Control Panels > Software Update (**Figure 59**) to display the Software Update control panel (**Figure 60**).
3. Click Update Now. Your computer connects to the Internet and queries Apple's servers for information about updates. If an update is available, it displays it in a list in an Install Software window (**Figure 61**).
4. Turn on the check box beside each update item you want to download and install.
5. Click Install.
6. If a Software License Agreement dialog appears, click OK.
7. Wait while your computer downloads and installs the updates.
8. If prompted to restart your computer, click Restart.

✔ Tips

- In step 4, if you select an item, a description of it appears in the bottom half of the window.
- You don't have to install all items that appear in the Install Software window (**Figure 61**). If you skip an item, you will be offered another chance to download and install it the next time you check for updates with Software Update.

Finder Basics

2

The Finder & Desktop

The *Finder* is a program that is part of Mac OS. It launches automatically when you start your computer.

The Finder provides a graphic user interface called the *desktop* (**Figure 1**) that you can use to open, copy, delete, list, organize, and perform other operations on computer files.

This chapter provides important instructions for using the Finder and items that appear on the Mac OS X desktop. It's important that you understand how to use these basic Finder techniques, since you'll use them again and again every time you work with your computer.

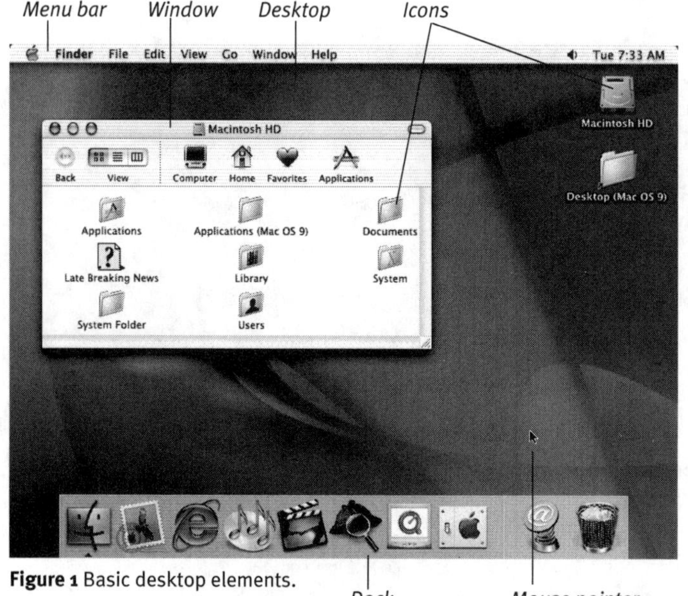

Figure 1 Basic desktop elements.

✔ Tips

- You never have to manually launch the Finder; it always starts automatically.
- Under normal circumstances, you cannot quit the Finder.
- If you're new to Mac OS, don't skip this chapter. It provides the basic information you'll need to use your computer successfully.

The Mouse

Mac OS, like most graphic user interface systems, uses the mouse as an input device. There are several basic mouse techniques you must know to use your computer:

- **Point** to a specific item on screen.
- **Click** an item to select it.
- **Double-click** an item to open it.
- **Press** an item to activate it.
- **Drag** to move an item or select multiple items.

✔ Tip

- Some computers use either a trackball or a trackpad instead of a mouse.

To point

1. Move the mouse on the work surface or mouse pad.

   or

   Use your fingertips to move the ball of the trackball.

   or

   Move the tip of one finger (usually your forefinger) on the surface of the trackpad.

   The mouse pointer, which usually looks like an arrow (**Figure 2**), moves on your computer screen.

2. When the tip of the mouse pointer's arrow is on the item to which you want to point (**Figure 3**), stop moving it.

✔ Tip

- The tip of the mouse pointer is its "business end."

Figure 2 The mouse pointer usually looks like an arrow pointer when you are working in the Finder.

Figure 3 Move the mouse pointer so the arrow's tip is on the item to which you want to point.

Figure 4 Click to select an icon...

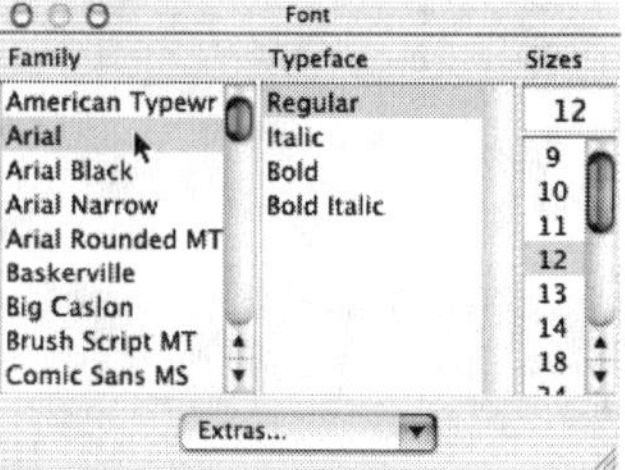

Figure 5 ...or an item in a list.

Figure 6 Press a scroll bar arrow to activate it.

Figure 7 Drag to move items such as folders.

To click

1. Point to the item you want to click.
2. Press (and release) the mouse button once. The item you clicked becomes selected (**Figures 4** and **5**).

To double-click

1. Point to the item you want to double-click.
2. Press (and release) the mouse button twice quickly. The item you double-clicked opens.

✔ Tip

- Keep the mouse pointer still while double-clicking. If you move the mouse pointer during the double-click process, you may move the item instead of double-clicking it.

To press

1. Point to the item you want to press.
2. Press and hold the mouse button without moving the mouse. The item you are pressing is activated (**Figure 6**).

✔ Tip

- The press technique is often used when working with scroll bars, as shown in **Figure 6**, where pressing is the same as clicking repeatedly.

To drag

1. Point to the item you want to drag.
2. Press the mouse button down.
3. While holding the mouse button down, move the mouse pointer. The item you are dragging moves (**Figure 7**).

Menus

The Finder—and most other Mac OS programs—offers menus full of options. There are four types of menus in Mac OS X:

- A **pull-down menu** appears on the menu bar at the top of the screen (**Figure 8**).
- A **submenu** appears when a menu option with a right-pointing triangle is selected (**Figure 9**).
- A **pop-up menu**, which displays a pair of triangles (or double arrow), appears within a window (**Figures 10** and **11**).
- A **contextual menu** appears when you hold down Control while clicking an item (**Figure 12**).

✔ Tips

- A menu option followed by an ellipsis (...) (**Figure 8**) will display a dialog when chosen. Dialogs are discussed in detail in **Chapter 5**.
- A menu option that is dimmed or gray cannot be chosen. The commands that are available vary depending on what is selected on the desktop or in a window.
- A menu option preceded by a check mark (**Figure 8**) is selected, or "turned on."
- A menu option followed by a series of keyboard characters (**Figure 8**) has a keyboard equivalent. Keyboard equivalents are discussed later in this chapter.
- Contextual menus only display options that apply to the item to which you are pointing.
- In Mac OS X, menus are translucent. Although this makes them look cool on screen, it doesn't always look good when illustrated on paper.

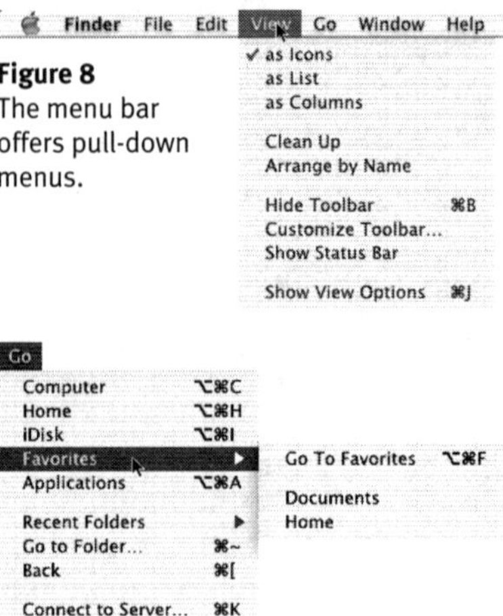

Figure 8 The menu bar offers pull-down menus.

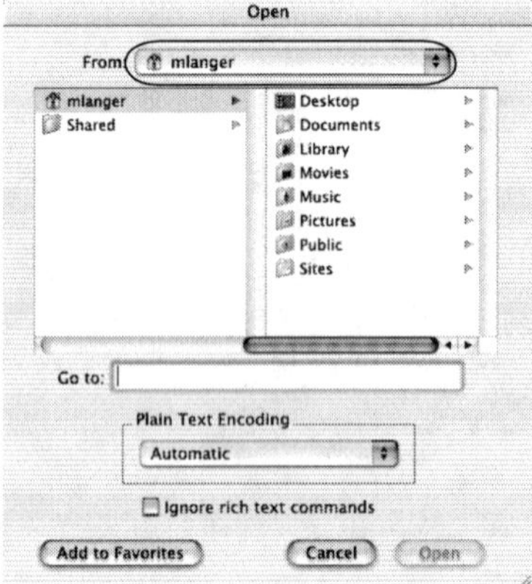

Figure 9 A submenu appears when you select a menu option with a right-pointing triangle beside it.

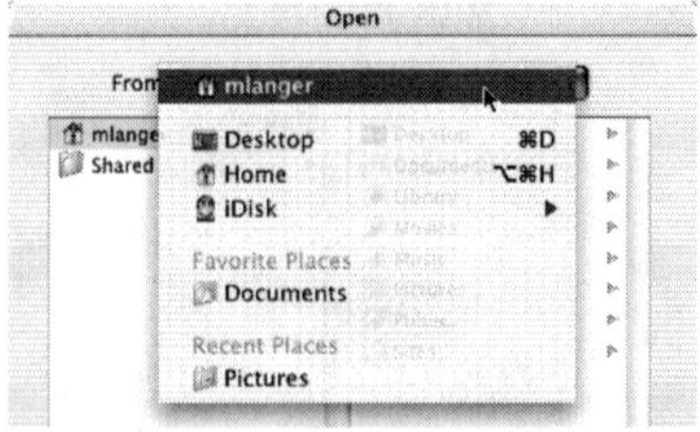

Figure 10 Pop-up menus can appear within dialogs.

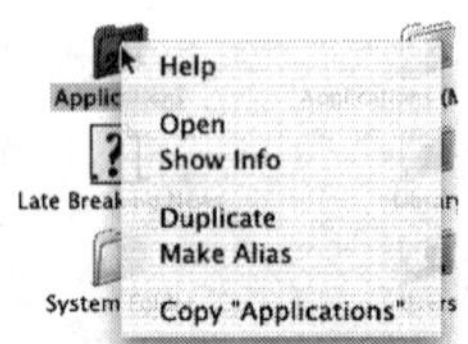

Figure 11 To display a pop-up menu, click it.

Figure 12 A contextual menu appears when you hold down Control while clicking.

Figure 13 Point to the menu name.

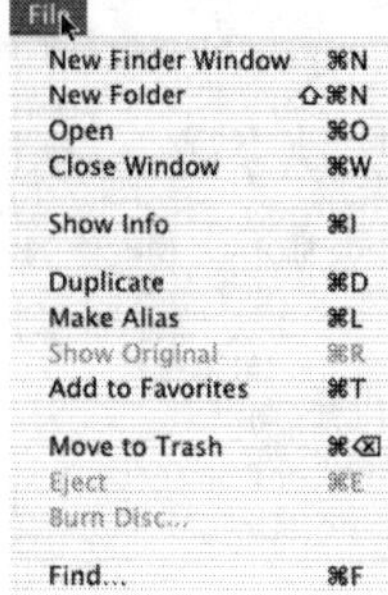

Figure 14 Click (or press) to display the menu.

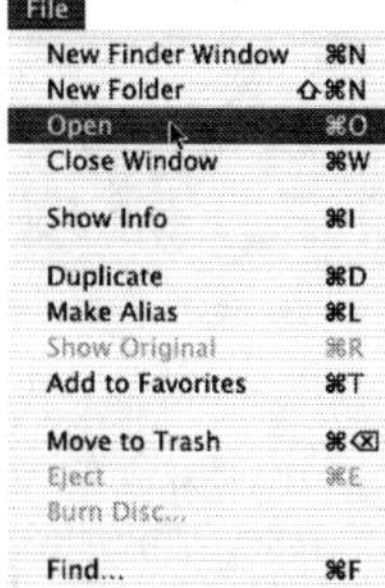

Figure 15 Click (or drag) to select the menu option you want.

Figure 16 Hold down [Control] while pointing to an item.

Figure 17 A contextual menu appears when you click.

Figure 18 Click (or drag) to select the option you want.

To use a menu

1. Point to the name of the menu (**Figure 13**).
2. Click. The menu opens, displaying its options (**Figure 14**).
3. Point to the menu option you want (**Figure 15**).
4. Click to choose the selected option. The menu disappears.

✔ Tips

- Mac OS X's menus are "sticky menus"—each menu opens and stays open when you click its name.
- To close a menu without choosing an option, click outside the menu.
- This book uses the following notation to indicate menu commands: *Menu Name* > *Submenu Name* (if necessary) > *Command Name*. For example, the instructions for choosing the Documents command from the Favorites submenu under the Go menu (**Figure 9**) would be: "choose Go > Favorites > Documents."

To use a contextual menu

1. Point to the item on which you want to act.
2. Press and hold down [Control]. A tiny contextual menu icon appears beside the mouse pointer (**Figure 16**).
3. Click. A contextual menu appears at the item (**Figure 17**).
4. Click the menu option you want (**Figure 18**).

The Keyboard

The keyboard offers another way to communicate with your computer. In addition to typing text and numbers, you can also use it to choose menu commands.

There are three types of keys on a Mac OS keyboard:

- **Character keys**, such as letters, numbers, and symbols, are for typing information. Some character keys have special functions, as listed in **Table 1**.
- **Modifier keys** alter the meaning of a character key being pressed or the meaning of a mouse action. Modifier keys are listed in **Table 2**.
- **Function keys** perform specific functions in Mac OS or an application. Dedicated function keys, which always do the same thing, are listed in **Table 3**. Function keys labeled F1 through F15 on the keyboard can be assigned specific functions by applications.

✓ Tips

- ⌘ is called the *Command key* (not the Apple key).
- Contextual menus are discussed on the previous page.

Table 1

Special Character Keys

Key	Function
Enter	Enters information or "clicks" a default button.
Return	Begins a new paragraph or line or "clicks" a default button.
Tab	Advances to the next tab stop or the next item in a sequence.
Delete	Deletes a selection or the character to the left of the insertion point.
Del	Deletes a selection or the character to the right of the insertion point.
Clear	Deletes a selection.
Esc	"Clicks" a Cancel button or ends the operation that is currently in progress.

Table 2

Modifier Keys

Key	Function
Shift	Produces uppercase characters or symbols. Also works with the mouse to extend selections and to restrain movement in graphic applications.
Option	Produces special symbols.
⌘	Accesses menu commands via keyboard equivalents.
Control	Modifies the functions of other keys and displays contextual menus.

Table 3

Dedicated Function Keys

Key	Function
Help	Displays onscreen help.
Home	Scrolls to the beginning.
End	Scrolls to the end.
Page Up	Scrolls up one page.
Page Down	Scrolls down one page.
← → ↑ ↓	Moves the insertion point or change the selections.

To use a keyboard equivalent

1. Hold down the modifier key(s) in the sequence. This is usually [⌘], but can be [Option], [Control], or [Shift].
2. Press the letter, number, or symbol key in the sequence.

For example, to choose the Open command, which can be found under the File menu (**Figure 15**), hold down [⌘] and press [O].

✔ Tips

- You can learn keyboard equivalents by observing the key sequences that appear to the right of some menu commands (**Figures 8** and **9**).
- Some commands include more than one modifier key. You must hold all modifier keys down while pressing the letter, number, or symbol key for the keyboard equivalent.
- You can find a list of all Finder keyboard equivalents in **Appendix A**.
- Some applications refer to keyboard equivalents as *shortcut keys*.

Icons

Mac OS uses icons to graphically represent files and other items on the desktop, in the Dock, or within Finder windows:

- **Applications** (**Figure 19**) are programs you use to get work done. **Chapters 5** through **7** discuss working with applications.
- **Documents** (**Figure 20**) are the files created by applications. **Chapter 5** covers working with documents.
- **Folders** (**Figure 21**) are used to organize files. **Chapters 3** and **4** discuss using folders.
- **Disks** (**Figure 22**), including removable media, are used to store files. **Chapter 3** covers working with disks.
- The **Trash** (**Figure 23**), which is in the Dock, is for discarding items you no longer want and for ejecting removable media. The Trash is covered in **Chapter 3**.

✔ Tip

- Icons can appear a number of different ways, depending on the view and view options chosen for a window. Windows are discussed later in this chapter; views are discussed in **Chapter 3**.

Figure 19 Application icons.

Figure 20 Document icons, including a TextEdit document, a Preview document, and a Word document.

Figure 21 Folder icons.

Figure 22 Three different disk icons: hard disk, CD-ROM disc, and networked disk.

Figure 23 The three faces of the Trash icon in the Dock: empty, full, and while dragging removable media.

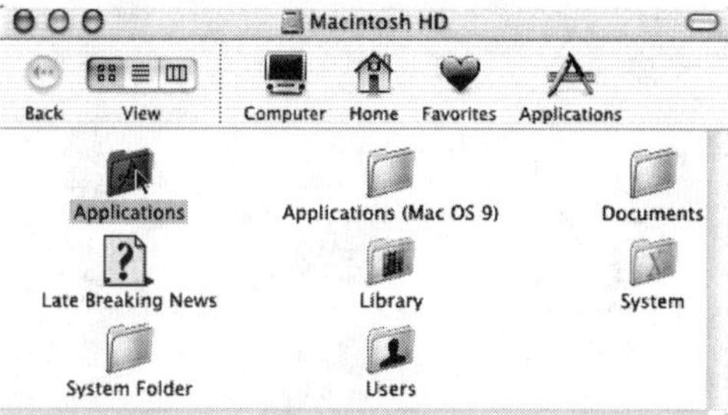

Figure 24 To select an icon, click it.

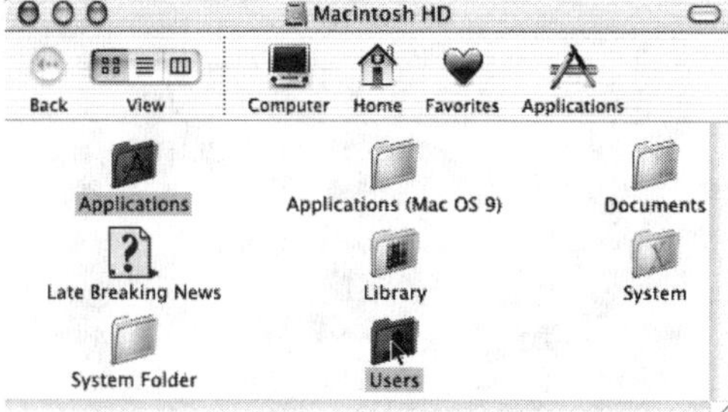

Figure 25 Hold down Shift while clicking other icons to add them to a multiple selection.

To select an icon

Click the icon that you want to select. The icon darkens, and its name becomes highlighted (**Figure 24**).

✔ Tip

- You can also select an icon in an active window by pressing the keyboard key for the first letter of the icon's name or by pressing Tab, Shift Tab, ←, →, ↑, or ↓ until the icon is selected.

To deselect an icon

Click anywhere in the window or on the Desktop other than on the selected icon.

✔ Tips

- If you select one icon and then click another icon, the originally selected icon is deselected and the icon you clicked becomes selected instead.
- Windows are discussed later in this chapter.

To select multiple icons by clicking

1. Click the first icon that you want to select.
2. Hold down Shift or ⌘ and click another icon that you want to select (**Figure 25**).
3. Repeat step 2 until all icons that you want to select have been selected.

✔ Tip

- Icons that are part of a multiple selection must be in the same window. Windows are discussed later in this chapter.

To select multiple icons by dragging

1. Position the mouse pointer slightly above and to the left of the first icon in the group that you want to select (**Figure 26**).
2. Press the mouse button down, and drag diagonally across the icons you want to select. A shaded box appears to indicate the selection area, and the items within it become selected (**Figure 27**).
3. When all the icons that you want to select are included in the selection area, release the mouse button (**Figure 28**).

✔ Tip

■ To select multiple icons by dragging, the icons must be adjacent.

To select all icons in a window

Choose Edit > Select All (**Figure 29**), or press [⌘][A].

All icons in the active window are selected.

✔ Tip

■ Activating windows is covered later in this chapter.

To deselect one icon in a multiple selection

Hold down [Shift] or [⌘] while clicking the icon that you want to deselect. That icon is deselected while the others remain selected.

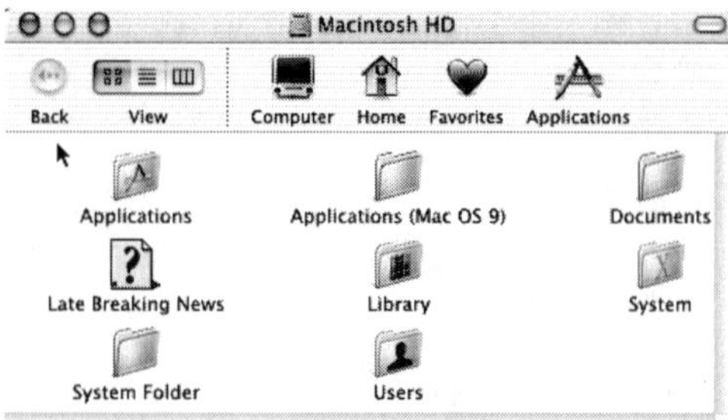

Figure 26 Position the mouse pointer above and to the left of the first icon that you want to select.

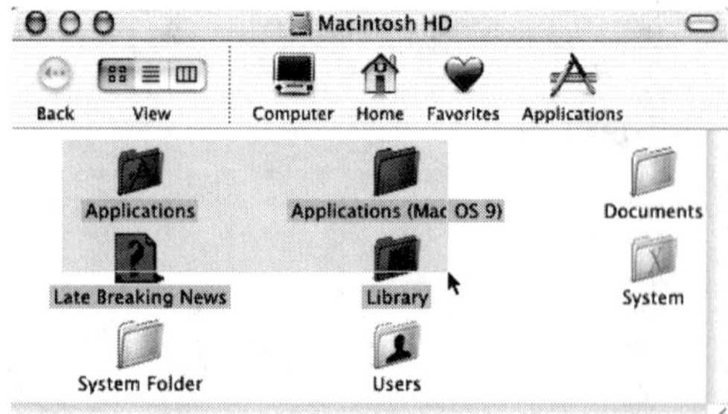

Figure 27 Drag to draw a shaded selection box around the icons that you want to select.

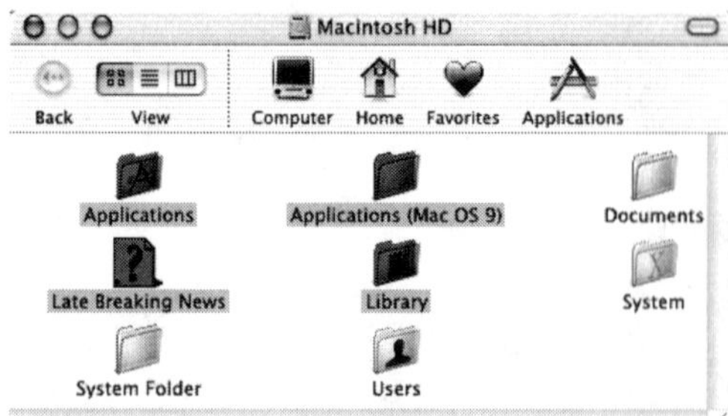

Figure 28 Release the mouse button to complete the selection.

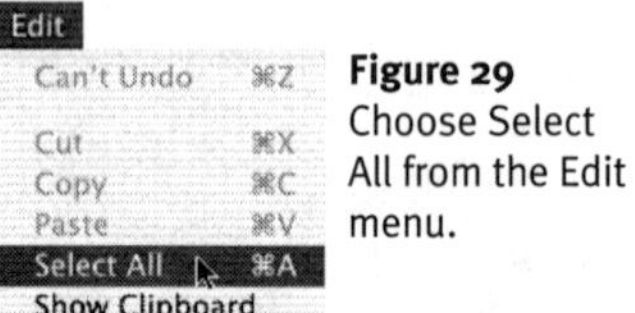

Figure 29 Choose Select All from the Edit menu.

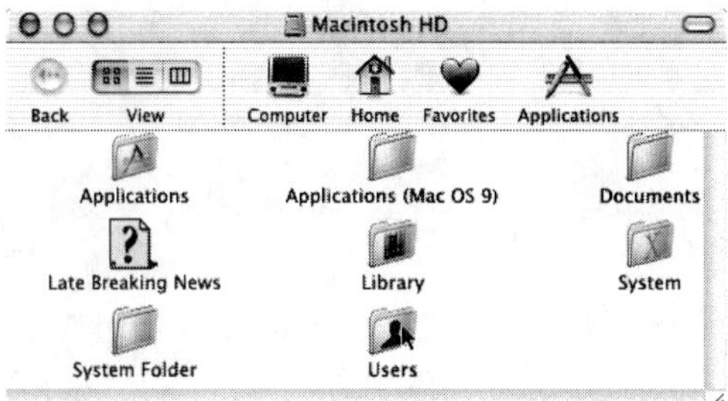

Figure 30 Point to the icon that you want to move.

Figure 31 Drag the icon to the new location.

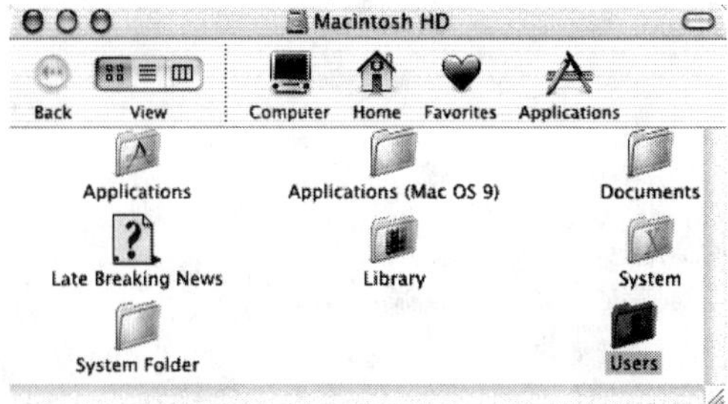

Figure 32 When you release the mouse button, the icon moves.

To move an icon

1. Position the mouse pointer on the icon that you want to move (**Figure 30**).
2. Press the mouse button down, and drag the icon to the new location. As you drag, a shadowy image of the icon moves with the mouse pointer (**Figure 31**).
3. Release the mouse button when the icon is in the desired position. The icon moves (**Figure 32**).

✔ Tips

- You cannot drag to reposition icons within windows set to list or column view. Views are discussed in **Chapter 3**.
- You move icons to rearrange them in a window or on the Desktop, or to copy or move the items they represent to another folder or disk. Copying and moving items is discussed in **Chapter 3**.
- You can also move multiple icons at once. Simply select the icons first, then position the mouse pointer on one of the selected icons and follow steps 2 and 3 above. All selected icons move together.

To open an icon

1. Select the icon you want to open (**Figure 33**).
2. Choose File > Open (**Figure 34**), or press [⌘ O].

or

Double-click the icon that you want to open.

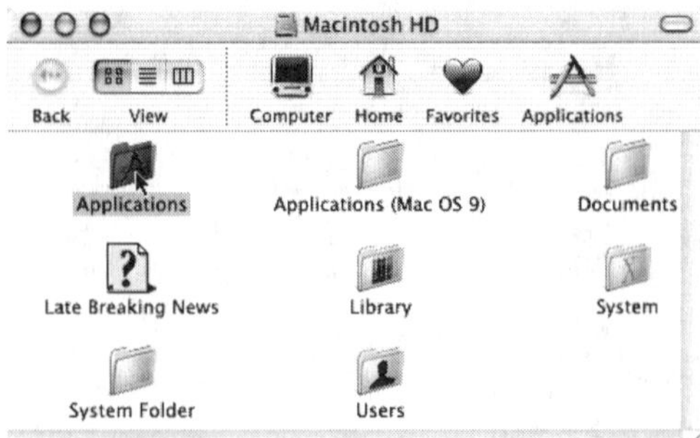

Figure 33 Select the icon.

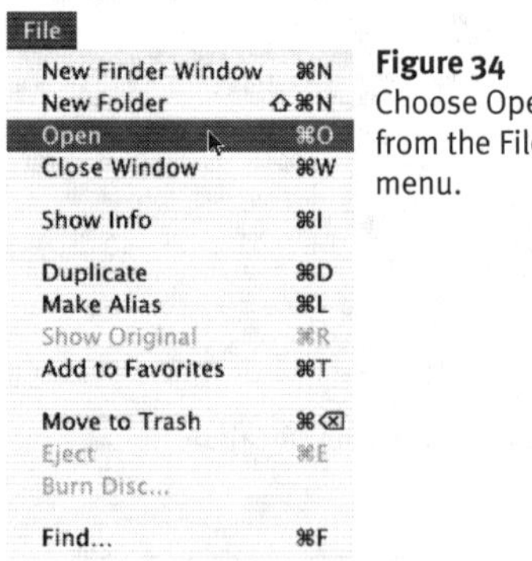

Figure 34 Choose Open from the File menu.

✔ Tips

- Only one click is necessary when opening an item in a Finder window toolbar or the Dock. The toolbar and Dock are covered in detail later in this chapter.
- What happens when you open an icon depends on the type of icon you open. For example:
  - Opening a folder icon displays the contents of the folder in the same Finder window (**Figure 35**). Windows are discussed next.
  - Opening an application icon launches the application so that you can work with it. Working with applications is covered in **Chapter 5** and elsewhere in this book.
  - Opening a document icon launches the application that created that document and displays the document so you can view or edit it. Working with documents is covered in **Chapter 5**.
  - Opening the Trash displays items that will be deleted when you empty the Trash. Using and emptying the Trash is discussed in **Chapter 3**.
- To open a folder or disk in a new Finder window, hold down [⌘] while opening it.

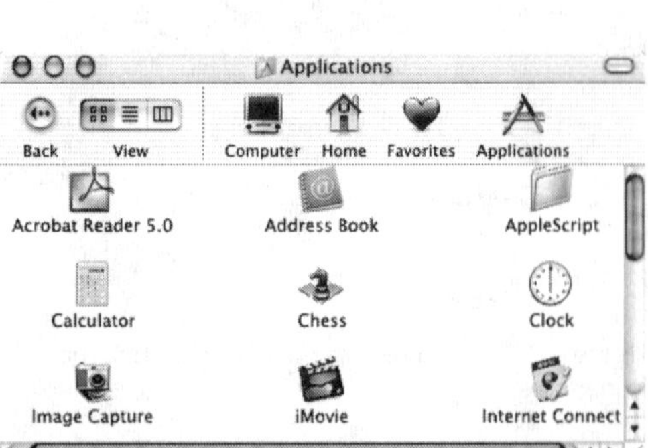

Figure 35 Opening a folder icon opens a window that displays the contents of the folder.

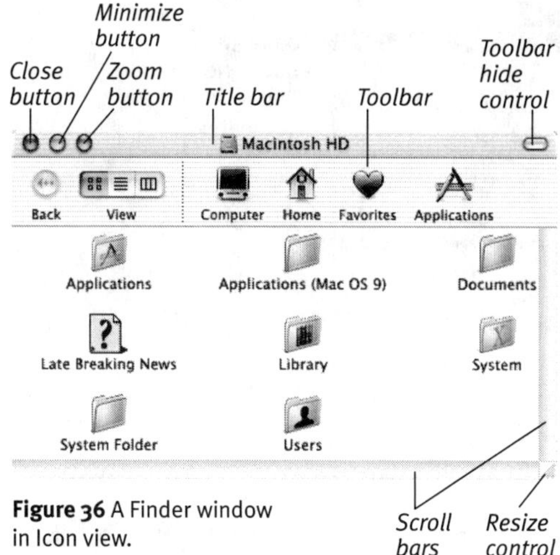

Figure 36 A Finder window in Icon view.

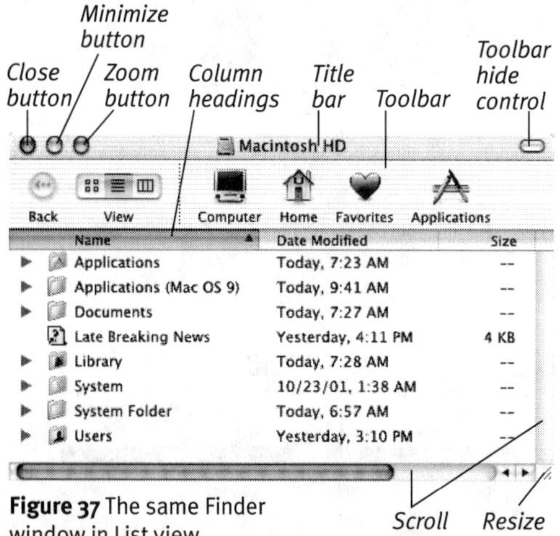

Figure 37 The same Finder window in List view.

Windows

Mac OS makes extensive use of windows for displaying icons and other information in the Finder and documents in other applications. **Figures 36** and **37** show two different views of a Finder window.

Each window includes a variety of controls you can use to manipulate it:

- The **title bar** displays the window's icon and name and can be used to move the window. (You can also move a window by dragging any of its edges.)
- The **close button** closes the window.
- The **minimize button** collapses the window to an icon in the Dock.
- The **zoom button** toggles the window's size between full size and a custom size.
- The **resize control** enables you to set a custom size for the window.
- **Scroll bars** scroll the contents of the window.
- **Column headings** (in list view only) display the names of the columns and let you quickly sort by a column. (The selected column heading is the column by which the list is sorted.)

✔ Tips

- The Finder's three window views are discussed in **Chapter 3**.
- By default, when you open a folder or disk icon, its contents appear in the currently active window. You can use Finder Preferences to set up Mac OS X so it always opens folders in new windows, like previous versions of Mac OS. Finder Preferences are discussed in **Chapter 4**.

To open a new Finder window

Choose File > New Finder Window (**Figure 38**), or press ⌘ N. A new top-level window appears (**Figure 39**).

✔ Tip

- The top-level window is discussed in **Chapter 3**.

To open a folder or disk in a new Finder window

Hold down ⌘ while opening a folder or disk icon. A new window containing the contents of the folder or disk appears.

✔ Tip

- Opening folders and disks is explained earlier in this chapter.

To close a window

Click the window's close button (**Figures 36** and **37**).

or

Choose File > Close Window (**Figure 40**), or press ⌘ W.

To close all open windows

Hold down Option while clicking the active window's close button (**Figures 36** and **37**).

or

Hold down Option while choosing File > Close All (**Figure 41**), or press ⌘ Option W.

✔ Tip

- The Close Window/Close All commands (**Figures 40** and **41**) are examples of *dynamic menu items*—pressing a modifier key (in this case, Option), changes the menu command from Close Window (**Figure 40**) to Close All (**Figure 41**).

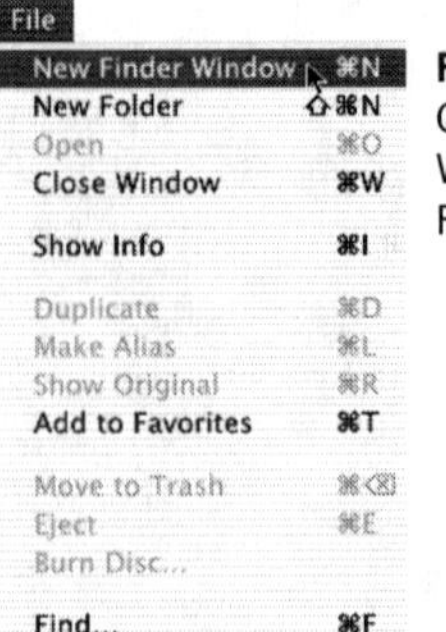

Figure 38 Choose New Finder Window from the File menu.

Figure 39 The active window's title bar includes color and appears atop all other windows.

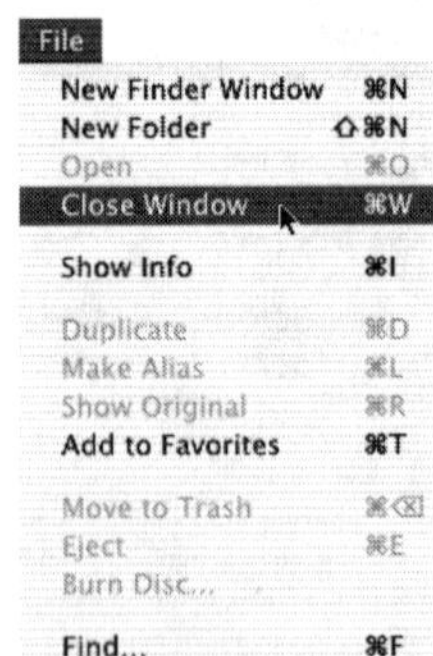

Figure 40 Choose Close Window from the File menu...

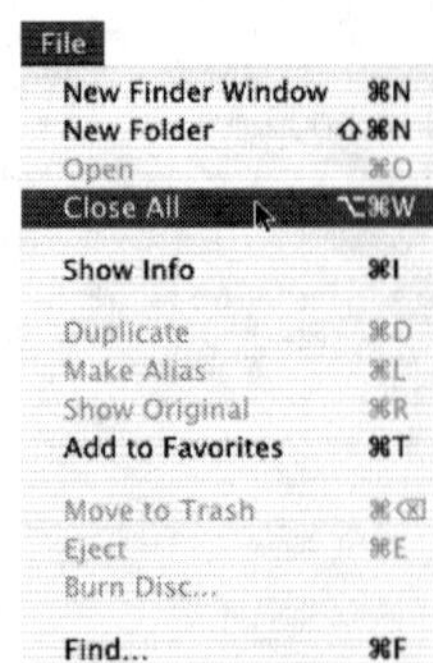

Figure 41 ...or hold down Option and choose Close All from the File menu.

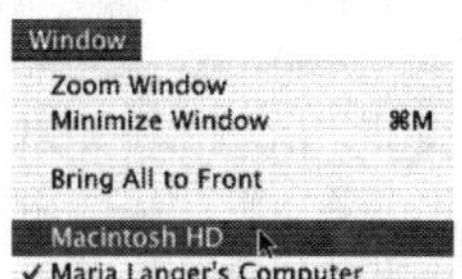

Figure 42 The Window menu lists all open Finder windows.

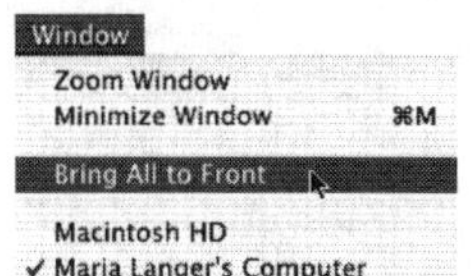

Figure 43 The Bring All to Front command brings all Finder windows to the top.

To activate a window

Click anywhere in or on the window.

or

Choose the name of the window you want to activate from the Window menu (**Figure 42**).

✔ Tips

- It's important to make sure that the window you want to work with is open and active *before* using commands that work on the active window—such as Close Window, Select All, and View menu options.
- You can distinguish between active and inactive windows by the appearance of their title bars; the active window's title bar includes color (**Figure 39**). In addition, a check mark appears beside the active window's name in the Window menu (**Figure 42**).
- When two or more windows overlap, the active window will always be on top of the stack (**Figure 39**).

To bring all Finder windows to the top

Choose Window > Bring All to Front (**Figure 43**). All open Finder windows that are not minimized become the top windows.

✔ Tip

- In Mac OS X, Finder windows can be intermingled with other applications' windows. The Bring All to Front command gathers the windows together in the top layers. You may find this command useful when working with many windows from several different applications.

To move a window

1. Position the mouse pointer on the window's title bar (**Figure 44**).
2. Press the mouse button and drag the window to a new location. As you drag, the window moves along with your mouse pointer (**Figure 45**).
3. When the outline of the window is in the desired position, release the mouse button.

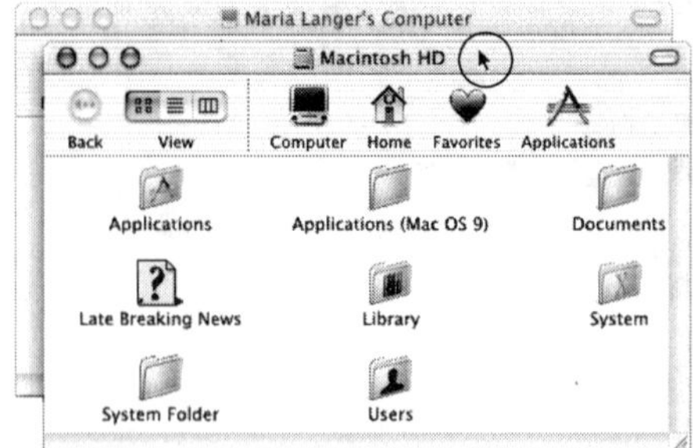

Figure 44 Position the mouse pointer on the title bar.

Figure 45 As you drag, the window moves.

To resize a window

1. Position the mouse pointer on the resize control in the lower right corner of the window (**Figure 46**).
2. Press the mouse button and drag. As you drag, the resize control moves with the mouse pointer, changing the size and shape of the window (**Figure 47**).
3. When the window is the desired size, release the mouse button.

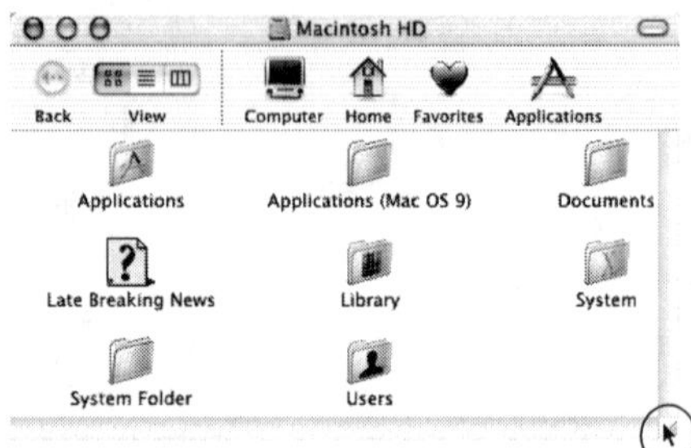

Figure 46 Position the mouse pointer on the resize control.

Figure 47 As you drag, the window's size and shape changes.

✔ Tips

- The larger a window is, the more you can see inside it.
- By resizing and repositioning windows, you can see inside more than one window at a time. This comes in handy when moving or copying the icons for files and folders from one window to another. Moving and copying files and folders is covered in **Chapter 3**.

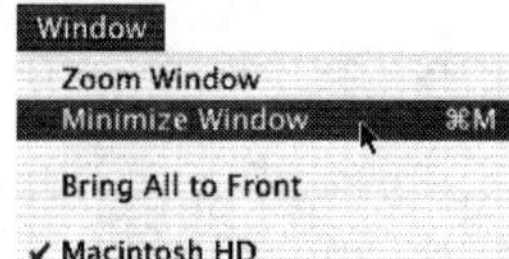

Figure 48 The Minimize Window command minimizes the active window.

Figure 49 Minimized windows shrink down into icons in the Dock.

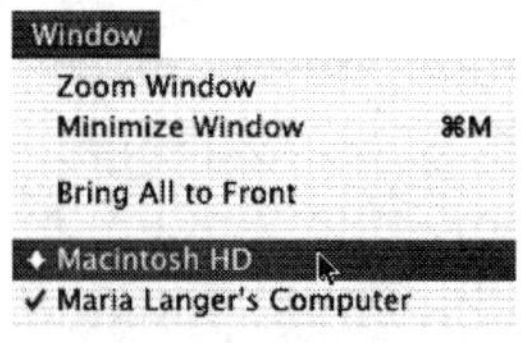

Figure 50 A diamond beside a window name indicates that the window has been minimized.

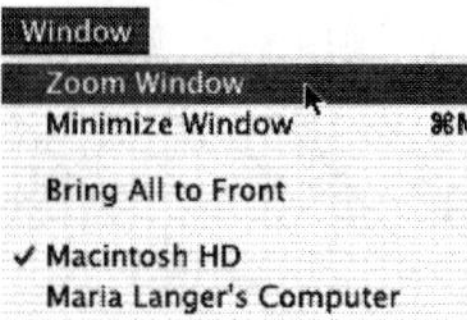

Figure 51 You can zoom the active window by choosing Zoom Window from the Window menu.

To minimize a window

Click the window's minimize button (**Figures 36** and **37**).

or

Choose Window > Minimize Window (**Figure 48**), or press ⌘ M.

or

Double-click the window's title bar.

The window shrinks into an icon and slips into the Dock at the bottom of the screen (**Figure 49**).

To redisplay a minimized window

Click the window's icon in the Dock (**Figure 49**).

or

Choose the window's name from the Window menu (**Figure 50**).

To zoom a window

Click the window's zoom button (**Figures 36** and **37**).

or

Choose Window > Zoom Window (**Figure 51**).

Each time you click the zoom button, the window's size toggles between two sizes:

- **Standard state** size is the largest possible size that would accommodate the window's contents (**Figure 46**).
- **User state** size, which is the size you specify with the resize control (**Figure 47**).

To scroll a window's contents

Click one of the scroll bar arrows (**Figure 52**) as follows:

- To scroll the window's contents up, click the down arrow on the vertical scroll bar.
- To scroll the window's contents down, click the up arrow on the vertical scroll bar.
- To scroll the window's contents to the left, click the right arrow on the horizontal scroll bar.
- To scroll the window's contents to the right, click the left arrow on the horizontal scroll bar.

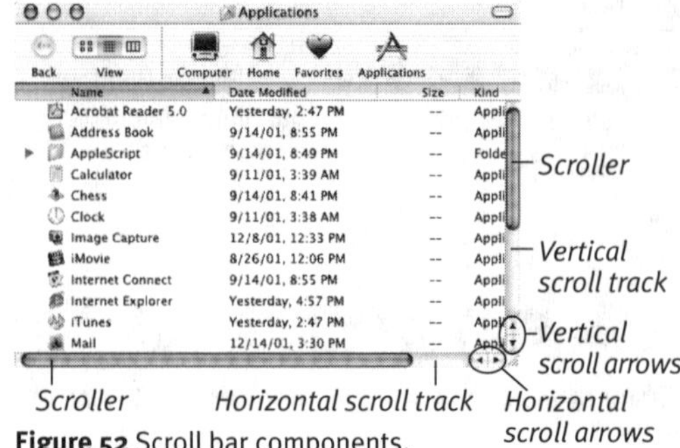

Figure 52 Scroll bar components.

✔ Tips

- If you have trouble remembering which scroll arrow to click, think of it this way:
  - Click down to see down.
  - Click up to see up.
  - Click right to see right.
  - Click left to see left.
- You can also scroll a window's contents by either clicking in the scroll track on either side of the scroller or by dragging the scroller to a new position on the scroll bar. Both of these techniques enable you to scroll a window's contents more quickly.
- If all of a window's contents are displayed, you will not be able to scroll the window. A window that cannot be scrolled will have flat or empty looking scroll bars (**Figure 46**).
- The scrollers in Mac OS X are proportional—this means that the more of a window's contents you see, the more space the scroller will take up in its scroll bar.

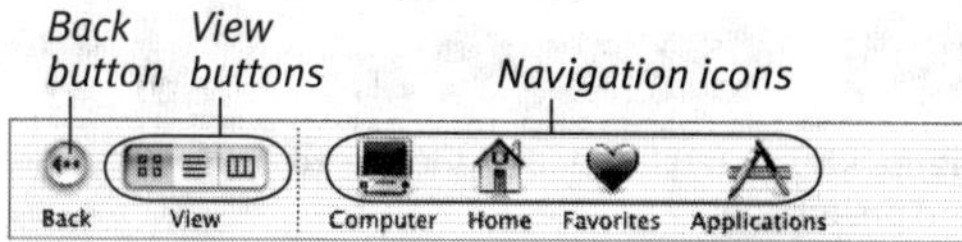

Figure 53 The toolbar.

Figure 54 When the window is narrow, some toolbar buttons may be hidden.

Figure 55 Click the double arrow to display a menu of hidden buttons.

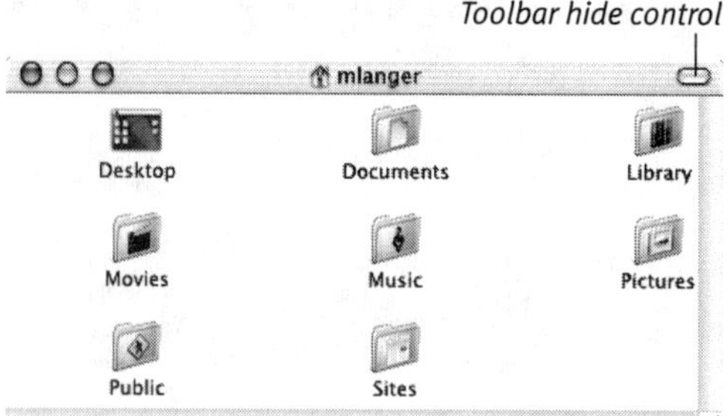

Figure 56 The toolbar hide control button can hide the toolbar...

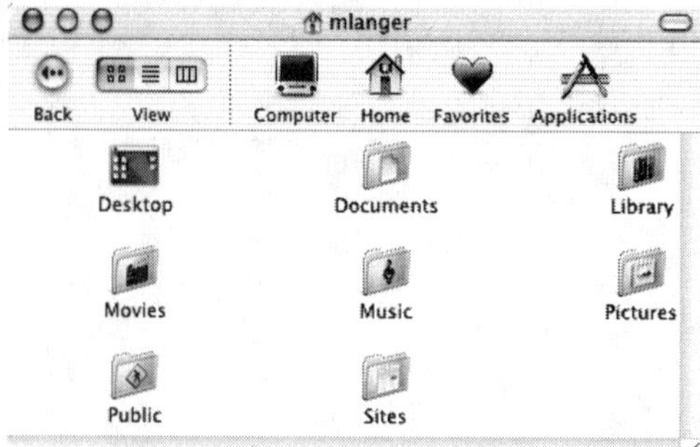

Figure 57 ...or display it.

The Toolbar

The Toolbar (**Figure 53**), which is new in Mac OS X, offers navigation tools and view buttons within Finder windows:

- The **Back button** displays the previous window's contents.
- **View buttons** enable you to change the window's view.
- **Navigation icons** open specific Finder windows.

✔ Tips

- The toolbar can be customized to show the items you use most; **Chapter 4** explains how.
- Views are covered in detail in **Chapter 4**; file management and navigation is discussed in **Chapter 3**.
- If the window is not wide enough to show all toolbar buttons, a double arrow appears on the right side of the toolbar (**Figure 54**). Click the arrow to display a menu of missing buttons (**Figure 55**) and select the button you want.

To hide or display the toolbar

Click the toolbar hide control button (**Figure 56**).

If the toolbar is displayed, it disappears (**Figure 56**); if the toolbar is not displayed, it appears (**Figure 57**).

To use a toolbar button

Click the button once.

The Dock

The Dock (**Figure 58**) offers easy access to often-used applications and documents, as well as minimized windows.

Figure 58 The Dock displays often-used applications and documents.

✔ Tip

- The Dock can be customized; **Chapter 4** explains how.

Figure 59 Point to an icon to see what it represents.

To identify items in the Dock

Point to the item. The name of the item appears above the Dock (**Figure 59**).

Figure 60 An item's icon bounces while it is being opened.

To identify items in the Dock that are running

Look at the Dock. A triangle appears beneath each item that is running.

To open an item in the Dock

Click the icon for the item you want to open. One of four things happens:

- If the icon is for an application that is running, the application becomes the active application.
- If the icon is for an application that is not running, the application launches. While it launches, the icon in the Dock bounces (**Figure 60**) so you know something is happening.
- If the icon is for a minimized window, the window is displayed.
- If the icon is for a document that is not open, the application that created the document launches (if necessary) and the document opens.

✔ Tip

- Using applications and opening documents is discussed in greater detail in **Chapter 5**; minimizing and displaying windows is discussed earlier in this chapter.

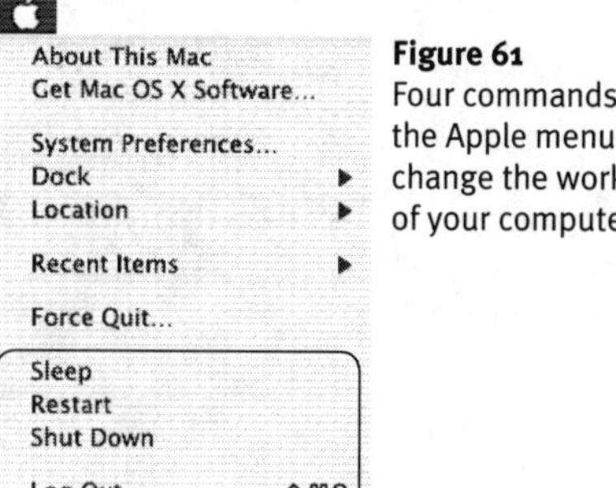

Figure 61 Four commands under the Apple menu let you change the work state of your computer.

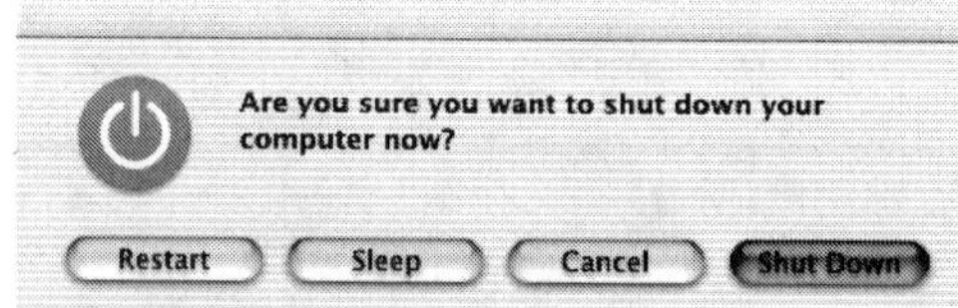

Figure 62 Pressing the Power key on some Mac OS computers displays a dialog like this one.

Sleeping, Restarting, & Shutting Down

The Apple menu (**Figure 61**) offers several options that change the work state of your computer:

- **Sleep** puts the computer into a state where it uses very little power. The screen goes blank and the hard disk may stop spinning.
- **Restart** instructs the computer to shut down and immediately start back up.
- **Shut Down** closes all open documents and programs, clears memory, and cuts power to the computer.

✔ Tips

- If your computer's keyboard includes a power key, pressing it displays a dialog with buttons for the Restart, Sleep, and Shut Down commands (**Figure 62**). This feature, however, does not work with all Mac OS-computer models.
- Do *not* restart or shut down a computer by simply flicking off the power switch. Doing so prevents the computer from properly closing files, which may result in file corruption and related problems.
- Mac OS X also includes a screen saver, which automatically starts up when your computer is inactive for five minutes. Don't confuse the screen saver with System or display sleep—it's different. To display the screen again, simply move the mouse or press any key. You can customize screen saver settings with the Screen Saver preferences pane, which is covered in the sequel to this book, *Mac OS X Advanced: Visual QuickPro Guide.*

To put your computer to sleep

Choose Apple > Sleep (**Figure 61**).

or

1. Press the Power key on the keyboard.
2. In the dialog that appears (**Figure 62**), click Sleep.

✔ Tips

- Not all computers support sleep mode. If your computer does not support sleep mode, the Sleep command will not appear on the Apple menu.
- When you put your computer to sleep, everything in memory is preserved. When you wake the computer, you can quickly continue working where you left off.
- Sleep mode is an effective way to conserve the battery life of a PowerBook or iBook without turning it off.
- By default, Mac OS X automatically puts a computer to sleep when it is inactive for 20 minutes. You can change this setting in the Energy Saver preferences pane, which is discussed in detail in the sequel to this book, *Mac OS X Advanced: Visual QuickPro Guide.*

To wake a sleeping computer

Press any keyboard key. You may have to wait several seconds for the computer to fully wake.

✔ Tips

- It's much quicker to wake a sleeping computer than to restart a computer that has been shut down.
- On some computer models, pressing Caps Lock or certain other keys may not wake the computer. When in doubt, press a letter key—they always work.

To restart your computer

Choose Apple > Restart (**Figure 61**).

or

1. Press the Power key on the keyboard.
2. In the dialog that appears (**Figure 62**), click Restart.

✔ Tip

- Restarting the computer clears memory and reloads all system files.

To shut down your computer

Choose Apple > Shut Down (**Figure 61**).

or

1. Press the Power key on the keyboard.
2. In the dialog that appears (**Figure 62**), click Shut Down or press Return or Enter.

✔ Tip

- On most computers, the Shut Down command will cut power to the computer as part of the shut down process. If it doesn't, a dialog will appear on screen, telling you it's safe to turn off your computer. You can then use the power switch to cut power to the computer.

Logging Out & In

If your computer is shared by multiple users, you may find it more convenient to log out when you're finished working. The Log Out command under the Apple menu (**Figure 61**) closes all applications and documents and closes your account on the computer. The computer remains running, making it quick and easy for the next person to log in and get right to work.

✔ Tip

- If you are your computer's only user, you'll probably never use the Log Out command. (I hardly ever do.)

To log out

1. Choose Apple > Log Out (**Figure 61**), or press Shift ⌘ Q.
2. A confirmation dialog like the one in **Figure 63** appears. Click Log Out.

   Your computer closes all applications and documents, then displays the Login Screen (**Figure 64** or **65**).

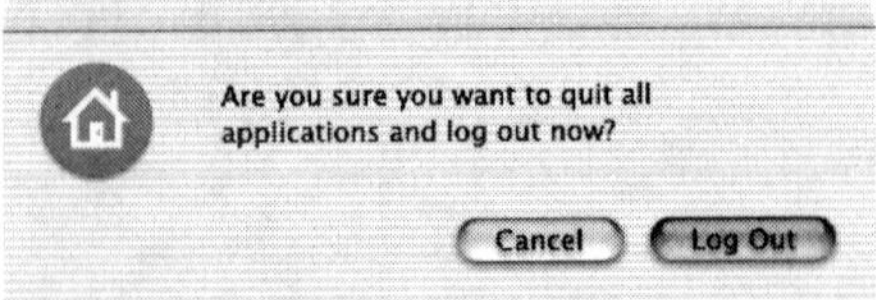

Figure 63 A dialog like this one confirms that you really do want to log out.

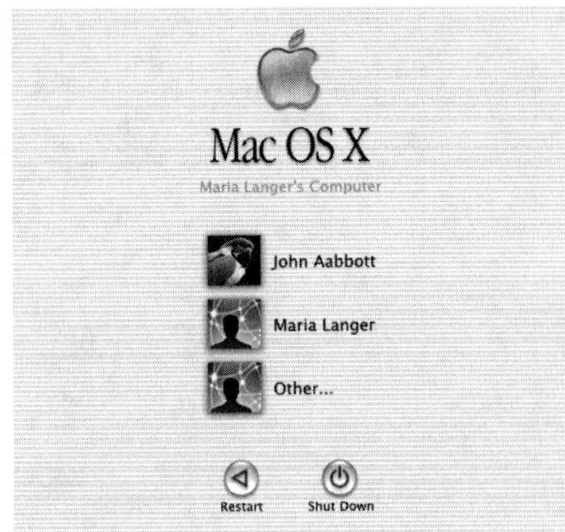

Figure 64 A typical Login Screen might list the computer's users...

Figure 65 ... or it might just provide text boxes for entering the Name and Password for a valid account.

Figure 66 If a Password box does not appear in the initial Login Screen (**Figure 64**), it appears when you select a user account.

To log in

1. If a Login Screen like the one in **Figure 64** appears, click the icon for your user account.
2. Enter your password in the Password box that appears (**Figure 66**).
3. Click Log In.

or

1. If a Login Screen like the one in **Figure 65** appears, enter your full or short account name in the Name box and your password in the Password box.
2. Click Log In.

Your Mac OS desktop appears, looking the same as it did when you logged out or shut down your computer.

✔ Tip

- The appearance of the Login Screen (**Figures 64** and **65**) varies depending on how the Users and Login preference panes have been configured by the system administrator. Users and Login options are advanced topics, which are discussed in detail in the sequel to this book, *Mac OS X Advanced: Visual QuickPro Guide.*

File Management

File Management

In Mac OS, you use the Finder to organize and manage your files.

- View the contents of your disks in windows in a variety of ways.
- Automatically sort items by name, kind, creation date, or other criteria in ascending or descending order.
- Rename items.
- Create folders to store related items.
- Move items stored on disk to organize them so they're easy to find and back up.
- Copy items to other disks to back them up or share them with others.
- Delete items you no longer need.
- Mount and eject disks.
- Write to, or "burn," CD-ROM discs.

✔ Tip

- If you're brand new to Mac OS, be sure to read the information in **Chapter 2** before working with this chapter. That chapter contains information and instructions about techniques that are used throughout this chapter.

Mac OS X Disk Organization

Like previous versions of Mac OS and most other computer operating systems, Mac OS X uses a hierarchical filing system (HFS) to organize and store files, including system files, applications, and documents.

The top level of the filing system is the computer level. You can view the computer level window (**Figure 1**) by clicking the Computer icon in the toolbar of any Finder window. This level shows the computer's internal hard disk, any other disks the computer has access to, and the Network icon.

The next level down is the computer's hard disk level. You can view this level by opening the hard disk icon in the computer level window (**Figure 1**) or on the desktop. While the contents of your hard disk may differ from what's shown in **Figure 2**, some elements should be the same:

- **Applications** contains Mac OS X applications.
- **Applications (Mac OS 9)** contains applications that run under the Classic environment.
- **System** contains the Mac OS X system files.
- **System Folder** contains the Mac OS 9.x system files for running the Classic environment.
- **Documents** contains documents you saved on your hard disk before upgrading to Mac OS X.
- **Users** (**Figure 3**) contains individual folders for each of the computer's users, as well as a Shared folder.

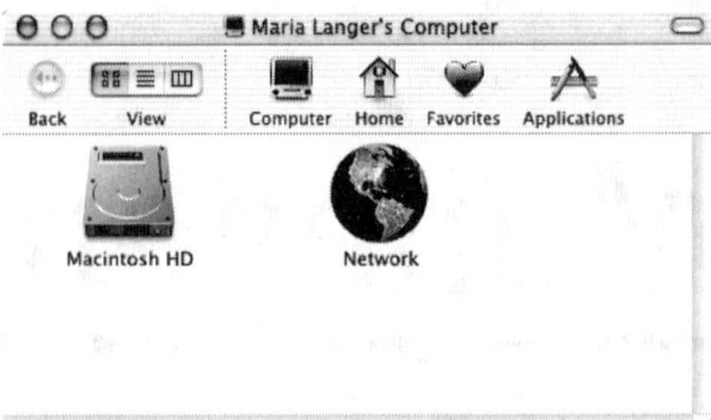

Figure 1 The top level of your computer shows all mounted disks and a Network icon.

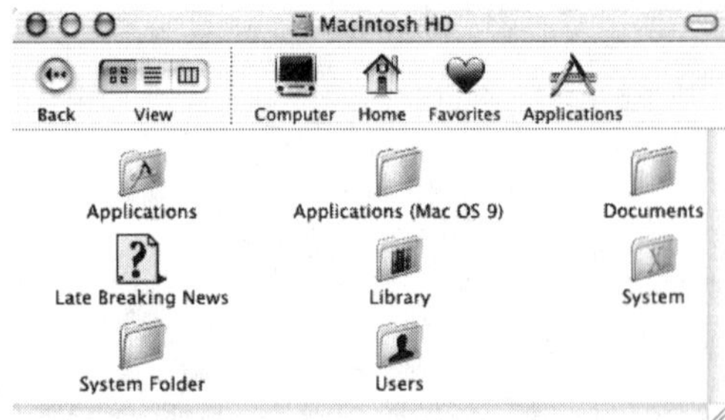

Figure 2 A typical hard disk window might look like this.

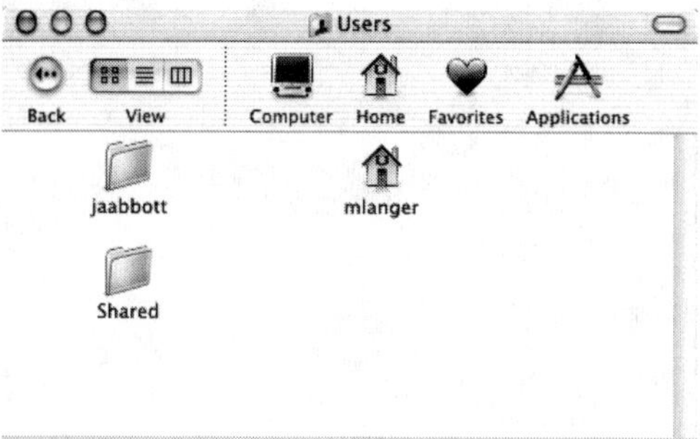

Figure 3 The Users folder contains a home folder for each user, as well as a Shared folder.

Figure 4 Your home folder is preconfigured with folders for storing a variety of item types.

By default, a Mac OS X hard disk is organized for multiple users. Each users has his or her own "home" folder, which is stored in the Users folder (**Figure 3**). You can view the items inside your home folder by opening the house icon with your name on it inside the Users folder (**Figure 3**) or by clicking the Home icon in the toolbar of any Finder window. Your home folder is preconfigured with folders for all kinds of items you may want to store on disk (**Figure 4**).

✔ Tips

- Applications and the Classic environment are discussed in greater detail in **Chapter 5.**
- When you install new applications on your computer, you should install Mac OS X-compatible applications in the Applications folder and Mac OS 9.x-compatible applications in the Applications (Mac OS 9) folder.
- If you upgraded from a previous version of Mac OS to Mac OS X, you may want to move the contents of the Documents folder on your hard disk (**Figure 2**) to the Documents folder inside your home folder (**Figure 4**) to keep your documents together and easier to find.
- Unless you are an administrator, you cannot access the files in any other user's home folder except those in the user's Public and Sites folders.
- If you place an item in the Shared folder inside the Users folder (**Figure 3**), it can be opened by anyone who uses the computer.
- Sharing computers and networking is beyond the scope of this book. For more information about these advanced topics, consult this book's sequel, *Mac OS X Advanced: Visual QuickPro Guide.*

Pathnames

A *path* or *pathname* is a kind of address for a file on disk. It includes the name of the disk on which the file resides, the names of the folders the file is stored within, and the name of the file itself. For example, the pathname for a file named *Letter.rtf* in the Documents folder of the mlanger folder shown in **Figure 4** would be: `Macintosh HD/Users/mlanger/Documents/Letter.rtf`

When entering a pathname from a specific folder, you don't have to enter the entire pathname. Instead, enter the path as it relates to the current folder. For example, the path to the above-mentioned file from the mlanger folder would be: `Documents/Letter.rtf`

To indicate a specific user folder, use the tilde (~) character followed by the name of the user account. So the path to the mlanger folder (**Figure 4**) would be: `~mlanger`. (You can omit the user name if you want to open your own user folder.)

To indicate the top level of your computer, use a slash (/) character. So the path to Maria Langer's Computer (**Figure 1**) would be: `/`

When used as part of a longer pathname, the slash character indicates the *root level* of your hard disk. So `/Applications/AppleScript` would indicate the AppleScript folder inside the Applications folder on your hard disk.

Don't worry if this sounds confusing to you. Fortunately, you don't really need to know it to use Mac OS X. It's just a good idea to be familiar with the concept of pathnames in case you run across it while working with your computer.

✔ Tip

- As discussed in **Chapter 5**, Mac OS X's Open dialogs support pathnames in the Go to field. If you decide to take advantage of this feature, use the guidelines above for entering pathnames.

Figure 5
The Go menu.

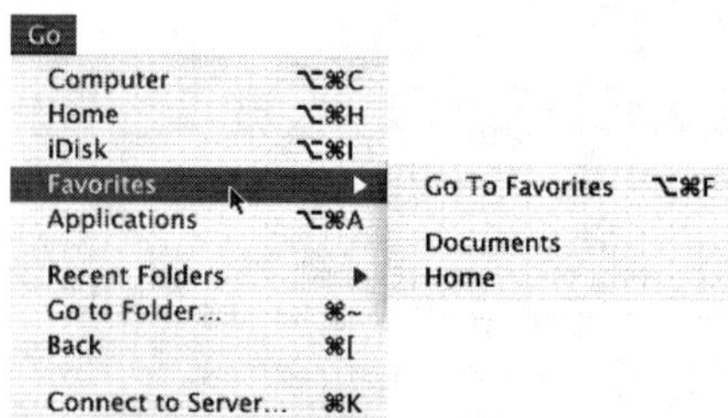

Figure 6 The Favorites submenu on the Go menu lists your favorite locations.

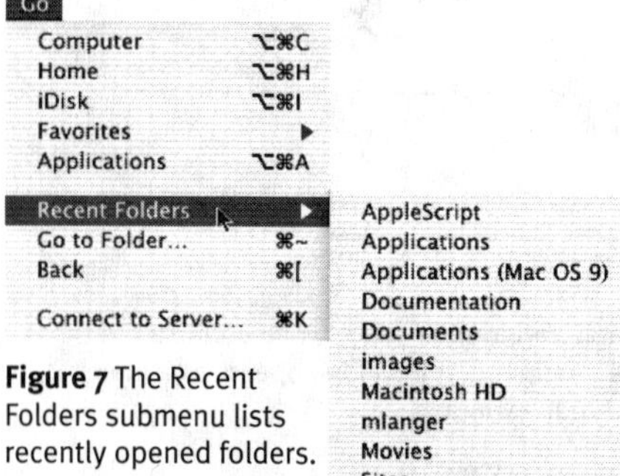

Figure 7 The Recent Folders submenu lists recently opened folders.

The Go Menu

The Go menu (**Figure 5**) offers a quick and easy way to open specific locations on your computer:

- **Computer** (Option ⌘ C) opens the top level window for your computer (**Figure 1**).
- **Home** (Option ⌘ H) opens your home folder (**Figure 4**).
- **iDisk** (Option ⌘ I) offers access to folders stored on Apple's server via the Internet and iDisk.
- **Favorites** displays a submenu of favorite locations (**Figure 6**).
- **Applications** (Option ⌘ A) opens the Applications folder.
- **Recent Folders** displays a submenu of recently opened folders (**Figure 7**).
- **Go to Folder** (Option ⌘ ~) enables you to open any folder your computer has access to.
- **Back** (⌘ [) opens the parent folder for the active window's folder. This command is only available if a window is active and if the window was used to display the contents of a folder within a folder.
- **Connect to Server** (⌘ K) enables you to open a server accessible via network.

✔ Tip

- iDisk is discussed in **Appendix B**, favorites are covered in **Chapter 4**, pathnames are discussed on the previous page.

To open a Go menu item

Choose the item's name from the Go menu (**Figure 5**) or one of its submenus (**Figures 6** and **7**).

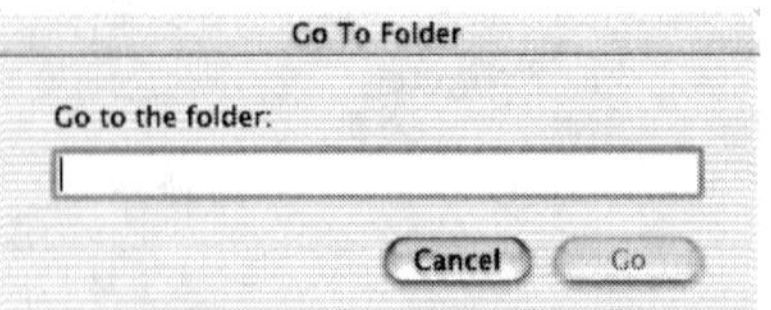

Figure 8 Use the Go To Folder dialog to enter the pathname of the folder you want to open.

To go to a folder

1. Choose Go > Go to Folder (**Figure 5**), or press [⌘ ⌘][~].
2. In the Go To Folder dialog that appears (**Figure 8**), enter the pathname for the folder you want to open.
3. Click Go.

   If you entered a valid pathname, the folder opens in a Finder window.

   or

   If you did not enter a valid pathname, an error message appears in the Go To Folder dialog (**Figure 9**). Repeat steps 2 and 3 to try again or click Cancel to dismiss the dialog.

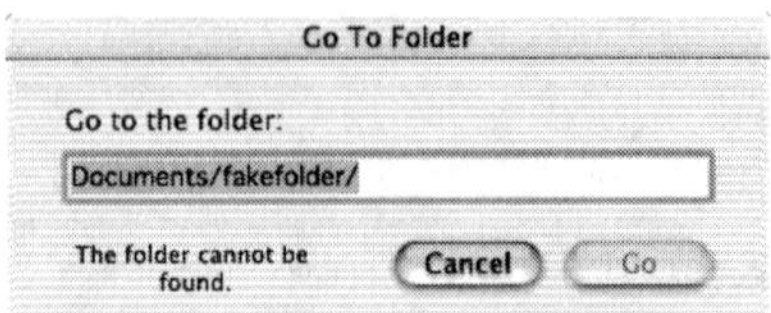

Figure 9 An error message appears in the Go To Folder window if you enter an invalid pathname.

✔ Tip

- If a window is active when you use the Go to Folder command, the Go To Folder dialog will appear as a dialog *sheet* attached to the window (**Figure 10**). The pathname you enter must be relative to that window's folder location on your hard disk.

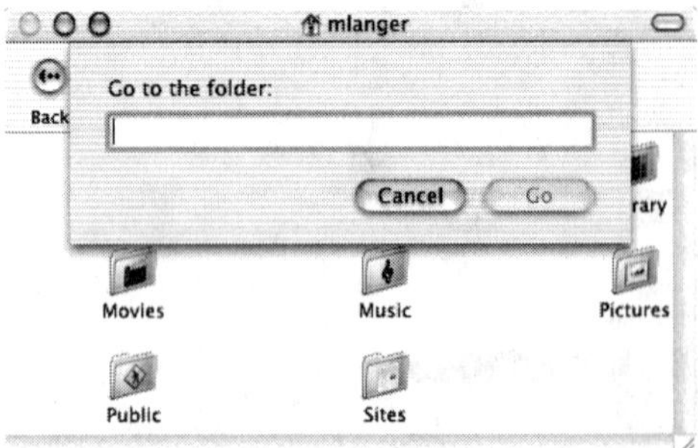

Figure 10 If a window is active when you use the Go to Folder command, the dialog appears as a sheet attached to the window.

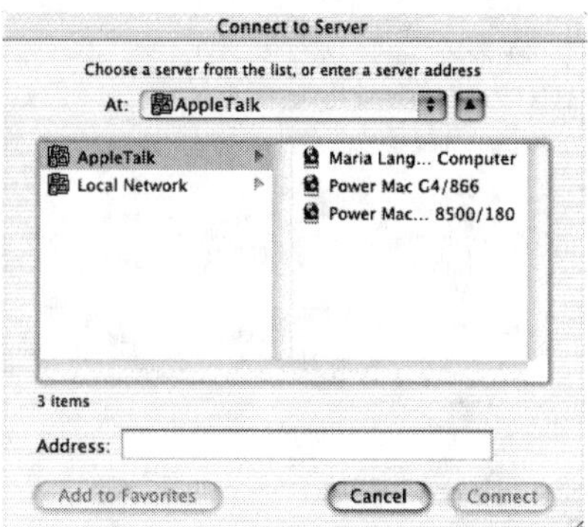

Figure 11 The Connect to Server dialog with servers accessible via AppleTalk displayed.

Figure 12 To connect to a server, you must provide log in information.

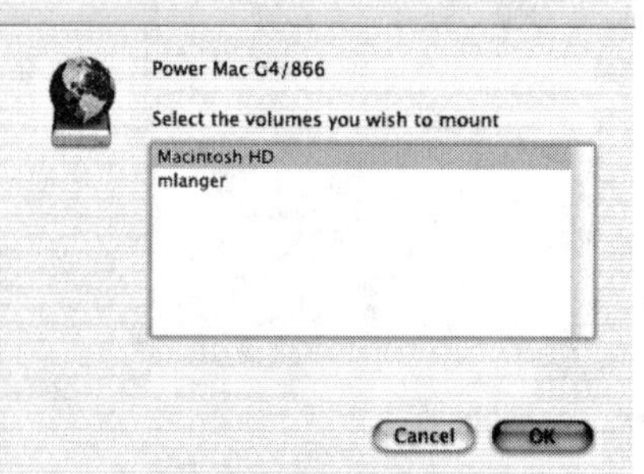

Figure 13 If more than one volume is available, choose the one you want to access.

Figure 14 The volume you connected to appears on your desktop.

To connect to a server

1. Choose Go > Connect to Server (**Figure 5**), or press [Cmd K].
2. In the Connect to Server dialog that appears, select a type of network connection in the list on the left. A list of available servers appears on the right (**Figure 11**).
3. Select the name of the computer you want to connect to.
4. Click Connect.
5. A log in window like the one in **Figure 12** appears. Enter your account information for the server in the appropriate boxes, and click Connect.
6. If the server has multiple volumes, a dialog like the one in **Figure 13** appears. Select the volume you want to open, and click OK.

   The icon for the server you connected to appears on your desktop (**Figure 14**).

✔ Tips

- A networked computer does not need to run special server software to be considered a "server" by Mac OS. For example, the computers shown in **Figure 11** are accessible via simple file sharing.
- As shown in **Figure 11**, your computer may appear in the list of available servers.
- To connect to a server using TCP/IP, enter the TCP/IP address for the server in step 2 and skip step 3.
- In step 6, a Mac OS X computer will display its hard disk and a separate volume for each user account you have access to.
- A more complete discussion of sharing computers and networking is beyond the scope of this book. For more information about these topics, consult *Mac OS X Advanced: Visual QuickPro Guide.*

Views

A Finder window's contents can be displayed using three different views:

- **Icons** displays the window's contents as small or large icons (**Figure 15**).
- **List** displays the window's contents as a sorted list (**Figure 16**).
- **Columns** displays the window's contents with a multiple-column format that shows the currently selected disk or folder and the items within it (**Figure 17**).

✔ Tip

- You can customize views by setting view options globally or for individual windows. I explain how in **Chapter 4**.

To change a window's view

1. If necessary, activate the window whose view you want to change.
2. Choose the view option you want from the View menu (**Figure 18**).

   or

   Click the toolbar's view button for the view you want (**Figure 19**).

The view of the window changes.

✔ Tips

- Commands on the View menu (**Figure 18**) work on the active window only.
- A check mark appears on the View menu beside the name of the view applied to the active window (**Figure 19**).
- You can set the view for each window individually.

Figure 15 You can display a window's contents as icons,...

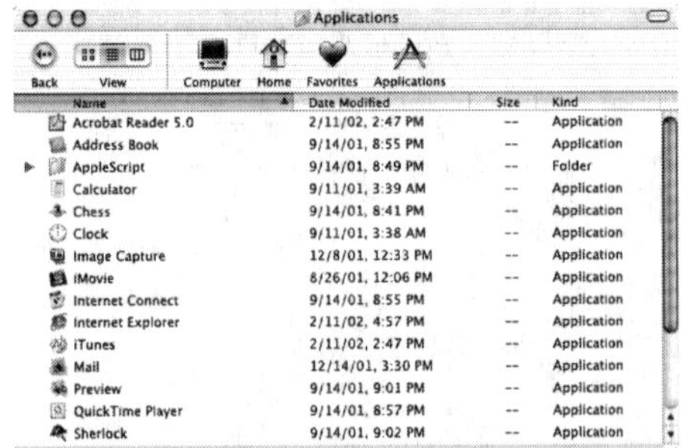

Figure 16 ...as a list,...

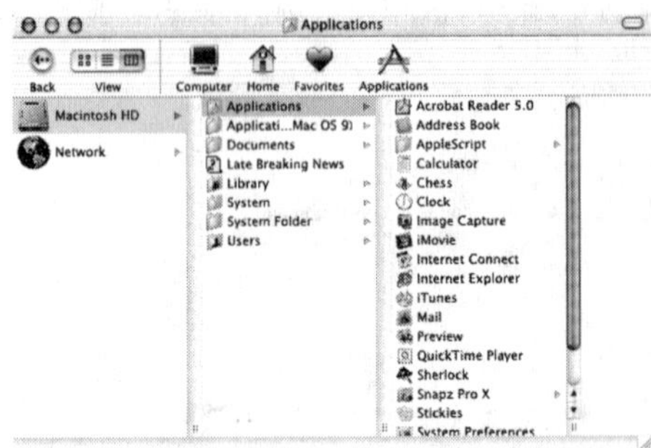

Figure 17 ...or as columns.

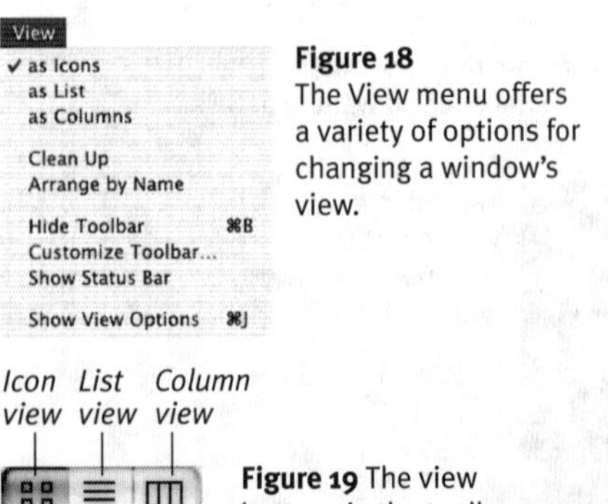

Figure 18 The View menu offers a variety of options for changing a window's view.

Figure 19 The view buttons in the toolbar.

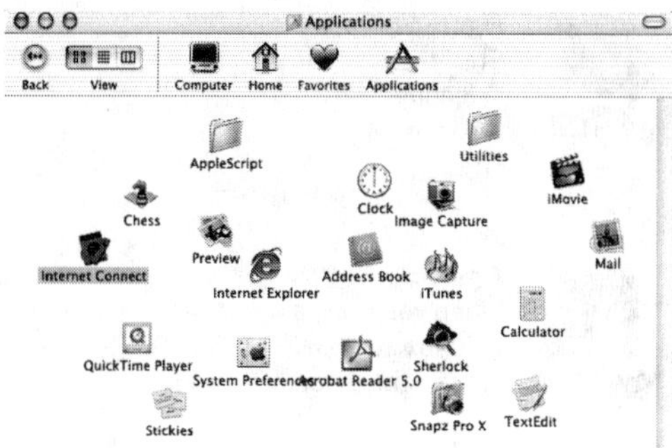

Figure 20 Start with a messy window like this one...

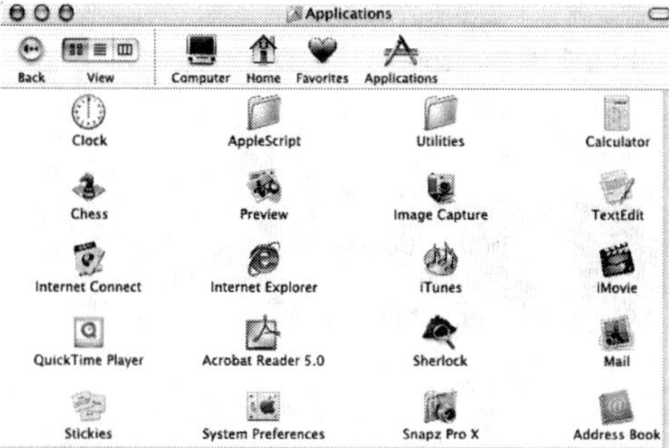

Figure 21 ...and use the Clean Up command to put the icons in place.

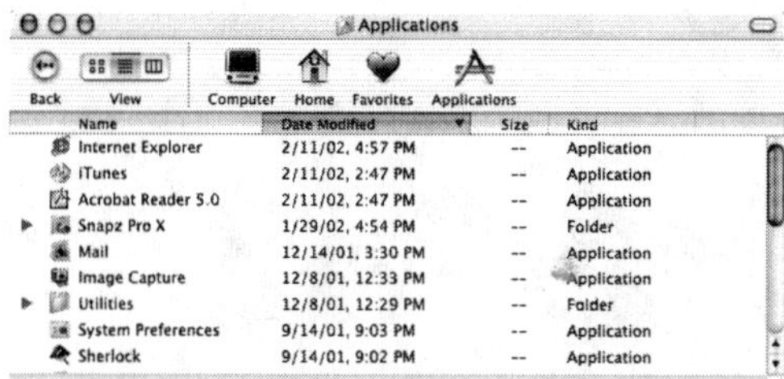

Figure 22 Click a column heading to sort by that column.

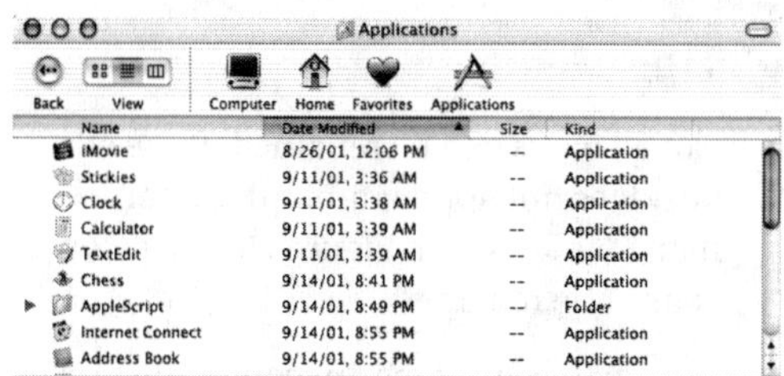

Figure 23 Click the same column heading to reverse that column's sort order.

To neatly arrange icons in icon view

1. Activate the window that you want to clean up (**Figure 20**).
2. Choose one or both of the following commands from the View menu (**Figure 18**):
   - ▲ **Clean Up** neatly arranges icons or buttons in the window's invisible grid (**Figure 21**).
   - ▲ **Arrange by Name** sorts the icons and arranges them alphabetically by name (**Figure 15**).

✔ Tip

- You can manually position an icon in the window's invisible grid by holding down ⌘ while dragging it within the window.

To sort a window's contents in list view

Click the column heading for the column you want to sort by. The list is sorted by that column (**Figure 22**).

✔ Tips

- You can identify the column by which a list is sorted by its colored column heading (**Figures 16, 22, and 23**).
- You can reverse a window's sort order by clicking the sort column's heading a second time (**Figure 23**).
- You can determine the sort direction by looking at the arrow in the sort column. When it points up, the items are sorted in ascending order (**Figures 16 and 23**); when it points down, the items are sorted in descending order (**Figure 22**).
- To properly sort by size, you must turn on the Calculate all sizes option for the window. I explain how in **Chapter 4**.

Icon Names

Mac OS is very flexible when it comes to names for files, folders, and disks.

- A file or folder name can be up to 255 characters long. A disk name can be up to 27 characters long.
- A name can contain any character except a colon (:).

This makes it easy to give your files, folders, and disks names that make sense to you.

✔ Tips

- Normally, you name documents when you save them. Saving documents is covered in **Chapter 5**.
- A lengthy file name may appear truncated (or shortened) when displayed in windows and lists.
- No two documents in the same window can have the same name.
- Because slash characters (/) are used in pathnames, it's not a good idea to use them in names. In fact, some programs (such as Microsoft Word X) won't allow you to include a slash in a file name.
- Disks are covered later in this chapter.

To rename an icon

1. Click the icon to select it (**Figure 24**).
2. Point to the name of the icon, and click. After a brief pause, a box appears around the name and the name becomes selected (**Figure 25**).
3. Type the new name. The text you type automatically overwrites the selected text (**Figure 26**).
4. Press Return or Enter, or click anywhere else. The icon is renamed (**Figure 27**).

Figure 24 Start by selecting the icon.

Figure 25 When you click, an edit box appears around the name.

Figure 26 Type a new name for the icon.

Figure 27 When you press Return, the name changes.

✔ Tips

- Not all icons can be renamed. If the edit box does not appear around an icon name (as shown in **Figure 25**), that icon cannot be renamed.
- You can also rename an icon in the Info window, which is covered in **Chapter 4**.

Renaming Icons

Figure 28 Choose New Folder from the File menu.

Figure 29 A new folder appears.

Figure 30 Enter a name for the folder while the edit box appears around it.

Folders

Mac OS uses folders to organize files and other folders on disk. You can create a folder, give it a name that makes sense to you, and move files and other folders into it. It's a lot like organizing paper files and folders in a file cabinet.

✔ Tips

- A folder can contain any number of files and other folders.
- It's a very good idea to use folders to organize the files on your hard disk. Imagine a file cabinet without file folders—that's how your hard disk would appear if you never used folders to keep your files tidy.
- As discussed earlier in this chapter, your home folder includes folders set up for organizing files by type. You'll find that these folders often appear as default file locations when saving specific types of files from within software programs. Saving files from within applications is covered in **Chapter 5**.

To create a folder

1. Choose File > New Folder (**Figure 28**), or press Shift ⌘ N. A new untitled folder (**Figure 29**) appears in the active window.
2. While the edit box appears around the new folder's name (**Figure 29**), type a name for it (**Figure 30**) and press Return.

✔ Tips

- You can rename a folder the same way you rename any other icon. Renaming icons is discussed on the previous page.
- Working with windows is discussed in **Chapter 2**.

Moving & Copying Items

In addition to moving icons around within a window or on the desktop, which I discuss in **Chapter 2**, you can move or copy items to other locations on the same disk or to other disks by dragging them:

- When you drag an item to a location on the same disk, the item is moved to that location.
- When you drag an item to a location on another disk, the item is copied to that location.
- When you hold down Option while dragging an item to a location on the same disk, the item is copied to that location.

The next few pages provide instructions for all of these techniques, as well as instructions for duplicating items.

✔ Tips

- You can move or copy more than one item at a time. Begin by selecting all of the items that you want to move or copy, then drag any one of them to the destination. All items will be moved or copied.
- You can continue working with the Finder or any other application—even start more copy jobs—while a copy job is in progress.

Figure 31 Drag the icon onto the icon for the folder to which you want to move it...

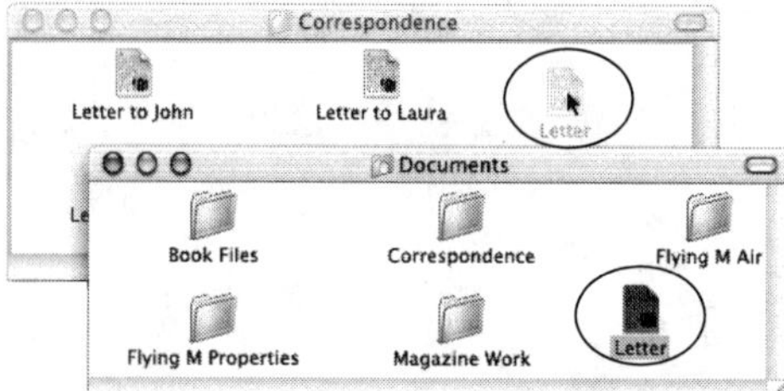

Figure 32 ...or drag the icon into the window in which you want to move it.

To move an item to another location on the same disk

1. Drag the icon for the item that you want to move as follows:
   - ▲ To move the item into a specific folder on the disk, drag the icon onto the icon for the folder. The destination folder icon becomes selected when the mouse pointer moves over it (**Figure 31**).
   - ▲ To move the item into a specific window on the disk, drag the icon into the window. A border appears around the inside of the destination window (**Figure 32**).
2. Release the mouse button. The item moves.

✔ Tip

- If the destination location is on another disk, the item you drag will be copied rather than moved. You can always delete the original after the copy is made. Deleting items is discussed later in this chapter.

To copy an item to another disk

1. Drag the icon for the item that you want to copy as follows:
   - ▲ To copy the item to the top (or *root*) level of a disk, drag the icon to the icon for the destination disk (**Figure 33**).
   - ▲ To copy the item into a folder on the disk, drag the icon to the icon for the folder on the destination disk (**Figure 34**).
   - ▲ To copy the item into a specific window on the disk, drag the icon into the window (**Figure 35**).

   When the item you are dragging moves on top of the destination location, a plus sign appears beside the mouse pointer. If the destination is an icon, the icon becomes selected.

2. Release the mouse button. A Copy window like the one in **Figure 36** appears. When it disappears, the copy is complete.

✔ Tips

- You cannot copy items to a disk that is write protected. I tell you about write-protecting disks later in this chapter.
- If a file with the same file name already exists in the destination location, an error message appears in the Copy window (**Figure 37**). Click **Stop** to dismiss the window without making the copy, or click **Replace** to replace the existing file with the one you are copying.

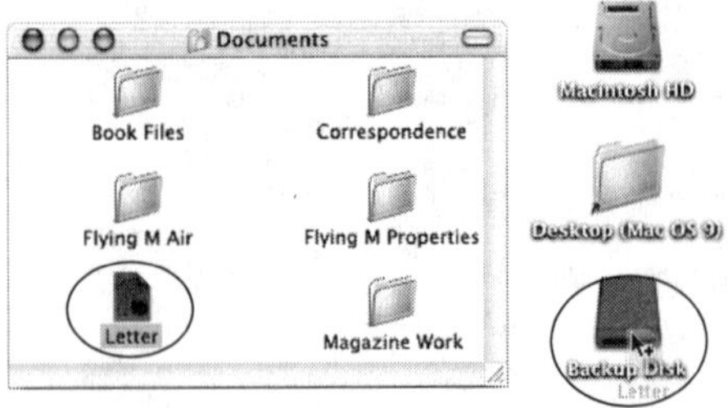

Figure 33 Drag the icon to the destination disk's icon...

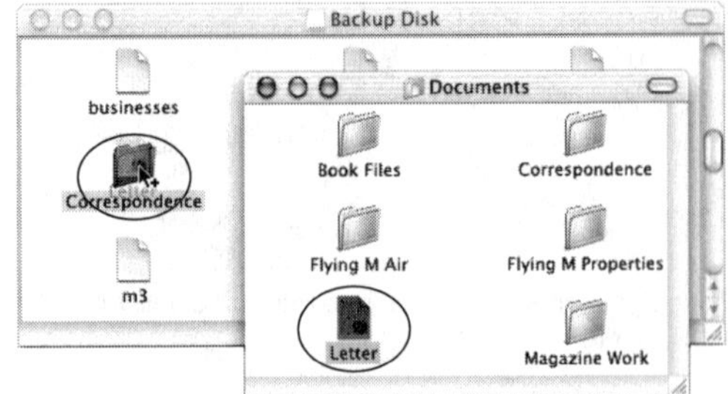

Figure 34 ...or to a folder icon in a window on the destination disk, ...

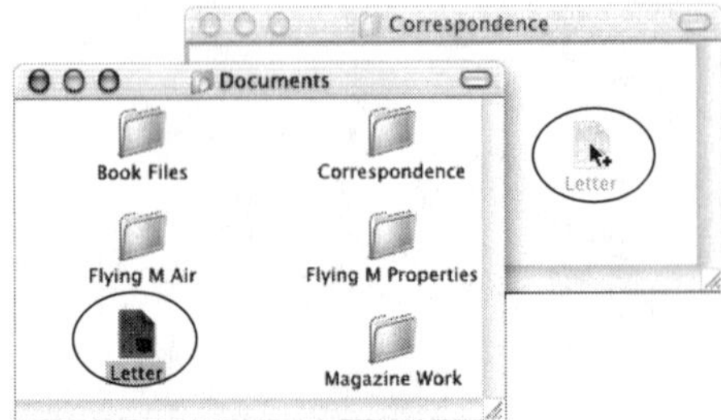

Figure 35 ...or to an open window on the destination disk.

Figure 36 A window like this indicates copy progress.

Figure 37 If a file with the same name already exists in the destination, Mac OS tells you.

Figure 38 Hold down Option while dragging the item onto a folder...

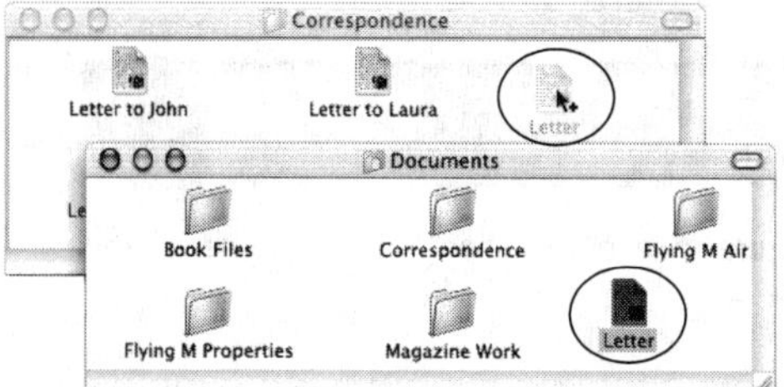

Figure 39 ...or into a window on the same disk.

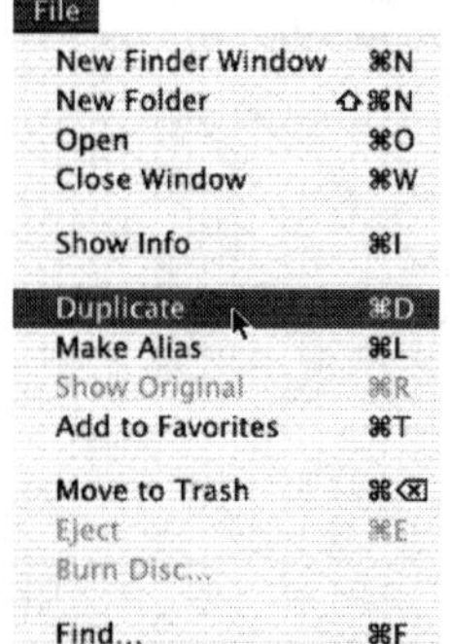

Figure 40 Choose Duplicate from the File menu.

Figure 41 A duplicate appears beneath the original.

To copy an item to another location on the same disk

1. Hold down Option while dragging the icon for the item that you want to copy onto a folder icon (**Figure 38**) or into a window (**Figure 39**).

   When the mouse pointer on the item you are dragging moves on top of the destination location, a plus sign appears beside it. If the destination is an icon, the icon becomes highlighted.

2. Release the mouse button. A Copy window like the one in **Figure 36** appears. When it disappears, the copy is complete.

✔ Tips

- When copying an item to a new location on the same disk, you *must* hold down Option. If you don't, the item will be moved rather than copied.
- If a file with the same file name already exists in the destination location, an error message appears in the Copy window (**Figure 37**). Click **Stop** to dismiss the window without making the copy, or click **Replace** to replace the existing file with the one you are copying.

To duplicate an item

1. Select the item that you want to duplicate.
2. Choose File > Duplicate (**Figure 40**), or press ⌘D.

or

Hold down Option while dragging the item that you want to duplicate to a different location in the same window.

A copy of the item you duplicated appears beside the original. The word *copy* appears at the end of the file name (**Figure 41**).

The Trash & Deleting Items

The Trash is a special place on your hard disk where you place items you want to delete. Items in the Trash remain there until you empty the Trash, which permanently deletes them. In Mac OS X, the Trash appears as an icon in the Dock.

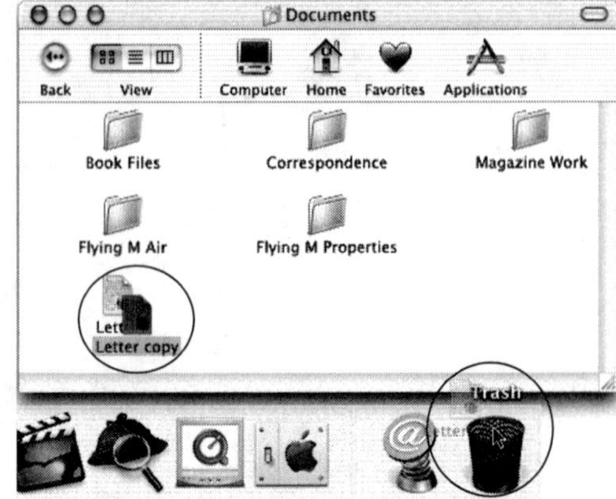

Figure 42 To move an item to the Trash, drag it there...

To move an item to the Trash

1. Drag the icon for the item you want to delete to the Trash icon in the Dock.
2. When the mouse pointer moves over the Trash icon, the Trash icon becomes selected (**Figure 42**). Release the mouse button.

or

1. Select the item that you want to delete.
2. Choose File > Move To Trash (**Figure 43**), or press [⌘ Delete].

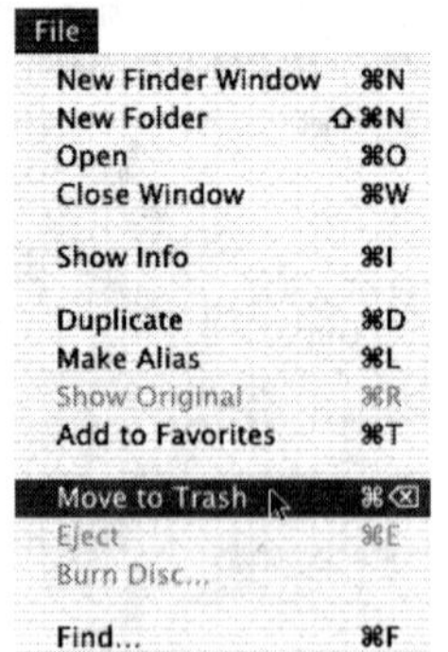

Figure 43 ...or select the item and choose Move to Trash from the File menu.

✔ Tips

- The Trash icon's appearance indicates its status:
  - ▲ If the Trash is empty, the Trash icon looks like an empty wire basket.
  - ▲ If the Trash is not empty, the Trash icon looks like a wire basket with crumpled papers in it (**Figure 44**).
- You can delete more than one item at a time. Begin by selecting all the items you want to delete, then drag any one of them to the Trash. All items will be moved to the Trash.
- Moving a disk icon to the Trash does not delete or erase it. Instead, it ejects, or *unmounts*, it. Working with disks is covered a little later in this chapter.

Figure 44 When an item has been moved to the Trash, the Trash icon looks full.

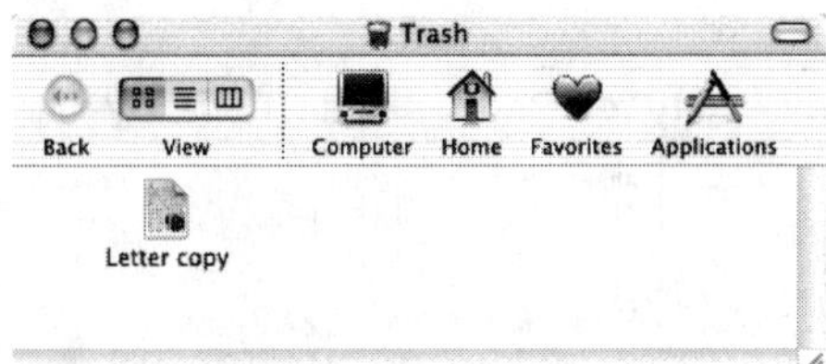

Figure 45 Opening the Trash displays the Trash window.

Figure 46 Choose Empty Trash from the Finder menu.

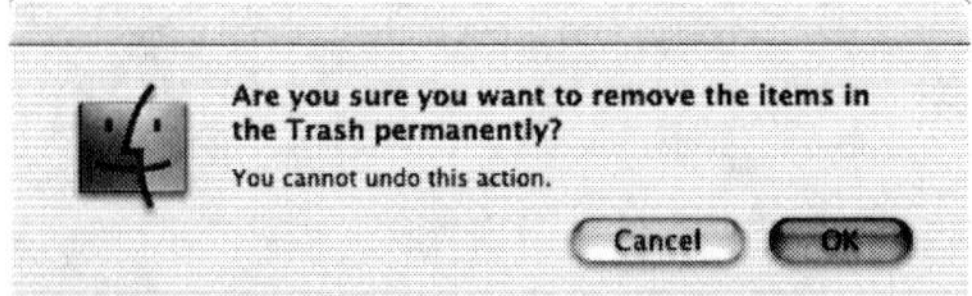

Figure 47 The Trash warning dialog asks you to confirm that you really do want to delete the items in the Trash.

Figure 48 When you point to the Trash icon in the Dock and hold the mouse button down, a menu with an Empty Trash option appears.

To move an item out of the Trash

1. Click the Trash icon in the Dock to open the Trash window (**Figure 45**).
2. Drag the item from the Trash window to the Desktop or to another window on your hard disk.

To empty the Trash

1. Choose Finder > Empty Trash (**Figure 46**), or press Shift ⌘ Delete.
2. A Trash warning dialog like the one in **Figure 47** appears. Click OK to permanently remove all items that are in the Trash.

or

1. Point to the Trash icon, press the mouse button, and hold it down until a menu appears (**Figure 48**).
2. Choose Empty Trash. The contents of the Trash are permanently deleted. No warning appears.

✔ Tip

- You can disable the Trash warning dialog (**Figure 47**) in the Finder Preferences window. I explain how in **Chapter 4**.

Storage Media

A Macintosh computer can read data from, or write data to, a wide range of storage media, including:

- **Hard disks**—high capacity magnetic media.
- **CD-ROM, CD-R, and DVD discs**—high capacity, removable optical media.
- **Zip, Jaz, or other disks or cartridges**—high capacity, removable magnetic media.
- **Floppy disks or diskettes**—low capacity, removable magnetic media.

To use storage media, it must be:

- **Mounted**—inserted, attached, or otherwise accessible to your computer.
- **Formatted** or **initialized**—specially prepared for use with your computer.

All of these things are covered in this section.

Table 1

Terminology for Storage Media Capacity

Term	Abbreviation	Size
byte	byte	1 character
kilobyte	KB	1,024 bytes
megabyte	MB	1,024 KB
gigabyte	GB	1,024 MB

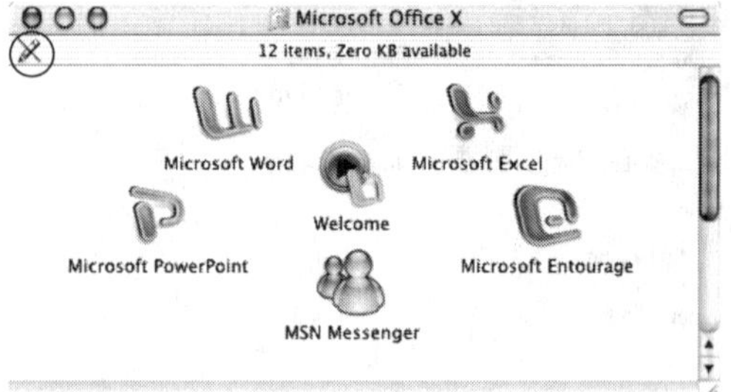

Figure 49 A write-protected icon appears in the status bar of CD-ROM discs and other write-protected media.

✔ Tips

- Don't confuse storage media with memory. The term *memory* usually refers to the amount of RAM in your computer, not disk space. RAM is discussed in **Chapter 5**.
- At a minimum, all new Macintosh computers include a hard disk and CD-ROM disc drives.
- Disk and other storage media drives can be internal (inside your computer) or external (attached to your computer by a cable).
- Some external storage devices must be properly connected and turned on *before* you start your computer or your computer may not recognize the device.
- Disk storage media capacity is specified in terms of bytes, kilobytes, megabytes, and gigabytes (**Table 1**).
- If a disk is *write-protected* or *locked*, files cannot be saved or copied to it. A pencil with a line through it appears in the status bar of write-protected or locked disks (**Figure 49**). I tell you more about the status bar in **Chapter 4**.
- You cannot write data to a CD-ROM. But if your Mac has a CD-Recordable (CD-R) drive or SuperDrive, you can use special software to create or *burn* your own CDs.
- Mac OS X may not recognize a built-in floppy drive. It does, however, recognize most third-party USB floppy drives.

Figure 50 Here's a desktop with a hard disk, floppy disk, CD-ROM disc, and network volume mounted.

Mounting Disks

You *mount* a disk by inserting it in the disk drive so it appears on the Mac OS desktop (**Figure 50**).

✔ Tips

- You must mount a disk to use it.
- To learn how to mount disks that are not specifically covered in this book, consult the documentation that came with the disk drive.
- Mounted disks appear on the desktop as well as in the top-level window for your computer (**Figure 50**).
- You mount a network volume by using the Connect to Server command under the Go menu (**Figure 5**). I explain how earlier in this chapter.

To mount a CD or DVD disc

1. Follow the manufacturer's instructions to open the CD or DVD disc tray or eject the CD or DVD caddy.
2. Place the CD or DVD disc in the tray or caddy, label side up.
3. Gently push the tray or caddy into the drive. After a moment, the disc icon appears on the desktop (**Figure 50**).

✔ Tip

- If your CD or DVD drive does not use a disc tray or caddy, consult its documentation for specific instructions.

To mount a floppy disk

Insert the disk in the floppy disk drive, label side up, metal side in. The disk's icon appears on the desktop (**Figure 50**).

To mount a Zip or Jaz disk

Insert the disk in the Zip or Jaz drive, label side up, metal side in. After a moment, the disk icon appears on the desktop.

Ejecting Disks

When you eject a disk, the disk is physically removed from the disk drive and its icon disappears from the desktop.

✔ Tip

- When the disk's icon disappears from the desktop, it is said to be *unmounted.*

To eject a disk

1. Click the disk's icon once to select it.
2. Choose File > Eject (**Figure 51**), or press ⌘ E.

or

1. Drag the disk's icon to the Trash (**Figure 52**). As you drag, the Trash icon turns into a rectangle with a triangle on top (**Figure 53**).
2. When the mouse pointer moves over the Trash icon, it becomes selected (**Figure 52**). Release the mouse button.

or

Press the Eject key on the keyboard.

✔ Tips

- If you try to eject a disk that contains one or more files that are in use by your computer, a dialog like the one in **Figure 54** appears. Click OK or press Return or Enter to dismiss the dialog, then quit the open application. You should then be able to eject the disk. Working with applications is covered in **Chapter 5.**
- Not all keyboards include an Eject key. On some keyboards, F12 may act as an Eject key.

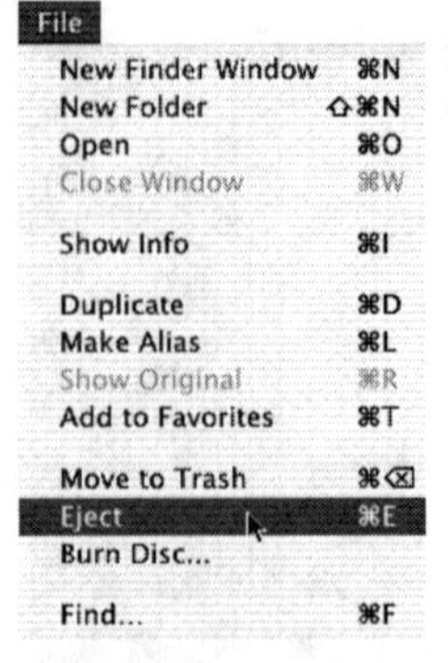

Figure 51 Select the disk, and then choose Eject from the File menu...

Figure 52 ...or drag the disk icon to the Trash.

Figure 53 When you drag a disk icon, the Trash icon transforms into an icon like this.

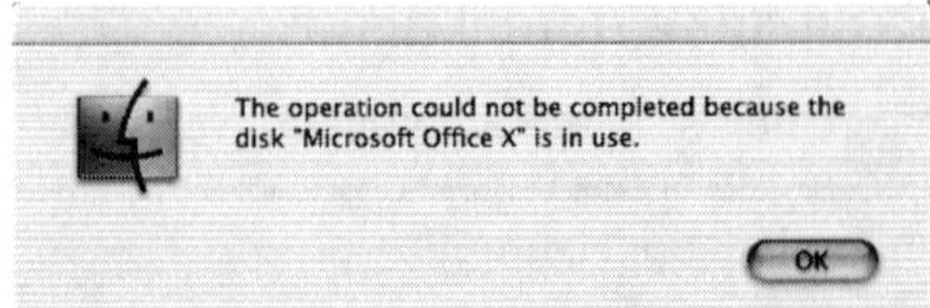

Figure 54 A dialog like this appears if you try to eject a disk that contains open files.

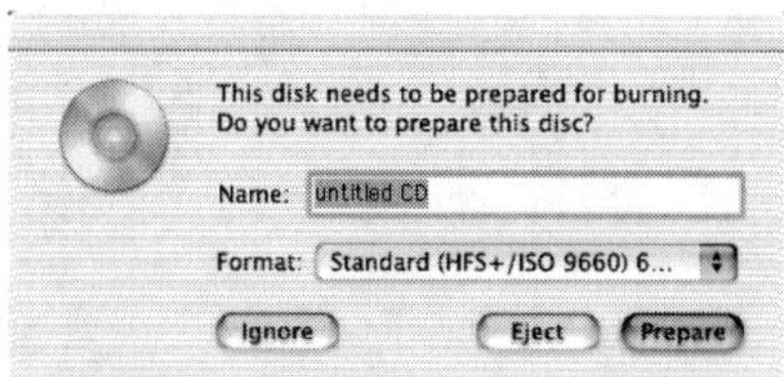

Figure 55 When you insert a blank CD-R disc, your Mac asks if it should prepare it.

Figure 56 An icon for the disc appears on the desktop.

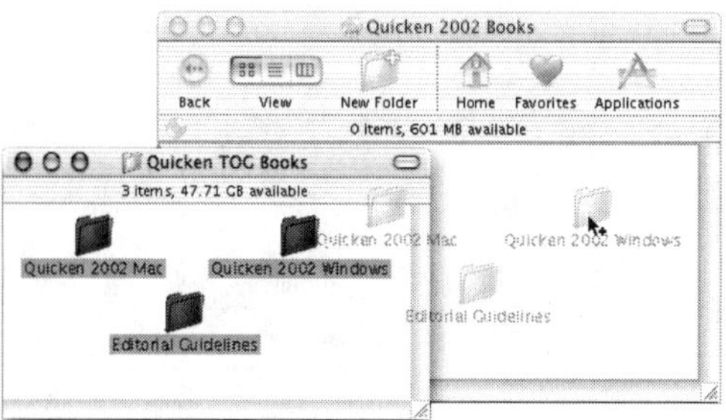

Figure 57 Copy the items you want to include on the disc to the disc's window.

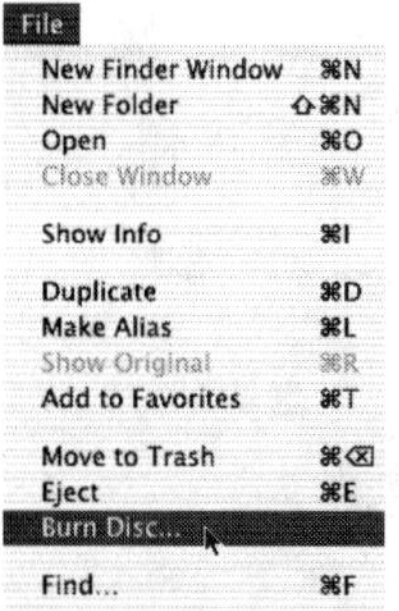

Figure 58 Choose Burn Disc from the File menu.

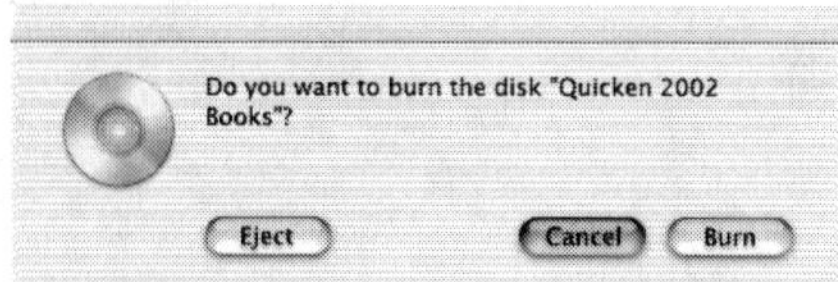

Figure 59 Your computer confirms that you want to burn the disc.

Figure 60 The Burn Disc window appears while the disc is being prepared, burned, and verified.

Burning CDs

If your Macintosh includes a CD-R drive or SuperDrive, you can write, or burn, files onto blank CD-R media. This is a great way to archive important files that you don't need on your computer's hard disk and to share files with other computer users.

✔ Tip

- This part of the chapter provides one technique for burning a CD with the Finder's Burn Disc command. You can also burn CDs or DVDs from within iTunes, iDVD, or other third party utilities, such as Roxio Toast. iTunes and iDVD are discussed in **Chapter 11**.

To burn a CD

1. Insert a blank CD-R disc into your computer's CD-R drive or SuperDrive.
2. A dialog like the one in **Figure 55** appears. Enter a suitable name for the disc in the edit box and click Prepare.
3. Wait while your computer prepares the disc. When it is finished, a CD disc icon appears on the desktop (**Figure 56**).
4. Drag the files you want to write on the disc onto the disc icon or into the open disc window (**Figure 57**).
5. Wait while your computer copies the files.
6. Repeat steps 4 and 5 until all files you want on the disc have been copied.
7. Choose File > Burn Disc (**Figure 58**).
8. A confirmation dialog like the one in **Figure 59** appears. Click Burn.
9. Wait while your computer prepares, burns, and verifies the disc. A Burn Disc window (**Figure 60**) reports its progress. When it disappears, the disk is ready.

Advanced Finder Techniques

4

✔ Tips

- If you're brand new to Mac OS, be sure to read the information in **Chapters 2** and **3** before working with this chapter. Those chapters contain information and instructions about techniques that are used throughout this chapter.
- This chapter is especially useful for experienced Mac OS users since it goes beyond the basics with new or advanced Mac OS features.

Advanced Finder Techniques

In addition to the basic Finder and file management techniques covered in **Chapters 2** and **3**, Mac OS X offers more advanced techniques you can use to customize the Finder, work with windows, and manage files:

- Customize the way the Finder and desktop look and work.
- Customize the toolbar to add buttons for the items you use most.
- Customize the Dock to add applications and documents you access often.
- Customize icon and list view windows to change the way contents are displayed.
- Use hierarchical outlines in list view windows.
- Use aliases to make frequently used files easier to access without moving them.
- Create and organize favorite items.
- Quickly reopen recently used items.
- Use the Info window to learn more about an item or set options for it.
- Undo actions you performed while working with the Finder.

This chapter covers all of these techniques.

Finder Preferences

The Finder Preferences window enables you to customize several aspects of the desktop and Finder.

Figure 1 Choose Preferences from the Finder menu.

✔ Tips

- Mac OS X 10.1 moved the icon arrangement settings from the Preferences window to the View Options window. View options are covered a little later in this chapter.
- Mac OS X 10.1 moved the Desktop Picture setting from the Finder Preferences window to the new Desktop preferences pane. System Preferences are discussed in detail in the sequel to this book, *Mac OS X Advanced: Visual QuickPro Guide*.

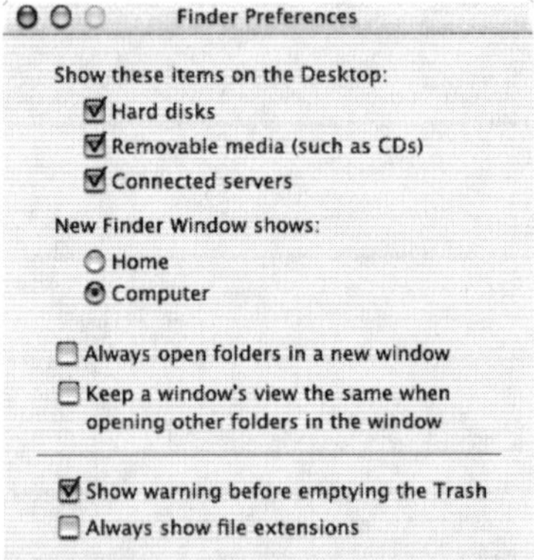

Figure 2 The Finder Preferences window offers options for customizing the desktop and Finder.

To set Finder Preferences

1. Choose Finder > Preferences (**Figure 1**) to display the Finder Preferences window (**Figure 2**).
2. Toggle check boxes to specify what items should appear on the desktop:
   - ▲ **Hard disks** displays icons for mounted hard disks.
   - ▲ **Removable media (such as CDs)** displays icons for removable media, including CDs, DVDs, Zip, Jaz, and floppy disks.
   - ▲ **Connected servers** displays icons for mounted server volumes.
3. Select a radio button to determine what should appear in a new Finder window (the window that appears when you choose File > New Finder Window):
   - ▲ **Home** displays the contents of your home folder (**Figure 3**).
   - ▲ **Computer** displays the icons for the network and all mounted volumes (**Figure 4**).

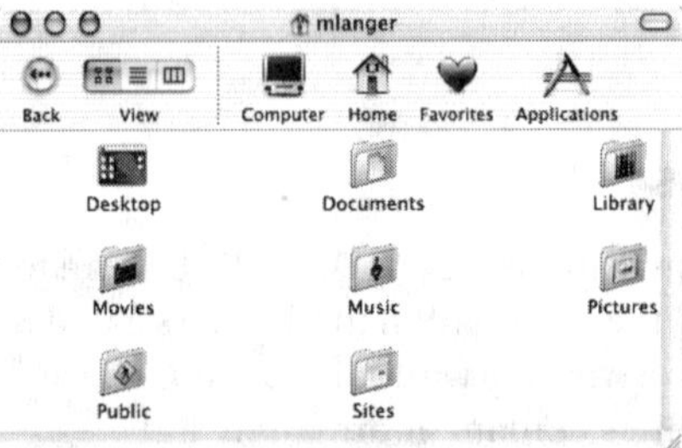

Figures 3 & 4 A new Finder window can display your home folder (above) or the items accessible by your computer (below).

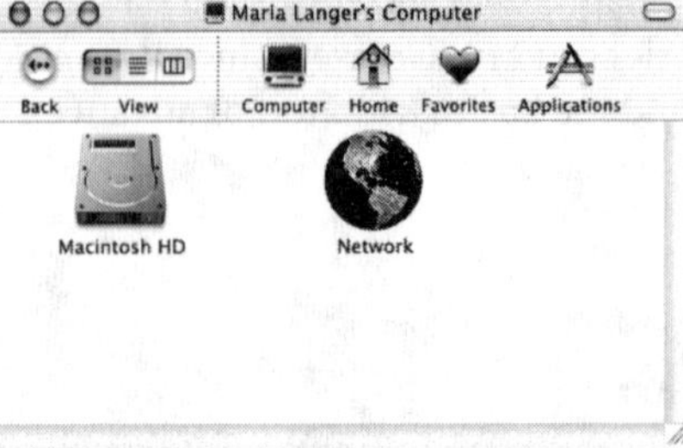

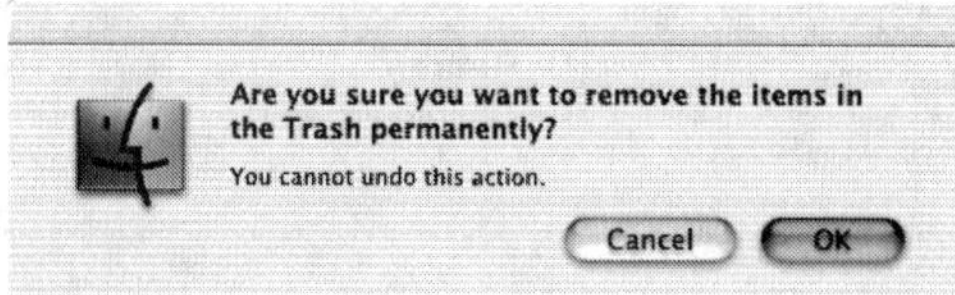

Figure 5 The Trash warning dialog.

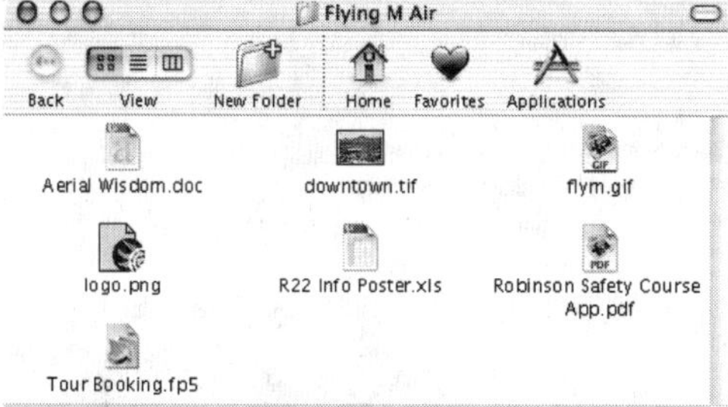

Figure 6 You can set up the Finder so it always displays file extensions as part of an item's name.

4. Toggle check boxes to set other options:
   - **Always open folders in a new window** opens a new window to display the contents of the folder you open. This makes Mac OS X work more like previous versions of Mac OS.
   - **Keep a window's view the same when opening other folders in the window** uses the same view—icon, list, or column—for all folders viewed in the same window.
   - **Show warning before emptying the Trash** displays a confirmation dialog (**Figure 5**) each time you choose Finder > Empty Trash. Turning off this check box prevents the dialog from appearing.
   - **Always show file extensions** displays file extensions in Finder windows (**Figure 6**).
5. Click the Finder Preferences window's close button to dismiss it and save your settings.

✔ Tip

- Disks, mounting disks, and the Trash are discussed in **Chapter 3**. Views are discussed in **Chapter 3** and again later in this chapter.

Customizing the Toolbar

The toolbar, which is discussed in **Chapter 2**, can be customized to include buttons and icons for a variety of commands and items.

✔ Tip

- When you customize the toolbar, your changes affect the toolbar in all windows in which the toolbar is displayed.

To customize the toolbar

1. With any Finder window open and the toolbar displayed, choose View > Customize Toolbar (**Figure 7**). Toolbar customization options appear in the current window (**Figure 8**).
2. To add an item to the toolbar, drag it from the center part of the window to the position you want it to occupy in the toolbar (**Figure 9**). When you release the mouse button, the item appears (**Figure 10**).
3. To remove an item from the toolbar, drag it from the toolbar into the center part of the window (**Figure 11**). When you release the mouse button, the item disappears (**Figure 12**).
4. To rearrange the order of items on the toolbar, drag them into the desired position (**Figure 13**). When you release the mouse button, the items are rearranged (**Figure 14**).
5. To specify how items should appear on the toolbar, choose an option from the Show pop-up menu at the bottom of the window (**Figure 15**):
   - ▲ **Icon & Text** displays both the icon and the icon's name (**Figure 14**).
   - ▲ **Icon Only** displays only the icon (**Figure 16**).
   - ▲ **Text Only** displays only the name of the icon (**Figure 17**).

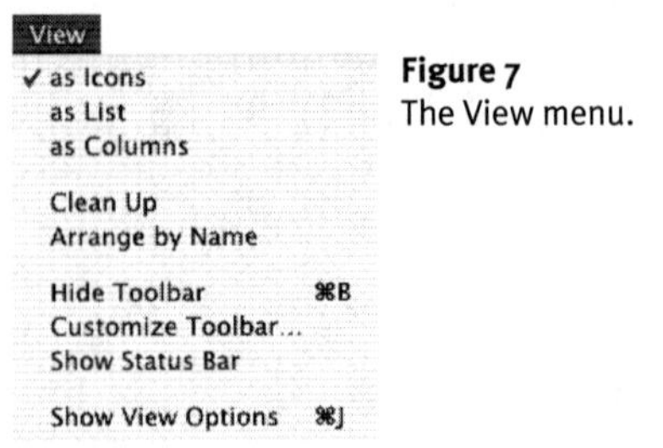

Figure 7 The View menu.

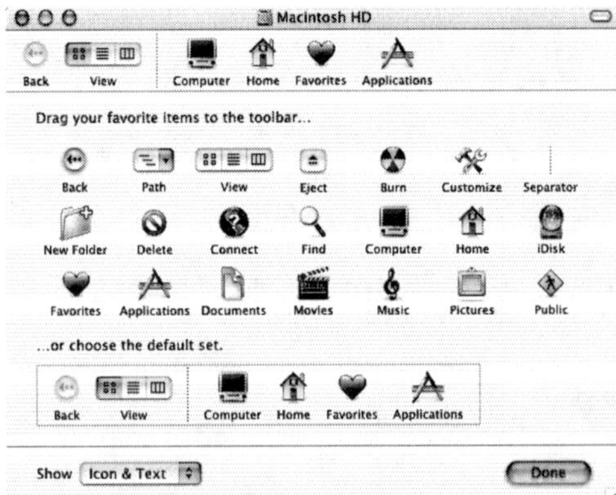

Figure 8 Toolbar customization options appear in the currently open window.

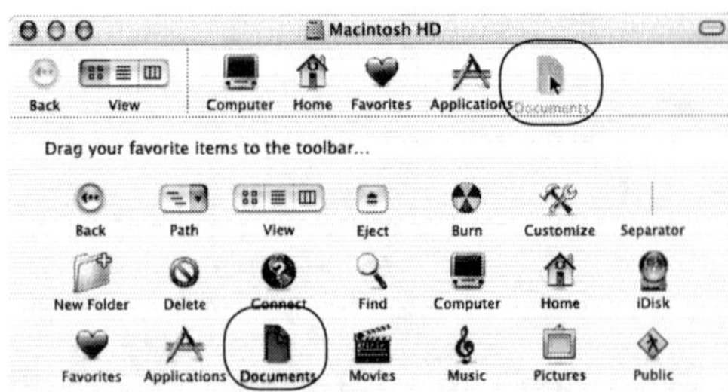

Figure 9 To add an item, drag it from the center part of the window to the toolbar.

Figure 10 When you release the mouse button, the item is added.

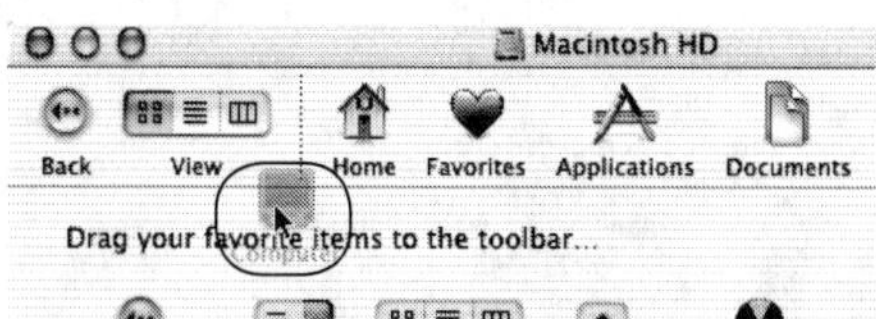

Figure 11 To remove an item, drag it from the toolbar into the center part of the window.

Figure 12 When you release the mouse button, the item is removed.

Figure 13 To rearrange toolbar items, drag them around the toolbar.

Figure 14 When you release the mouse button, the items are rearranged.

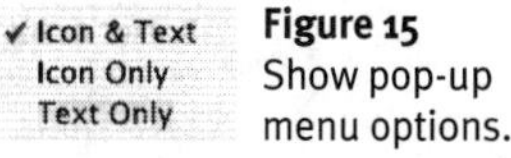

Figure 15 Show pop-up menu options.

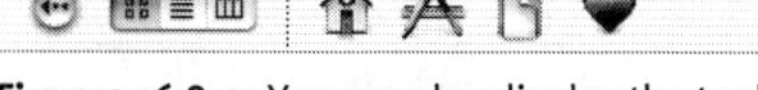

Figures 16 & 17 You can also display the toolbar as icons only (above) or as text only (below).

Back View Home Applications Documents Favorites

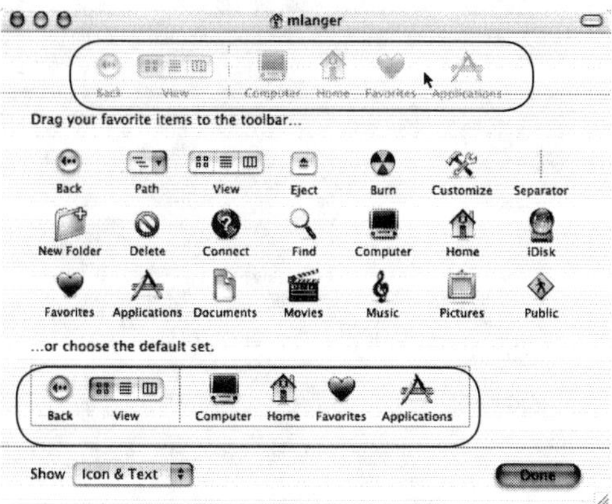

Figure 18 Drag the default set of icons to the toolbar.

6. When you are finished making changes, click Done to hide the toolbar customization options and return to your view of the window.

✔ Tip

- You can add *any* icon to the toolbar. Simply drag the icon from a window to the toolbar of the window. The item appears where you placed it. To remove the icon, drag it out of the toolbar. It is not necessary to display toolbar customization options.

To restore the toolbar to its default settings

1. With any Finder window displaying the toolbar open, choose View > Customize Toolbar (**Figure 7**). Toolbar customization options appear in the window (**Figure 8**).
2. Drag the group of items in a box near the bottom of the window to the toolbar (**Figure 18**). When you release the mouse button, the toolbar's default items appear (**Figure 8**).
3. Click Done to hide the toolbar customization options and return to your view of the window.

Customizing the Dock

The Dock, which is discussed in **Chapter 2**, can be customized to include icons for specific documents and applications that you use often. This makes them quick and easy to open any time you need them.

✔ Tips

- If you used the customizable Apple menu in previous versions of Mac OS, you may want to customize the Dock to include the items you previously included on the Apple menu.
- When you press the mouse button down on a Dock icon, a menu with commands that apply to that icon appears (**Figure 19**). You can select a command like any other menu command.
- When you press the mouse button down on a folder in the dock, it appears as a menu. Choose an item to open it or point to a folder within the menu to display a submenu of items within it. **Figure 20** shows an example of how you can use this feature.

Figure 19 Pressing the mouse button on a Dock item often displays a menu. In this example, pressing the Finder icon displays a menu of open Finder windows.

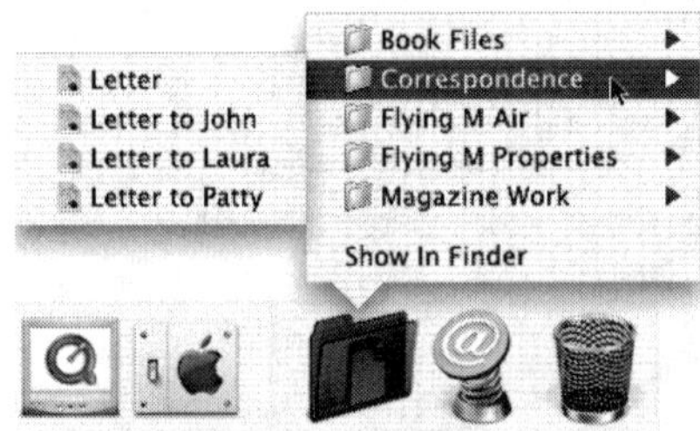

Figure 20 Creative use of folders in the Dock can put all your frequently used files at your fingertips—without turning the Dock into a cluttered mess.

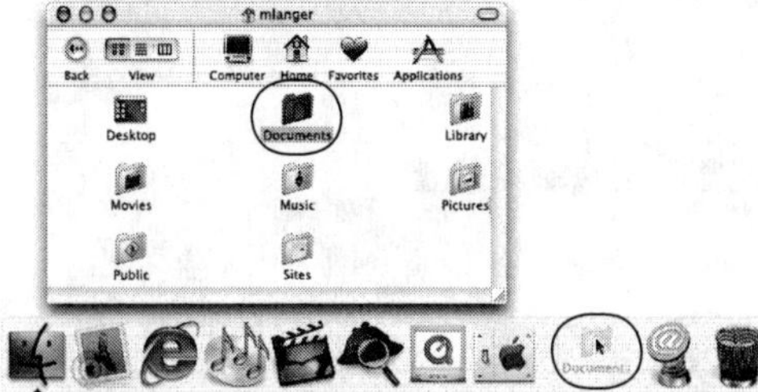

Figure 21 Drag an icon from the window to the Dock.

Figure 22 The Icon appears in the Dock.

Figure 23 Drag an icon off the Dock.

Figure 24 The icon is removed from the Dock.

To add an icon to the Dock

1. Open the window containing the icon you want to add to the Dock.
2. Drag the icon from the window to the Dock (**Figure 21**). When you release the mouse button, the icon appears (**Figure 22**).

✔ Tips

- Dragging an icon to the Dock does not remove it from its original location.
- When dragging items to the Dock, drag applications to the left of the divider and documents and folders to the right of the divider.

To remove an icon from the Dock

Drag the item from the Dock to the desktop (**Figure 23**). When you release the mouse button, the icon disappears in a puff of "smoke" and no longer appears in the Dock (**Figure 24**).

✔ Tips

- Removing an icon from the Dock does not delete it from disk.
- If you try to remove an icon for an application that is running, the icon will not disappear from the Dock until you quit the application.

To set basic Dock options

Choose options from the Dock menu under the Apple menu (**Figure 25**):

- **Turn Magnification On** magnifies a Dock icon when you point to it (**Figure 26**). With this option enabled, the command changes to **Turn Magnification Off**, which disables magnification.
- **Turn Hiding On** (Option ⌘ D) automatically hides the Dock until you point to where it should appear. This is a great way to regain screen real estate normally occupied by the Dock. With this option enabled, the command changes to **Turn Hiding Off**, which displays the Dock all the time.
- **Position on Left**, **Position on Bottom**, and **Position on Right** move the Dock to the left side, bottom, or right side of the screen. The option that is not available (Position on Bottom in **Figure 25**) is the one that is currently selected. When positioned on the left or right, the Dock fits vertically down the screen (**Figure 27**).
- **Dock Preferences** displays the Dock preferences pane, which includes a few additional options for customizing the Dock.

✔ Tips

- To change the size of the Dock, point to the divider line. When the mouse pointer turns into a line with two arrows (**Figure 28**), press the mouse button down and drag up to make the Dock bigger or drag down to make the Dock smaller.
- System Preferences, including the Dock preferences pane, is covered in detail in the sequel to this book, *Mac OS X Advanced: Visual QuickPro Guide.*

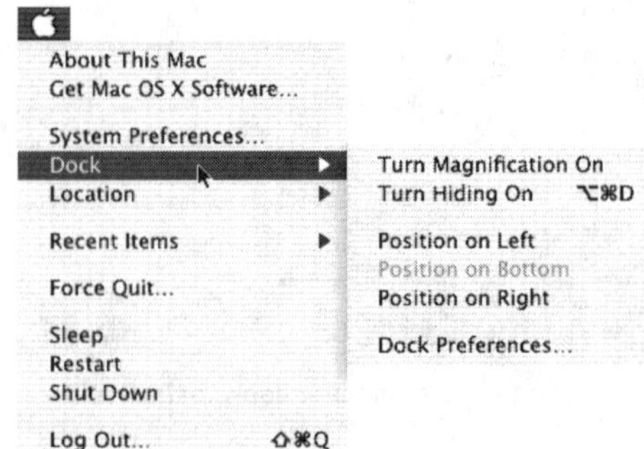

Figure 25 The Dock submenu under the Apple menu offers options for customizing the way the Dock looks and works.

Figure 26 When magnification is turned on, pointing to an icon enlarges it.

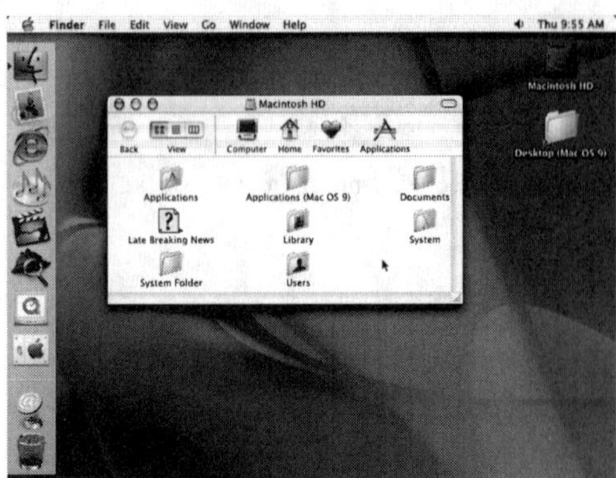

Figure 27 You can position the Dock on the side of the screen instead of the bottom.

Figure 28 You can resize the dock by pointing to the divider line and dragging.

SETTING BASIC DOCK OPTIONS

Customizing Window & Desktop Views

As discussed in **Chapter 3**, a window's view determines how icons and other information appear within it. Mac OS X remembers a window's view settings and uses them whenever you display the window.

You can customize views a number of ways:

- Change the settings for the default, or *global*, view for icon and list views.
- Change the settings for an individual window's icon or list view.
- Change the view for the desktop.

View settings include a number of options:

- Icon view settings include icon size, arrangement, and background.
- List view settings include columns, date format, item size calculation, and icon size, as well as column width and the order in which columns appear.
- Desktop view settings include icon size and arrangement.

You can also display a status bar with disk information in any Finder window.

This part of the chapter explains how to do all of these things.

✔ Tip

- The only time the Finder does not use a window's custom view is when you have the Keep a window's view the same when opening other folders in the window option set in the Finder Preferences window (**Figure 2**). I tell you about this option and the rest of Finder Preferences earlier in this chapter.

To set icon view options

1. To set icon view options for a specific window, activate that window and make sure it is displayed in icon view.

   or

   To set default icon view options, activate any window that is displayed in icon view.

2. Choose View > Show View Options (**Figure 7**), or press ⌘J.

3. In the view options window that appears (**Figure 29**), select the radio button for the type of option you want to set:

   ▲ **This window only** customizes the settings for the active window.

   ▲ **Global** sets options for all icon view windows that do not have custom settings.

4. Use the Icon Size slider to set the size of icons:

   ▲ Drag the slider to the left to make the icon size smaller.

   ▲ Drag the slider to the right to make the icon size larger.

5. Select an Icon Arrangement option:

   ▲ **None** removes any automatic icon arrangement.

   ▲ **Always snap to grid** forces icons to snap to an invisible grid within the window.

   ▲ **Keep arranged by** automatically arranges icons in a certain order. If you select this option, choose a sort order from the pop-up menu beneath it (**Figure 30**).

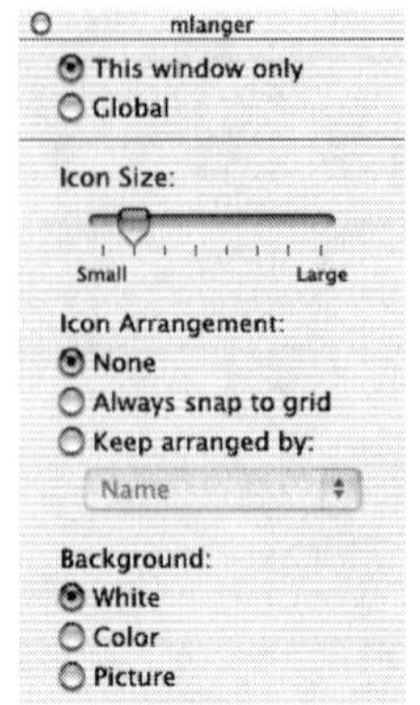

Figure 29 The view options for icon view.

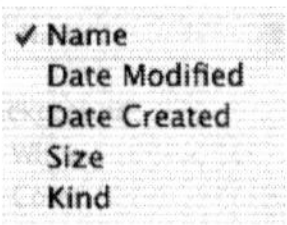

✓ Name
Date Modified
Date Created
Size
Kind

Figure 30 Use this pop-up menu to specify an automatic arrangement order.

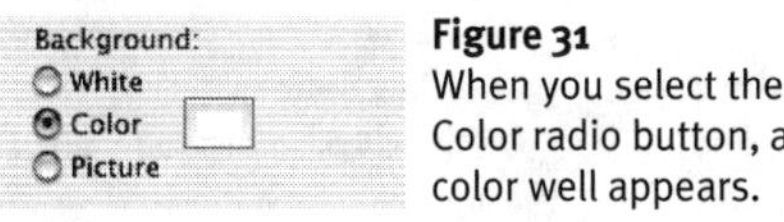

Figure 31 When you select the Color radio button, a color well appears.

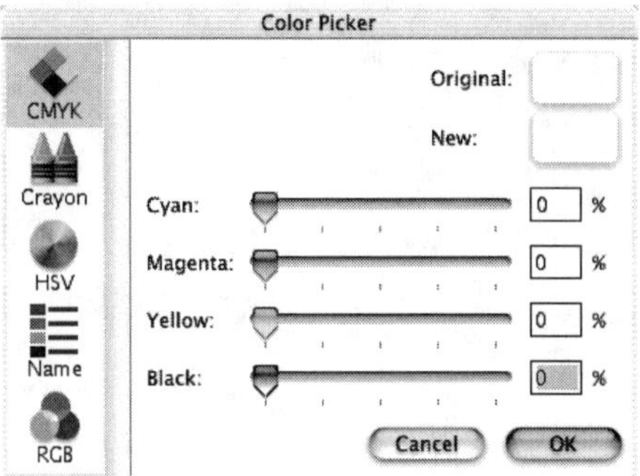

Figure 32 Use the Color Picker to select a new background color.

Figure 33 When you select the Picture radio button, a Select button appears.

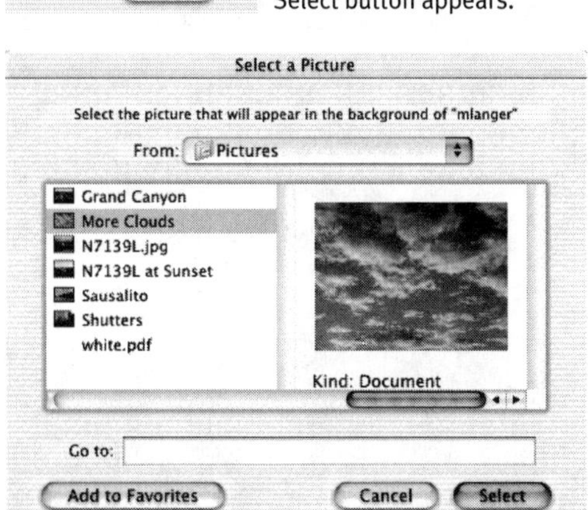

Figure 34 Use the Select a Picture dialog to locate and select a background picture.

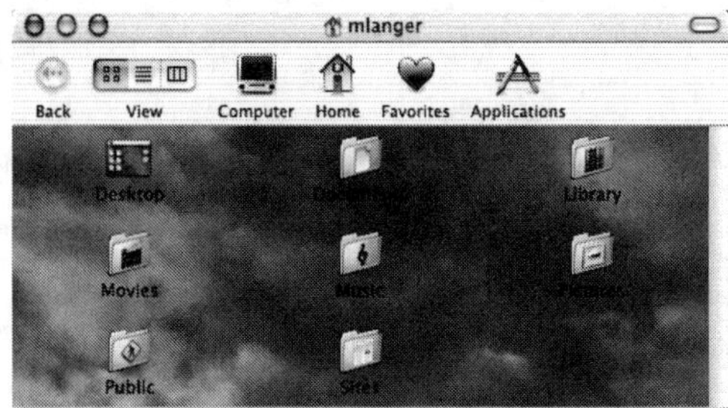

Figure 35 A background picture appears behind icons.

6. Select a Background option:
   - ▲ **White** makes the background white.
   - ▲ **Color** enables you to select a background color for the window. If you select this option, click the color well that appears beside it (**Figure 31**), use the Color Picker that appears (**Figure 32**) to select a color, and click OK.
   - ▲ **Picture** enables you to set a background picture for the window. If you select this option, click the Select button that appears beside it (**Figure 33**), use the Select a Picture dialog that appears to locate and select a background picture (**Figure 34**), and click Select.
7. When you're finished setting options, click the view option window's close button to dismiss it.

✔ Tips

- To restore the current window's options to the default or global settings for all icon view windows, select the Global radio button in step 3.
- Working with dialogs is discussed in **Chapter 5**.
- A background picture fills the window's background behind the icons (**Figure 35**).

To set list view options

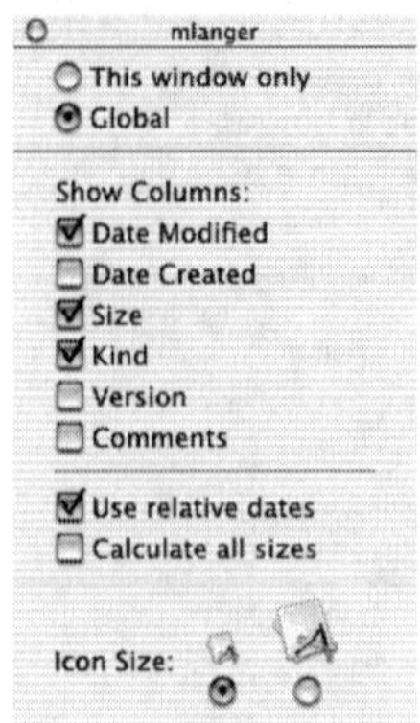

Figure 36 The view options for list view.

1. To set list view options for a specific window, activate that window and make sure it is displayed in list view.

   or

   To set default list view options, activate any window that is displayed in list view.

2. Choose View > Show View Options (**Figure 7**), or press [⌘ J].

3. In the view options window that appears (**Figure 36**), select the radio button for the type of option you want to set:

   ▲ **This window only** customizes the settings for the active window.

   ▲ **Global** sets options for all list view windows that do not have custom settings.

4. Select the columns you want to appear in list view by turning Show Columns check boxes on or off:

   ▲ **Date Modified** is the date and time an item was last changed.

   ▲ **Date Created** is the date and time an item was first created.

   ▲ **Size** is the amount of disk space the item occupies.

   ▲ **Kind** is the type of item. I tell you about types of icons in **Chapter 2**.

   ▲ **Version** is the item's version number.

   ▲ **Comments** is the information you entered in the comments field of the Info window. I tell you about the Info window later in this chapter.

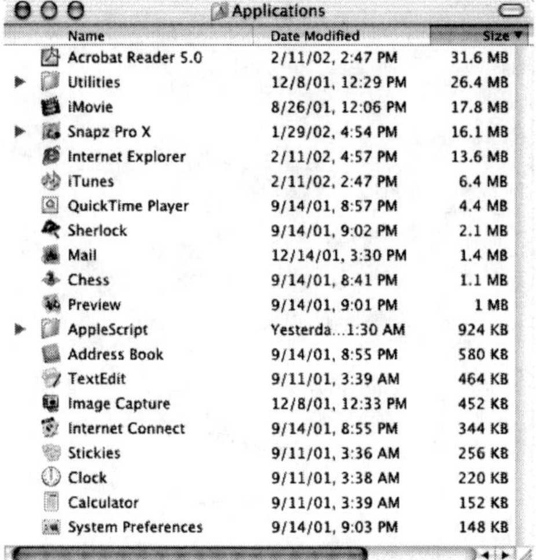

Figure 37 When you turn on the Calculate all sizes in the list view options for a window, you can sort the window's contents by size.

5. To display the date in relative terms (that is, using the words "today" and "yesterday"), turn on the Use relative dates check box.

6. To display the disk space occupied by items and the contents of folders in the list, turn on the Calculate all sizes check box.

7. Select an Icon Size option by clicking the radio button beneath the size you want.

8. When you're finished setting options, click the view option window's close button to dismiss it.

✔ Tip

- Turning on the Calculate all sizes check box in step 6 makes it possible to sort a window's contents by size (**Figure 37**). Sorting window contents is covered in **Chapter 3**.

To set desktop view options

1. Click anywhere on the desktop to activate it.
2. Choose View > Show View Options (**Figure 7**) or press [⌘ J] to display the Desktop view options window (**Figure 38**).
3. Use the Icon Size slider to set the size of icons:
   - ▲ Drag the slider to the left to make the icon size smaller.
   - ▲ Drag the slider to the right to make the icon size larger.
4. Select an Icon Arrangement option:
   - ▲ **None** removes any automatic icon arrangement.
   - ▲ **Always snap to grid** forces icons to snap to an invisible grid within the window.
   - ▲ **Keep arranged by** automatically arranges icons in a certain order. If you select this option, choose a sort order from the pop-up menu beneath it (**Figure 30**).
5. When you're finished setting options, click the view option window's close button to dismiss it.

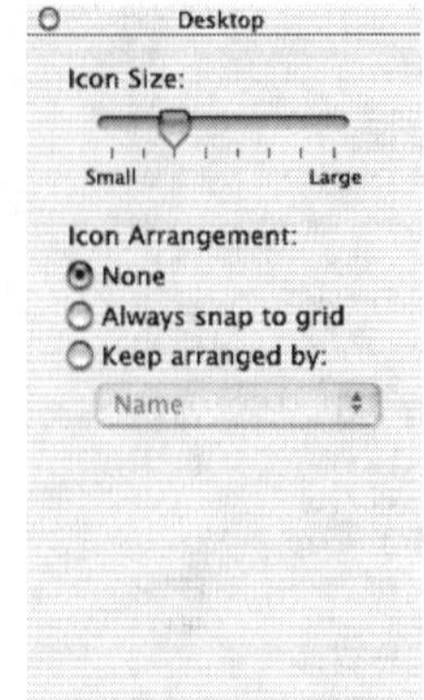

Figure 38
View options for the desktop.

✔ Tip

- ▲ You can set the desktop background pattern in the Desktop preferences pane. System Preferences, including the Desktop preferences pane, are covered in detail in the sequel to this book, *Mac OS X Advanced: Visual QuickStart Guide*.

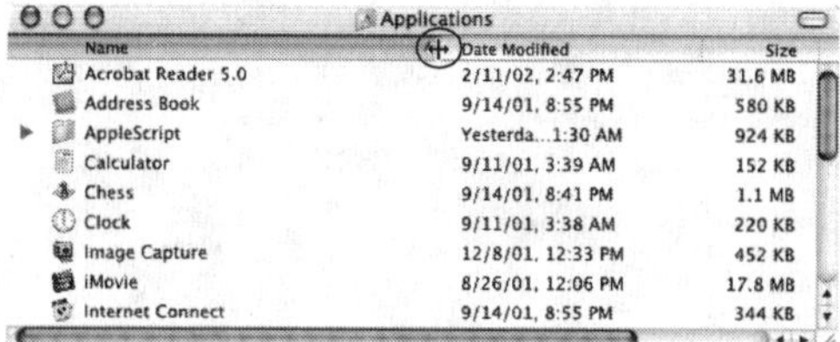

Figure 39 Position the mouse pointer on the column border.

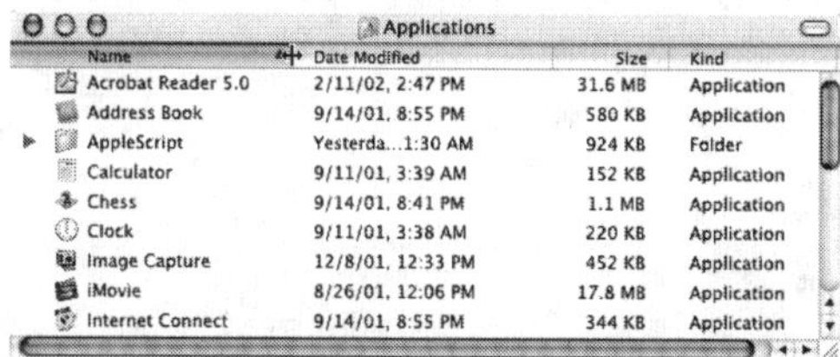

Figure 40 When you press the mouse button down and drag, the column's width changes.

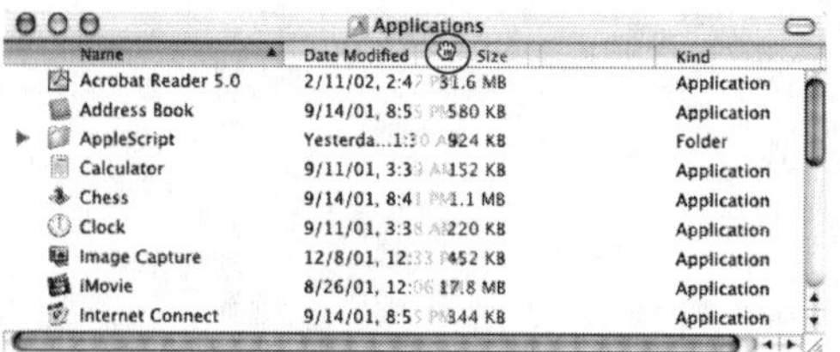

Figure 41 Drag a column border...

Figure 42 ...to change the column's position.

To change a column's width

1. Position the mouse pointer on the line between the heading for the column whose width you want to change and the column to its right. The mouse pointer turns into a vertical bar with two arrows (**Figure 39**).
2. Press the mouse button down and drag:
   - ▲ To make the column narrower, drag to the left.
   - ▲ To make the column wider, drag to the right (**Figure 40**).
3. When the column is displayed at the desired width, release the mouse button.

✔ Tip

- If you make a column too narrow to display all of its contents, information may be truncated or condensed.

To change a column's position

1. Position the mouse pointer on the heading for the column you want to move.
2. Press the mouse button down and drag:
   - ▲ To move the column to the left, drag to the left (**Figure 41**).
   - ▲ To move the column to the right, drag to the right.

   As you drag, the other columns shift to make room for the column you're dragging.
3. When the column is in the desired position, release the mouse button. The column changes its position (**Figure 42**).

✔ Tip

- You cannot change the position of the Name column.

To display the status bar

Choose View > Show Status Bar (**Figure 7**).

The status bar appears above the window's contents (**Figure 43**).

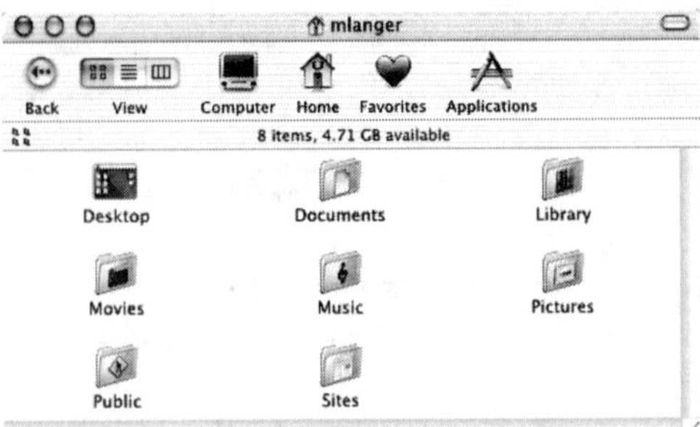

Figure 43 The status bar appears above a window's content, but below the toolbar (if displayed).

✔ Tips

- As shown in **Figure 43**, the status bar shows the number of items in the window and the total amount of space available on the disk.
- When the status bar is displayed, it appears in all Finder windows.

To hide the status bar

Choose View > Hide Status Bar (**Figure 44**).

The status bar disappears.

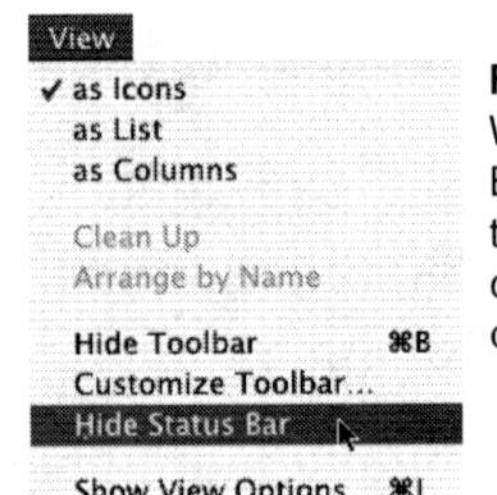

Figure 44 When the Status Bar is displayed, the Hide Status Bar command appears on the View menu.

Click a right-pointing triangle to expand the outline.

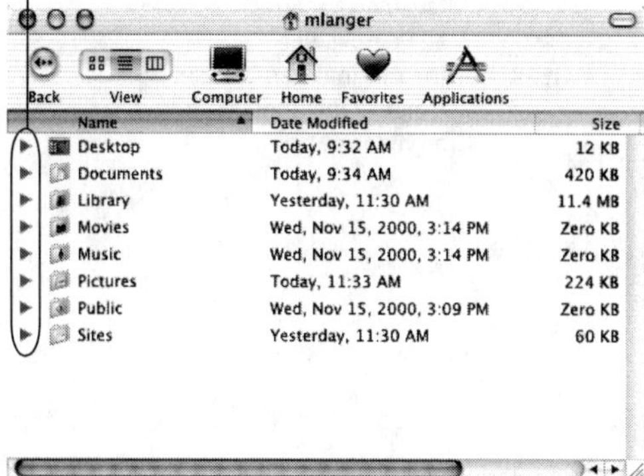

Figure 45 Right-pointing triangles indicate collapsed outlines.

Click a down-pointing triangle to collapse an outline.

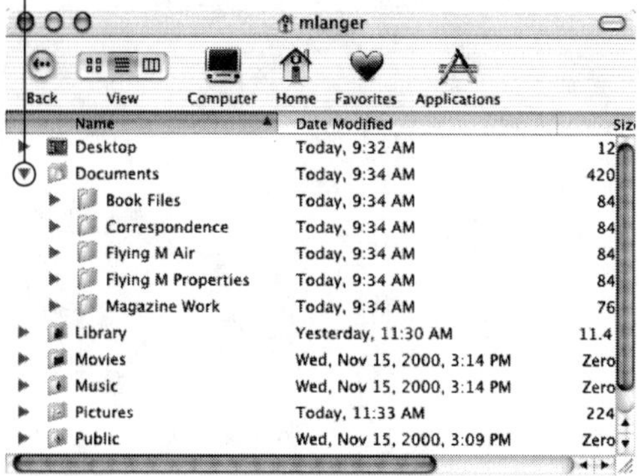

Figure 46 Folder contents can be displayed as an outline...

Figure 47 ...that can show several levels.

Outlines in List View

Windows displayed in list view have a feature not found in icon or column views: They can display the contents of folders within the window as an outline (**Figures 46** and **47**).

✔ Tip

- Views are discussed in detail in **Chapter 3** and earlier in this chapter.

To display a folder's contents

Click the right-pointing triangle beside the folder (**Figure 45**).

or

Click the folder once to select it, and press ⌘ →.

The items within that folder are listed below it, slightly indented (**Figure 46**).

✔ Tip

- As shown in **Figure 47**, you can use this technique to display multiple levels of folders in the same window.

To hide a folder's contents

Click the down-pointing triangle beside the folder (**Figure 46**).

or

Click the folder once to select it, and press ⌘ ←.

The outline collapses to hide the items in the folder (**Figure 45**).

Aliases

An *alias* (**Figure 48**) is a pointer to an item. You can make an alias of an item and place it anywhere on your computer. Then, when you need to open the item, just open its alias.

Figure 48
The icon for an alias looks like the original item's icon but includes a tiny arrow.

✔ Tips

- It's important to remember that an alias is not a copy of the item—it's a pointer. If you delete the original item, the alias will not open.
- You can use the Fix Alias dialog (**Figure 71**) to reassign an original to an alias, as explained later in this chapter.
- By putting aliases of frequently used items together where you can quickly access them—such as on the desktop—you make the items more accessible without actually moving them.
- The Favorites and Recent Items features work with aliases. These features are discussed a little later in this chapter.
- You can name an alias anything you like, as long as you follow the file naming guidelines discussed in **Chapter 3**. An alias's name does not need to include the word *alias*.
- The icon for an alias looks very much like the icon for the original item but is slightly lighter in appearance and includes a tiny arrow (**Figure 48**).
- You can move, copy, rename, open, and delete an alias just like any other file.

Figure 49 To create an alias, begin by selecting the item for which you want to make an alias.

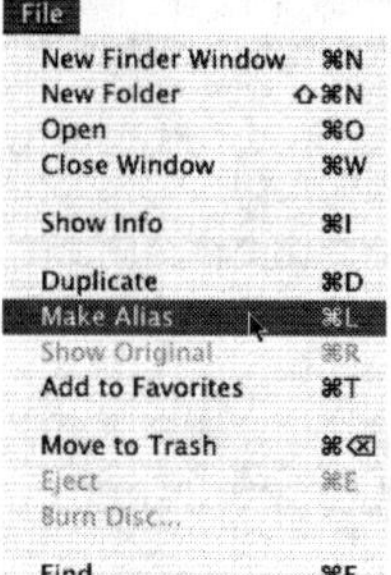

Figure 50 Choose Make Alias from the File menu.

Figure 51 The alias appears with the original.

Figure 52 Select the alias's icon.

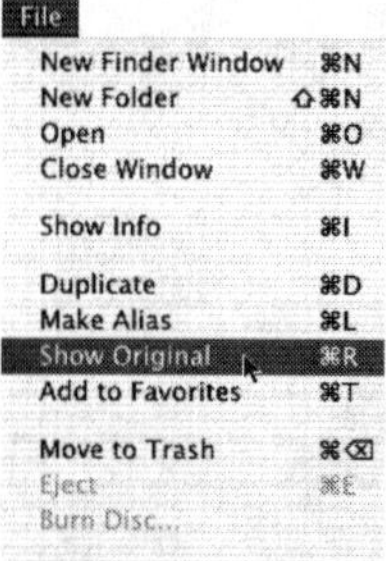

Figure 53 Choose Show Original from the File menu.

Figure 54 The original item appears selected in its window.

To create an alias

1. Select the item you want to make an alias for (**Figure 49**).
2. Choose File > Make Alias (**Figure 50**), or press [⌘ L].

   The alias appears right beneath the original item (**Figure 51**).

or

Hold down [⌘ Option] and drag the item for which you want to make an alias to a new location. The alias appears in the destination location.

✔ Tip

- An alias's name is selected right after it is created (**Figure 51**). If desired, you can immediately type a new name to replace the default name.

To find an alias's original file

1. Select the alias's icon (**Figure 52**).
2. Choose File > Show Original (**Figure 53**), or press [⌘ R].

   The original item appears selected in the window in which it resides on disk (**Figure 54**).

Favorites

Favorites enables you to add frequently used documents, applications, and other items to the Favorites submenu on the Go menu (**Figure 55**). This makes these items quick and easy to access.

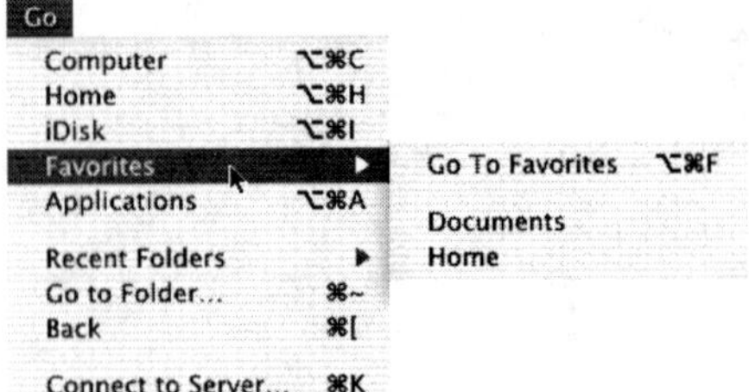

Figure 55 Favorites are listed on the Favorites submenu on the Go menu.

✔ Tips

- Favorites also appear in the Open and Save Location dialogs, which are discussed in **Chapter 5**.
- The favorites feature works with aliases, which are discussed on the previous two pages.
- Your favorite item aliases are stored in the Favorites folder, in the Library folder, inside your home folder. You can learn more about your home folder in **Chapter 3**.
- The Mac OS X installer creates favorites for two items (**Figure 55**):
  - ▲ **Documents** is an alias to your Documents folder, which is the default location for storing documents.
  - ▲ **Home** is an alias to your home folder.

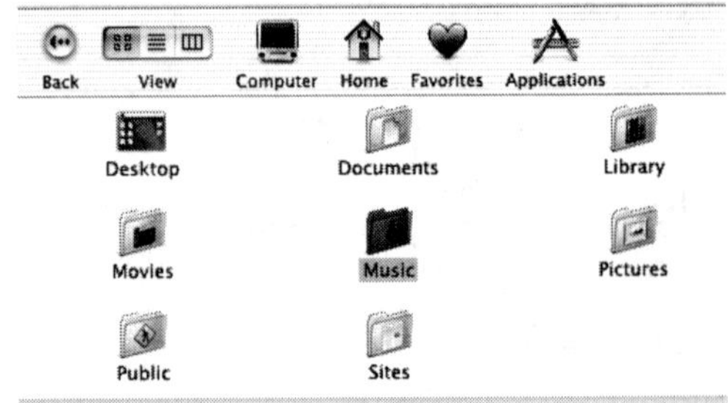

Figure 56 Select the item that you want to add as a favorite item.

To add a favorite item

1. In the Finder, select the icon for the item that you want to add as a favorite item (**Figure 56**).
2. Choose File > Add to Favorites (**Figure 57**), or press ⌘ T.

   The item is added to the Favorites submenu on the Go menu (**Figure 58**).

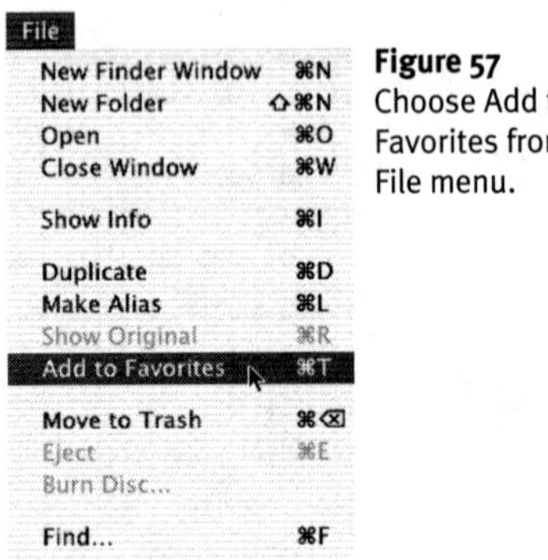

Figure 57 Choose Add to Favorites from the File menu.

✔ Tip

- You can also add a currently selected folder to favorites by clicking the Add to Favorites button in the Open or expanded Save Location (**Figure 59**) dialogs. These dialogs are covered in **Chapter 5**.

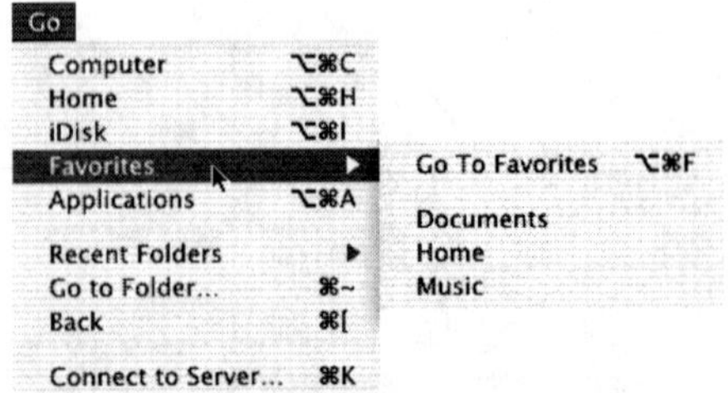

Figure 58 The item is added to the Favorites submenu on the Go menu.

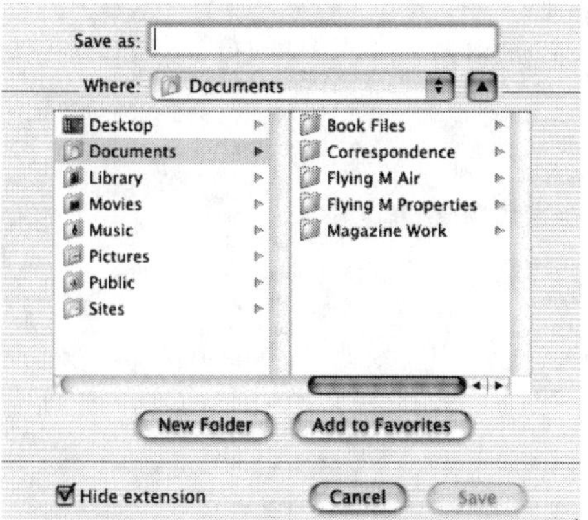

Figure 59 You can click the Add to Favorites button in a Save Location dialog like this one to add the currently selected folder to your favorite items.

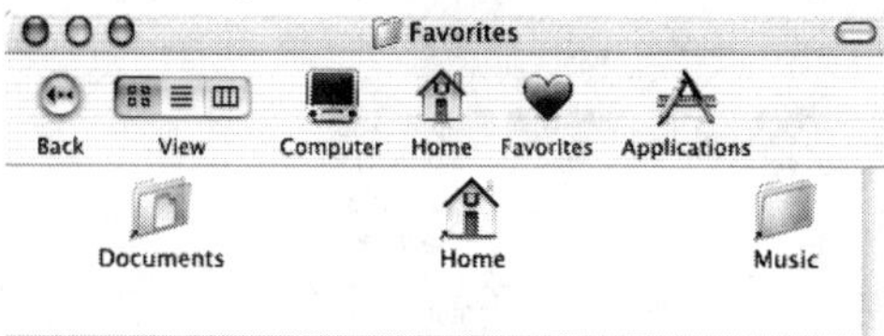

Figure 60 The Favorites folder contains icons for all your favorite items.

To use a favorite item

From the Favorites submenu on the Go menu (**Figures 55** and **58**), choose the item you want to open.

To remove a favorite

1. Click the Favorites button in the toolbar of any Finder window.

   or

   Choose Go > Favorites > Go To Favorites (**Figures 55** and **58**), or press Option ⌘ F.

   The Favorites folder window opens (**Figure 60**).

2. Drag the item that you want to remove out of the window.

3. Close the Favorites folder window.

   The item is removed from the Favorites submenu.

Recent Items

Mac OS automatically tracks the things you open. It creates submenus of the most recently opened items in three categories—applications, documents, and folders—making it quick and easy to open them again.

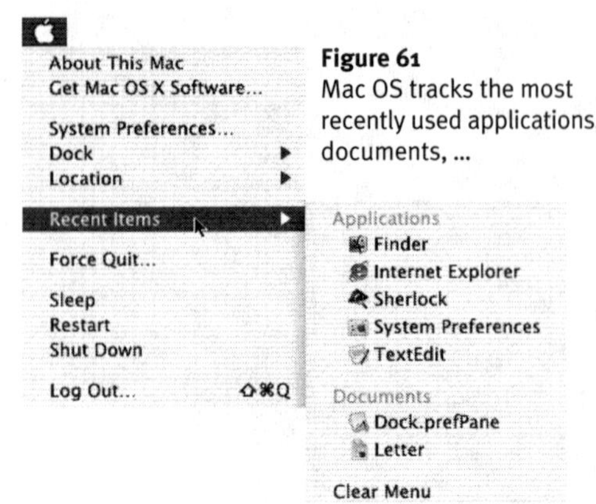

Figure 61
Mac OS tracks the most recently used applications, documents, ...

To open recent items

To open a recently used application or document, choose its name from the Recent Items submenu under the Apple menu (**Figure 61**).

or

To open a recently used folder, choose its name from the Recent Folders submenu under the Go menu (**Figure 62**).

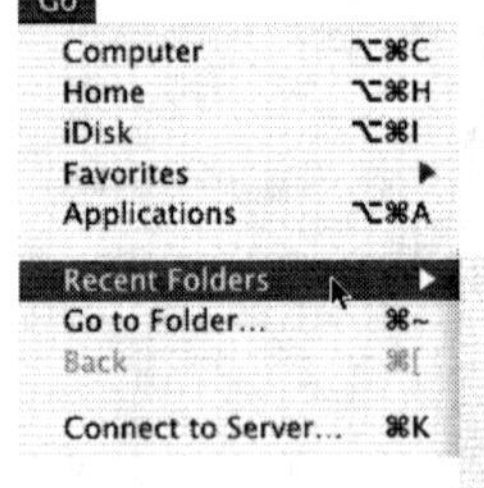

Figure 62
...and folders.

✔ Tips

- The favorites feature works with aliases, which are discussed earlier in this chapter.
- Working with applications and documents is discussed in **Chapter 5**.

To clear the Recent Items submenu

Choose Apple > Recent Items > Clear Menu (**Figure 61**).

✔ Tip

- Clearing the Recent Items submenu does not delete any application or document files.

The Info Window

You can learn more about an item by opening its Info window (**Figures 63** through **66**). Depending on the type of icon (disk, folder, application, document, alias, etc.), the General Information in the Info window will provide some or all of the following information:

- **Icon** that appears in the Finder.
- **Name** of the item.
- **Kind** or type of item.
- **Size** of item or contents (folders and files only).
- **Where** item is on disk.
- **Created** date and time.
- **Modified** date and time.
- **Format** of item (disks only).
- **Capacity** of item (disks only).
- **Version** number or copyright date (files only).
- **Original** location on disk (aliases only).
- **Stationery Pad** check box to convert the file into a stationery format file, which is like a document template. (This option appears for documents only.)
- **Locked** check box to prevent the file from being deleted or overwritten (folders and files only).
- **Comments** entered by users (like you).

✔ Tip

- Other types of information available for a disk, folder, or file can be displayed by choosing an option from the pop-up menu.

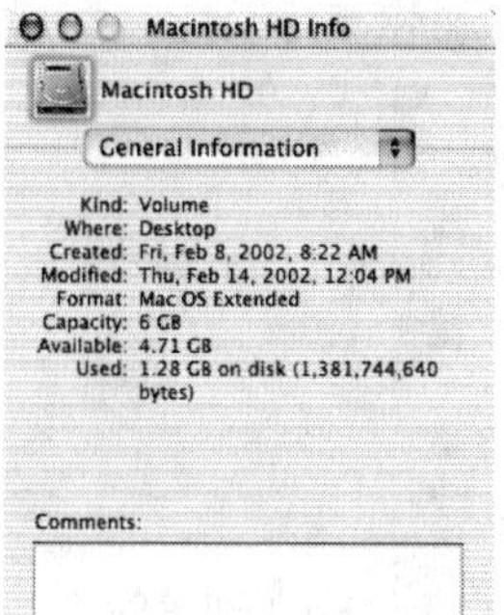

Figure 63 The Info window for a hard disk.

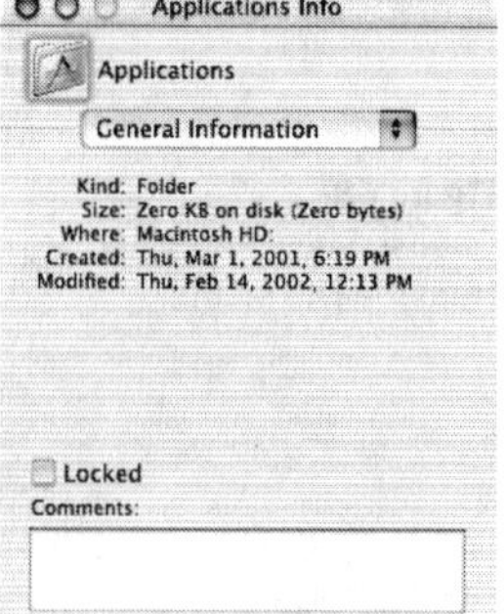

Figure 64 The Info window for a folder.

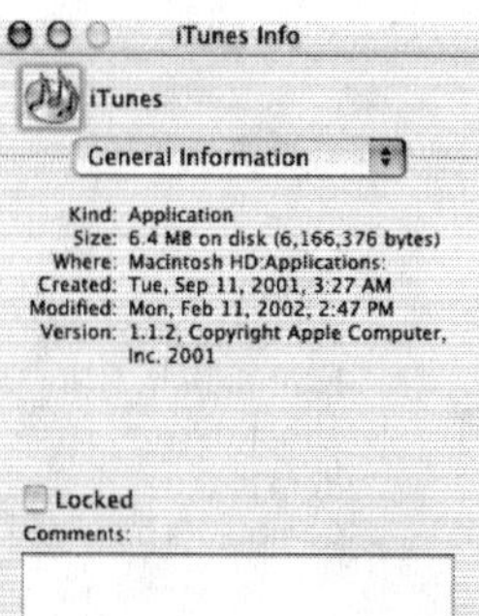

Figure 65 The Info window for an application.

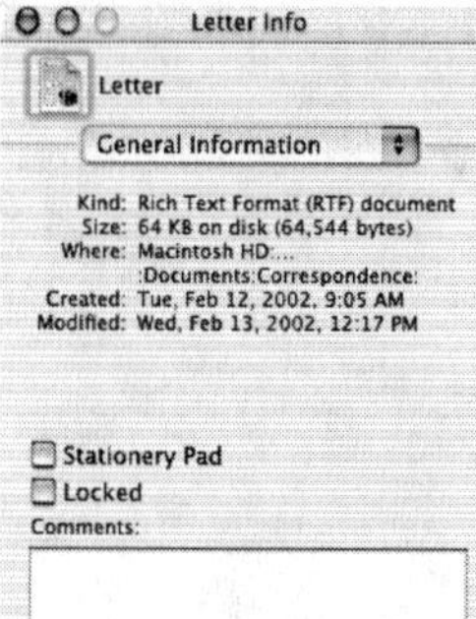

Figure 66 The Info window for a document.

To open the Info window

1. Select the item for which you want to open the Info window (**Figure 67**).
2. Choose File > Show Info (**Figure 68**), or press [⌘ I].

   The Info window for that item appears (**Figure 64**).

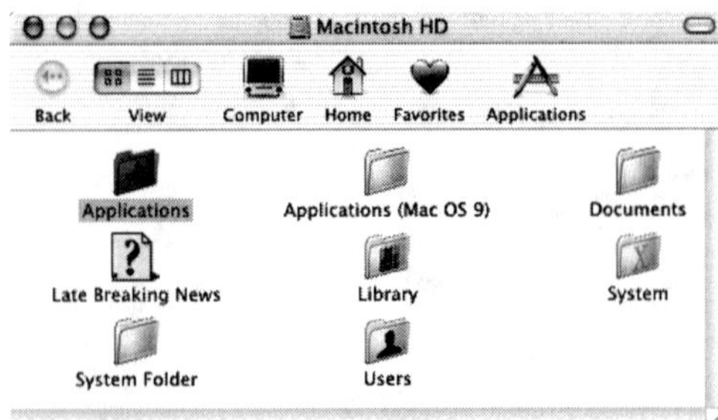

Figure 67 Select the item for which you want to open the Info window.

✔ Tip

- When the Info window is open, clicking a different icon displays the information for that icon.

To enter comments in the Info window

1. Open the Info window for the item for which you want to enter comments.
2. Click in the Comments box to position the blinking insertion point there.
3. Type your comments (**Figure 69**). They are automatically saved.

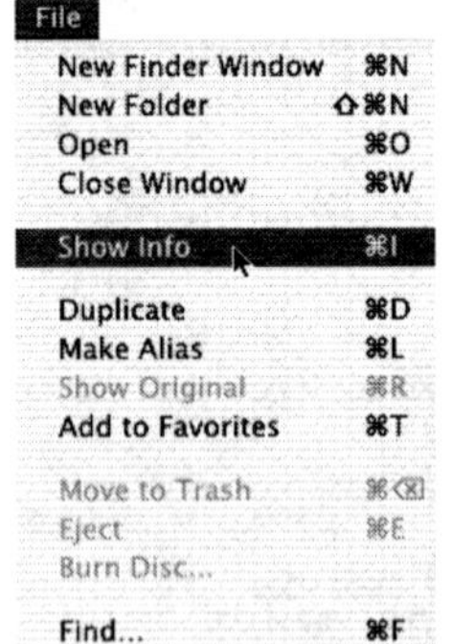

Figure 68 Choose Show Info from the File menu.

✔ Tip

- As discussed earlier in this chapter, you can set a window's list view to display comments entered in the Info window.

To lock an application or document

1. Open the Info window for the item you want to lock (**Figures 64** through **66** and **69**).
2. Turn on the Locked check box.

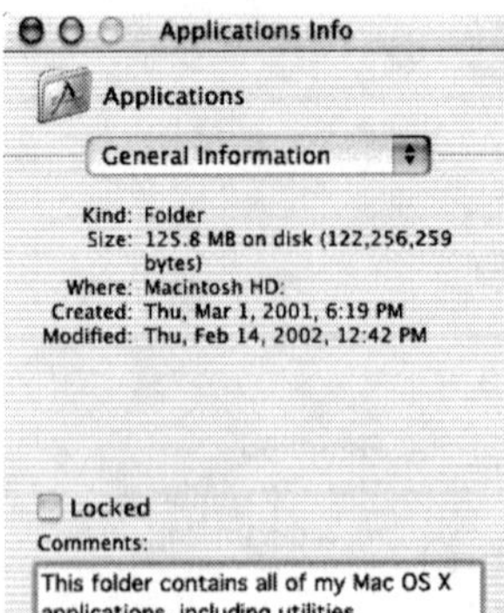

Figure 69 You can enter information about the item in the Comments box.

✔ Tip

- Locked items cannot be deleted or overwritten. They can, however, be moved.

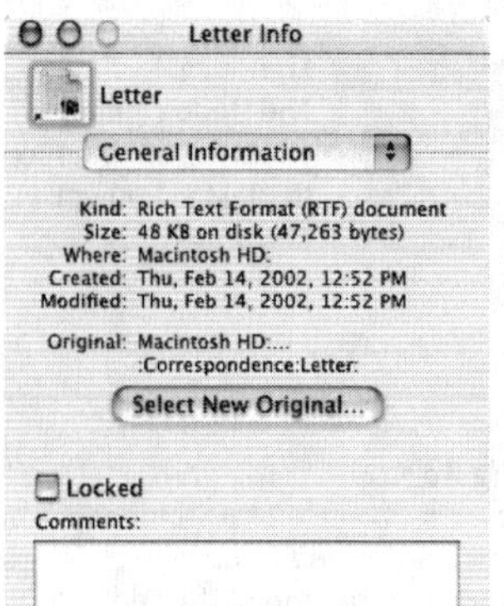

Figure 70 You can click the Select New Original button in the Info window for an alias to assign a new original to the alias.

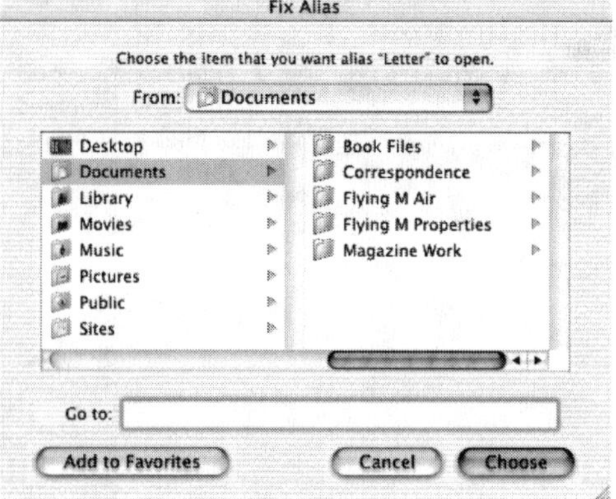

Figure 71 Use the Fix Alias dialog to locate and choose a new original for an alias.

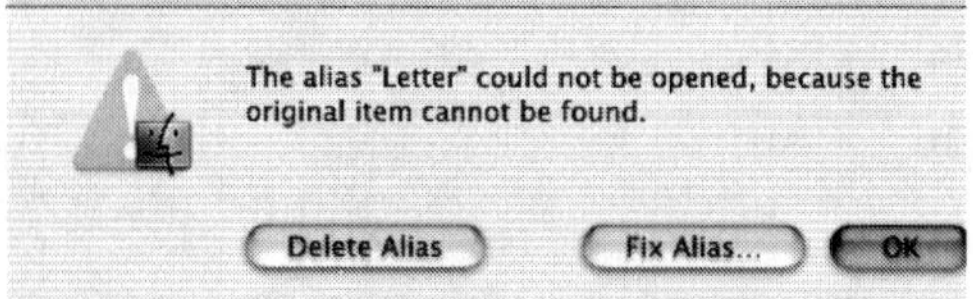

Figure 72 This dialog appears when you attempt to open an alias for which the original cannot be found.

To select a new original item for an alias

1. In the Info window for the alias (**Figure 70**), click the Select New Original button.
2. Use the Fix Alias dialog that appears (**Figure 71**) to locate and select the item that you want to use as the original for the alias.
3. Click Choose. The item you selected is assigned to the alias.

✔ Tips

- The Fix Alias dialog is similar to an Open dialog, which is covered in **Chapter 5**.
- If you try to open an alias for which the original cannot be found, a dialog like the one in **Figure 72** appears. Click Fix Alias to display the Fix Alias dialog (**Figure 71**) and select a new original.
- Aliases are discussed in detail earlier in this chapter.

To close the Info window

Click the Info window's close button.

or

1. Activate the Info window.
2. Choose File > Close Window, or press ⌘W.

✔ Tip

- Closing the Info window saves all changes you made to its contents.

Undoing Finder Actions

The Mac OS X Finder includes limited support for the Undo command, which can reverse the most recently completed action. Say, for example, that you move a file from one window to another. If you immediately change your mind, you can choose Edit > Undo Move (**Figure 73**) to put the file back where it was.

✔ Tips

- Don't depend on the Undo command. Unfortunately, it isn't available for all actions (**Figure 74**).
- The exact wording of the Undo command varies depending on the action and the item it was performed on. In **Figure 73**, for example, the command is Undo Move of "Letter to John" because the last action was to move a document icon named *Letter to John.*
- The Undo command is also available (and generally more reliable) in most Mac OS applications. You'll usually find it at the top of the Edit men.

To undo an action

Immediately after performing an action, choose Edit > Undo *action description* (**Figure 73**). The action is reversed.

To redo an action

Immediately after undoing an action, choose Edit > Redo *action description* (**Figure 75**). The action is redone—as if you never used the Undo command.

✔ Tip

- Think of the Redo command as the Undo-Undo command since it undoes the Undo command.

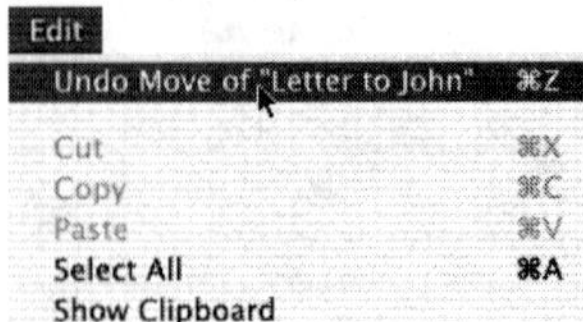

Figure 73 The Undo command enables you to undo the last action you performed.

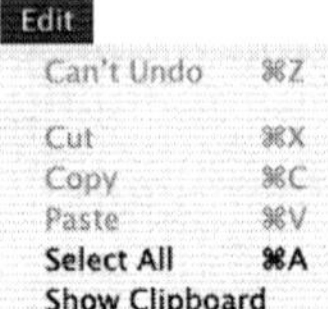

Figure 74 If an action cannot be undone, the words *Can't Undo* will appear at the top of the Edit menu in gray.

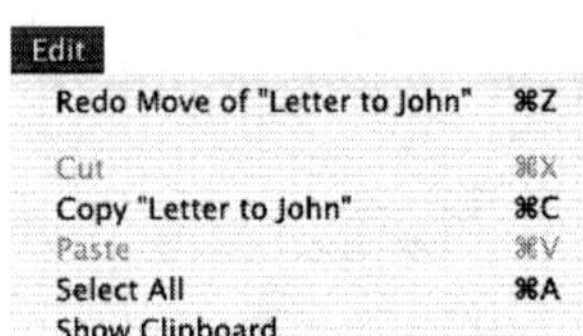

Figure 75 The Redo command undoes the Undo command.

Application Basics

5

Applications

Applications, which are also known as *programs*, are software packages you use to get work done. Here are some examples:

- **Word processors**, such as TextEdit and Microsoft Word, are used to write letters, reports, and other text-based documents.
- **Spreadsheets**, such as Microsoft Excel, have built-in calculation features that are useful for creating number-based documents such as worksheets and charts.
- **Databases**, such as FileMaker Pro, are used to organize information, such as the names and addresses of customers or the artists and titles in a record collection.
- **Graphics** and **presentation** programs, such as Adobe Photoshop and Microsoft PowerPoint, are used to create illustrations, animations, and presentations.
- **Communications** programs, such as Internet Connect and Microsoft Internet Explorer, are used to connect to other computers, including the Internet.
- **Integrated** software, such as AppleWorks, combines "lite" versions of several types of software into one application.
- **Utility** software, such as Disk Utility and StuffIt Expander, performs tasks to manage computer files or keep your computer in good working order.

✔ Tips

- Your Macintosh comes with some application software, some of which is discussed throughout this book.
- Make sure the software you buy is Mac OS-compatible, and if possible, labeled "Built for Mac OS X." You may see Mac OS X applications referred to as *Carbon* or *Cocoa* applications. (Carbon and Cocoa are two methods for writing Mac OS X software.)

Mac OS X Applications vs. Classic Applications

Mac OS X supports two types of Mac OS applications:

- **Mac OS X applications** are those written specifically for Mac OS X. These programs take advantage of many of the new features of Mac OS X and use its new interface for menus, commands, and onscreen display. You can usually identify Mac OS X applications by the "Built for Mac OS X" label on them.
- **Classic applications** are those written for Mac OS 9.x and earlier but not rewritten for Mac OS X. These programs must be run in the Classic environment, which utilizes Mac OS 9.x.

You don't have to do anything special to run a Classic application. Mac OS X will automatically launch the Classic environment when it needs to.

✔ Tips

- All of the applications that come with Mac OS X are Mac OS X applications.
- If you upgraded to Mac OS X from a previous version of Mac OS, all of the applications that were on your computer before the upgrade are probably Classic applications.
- Whenever possible, you should use Mac OS X applications. You'll find that applications run better and faster under Mac OS X than in the Classic environment.
- Classic applications are covered in greater detail near the end of this chapter.
- The hard disk window should include two applications folders, as shown in **Figure 1**: Applications and Applications (Mac OS 9).

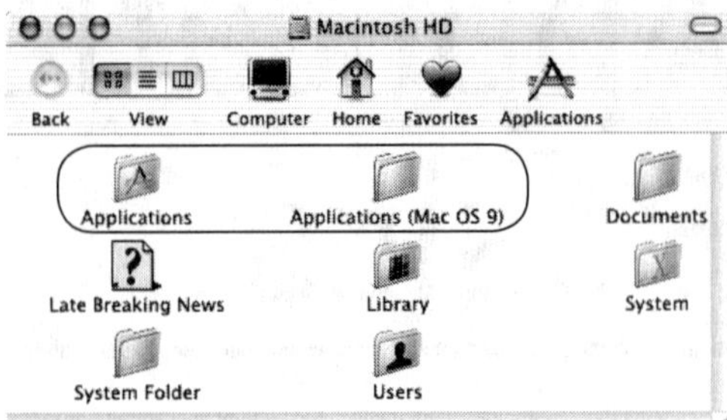

Figure 1 A typical Mac OS X setup includes two Applications folders.

Figure 2 A tiny triangle appears beneath each open application. Click an icon to make its application active.

Multitasking & the Dock

Mac OS uses a form of *multitasking,* which makes it possible for more than one application to be open at the same time. Only one application, however, can be *active.* You must make an application active to work with it.

Mac OS X features *preemptive multitasking,* a type of multitasking in which the operating system can interrupt a currently running task in order to run another task, as needed.

As discussed in **Chapter 2**, you can identify open applications by looking at the Dock; a tiny triangle appears beneath each application that is running (**Figure 2**).

You can also use the Dock to switch from one open application to another; simply click the application's icon in the Dock to make the application active.

✔ Tips

- Mac OS 8 and 9 use *cooperative multitasking,* a type of multitasking in which a running program can receive processing time only if other programs allow it. Each application must "cooperate" by giving up control of the processor in order to allow others to run.
- Mac OS X also features *protected memory,* a memory management system in which each program is prevented from modifying or corrupting the memory partition of another program. This means that if one application freezes up or bombs, your computer won't freeze up. You can continue using the other applications that are running.
- One application that is always open is Finder, which I cover in detail in **Chapters 2** through **4**.
- The active application is the one whose name appears at the top of the application menu—the menu to the right of the Apple menu—on the menu bar. The application menu is covered in more detail a little later in this chapter.
- Another way to activate an application is to click any of its windows. This brings the window to the foreground onscreen and makes the application active.

Using Applications & Creating Documents

You use an application by opening, or *launching*, it. It loads into the computer's memory. Its menu bar replaces the Finder's menu bar and offers commands that can be used only with that application. It may also display a document window and tools specific to that program.

Most applications create *documents*—files written in a format understood by the application. When you save documents, they remain on disk so you can open, edit, print, or just view them at a later date.

For example, you may use Microsoft Word to write a letter. When you save the letter, it becomes a Word document file that includes all the text and formatting you put into the letter, written in a format that Microsoft Word can understand.

Your computer keeps track of applications and documents. It automatically associates documents with the applications that created them. That's how your computer is able to open a document with the correct application when you open the document from the Finder.

✔ Tips

- You can launch an application by opening a document that it created.
- A document created by an application that is not installed on your computer is sometimes referred to as an *orphan* document since no *parent* application is available. An orphan document usually has a generic document icon (**Figure 3**).

Figure 3 An orphan document often has a generic document icon like this one.

Figure 4 Select the icon for the application that you want to open.

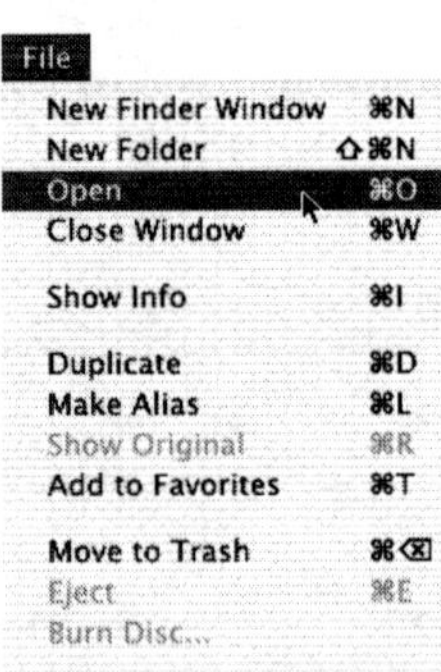

Figure 5 Choose Open from the File menu.

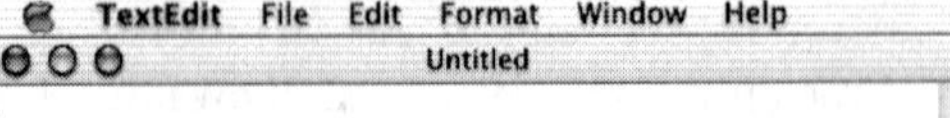

Figure 6 When you launch TextEdit by opening its application icon, it displays an empty document window.

Figure 7 Select the icon for the document you want to open.

TextEdit File Edit Format Window Help

Letter to Laura

February 16, 2002

Dear Laura,

I just got my dress for Norb and Missy's wedding. It's a lot nicer than I thought it would be. And fortunately, it fits! I just have to have it taken up. This is the first time in my life that I've ever had to had something shortened—I'm sure you know what I mean.

Although I won't be back in New Jersey for the wedding shower, I'll be back at least a few days before the wedding. I hope we can spend some time together. Perhaps you can take me to your hairdresser to get my hair done before the wedding? I wouldn't mind a manicure, too—if I have any nails left.

Don't tell Ma, but I'm thinking about flying my helicopter to New Jersey for the wedding. The trip would take about a week, but I'd allow myself more time just in case I get stuck somewhere due to weather. I ordered all the charts I need to plan the trip and should be able to make a decision on whether to attempt it later this month. I'm very excited about the possibility of making such a long solo flight. I think it would be a good experience for me.

Well, it's time to get back to work! I'll write more later.

Love,
Maria

Figure 8 When you launch TextEdit by opening one of its documents, it displays the document.

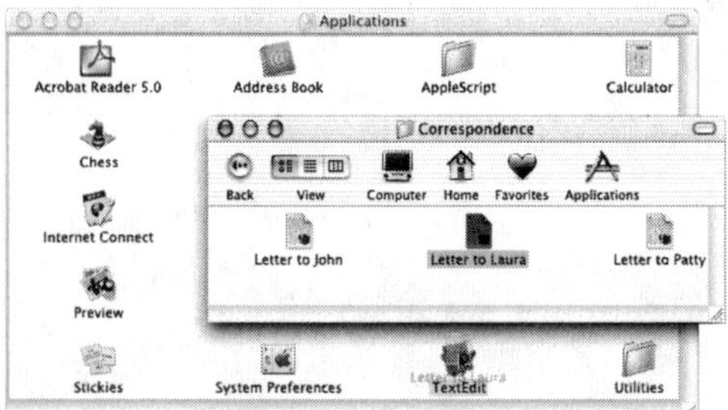

Figure 9 Drag the icon for the document you want to open onto the icon for the application you want to open it with.

To launch an application

Double-click the application's icon.

or

1. Select the application's icon (**Figure 4**).
2. Choose File > Open (**Figure 5**), or press ⌘O.

The application opens (**Figure 6**).

To launch an application & open a document at the same time

Double-click the icon for the document that you want to open.

or

1. Select the icon for the document that you want to open (**Figure 7**).
2. Choose File > Open (**Figure 5**), or press ⌘O.

If the application that created the document is not already running, it launches. The document appears in an active window (**Figure 8**).

To open a document with drag & drop

1. Drag the icon for the document that you want to open onto the icon for the application with which you want to open it.
2. When the application icon becomes selected (**Figure 9**), release the mouse button. The application launches and displays the document (**Figure 8**).

✔ Tips

- Drag and drop is a good way to open a document with an application other than the one that created it.
- Not all applications can read all documents. Dragging a document icon onto the icon for an application that can't open it either won't launch the application or will display an error message.

Standard Application Menus

Apple's Human Interface Guidelines provide basic recommendations to software developers to ensure consistency from one application to another. Nowhere is this more obvious than in the standard menus that appear in most applications: the application, File, Edit, Window, and Help menus. You'll see these menus with the same kinds of commands over and over in most of the applications you use. This consistency makes it easier to learn Mac OS applications.

The next few pages provide a closer look at the standard menus you'll find in most applications.

✔ Tips

- The Finder, which is covered in **Chapters 2 through 4**, has standard menus similar to the ones discussed here.
- The Finder rules regarding the ellipsis character (...) and keyboard commands displayed on menus also apply to applications. **Chapter 2** explains these rules.

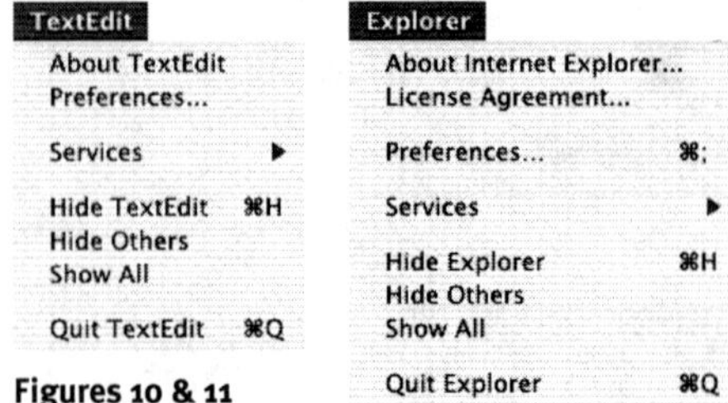

Figures 10 & 11 The TextEdit application menu (left), and the Internet Explorer application menu (right).

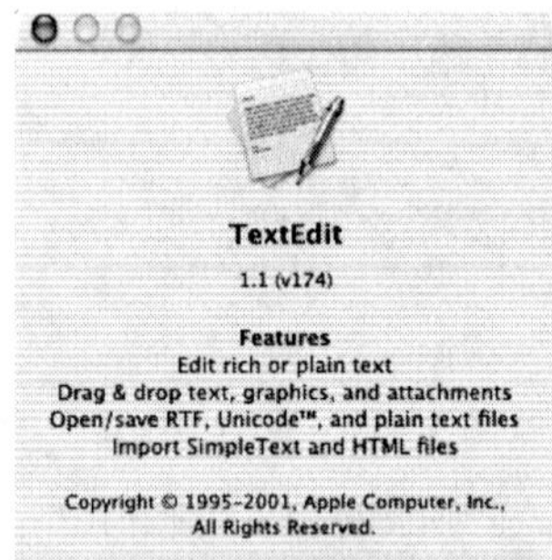

Figure 12 The About window for TextEdit provides its version number and other information.

The Application Menu

The application menu is named for the application—for example, the TextEdit application menu (**Figure 10**) or the Internet Explorer application menu (**Figure 11**). It includes commands for working with the entire application.

To learn about an application

1. From the application menu, choose About *application name* (**Figures 10** and **11**).
2. A window with version and other information appears (**Figure 12**). Read the information it contains.
3. When you're finished reading about the application, click the window's close button.

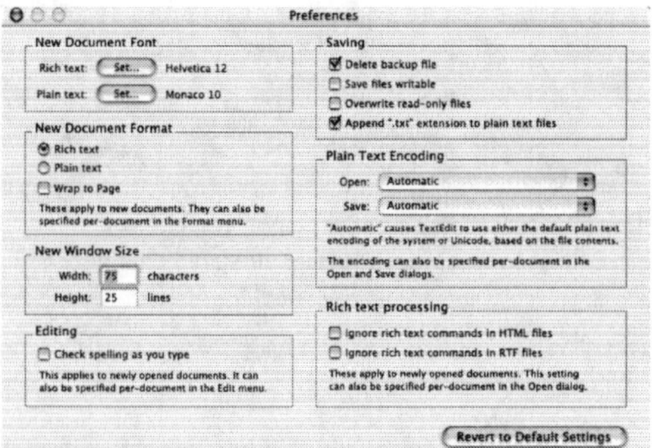

Figure 13 TextEdit's Preferences window offers a number of options you can set to customize the way TextEdit works.

To display a hidden application

Click the application's icon (or any of its document icons) in the Dock (**Figure 2**).

To unhide all applications

From the Application menu, choose Show All (**Figures 10** and **11**).

To set application preferences

1. From the application menu, choose Preferences (**Figures 10** and **11**).
2. The application's Preferences window (**Figure 13**) or dialog appears. Set options as desired.
3. Click the window's close button.

   or

   Click the dialog's OK or Save button.

✔ Tip

- Preference options vary greatly from one application to another. To learn more about an application's preferences, check its documentation or online help.

To hide an application

From the application menu, choose Hide *application name* (**Figures 10** and **11**) or press [⌘ H]. All of the application's windows, as well as its menu bar, are hidden from view.

✔ Tip

- You cannot hide the active application if it is the only application that is open (the Finder) or if all the other open applications are already hidden.

To hide all applications except the active one

From the application menu, choose Hide Others (**Figures 10** and **11**).

To hide the active application while displaying another application

Hold down [Option] while displaying or switching to another application.

To quit an application

1. From the application menu, choose Quit *application name* (**Figures 10** and **11**), or press [⌘ Q].
2. If unsaved documents are open, a dialog like the one in **Figure 14** appears for each unsaved document.
   - ▲ Click Don't Save to quit without saving the document.
   - ▲ Click Cancel or press [Esc] to return to the application without quitting.
   - ▲ Click Save or press [Return] or [Enter] to save the document.

   The application closes all windows, saves preference files (if applicable), and quits.

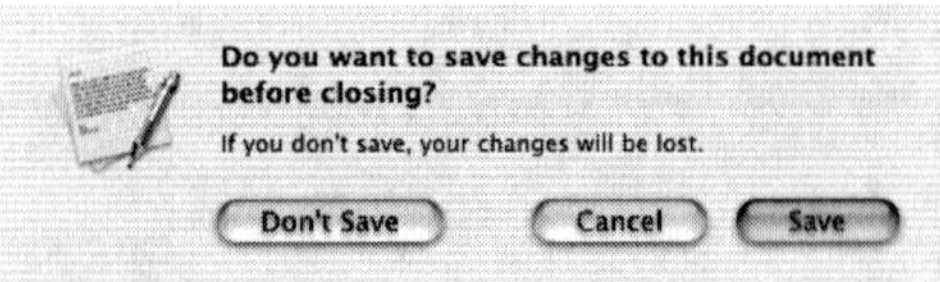

Figure 14 This dialog appears when you close a TextEdit document that contains unsaved changes.

✔ Tips

- Closing all of an application's open windows is not the same as quitting. An application is still running until you quit it.
- I tell you more about saving documents later in this chapter.
- In Classic applications, the Quit command is on the File menu.
- If an application is unresponsive and you cannot access its menus or commands, you can *force quit* it. I explain how near the end of this chapter.

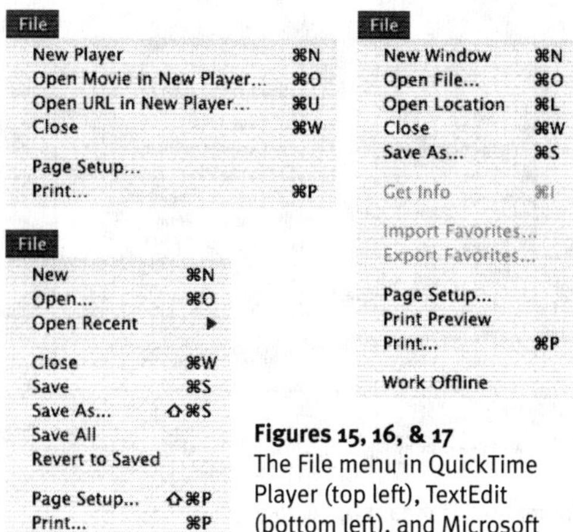

Figures 15, 16, & 17 The File menu in QuickTime Player (top left), TextEdit (bottom left), and Microsoft Internet Explorer (above).

Figure 18 TextEdit's New command displays a new, untitled document window.

Figure 19 Internet Explorer's New Window command opens a new Web browser window displaying the default Home page.

The File Menu

The File menu (**Figures 15**, **16**, and **17**) includes commands for working with files or documents. This section discusses the commands most often found under the File menu: New, Open, Close, and Save.

✔ Tip

- The Page Setup and Print commands are also found on the File menu. These commands are discussed in detail in **Chapter 8**.

To create a new document or window

Choose File > New (**Figure 16**).

or

Choose File > New Window (**Figure 17**).

or

Press ⌘ N.

A new untitled document (**Figure 18**) or window (**Figure 19**) appears.

✔ Tip

- As shown in **Figures 15**, **16**, and **17**, the exact wording of the command for creating a new document or window varies depending on the application and what the command does. This command, however, is usually the first one on the File menu.

To open a file

1. Choose File > Open (**Figures 15, 16,** and **17**) or press ⌘ O to display the Open dialog (**Figure 20**).

2. Use any combination of the following techniques to locate the document you want to open:
   - ▲ Use the From pop-up menu (**Figure 21**) to select a specific location.
   - ▲ Click one of the items in either list to view its contents in the list on the right side of the window. (The list containing the item you clicked shifts to the left if necessary.)
   - ▲ Use the scroll bar at the bottom of the two lists to shift lists. Shifting lists to the right enables you to see your path from the root directory (usually your hard disk).
   - ▲ In the Go to field, enter the path from the currently selected folder to the folder you want to open. (This is an advanced technique that requires you to know the exact location of a folder or file.)

3. When the name of the file you want to open appears in the list on the right side of the window, use one of the following techniques to open it:
   - ▲ Select it and then click Open or press Return or Enter.
   - ▲ Double-click it.

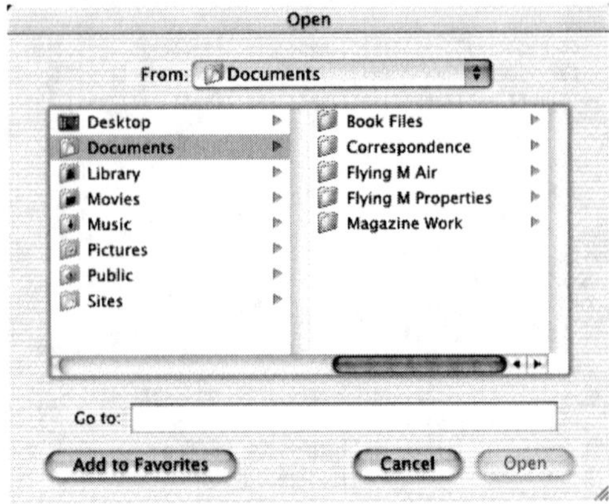

Figure 20 A standard Open dialog.

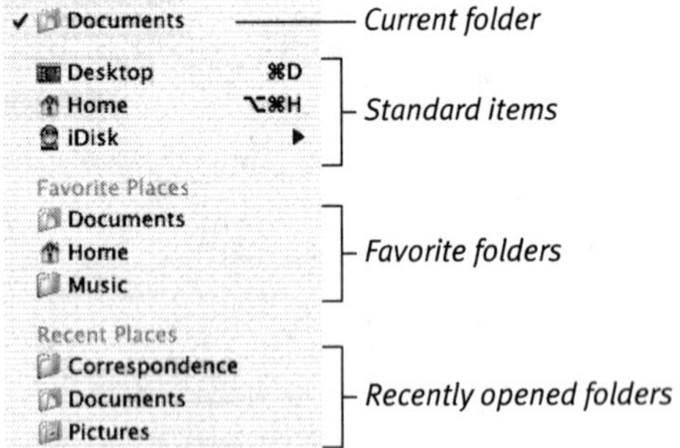

Figure 21 The From (and Where) pop-up menu includes several standard items, as well as your Favorite folders and up to five of the folders most recently accessed by the application.

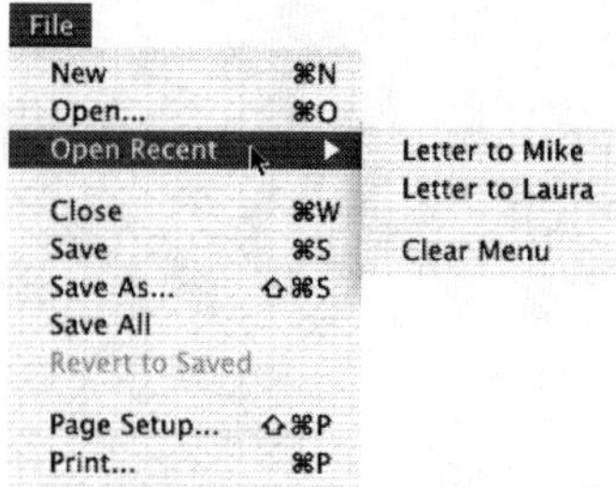

Figure 22 TextEdit's Open Recent submenu makes it easy to reopen a recently opened document.

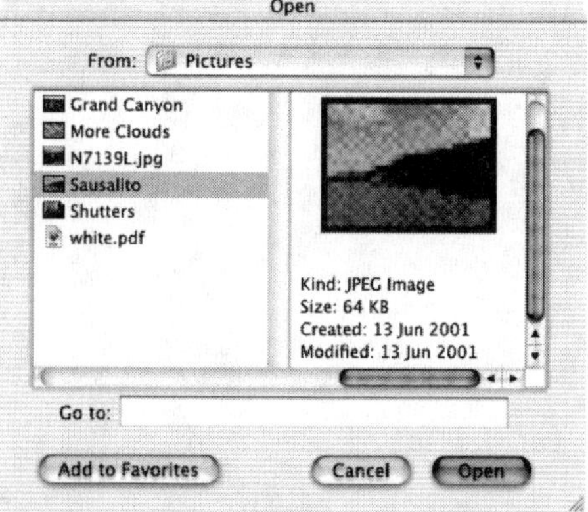

Figure 23 When you select a file in the Open dialog, the file's icon or a preview and other information for the file appears. This example shows the Open dialog for Preview with a JPEG format file selected. The image in the right side of the dialog is the file's custom icon, which was created automatically by Photoshop when the image was saved.

✓ Tips

- The exact wording of the Open command varies depending on the application and what you want to open. For example, the Open command on QuickTime Player's File menu (**Figure 15**) is Open Movie in New Player and the Open command on Internet Explorer's File menu (**Figure 17**) is Open File.
- The Open Recent command, which is available on the File menu of some applications (**Figure 16**), displays a submenu of recently opened items (**Figure 22**). Choose the item you want to open it again.
- The Open dialog (**Figure 20**) has many standard elements that appear in all Open dialogs.
- In step 2, you can make a selected folder into a favorite item by clicking the Add to Favorites button.
- In step 3, you can only select the files that the application can open; other files will either not appear in the list or will appear in gray. Some applications include a Show menu that enables you to display the types of files that appear in the Open dialog.
- In step 3, selecting a file's name in the Open dialog displays its icon or a preview and other information for the file on the right side of the dialog (**Figure 23**).
- Favorites are covered in **Chapter 4** and file paths are discussed in **Chapter 3**. iDisk is covered in detail in the sequel to this book, *Mac OS X Advanced: Visual QuickPro Guide*.

To close a window

1. Choose File > Close (**Figures 15, 16, and 17**), or press [⌘][W].

   or

   Click the window's close button.

2. If the window contains a document with changes that have not been saved, a dialog sheet like the one in **Figure 14** appears.
   - ▲ Click Don't Save to close the window without saving the document.
   - ▲ Click Cancel or press [Esc] to keep the window open.
   - ▲ Click Save or press [Return] or [Enter] to save the document.

✔ Tip

- The exact appearance of the dialog sheet that appears when you close a document with unsaved changes varies depending on the application. All versions of the dialog should offer the same three options, although they may be worded differently. **Figure 14** shows the dialog that appears in TextEdit.

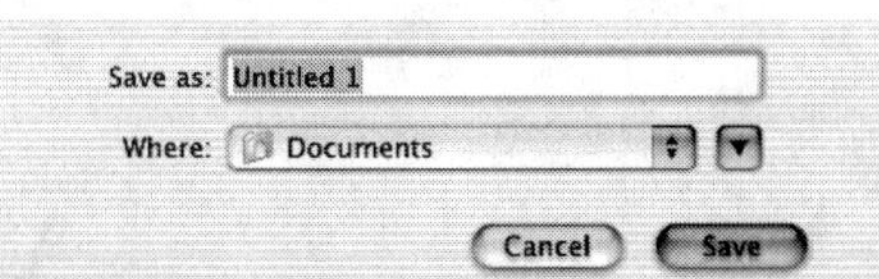

Figure 24 The Save dialog sheet can be collapsed to offer fewer options...

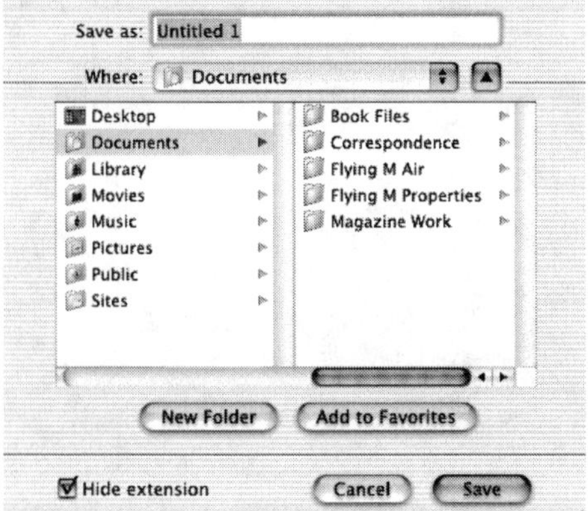

Figure 25 ...or expanded to offer more options.

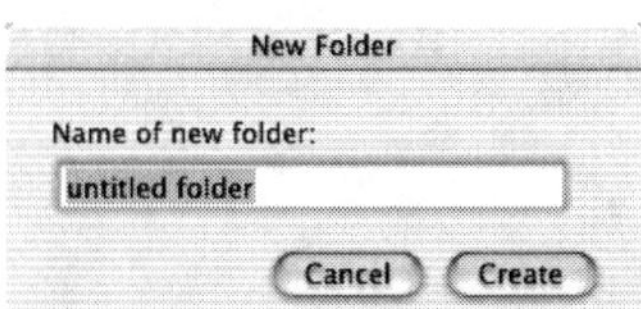

Figure 26 Use the New Folder dialog to enter a name for a new folder.

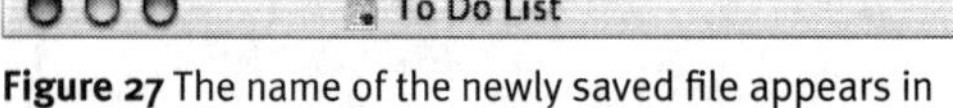

Figure 27 The name of the newly saved file appears in the window's title bar.

To save a document for the first time

1. Choose File > Save (**Figure 16**) or press [⌘S] to display the Save dialog (**Figure 24** or **25**).
2. Use the Where pop-up menu (**Figure 21**) to select a location in which to save the document.

   or

   If necessary, click the triangle beside the Where pop-up menu (**Figure 24**) to expand the dialog (**Figure 25**). Then use any combination of the following techniques to select a location in which to save the document:
   - ▲ Click one of the items in either list to view its contents on the right side of the dialog. (The list containing the item you clicked shifts to the left if necessary.)
   - ▲ Use the scroll bar at the bottom of the two lists to shift lists. Shifting lists to the right enables you to see your path from the root directory (usually your hard disk).
   - ▲ Click the New Folder button to create a new folder inside the currently selected folder. Enter a name for the folder in the New Folder dialog that appears (**Figure 26**), and click Create.
3. When the name of the folder in which you want to save the document appears on the Where pop-up menu, enter a name for the document in the Save as edit box and click Save.

   The document is saved in the location you specified. The name of the file appears in the document window's title bar (**Figure 27**).

Continued on next page...

Continued from previous page.

✔ Tips

- Not all applications enable you to save documents. The standard version of QuickTime Player, for example, does not include a Save command on its File menu (**Figures 15**).
- The Save dialog (**Figure 24**) is also known as the Save Location dialog because it enables you to select a location in which to save a file.
- In step 1, you can also use the Save As command. The first time you save a document, the Save and Save As commands do the same thing: display the Save dialog.
- In step 2, you can make a selected folder into a favorite item by clicking the Add to Favorites button.
- Some applications automatically append a period and a three-character *extension* to a file's name when you save it. Extensions are used by Mac OS X and Windows applications to identify the file type.
- Favorites are covered in **Chapter 4** and file paths are discussed in **Chapter 3**.

Close button

To Do List

Figure 28 A bullet in the close button of a document window indicates that the document has unsaved changes.

To save changes to a document

Choose File > Save (**Figure 16**), or press [⌘ S].

The document is saved in the same location with the same name, thus overwriting the existing version of the document with the new version.

✔ Tip

- Mac OS X includes two ways to indicate whether a window contains unsaved changes:
  - ▲ A bullet character appears in the close button on the title bar of the window for a document with unsaved changes (**Figure 28**).
  - ▲ A bullet character appears in the Window menu beside the name of the window for a document with unsaved changes (**Figure 32**). The Window menu is discussed a little later in this chapter.

To save a document with a new name or in a new location

1. Choose File > Save As (**Figures 16** and **17**) to display the Save dialog sheet (**Figure 24** or **25**).
2. Follow steps 2 and 3 in the section titled "To save a document for the first time" to select a location, enter a name, and save the document.

✔ Tips

- Saving a document with a new name or in a new location creates a copy of the existing document. From that point forward, you work with the copy, not the original.
- If you use the Save dialog to save a document with the same name as a document in the selected location, a confirmation dialog like the one in **Figure 29** appears. You have two options:
  - ▲ Click Cancel or press Esc to return to the Save dialog and either change the document's name or the save location.
  - ▲ Click Replace or press Return or Enter to replace the document on disk with the current document.

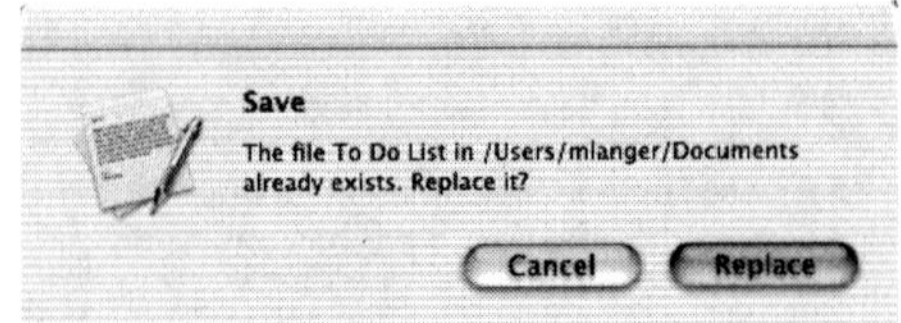

Figure 29 This dialog appears when you try to save a file with the same name as another file in a folder.

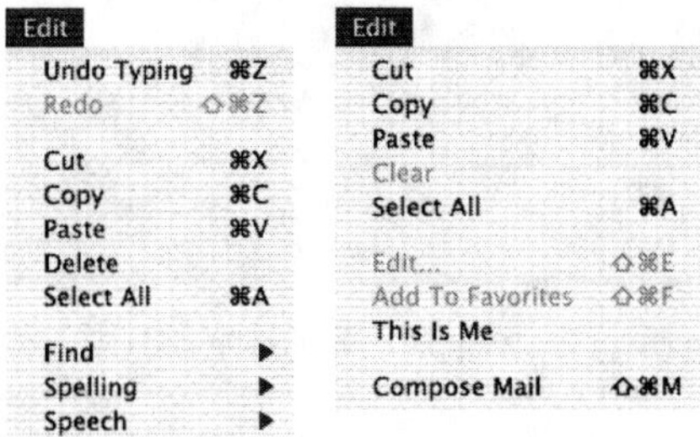

Figures 30 & 31 The Edit menus for TextEdit (left) and Address Book (right).

The Edit Menu

The Edit menu (**Figures 30** and **31**) includes commands for modifying the contents of a document. Here's a quick list of the commands you're likely to find, along with their standard keyboard equivalents:

- **Undo** (⌘ Z) reverses the last editing action you made.
- **Redo** reverses the last undo.
- **Cut** (⌘ X) removes a selection from the document and puts a copy of it in the Clipboard.
- **Copy** (⌘ C) puts a copy of a selection in the Clipboard.
- **Paste** (⌘ V) inserts the contents of the Clipboard into the document at the insertion point or replaces selected text in the document with the contents of the Clipboard.
- **Clear** or **Delete** removes a selection from the document. This is the same as pressing Delete when document contents are selected.
- **Select All** (⌘ A) selects all text or objects in the document.

✔ Tips

- As you can see in **Figures 30** and **31**, not all Edit menu commands are available in all applications at all times.
- Edit menu commands work with selected text or graphic objects in a document.
- Most Edit menu commands are discussed in greater detail in **Chapter 7**, which covers TextEdit.

The Window Menu

The Window menu (**Figures 32** and **33**) includes commands for working with open document windows as well as a list of the open windows.

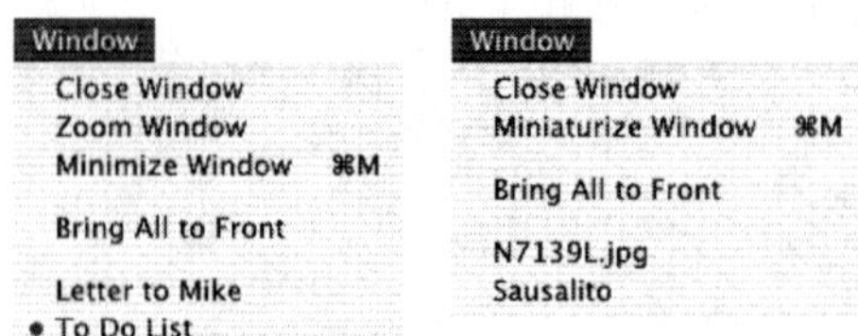

Figures 32 & 33 The Window menus for TextEdit (left) and Preview (right).

✔ Tips

- The windows within applications have the same basic parts and controls as Finder windows, which are discussed in detail in **Chapter 2**.
- A bullet character beside the name of a window in the Window menu indicates that the window contains a document with unsaved changes.

To close a window

1. Choose Window > Close Window (**Figures 32** and **33**).
2. If the window contains a document with changes that have not been saved, a Save Changes dialog sheet like the one in **Figure 14** appears.
   - ▲ Click Don't Save to close the window without saving the document.
   - ▲ Click Cancel or press Esc to keep the window open.
   - ▲ Click Save or press Return or Enter to save the document.

To zoom a window

Choose Window > Zoom Window (**Figure 32**).

The window toggles between its full size and a custom size you create with the window's resize control.

Figure 34 The icon for a minimized window appears in the Dock.

To minimize a window

Choose Window > Minimize Window (**Figure 32**).

or

Choose Window > Miniaturize Window (**Figure 33**).

or

Press [⌘] [M].

An animation shows the window shrink down to the size of an icon and slip into the Dock (**Figure 34**).

To display a minimized window

With the application active, choose the window's name from the Window menu (**Figures 32** and **33**).

or

Click the window's icon in the Dock (**Figure 34**).

The window expands out of the Dock and appears onscreen.

To bring all of an application's windows to the front

Choose Window > Bring All to Front (**Figures 32** and **33**).

All of the application's open windows are displayed on top of open windows for other applications.

✔ Tip

- This concept is new in Mac OS X, which allows an application's windows to be mingled in layers with other applications' windows.

To activate a window

Choose the window's name from the Window menu (**Figures 32** and **33**).

The Help Menu

The Help menu (**Figures 35** and **36**) includes commands for viewing onscreen help information specific to the application. Choosing the primary Help command launches the Help Viewer application with help information and links (**Figures 37** and **38**).

✔ Tips

- Onscreen help is covered in detail in **Chapter 13**.
- Although the Help menu may only have one command for a simple application (**Figures 35** and **36**), it can have multiple commands to access different kinds of help for more complex applications.

Figures 35 & 36 The Help menu for Sherlock (left) and TextEdit (right).

Figure 37 Choosing Sherlock Help from Sherlock's Help menu displays this window,...

Figure 38 ...while choosing TextEdit Help from TextEdit's Help menu displays this window.

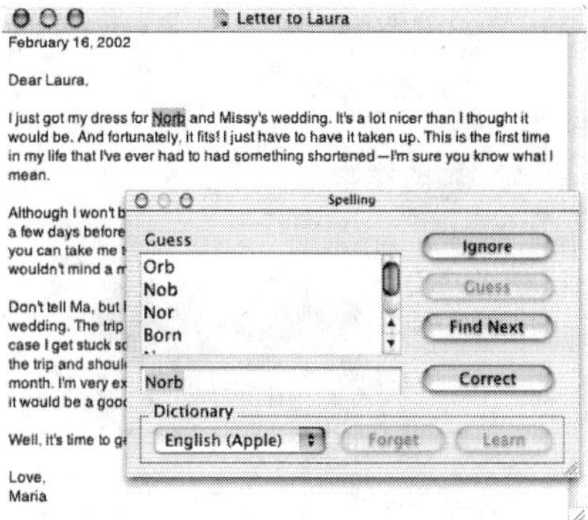

Figure 39 This Spelling dialog in TextEdit is an example of a modeless dialog—you can interact with the document while the dialog is displayed.

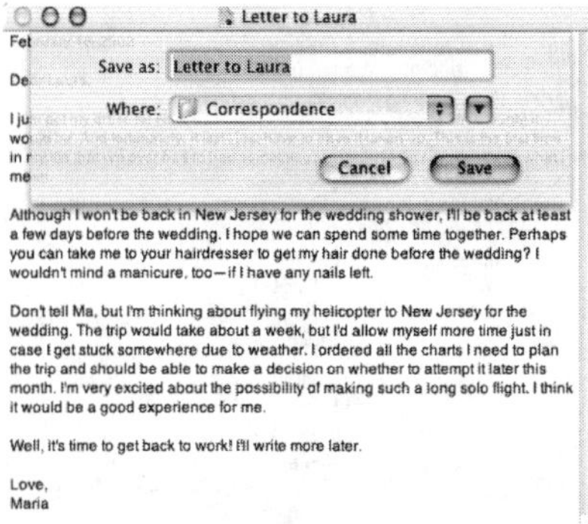

Figure 40 A standard Save Location dialog sheet is an example of a document modal dialog—you must address and dismiss it before you can continue working with the document it is attached to.

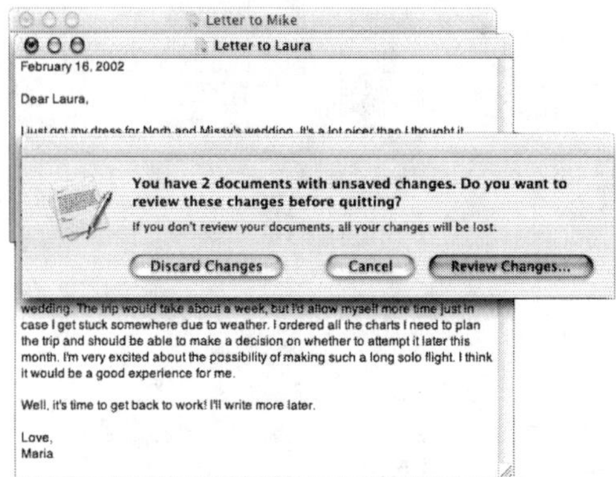

Figure 41 An application modal dialog like this Quit dialog requires your attention before you can continue working with the application.

Dialogs

Mac OS applications use *dialogs* to tell you things and get information from you. Think of them as the way your computer has a conversation—or dialog—with you.

Mac OS X has three main types of dialogs:

- *Modeless* dialogs enable you to work with the dialog while interacting with document windows. These dialogs usually have their own window controls to close and move them (**Figure 39**).
- *Document modal* dialogs usually appear as dialog *sheets* attached to a document window (**Figure 40**). You must address and dismiss these dialogs before you can continue working with the window, although you can switch to another window or application while the dialog is displayed.
- *Application modal* dialogs appear as movable dialogs (**Figure 41**). These dialogs must be addressed and dismissed before you can continue working with the application, although you can switch to another application while the dialog is displayed.

This part of the chapter identifies and explains the standard parts of a dialog that you'll see over and over in every application you use.

✔ Tips

- You don't need to remember *modeless* vs. *modal* terminology to work with Mac OS X. Just understand how the dialogs differ and what the differences mean.
- Some dialogs are very similar from one application to another. This chapter covers some of these standard dialogs , including Open (**Figure 20**), Save Location (**Figures 24, 25, and 40**), Save Changes (**Figure 14**), and Replace Confirmation (**Figure 29**). Two more standard dialogs—Page Setup and Print—are covered in **Chapter 8**.

To use dialog parts

- Click a *tab control* to view a *pane* full of related options (**Figure 42**).
- Enter text or numbers into *entry fields* (**Figure 44**), including those that are part of combination boxes (**Figure 43**).
- Use *scroll bars* to view the contents of *scrolling lists* (**Figure 43**). Click a list item once to select it or to enter it in a *combination box* (**Figure 43**).
- Click a *pop-up menu* (**Figures 43** and **44**) to display its options. Click a menu option to select it.
- Click a *check box* (**Figure 45**) to select or deselect it. (A check box is selected when a check mark or X appears inside it.)
- Click a *radio button* (**Figure 45**) to select it. (A radio button is selected when a bullet appears inside it.)
- Drag a *slider* thumb control (**Figure 45**) to change a setting.
- Consult a preview area (**Figure 42**) to see the effects of your changes.
- Drag an image file into an *image well* (**Figure 44**).
- Click a *push button* (**Figures 42** and **44**) to select it.

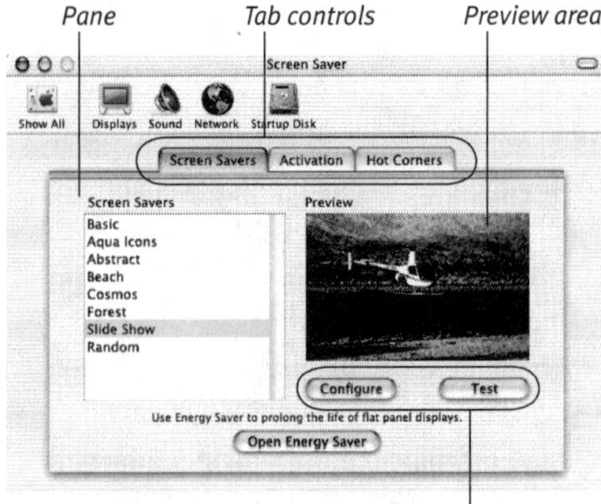

Figure 42 The Screen Saver pane of the System Preferences application.

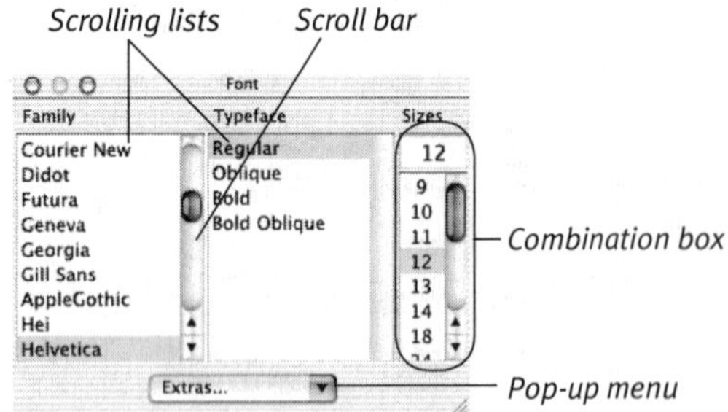

Figure 43 TextEdit's Font pane.

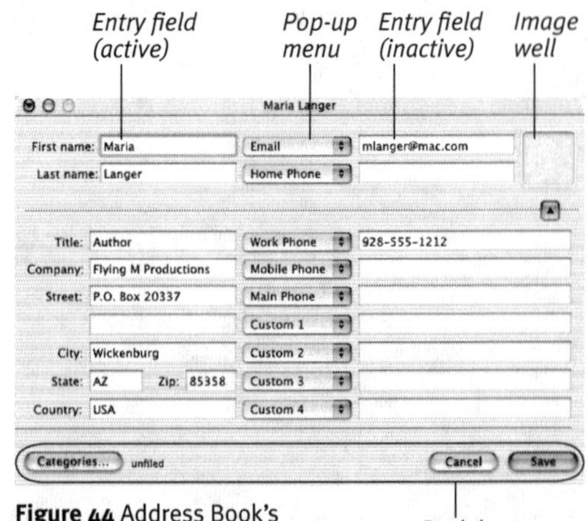

Figure 44 Address Book's Edit Address Card window.

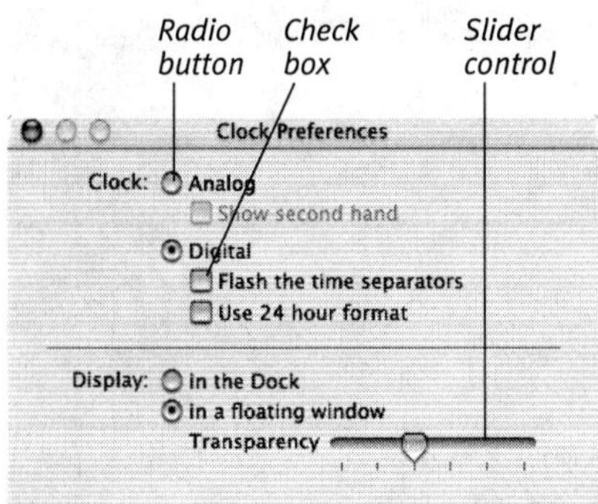

Figure 45 The Clock Preferences dialog for the Clock application.

✔ Tips

- An entry field with a dark border around it is the active field (**Figure 44**). Typing automatically enters text in this field. You can advance from one entry field to the next by pressing [Tab].
- If an entry field has a pair of arrows or triangles beside it you can click the triangles to increase or decrease a value already in the field.
- The default push button is the one that pulsates (such as the Save button in **Figure 44**). You can always select a default button by pressing [Enter] and often by pressing [Return].
- You can usually select a Cancel button (**Figure 44**) by pressing [Esc].
- You can select as many check boxes (**Figure 45**) in a group as you like.
- One and only one radio button in a group can be selected (**Figure 45**). If you try to select a second radio button, the first button becomes deselected.
- If you click the Cancel button in a dialog (**Figure 44**), any options you set are lost.
- To select multiple items in a scrolling list, hold down [⌘] while clicking each one. Be aware that not all dialogs support multiple selections in scrolling lists.
- There are other standard controls in Mac OS X dialogs. These are the ones you'll encounter most often.

Using Classic Applications

When you open an application that isn't Mac OS X-compatible, Mac OS X automatically launches the Classic environment, then opens the application within it. The application runs under Mac OS 9.x, which has slightly different interface elements.

This part of the chapter explains how you can manually start and stop the Classic environment, as well as how to use standard Open and Save As dialogs within Mac OS 9.x applications.

✔ Tips

- The Classic environment in Mac OS X is discussed in greater detail in the sequel to this book, *Mac OS X Advanced: Visual QuickPro Guide.*
- Other aspects of the Classic environment, including Apple menu options, networking, and control panels, are covered in *Mac OS 9.1: Visual QuickStart Guide.*

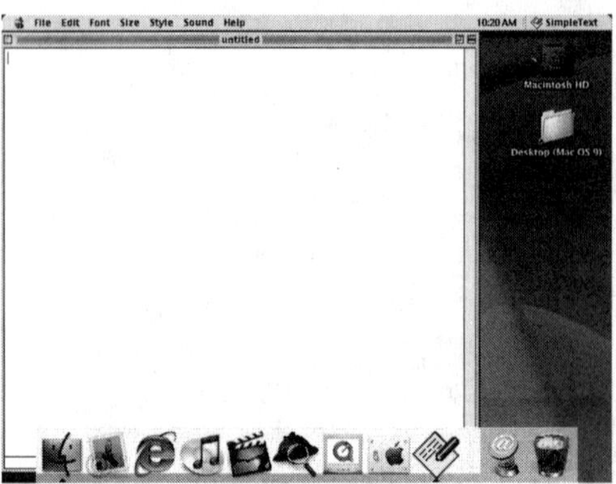

Figure 46 SimpleText running in the Classic environment.

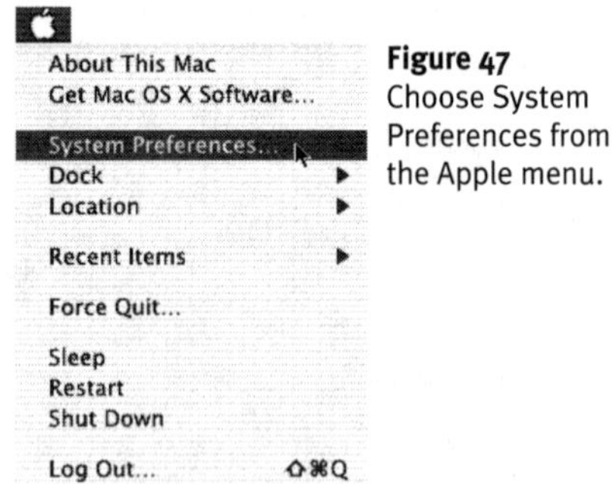

Figure 47 Choose System Preferences from the Apple menu.

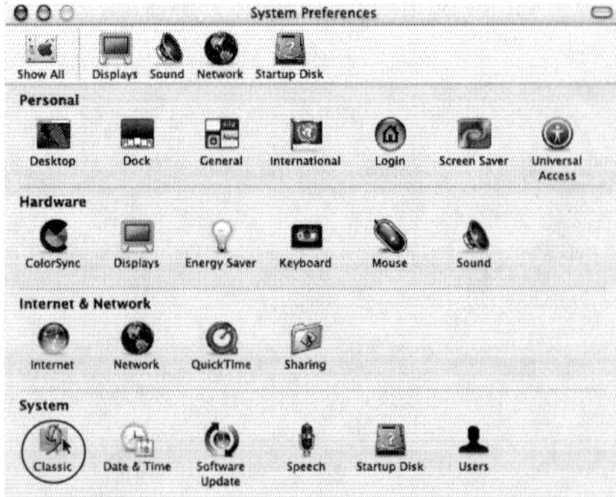

Figure 48 The Classic icon in the System Preferences window.

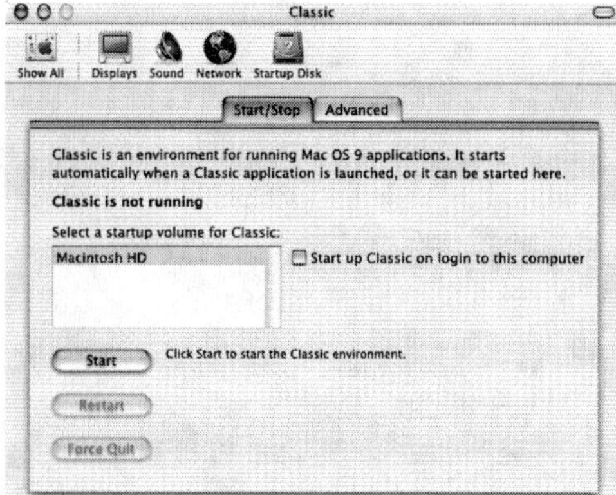

Figure 49 The Classic pane of System Preferences.

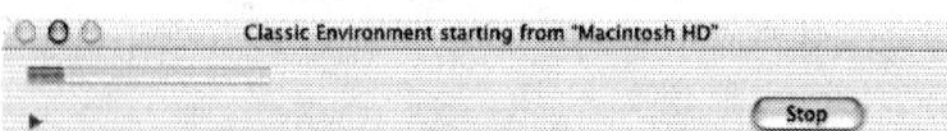

Figure 50 This window appears while the Classic environment starts up.

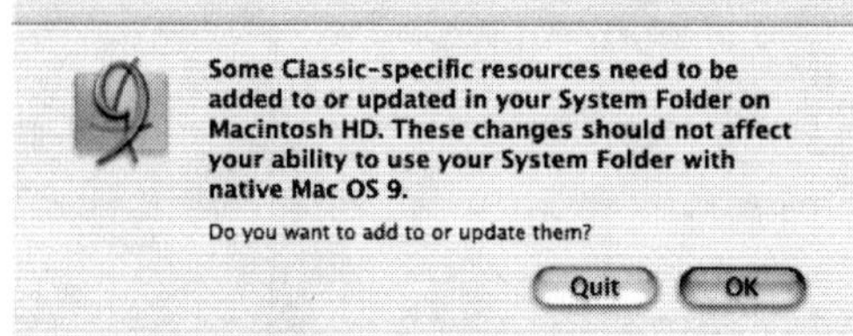

Figure 51 This dialog may appear the first time you start the Classic environment. If it does, click OK.

To start the Classic environment

Open any application that is not Mac OS X-compatible. The Classic environment launches automatically, and the application opens within it (**Figure 46**).

or

1. Choose Apple > System Preferences (**Figure 47**).
2. In the System Preferences window that appears, click the Classic icon (**Figure 48**) to display the Classic pane (**Figure 49**).
3. If necessary, select the hard disk on which Mac OS 9.x is installed.
4. Click the Start button.
5. Wait while the Classic environment starts. A window with a progress bar (**Figure 50**) tracks its progress. When it's finished, the progress window disappears and the message "Classic is running" appears in the Classic pane (**Figure 52**).

✔ Tips

- The first time you start the Classic environment, a dialog like the one in **Figure 51** may appear. Click OK.
- If you often use Mac OS 9.x applications, you can configure your computer to automatically start the Classic environment when you start or log in to your computer. Just turn on the Start up Classic on login to this computer check box in the Classic pane of System Preferences (**Figure 49**).

To stop the Classic environment

1. Choose Apple > System Preferences (**Figure 47**).
2. In the System Preferences window that appears, click the Classic icon (**Figure 48**) to display the Classic pane (**Figure 52**).
3. Click the Stop button.
4. Your computer switches to the Classic environment and attempts to Quit each open Mac OS 9.x application. Use any dialogs that appear to save changes to unsaved documents.

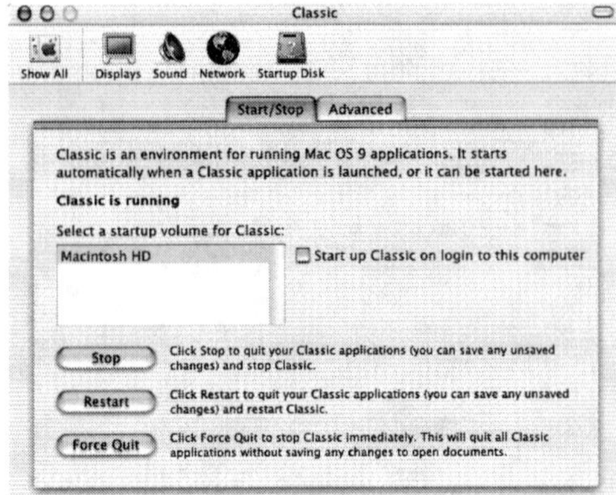

Figure 52 Once the Classic environment is running, you can use the Classic pane to stop it.

✔ Tip

- You don't have to stop the Classic environment when you're finished working with Classic applications. Doing so, however, frees up computer resources and may make your computer run faster in Mac OS X.

Figure 53 Choose Open from the application's—in this case SimpleText's—File menu.

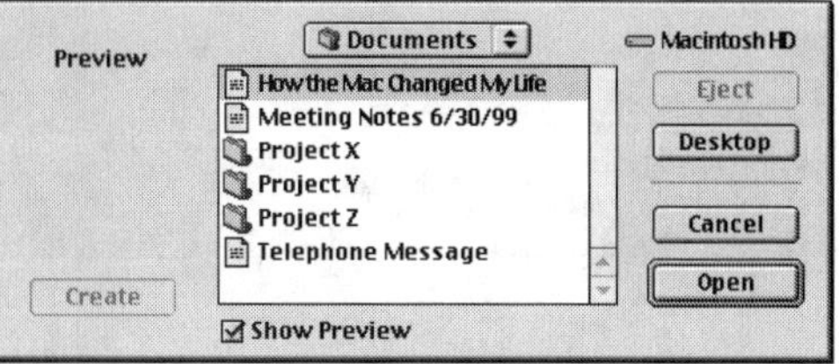

Figure 54 An Open dialog can look like this...

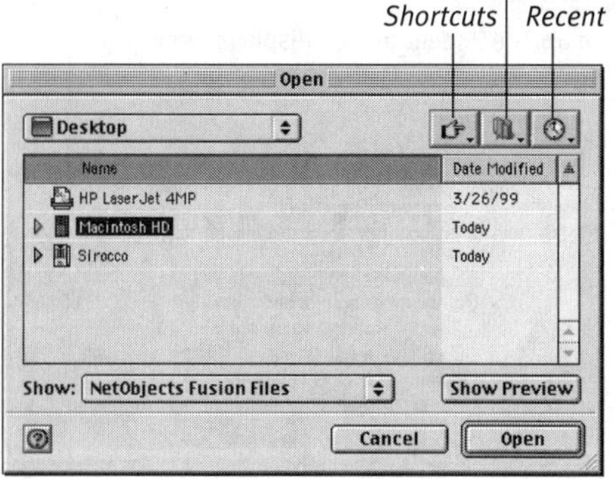

Figure 55 ...or like this.

Figure 56 Use the pop-up menu above the scrolling list to choose a different folder in the hierarchy.

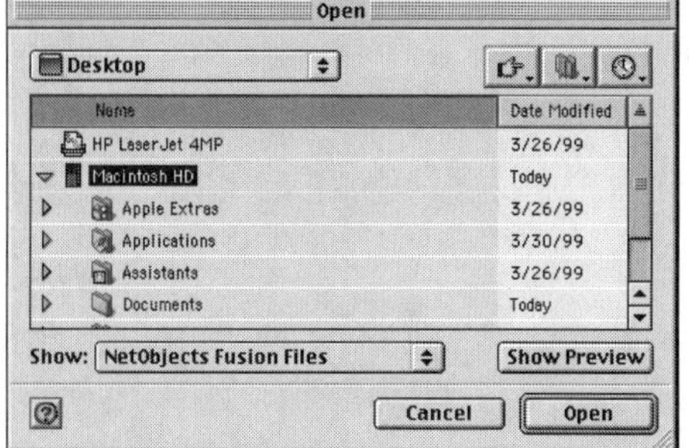

Figure 57 Click a triangle to display the items within its folder or disk.

To use a Mac OS 9.x Open dialog

1. Choose File > Open (**Figure 53**), or press ⌘ O.

   A dialog similar to the one in **Figure 54** or **55** appears.

2. Use any combination of these techniques to navigate to the file you want to open:

   ▲ To open an item in a scrolling list, click to select it and then click Open or double-click it.

   ▲ To back up out of the current folder to a previous folder in the file hierarchy, choose a folder from the pop-up menu above the scrolling list (**Figure 56**) or press ⌘ ↑ to back up one folder level at a time.

   ▲ Click the triangle to the left of the name of a disk or folder that you want to open (**Figure 55**) to display its contents along with the contents of other disks or folders (**Figure 57**).

   ▲ Open several files at once by holding down Shift while clicking the names of the files you want to open. (This only works in applications that support it.)

   ▲ Choose an option from the Shortcuts button menu (**Figure 58**) to quickly access the desktop, mounted disks, or disks available over the network or Internet.

   ▲ Choose an item from the Favorites button menu (**Figure 59**) to open a Favorite item.

   ▲ Choose an item from the Recent button menu (**Figure 60**) to open an item you recently opened with that application.

Continued on next page...

Continued from previous page.

3. Click to select the name of the file that you want to open, and then click Open (**Figure 61**) or press [Return] or [Enter].

   or

   Double-click the name of the file that you want to open.

✔ Tips

- To quickly view the items on the Desktop, click the Desktop button (**Figure 54**) or press [⌘ D]. This enables you to open folders, files, and other disks on your Desktop.
- Some Open dialogs offer a Show pop-up menu that lets you narrow down a file list by document or file type (**Figure 55**).

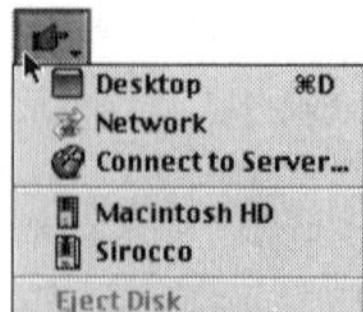

Figure 58 The Shortcuts button displays the desktop, network connections, and other mounted disks.

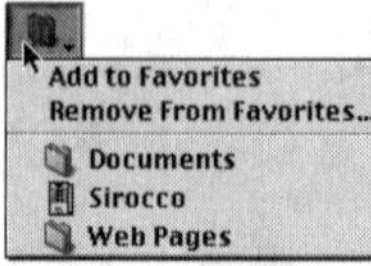

Figure 59 The Favorites button displays your Favorites.

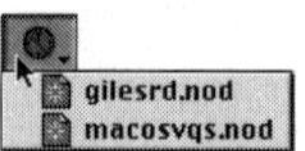

Figure 60 The Recent button displays items recently opened with that application.

Figure 61 Select the file's name and click Open to open it within the application.

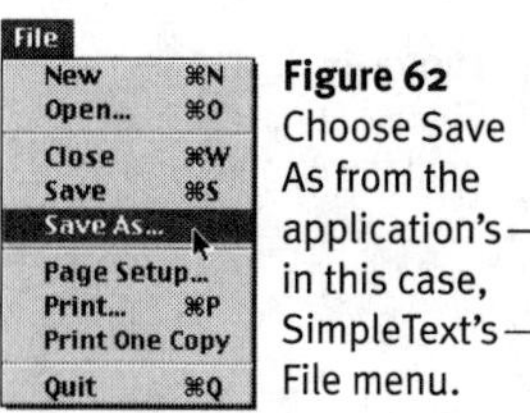

Figure 62 Choose Save As from the application's—in this case, SimpleText's—File menu.

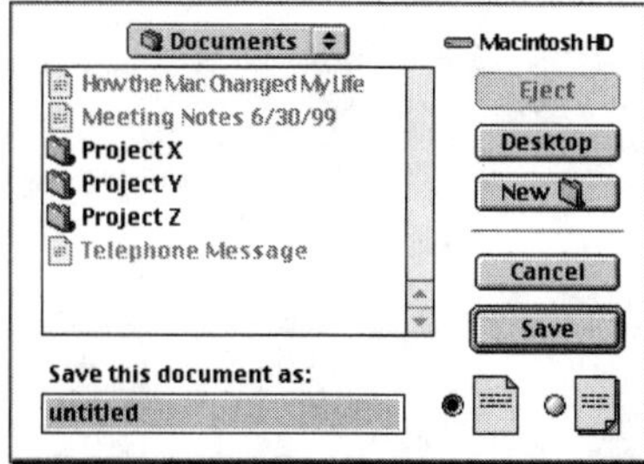

Figure 63 A Save As dialog could look like this...

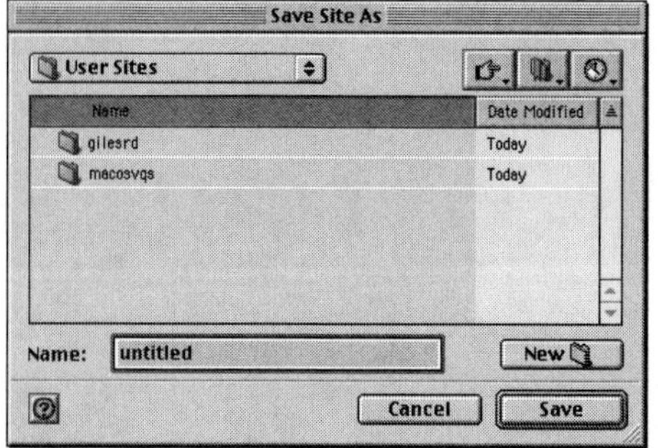

Figure 64 ...or like this.

To use the Mac OS 9.x Save As dialog

1. Choose File > Save As (**Figure 62**). A dialog similar to the one in **Figure 63** or **64** appears.
2. Use any combination of these techniques to navigate to the folder in which you want to save the document:
   - ▲ To open an item in a scrolling list, click to select it and then click Open or double-click it.
   - ▲ To back out of the current folder to a previous folder in the file hierarchy, choose a folder from the pop-up menu above the scrolling list (**Figure 56**) or press [⌘][↑] to back up one folder level at a time.
   - ▲ Choose an option from the Shortcuts button menu (**Figure 58**) to quickly access the desktop, mounted disks, or disks available over the network or Internet.
   - ▲ Choose an item from the Favorites button menu (**Figure 59**) to open a Favorite folder.
   - ▲ Choose an item from the Recent button menu (**Figure 60**) to open an folder you recently opened with that application.
3. In the edit box beneath the scrolling list, enter the name that you want to give the document.
4. Click Save, or press [Return] or [Enter].

✔ Tips

- If you have never saved the document, you can also choose Save from the application's File menu or press [⌘][S] to display the Save As dialog.
- To quickly view the items on the Desktop, click the Desktop button (**Figure 63**) or press [⌘][D]. This enables you to open folders and other disks on your Desktop.

Force Quitting Applications

Occasionally, an application may freeze, lock up, or otherwise become unresponsive. When this happens, you can no longer work with that application or its documents. Sometimes, you can't access any application at all!

Mac OS X includes the Force Quit command (**Figure 65**), which enables you to force an unresponsive application to quit. Then you can either restart it or continue working with other applications.

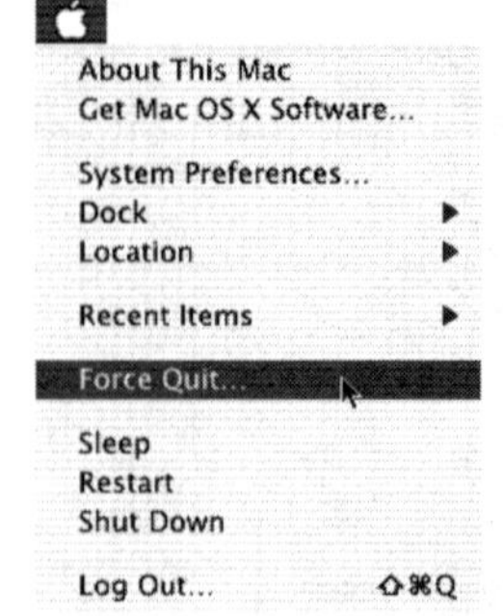

Figure 65 Choose Force Quit from the Apple menu.

✖ Warning!

- When you force quit an application, any unsaved changes in that application's open documents may be lost. Use the Force Quit command only as a last resort, when the application's Quit command cannot be used.

✔ Tips

- Mac OS X's protected memory, which is discussed at the beginning of this chapter, makes it possible for applications to continue running properly on your computer when one application locks up.
- If more than one application experiences problems during a work session, you might find it helpful to restart your computer. This clears out RAM and forces your computer to reload all applications and documents into memory. You can learn more about troubleshooting Mac OS X in **Chapter 13**.

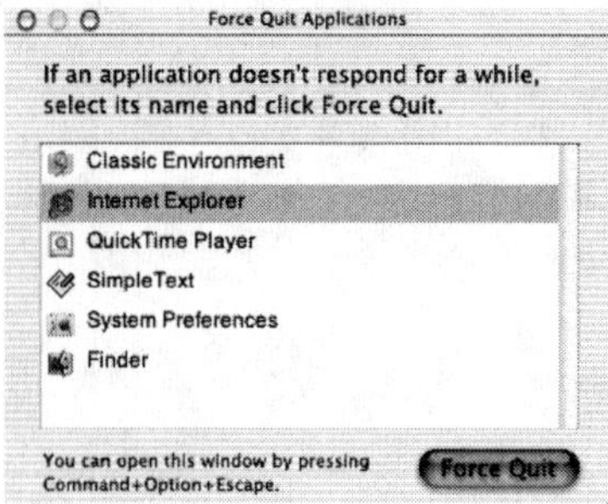

Figure 66 Select the application you want to force to quit.

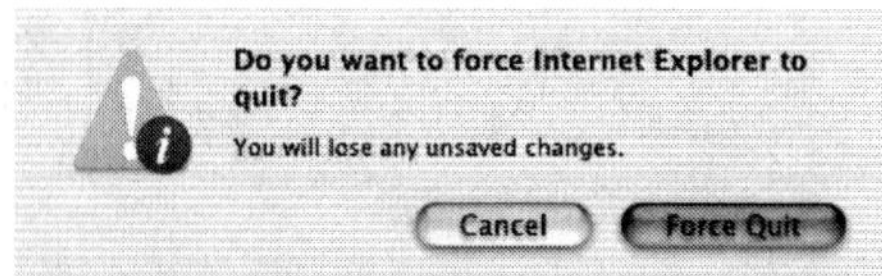

Figure 67 Use this dialog to confirm that you really do want to force quit the application.

To force quit an application

1. Choose Apple > Force Quit (**Figure 65**), or press Option ⌘ Esc.
2. In the Force Quit Applications window that appears (**Figure 66**), select the application you want to force to quit.
3. Click Force Quit.
4. A confirmation dialog like the one in **Figure 67** appears. Click Force Quit.

   The application immediately quits.

✔ Tip

- If you selected Finder in step 2, the button to click in step 3 is labeled Relaunch.

Using Mac OS X Applications

Figure 1 The Mac OS X 10.1 Applications folder.

Mac OS Software

Mac OS X includes a variety of applications that you can use to perform tasks on your computer.

This chapter covers the following Apple programs in the Applications folder (**Figure 1**):

- **Address Book**, which enables you to keep track of contact information for friends, family members, and business associates.
- **Calculator**, which enables you to perform quick calculations and graph formulas.
- **Chess**, which is a computerized version of the game of chess.
- **Clock**, which displays a live-action digital or analog clock.
- **Image Capture**, which enables you to download image files from a digital camera and save them on disk.
- **Preview**, which enables you to view images and PDF files.
- **QuickTime Player**, which enables you to view QuickTime movies and streaming video.
- **Stickies**, which enables you to place colorful notes on your computer screen.

✔ Tips

- Mac OS X includes a number of other applications that are discussed elsewhere in this book or in *Mac OS X Advanced: Visual QuickPro Guide*:
  - TextEdit is covered in **Chapter 7**.
  - Print Center is covered in **Chapter 8**.
  - Internet Connect, Internet Explorer, and Mail are covered in **Chapter 9**.
  - Sherlock is covered in **Chapter 10**.
  - iMovie and iTunes (as well as iPhoto and iDVD) are covered in **Chapter 11**.
  - AppleScript is covered in **Chapter 12**.
  - System Preferences are covered in *Mac OS X Advanced: Visual QuickPro Guide*.
  - Applications in the Utilities folder are covered in *Mac OS X Advanced: Visual QuickPro Guide*.

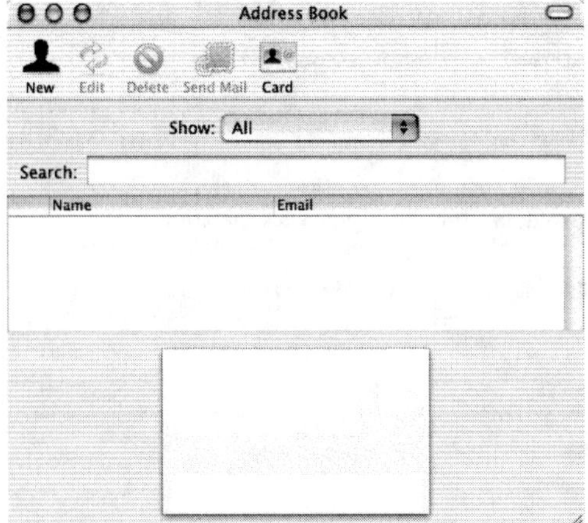

Figure 2 The main Address Book window.

Address Book

The Address Book application enables you to keep track of the names, addresses, phone numbers, and e-mail addresses of people you know. Once an e-mail address is stored within Address Book, you can use it to send e-mail messages with Mac OS X's Mail application.

✔ Tips

- You must have an Internet connection to send e-mail.
- Mac OS X's Mail application is covered in **Chapter 9**.

To launch Address Book

Double-click the Address Book icon in the Applications folder (**Figure 1**).

or

1. Click the Address Book icon in the Applications folder (**Figure 1**).
2. Choose File > Open, or press [⌘O].

Address Book's main window appears (**Figure 2**).

✔ Tip

- You can also open Address Book from within the Mail application, as discussed in **Chapter 9**.

To add a new contact record

1. Click the New button in the toolbar (**Figure 2**) to display an untitled address card window (**Figure 3** or **4**).
2. Enter information about the contact into appropriate fields. You can enter information into any combination of fields. Press Tab to move from field to field and use pop-up menus when necessary to identify information.
3. To set a category for the contact, click the Categories button to display the Choose Categories dialog sheet (**Figure 5**). Turn on the check box beside each category you want to assign to the record and click OK.
4. When you are finished entering data for the contact, click Save in the address card window. The information is saved and the contact appears in the main Address Book window (**Figure 6**).

✔ Tips

- By assigning categories to contacts, you can use the Show pop-up menu in the Address Book window to narrow down the contact list.
- You can add additional categories to Address Book by clicking the + button in the Choose Categories dialog sheet (**Figure 5**). This adds a blank category line (**Figure 7**), which you can fill in with the name of a category. Likewise, you can delete a custom category by selecting it and clicking the – button.

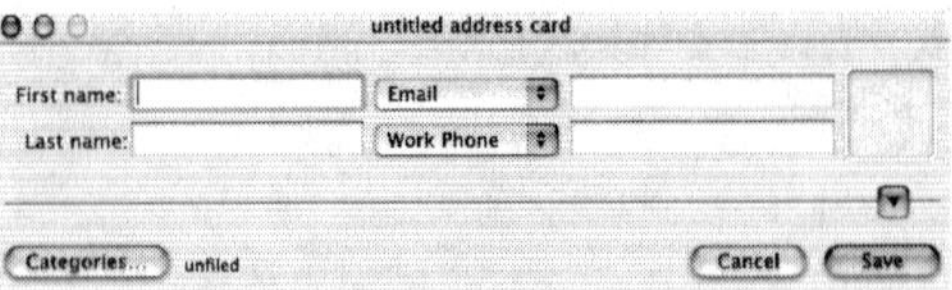

Figure 3 The untitled address card can appear collapsed, like this. When you click the arrow button, ...

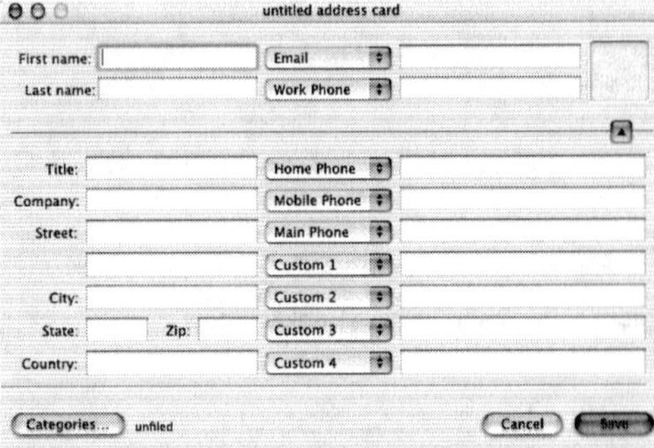

Figure 4 ...it expands to offer more entry fields, like this.

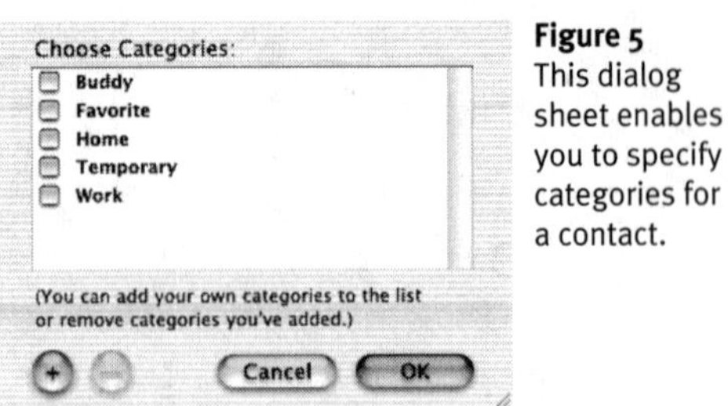

Figure 5 This dialog sheet enables you to specify categories for a contact.

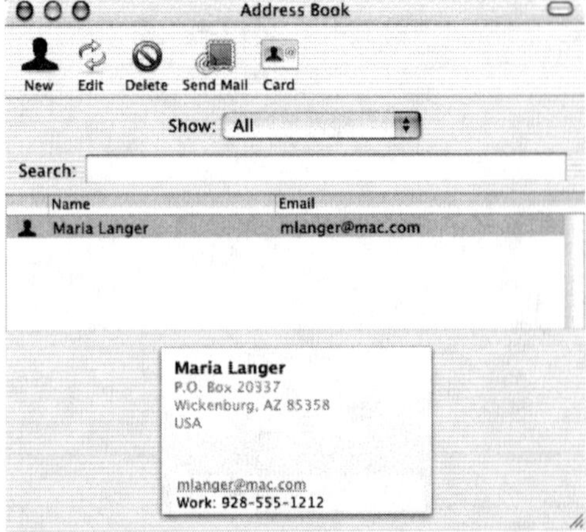

Figure 6 When you save the contact information, it appears in the Address Book window.

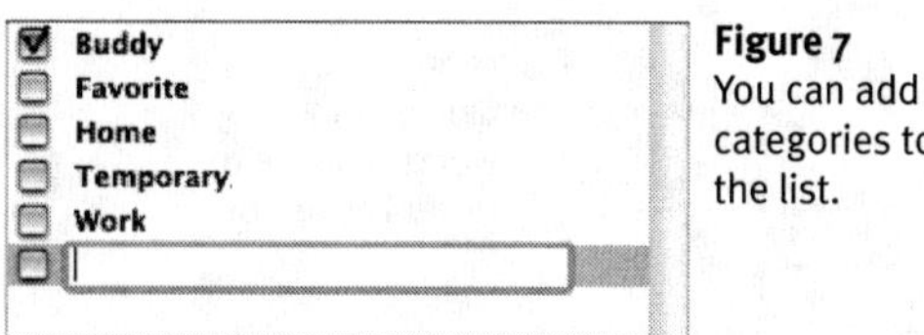

Figure 7 You can add categories to the list.

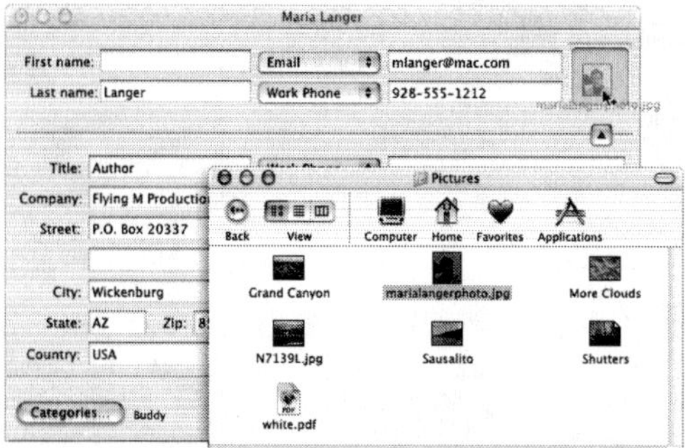

Figure 8 To add a picture for a record, simply drag its icon into the image well.

Figure 9 The picture is added to the record and appears in the Address Book window.

To edit a contact record

1. In the Address Book window, select the contact you want to edit.
2. Click the Edit button on the toolbar.
3. Use the address card window to make changes as desired to the contact's information.
4. When you are finished making changes, click Save. Your changes are saved with the contact record.

To add a photo or log to a contact record

1. Display the address card record for a new contact (**Figure 3** or **4**) or existing contact.
2. Drag the icon for the file containing the photo or logo you want to add from a Finder window to the image well in the address card window (**Figure 8**). When you release the mouse button, the image appears in the image well.
3. Click Save to save the image as part of the contact information.

✔ Tip

- The image appears in the Address Book main window when the contact is selected (**Figure 9**).

To delete a contact record

1. In the Address Book window, select the contact you want to delete.
2. Click the Delete button on the toolbar. The contact disappears.

✔ Tip

- Be sure you have selected the correct contact in step 1. Deleting a contact is permanent and cannot be undone.

Calculator

Calculator displays a simple calculator that can perform addition, subtraction, multiplication, and division.

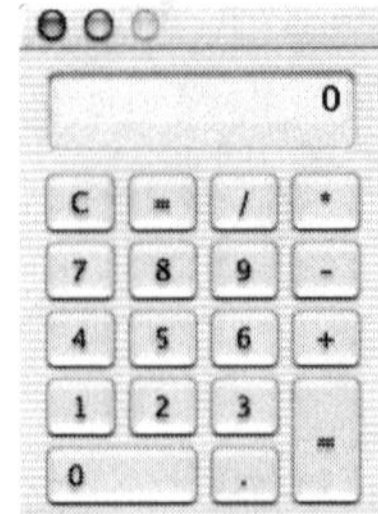

Figure 10
The Calculator looks and works just like a $3 pocket calculator.

✔ Tip

- The Calculator has been around since the Mac's early days. For Mac OS X, it got a facelift, but it still works the same way.

To launch Calculator

Double-click the Calculator icon in the Applications folder (**Figure 1**).

or

1. Click the Calculator icon in the Applications folder (**Figure 1**).
2. Choose File > Open, or press ⌘O.

The Calculator window appears (**Figure 10**).

To use the Calculator

Use your mouse to click buttons for numbers and operators.

or

Press keyboard keys corresponding to numbers and operators.

The numbers you enter and the results of your calculations appear at the top of the Calculator window.

✔ Tip

- You can use the Cut, Copy, and Paste commands to copy the results of calculations into documents. **Chapter 7** covers the Cut, Copy, and Paste commands.

Figure 11 The Chess window displays a three-dimensional chess board.

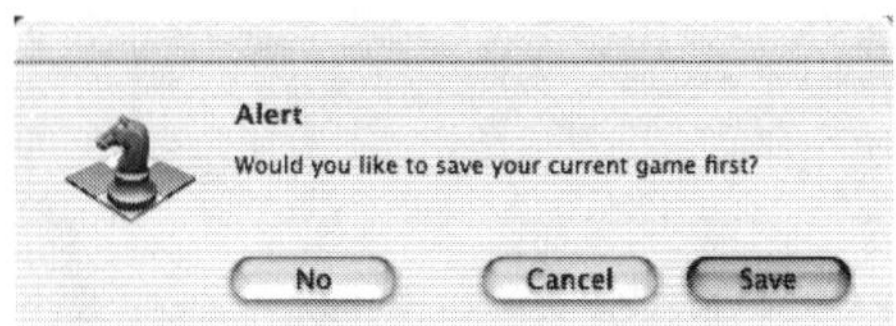

Figure 12 This Alert appears if you try to start a new game while another game is active.

Chess

Chess is a computerized version of the classic strategy game of chess. Your pieces are white and you go first; the computer's pieces are black.

To launch Chess

Double-click the Chess icon in the Applications folder (**Figure 1**).

or

1. Click the Chess icon in the Applications folder (**Figure 1**).
2. Choose File > Open, or press [⌘ O].

The Chess window appears (**Figure 11**).

To move a chess piece

Drag the piece onto any valid square on the playing board.

✔ Tips

- The computer moves automatically after each of your moves.
- If you attempt to make an invalid move, an alert sounds and the piece returns to where it was.
- If Speakable Items is enabled, you can use spoken commands to move chess pieces. You can learn about speakable items in *Mac OS X: Visual QuickPro Guide.*

To start a new game

1. Choose File > New.
2. If you are already in the middle of a game, an alert dialog (**Figure 12**) appears:
   - ▲ **No** starts a new game without saving the current one.
   - ▲ **Cancel** dismisses the dialog and returns you to the current game.
   - ▲ **Save** displays a Save Location dialog that you can use to save the game.

Clock

Clock displays an analog or digital clock, either in the Dock or in a floating window on screen.

Figure 13 The Clock in the Dock (not to be confused with the Cat in the Hat).

To launch Clock

Double-click the Clock icon in the Applications folder (**Figure 1**).

or

1. Click the Clock icon in the Applications folder (**Figure 1**).
2. Choose File > Open, or press [⌘ O].

The Clock either appears in the Dock (**Figure 13**) or as a floating window (**Figure 14**).

Figure 14 A floating analog clock window.

To set Clock preferences

1. Choose Clock > Preferences to display the Clock Preferences window (**Figure 15**).
2. Set Clock options by selecting a radio button and toggling check boxes as desired:
   - ▲ **Analog** displays an analog clock (**Figures 13 and 14**). Use the check box to determine whether you want the second hand to display.
   - ▲ **Digital** displays a digital clock (**Figure 16**). Use check boxes to determine whether it should flash time separators to mark seconds or use 24-hour format.
3. Set Display options as desired by selecting a radio button:
   - ▲ **In the Dock** displays the clock in the Dock (**Figure 13**).
   - ▲ **In a floating window** displays the clock in a floating window on screen (**Figures 14 and 16**). If you select this option, you can use the slider to set the transparency of the window.

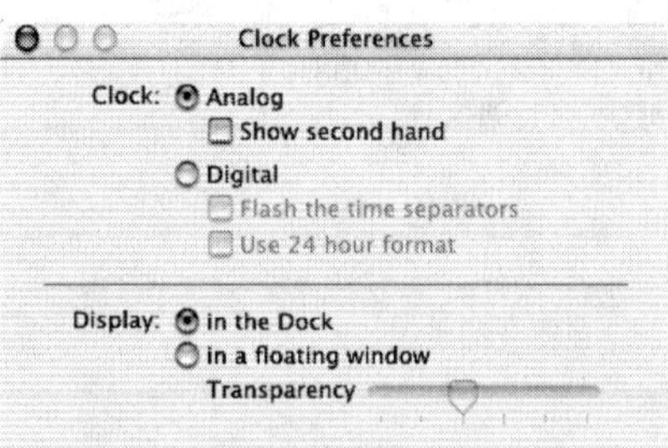

Figure 15 The Clock Preferences window.

Figure 16 A floating digital clock window.

✔ Tip

- The clock that appears in the menu bar can be customized with the Date & Time pane of System Preferences. System Preferences are covered in detail in the sequel to this book, *Mac OS X Advanced: Visual QuickPro Guide*.

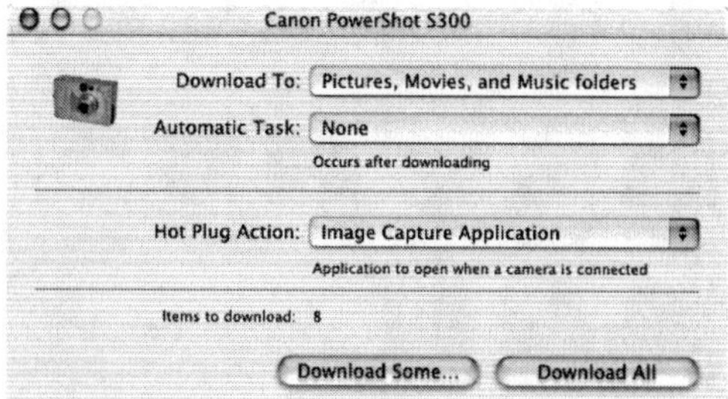

Figure 17 Image Capture's main window is named for the camera you have attached and turned on.

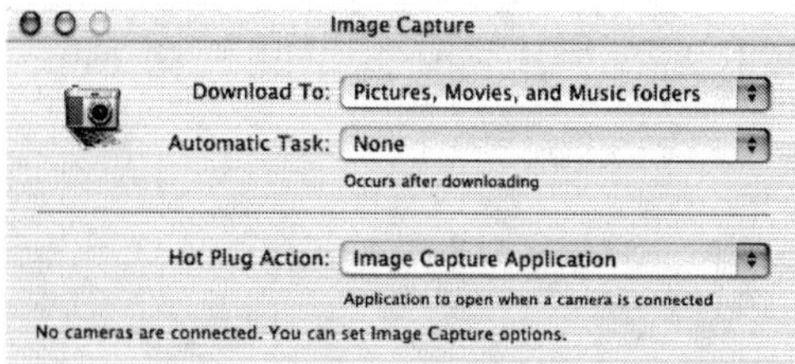

Figure 18 If no camera is attached when you launch Image Capture, its main window looks like this.

✔ Tip

- If no camera is attached when you launch Image Capture, its main window looks like the one in **Figure 18**. Although you cannot download images, you can still set Image Capture options.

Image Capture

Image Capture is an application that enables you to download image files from a digital camera to your computer's hard disk. What's cool about Image Capture is that it can sense when a camera is attached and turned on and launch itself automatically.

✔ Tips

- Not all digital cameras are compatible with Image Capture. Generally speaking, if Image Capture does not "see" your digital camera when it is connected and turned on, the camera is probably not compatible with Image Capture and Image Capture cannot be used. You can learn more on Apple's Web site at `www.apple.com/macosx/whatyoucando/applications/imagecapture.html`.
- You can also download images using iPhoto. I explain how in **Chapter 11**.

To launch Image Capture

1. Attach your digital camera to your computer's USB or Firewire port, using the applicable cable.
2. Turn the digital camera on and, if necessary, set it to review mode. The Image Capture window should appear (**Figure 17**). If it does not, then:

   Double-click the Image Capture icon in the Applications folder (**Figure 1**).

   or

   1. Click the Image Capture icon in the Applications folder (**Figure 1**).
   2. Choose File > Open, or press ⌘O.

To download images

To download all images on the camera, click the Download All button in the main Image Capture window (**Figure 17**).

or

1. To download some of the images on the camera, click the Download Some button in the main Image Capture window (**Figure 17**).
2. A window full of thumbnail images appears (**Figure 19**). Select the images you want to download. To select more than one image, hold down ⌘ while clicking each image.
3. Click the Download button.

A dialog sheet appears, showing the progress of the download (**Figure 20**). When it disappears, the download is complete and Image Capture displays the window(s) for the folder(s) in which it downloaded the pictures (**Figure 21**).

✔ Tip

- You can also use the thumbnail window (**Figure 19**) to delete images on the camera. Select the images you want to delete and click the Delete Picture button (the red circle with a line through it). Then click Delete in the confirmation dialog sheet that appears.

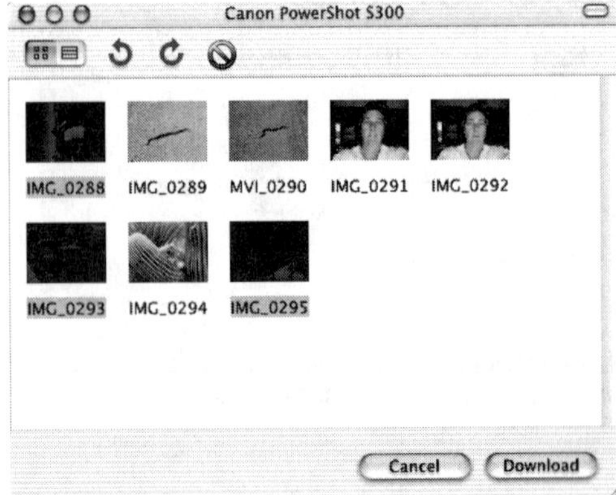

Figure 19 Use this window to select the images you want to download.

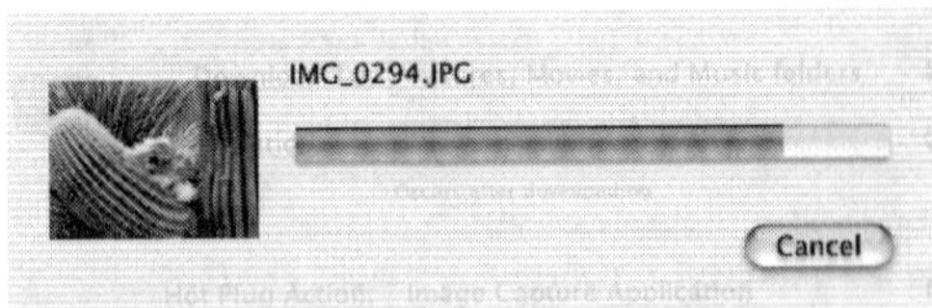

Figure 20 A progress window appears as the pictures are downloaded. (This is the bird's nest in the saguaro cactus outside my office window.)

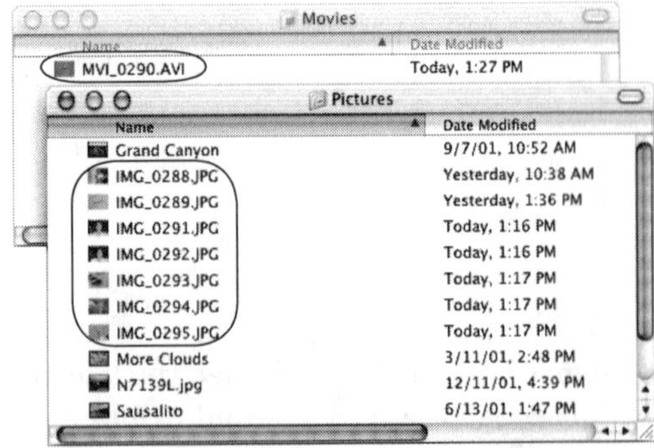

Figure 21 Image Capture displays the windows where it downloaded the images and/or movies. In this example, it has downloaded seven images and one movie from my Canon Digital Elph.

Figure 22 Here's an image file opened with Preview...

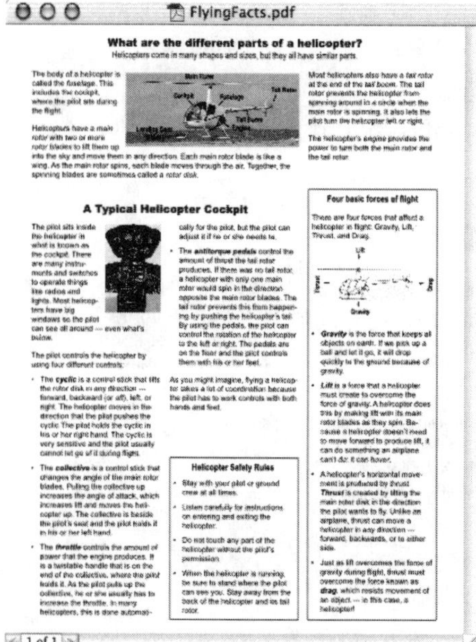

Figure 23 ...and here's a PDF file opened with Preview.

Preview

Preview is a program that enables you to open and view two kinds of files:

- **Image files** (**Figure 22**), including files in JPEG, TIFF, PICT, and GIF formats.
- **PDF** or **Portable Document Format files** (**Figure 23**) created with Mac OS X's Print command or Adobe Acrobat software.

✔ Tips

- I explain how to create PDF files with the Print command in **Chapter 8**.
- You can also open PDF files with Adobe Systems' Acrobat Reader, which may have been installed with Mac OS X 10.1. (Look for it in your Applications folder, **Figure 1**.) You can learn more about Acrobat Reader—and download a copy of the software, if you need it—on the Adobe Web site, `www.adobe.com`. Adobe Acrobat Reader is free.

To open a file with Preview

Drag the document file's icon onto the Preview icon in the Applications folder (**Figure 24**).

or

Double-click the icon for a Preview document (**Figure 25**).

Preview launches and displays the file in its window (**Figures 22** and **23**).

✔ Tips

- You can also use Preview's Open command to open any compatible file on disk. I explain how to use an application's Open command in **Chapter 5**.
- You can use options on Preview's Display menu (**Figure 26**) to zoom in or out or rotate the window's contents to better view the document.

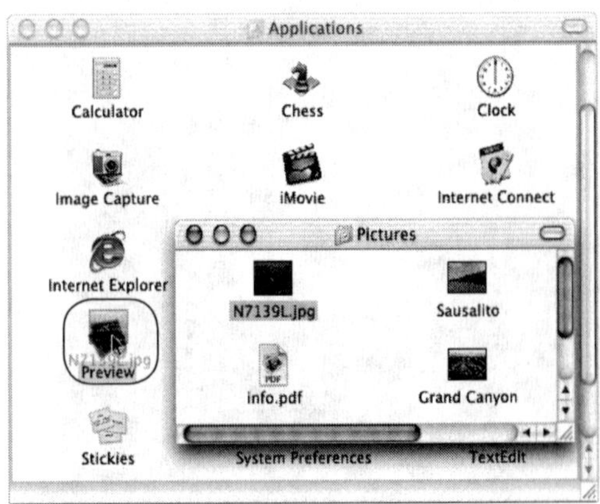

Figure 24 One way to open a file with Preview is to drag the file's icon onto the Preview icon.

info.pdf photo.jpg

Figure 25 You can also simply double-click a Preview document's file's icon.

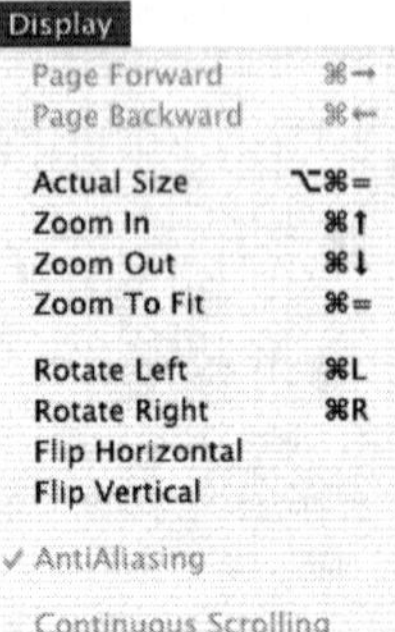

Figure 26 Here's the Display menu with an image file open. Other commands are available when a PDF file is open.

Figure 27 One way to launch QuickTime is to click its icon in the Dock.

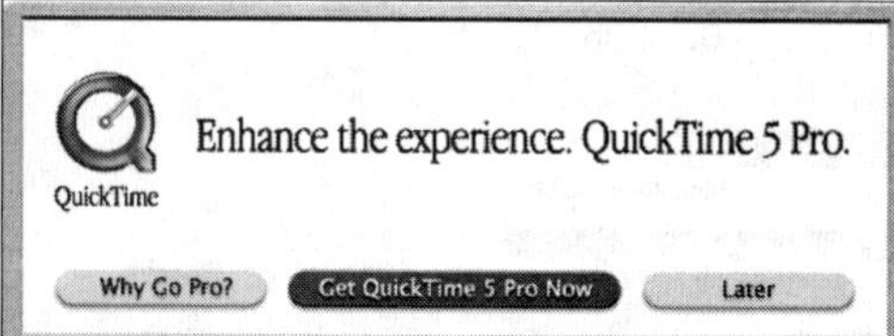

Figure 28 When you launch QuickTime Player, Apple tries to sell you QuickTime Pro.

Figure 29 QuickTime appears as either a window full of channels like this, ...

Figure 30 ... or, if you are connected to the Internet, as a window containing an advertisement (what else?) like this.

QuickTime Player

QuickTime is a video and audio technology developed by Apple Computer, Inc. It is widely used for digital movies as well as streaming audio and video available via the Internet. QuickTime Player is an application you can use to view QuickTime movies and streaming Internet content.

✔ Tips

- There are two versions of QuickTime Player: the standard version, which is included with Mac OS X, and the Pro version, which enables you to edit and save QuickTime files. You can learn more about QuickTime Pro on Apple's QuickTime Web site, `www.apple.com/quicktime/`, and in *QuickTime 5: Visual QuickStart Guide.*
- Internet access is covered in **Chapter 9**.

To launch QuickTime Player

Click the QuickTime Player icon in the Dock (**Figure 27**).

or

Open the QuickTime Player icon in the Applications folder (**Figure 1**).

A QuickTime Player window appears (**Figure 28** or **29**).

✔ Tips

- When you launch QuickTime Player, a dialog like the one in **Figure 28** may appear. Click Later to dismiss it.
- The first time you launch QuickTime Player, a dialog like the one in **Figure 31** may appear. Click OK to dismiss the dialog, then follow the instructions on the next page to set QuickTime Connection Speed preferences.

To set connection speed options

1. If a dialog like the one in **Figure 31** appears when you launch QuickTime, click OK.

   or

   Choose QuickTime Player > Preferences > QuickTime Preferences (**Figure 32**).
2. Mac OS X opens the System Preferences application and displays the QuickTime Preferences pane. Click the Connection tab to display its options (**Figure 33**).
3. Choose a speed from the Connection Speed pop-up menu (**Figure 34**).
4. Choose System Prefs > Quit System Prefs (**Figure 35**), or press ⌘Q.

✔ Tips

- The dialog in **Figure 31** automatically appears just the first time you launch QuickTime Player.
- Once set, you do not need to change the QuickTime connection speed options unless you change your Internet connection speed—for example, switch from dialup to DSL.
- System Preferences are covered in detail in *Mac OS X Advanced: Visual QuickPro Guide.*

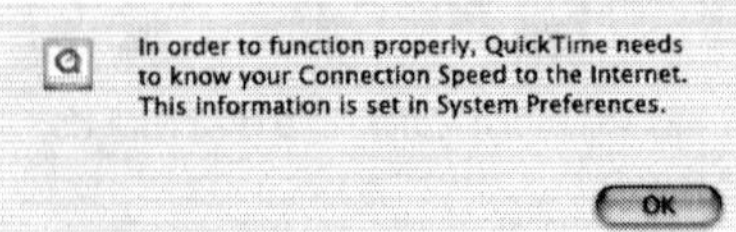

Figure 31 This dialog appears the first time you launch QuickTime Player.

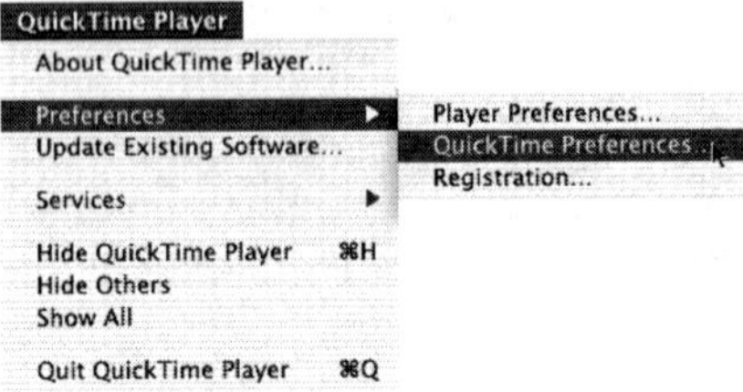

Figure 32 You can manually open the QuickTime preferences pane by choosing QuickTime Preferences from the Preferences submenu under the QuickTime Player menu.

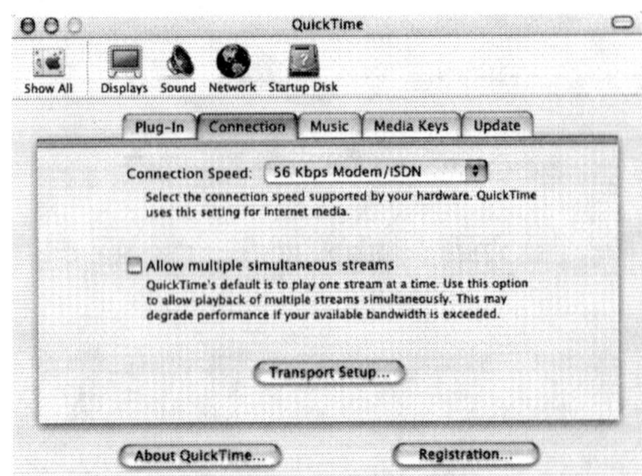

Figure 33 The Connection tab of the QuickTime preferences pane.

Figure 34 Connection Speed options.

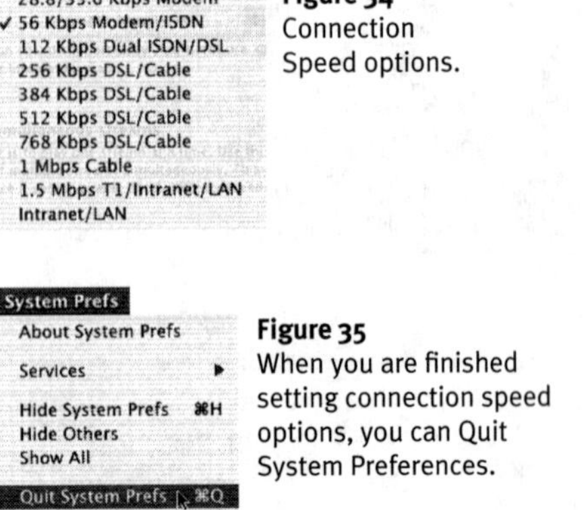

Figure 35 When you are finished setting connection speed options, you can Quit System Preferences.

Figure 36 A QuickTime movie file icon.

The Fellowship of The Ring

Movie

Time line

Graphic EQ

TV button

Volume Go To Start Fast Rewind Play / Pause Fast Forward Go To End

Figure 37 The first frame of the movie appears in a QuickTime Player window.

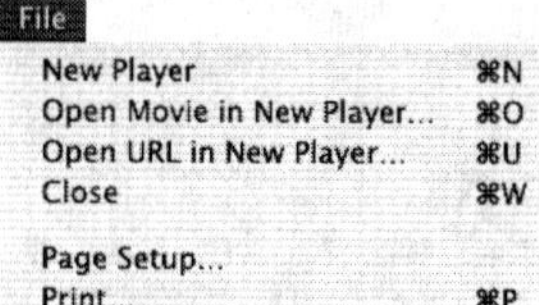

Figure 38 QuickTime Player's File menu. There are more menu commands in QuickTime Pro.

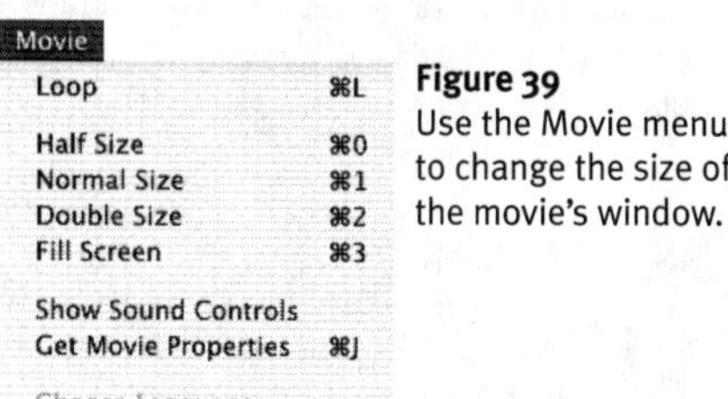

Figure 39 Use the Movie menu to change the size of the movie's window.

To open a QuickTime movie file

Double-click the QuickTime movie file icon (**Figure 36**).

If QuickTime Player is not already running, it launches. The movie's first frame appears in a window (**Figure 37**).

✔ Tip

- You can also open a QuickTime movie file by using the Open Movie in New Player command on QuickTime Player's File menu (**Figure 38**). The Open dialog is covered in **Chapter 5**.

To control movie play

You can click buttons and use controls in the QuickTime Player window (**Figure 37**) to control movie play:

- **Go To Start** displays the first movie frame.
- **Fast Rewind** plays the movie backward quickly, with sound.
- **Play** starts playing the movie. When the movie is playing, the Play button turns to a **Pause** button, which pauses movie play.
- **Fast Forward** plays the movie forward quickly, with sound.
- **Go To End** displays the last movie frame.
- **Time line** tracks movie progress. By dragging the slider, you can scroll through the movie without sound.
- **Volume** changes movie volume; drag the slider left or right.

To specify movie size

Select a size option from the Movie menu (**Figure 39**). The size of the movie's window changes accordingly.

To open QuickTime content on the Internet

1. If necessary, connect to the Internet.
2. Choose File > Open URL in New Player (**Figure 38**).
3. Enter the URL for the movie you want to watch in the Open URL dialog that appears, (**Figure 40**) and click OK.

   Your computer downloads the movie you specified and displays it in a QuickTime Player window.

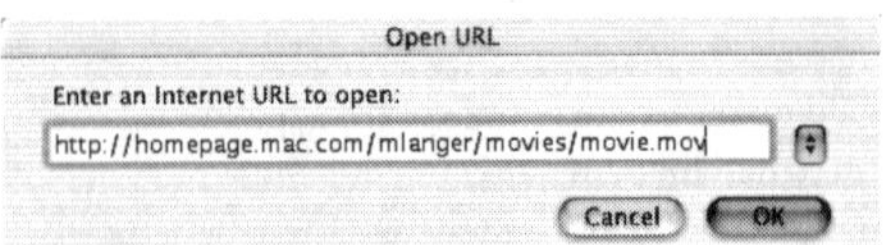

Figure 40 Use this dialog to enter the Internet address for the movie you want to watch.

To watch QuickTime TV

1. If necessary, connect to the Internet.
2. Choose one of the channels on the Quick-Time TV submenu on the QTV menu (**Figure 41**).

   or

   Click the TV button in a QuickTime window to display QuickTime TV channel buttons (**Figure 29**). Then click one of the channel buttons.
3. The main screen for the channel appears. It may include buttons to access specific content (**Figure 42**). Click a button for the content that interests you.

   Your computer downloads the content and displays it in a QuickTime Player steaming video window (**Figure 43**).

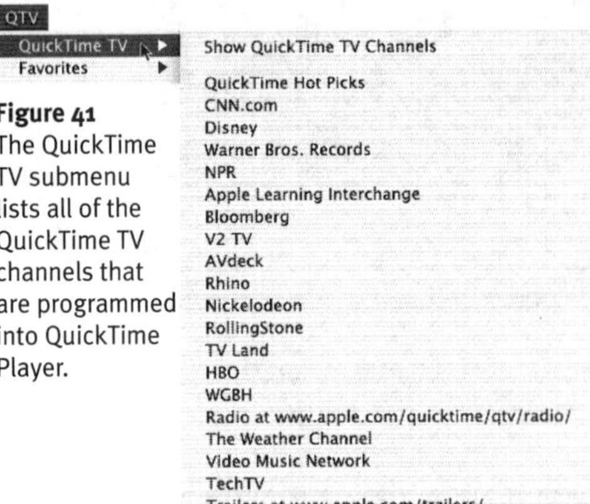

Figure 41 The QuickTime TV submenu lists all of the QuickTime TV channels that are programmed into QuickTime Player.

Figure 42 Here's what CNN.com's QuickTime TV channel looked like on the day I wrote this page.

Figure 43 A QuickTime TV news story.

✔ Tip

- Some QuickTime TV channels display *streaming* audio or video. This requires a constant connection to the Internet while content is downloaded to your computer. Streaming content will not stop downloading until you close its QuickTime Player window or quit QuickTime Player.

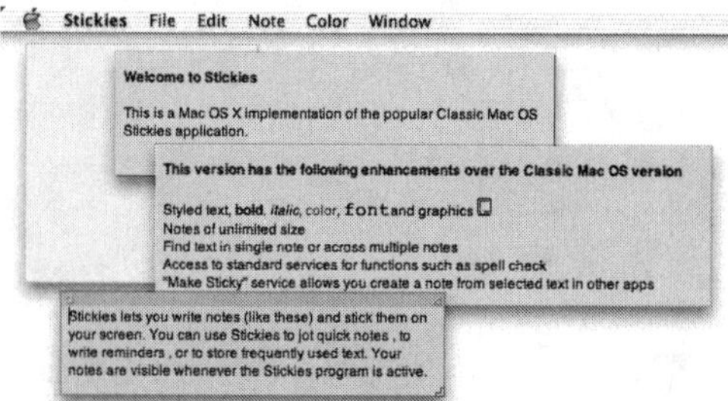

Figure 44 The default windows that appear when you first launch Stickies tell you a little about the program.

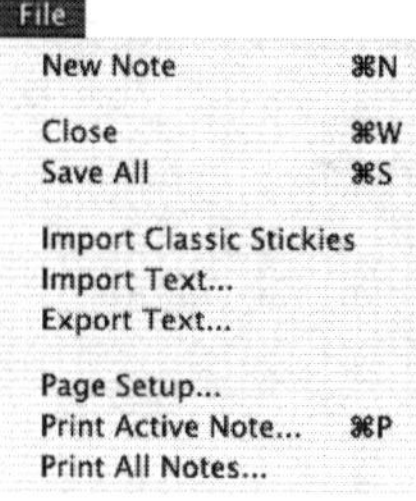

Figure 45 Stickies' File menu.

Figure 46 Here's a blank new sticky note...

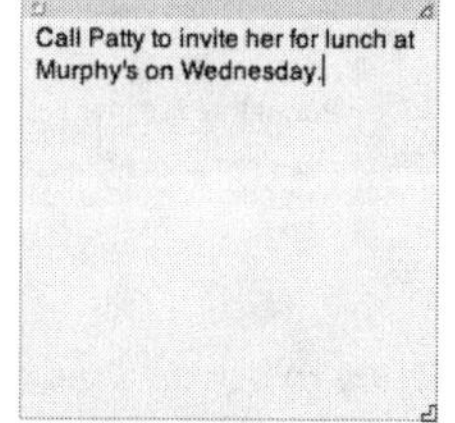

Figure 47 ...and here's the same note with a reminder typed in.

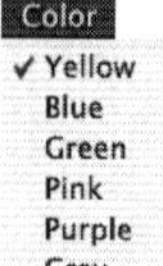

Figures 48 & 49 Use the Color and Note menus to change the appearance of notes.

Note
Font Panel... ⌘T
Bold ⌘B
Italic ⌘I
Copy Font ⌘3
Paste Font ⌘4
Use as Default
Text Colors...
Note Info ⇧⌘I

Stickies

Stickies is an application that displays computerized "sticky notes" that you can use to place reminders on your screen.

To launch Stickies

Double-click the Stickies icon in the Applications folder (**Figure 1**).

or

1. Click the Stickies icon in the Applications folder (**Figure 1**).
2. Choose File > Open, or press [⌘][O].

The default Stickies windows appear (**Figure 44**).

✔ Tips

- Read the text in the default Stickies windows (**Figure 44**) to learn more about Stickies and how the Mac OS X version differs from previous versions.
- Stickies notes remain on the Desktop until you quit Stickies.
- When you quit Stickies, all notes are automatically saved to disk and will reappear the next time you launch Stickies.

To create a sticky note

1. Choose File > New Note (**Figure 45**) or press [⌘][N] to display a blank new note (**Figure 46**).
2. Type the text that you want to include in the note (**Figure 47**).

✔ Tip

- You can use options under the Color and Note menus (**Figures 48** and **49**) to change the appearance of notes or note text. Formatting text is covered in **Chapter 7**.

To print sticky notes

1. To print just one sticky note, click it to activate it and then choose File > Print Active Note (**Figure 45**) or press ⌘P.

   or

   To print all sticky notes, choose File > Print All Notes (**Figure 45**).

2. Use the Print dialog that appears (**Figure 50**) to set options for printing and click the Print button.

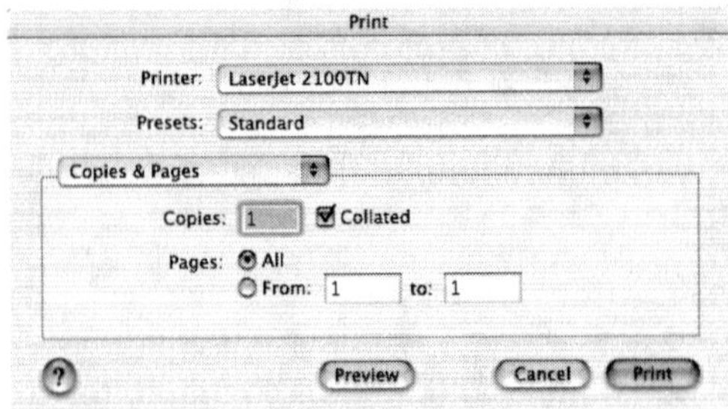

Figure 50 The Print dialog.

✔ Tip

- **Chapter 8** covers the Print dialog and printing.

To close a sticky note

1. Click the close box for the sticky note you want to close.

   or

   Activate the sticky note you want to close and choose File > Close (**Figure 45**) or press ⌘W.

2. A Close dialog like the one in **Figure 51** may appear.

   ▲ Don't Save closes the note without saving its contents.

   ▲ Cancel leaves the note open.

   ▲ Save displays the Export dialog (**Figure 52**), which you can use to save the note as plain or formatted text in a file on disk. Enter a name and select a disk location for the note's contents, then choose a file format and click Save.

Figure 51 The Close dialog asks if you want to save note contents.

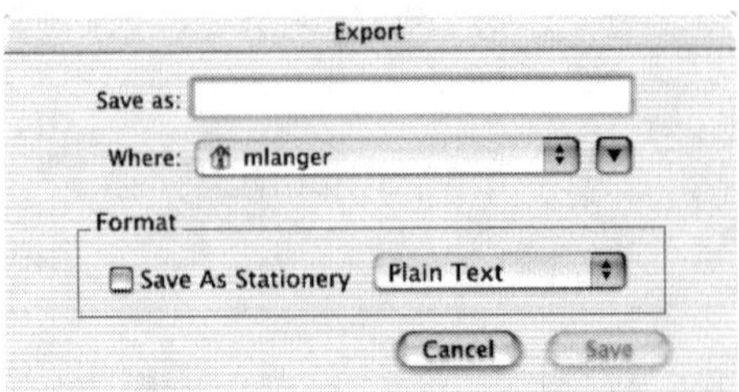

Figure 52 Use the Export dialog to save a note as plain or formatted text in a file on disk.

✔ Tip

- Once a sticky note has been saved to disk, it can be opened and edited with TextEdit or any other program capable of opening text files.

Using TextEdit

Figure 1 The TextEdit application icon.

Figure 2 A TextEdit document's icon.

TextEdit

TextEdit (**Figure 1**) is a basic text editing application that comes with Mac OS. As its name implies, TextEdit lets you create, open, edit, and print text documents (**Figure 2**), including the "Read Me" files that come with many applications.

This chapter explains how to use TextEdit to create, edit, format, open, and save documents.

✔ Tips

- Although TextEdit offers many of the basic features found in a word processing application, it falls far short of the feature list of word processors such as Microsoft Word and the word processing components of integrated software such as AppleWorks.
- If you're new to computers, don't skip this chapter. It not only explains how to use TextEdit, but it provides instructions for basic text editing skills—like text entry and the Copy, Cut, and Paste commands —that you'll use in all Mac OS-compatible applications.

Launching & Quitting TextEdit

Like any other application, you must launch TextEdit before you can use it. This loads it into your computer's memory so your computer can work with it.

To launch TextEdit

Double-click the TextEdit application icon.

or

1. Select the TextEdit application icon (**Figure 1**).
2. Choose File > Open (**Figure 3**), or press ⌘O.

   TextEdit launches. An untitled document window appears (**Figure 4**).

✔ Tips

- TextEdit is normally found in the Applications folder on your hard drive.
- As illustrated in **Figure 4**, the TextEdit document window has the same standard window parts found in Finder windows. I tell you how to use Finder windows in **Chapter 2**; TextEdit and other application windows work the same way.

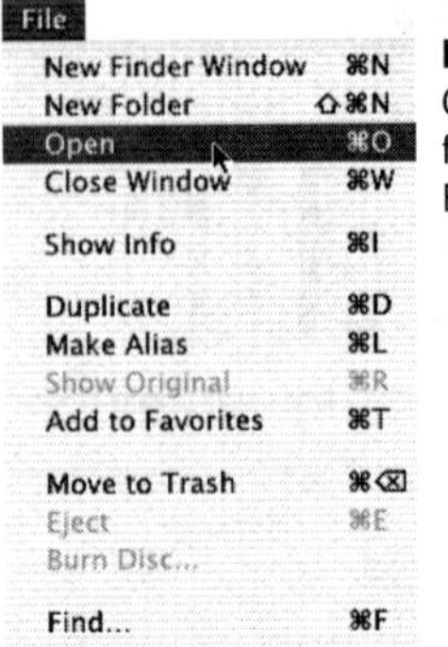

Figure 3 Choose Open from the Finder's File menu.

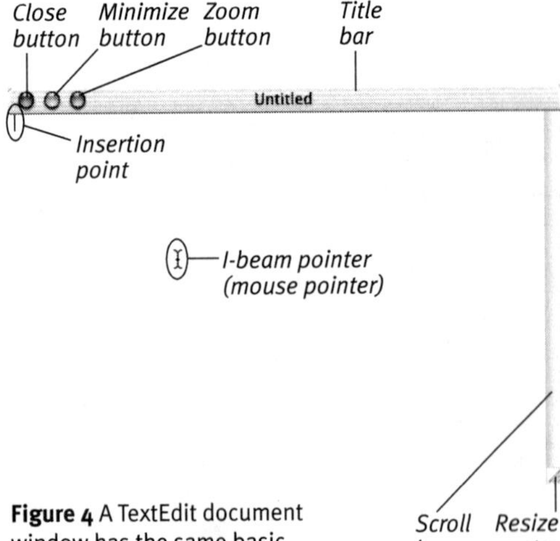

Figure 4 A TextEdit document window has the same basic parts as a Finder window.

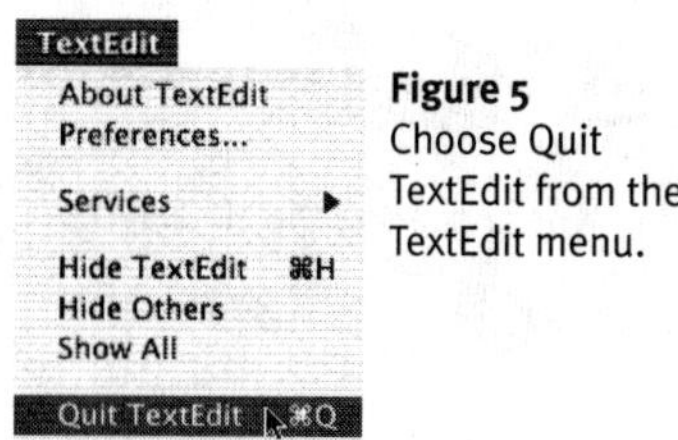

Figure 5 Choose Quit TextEdit from the TextEdit menu.

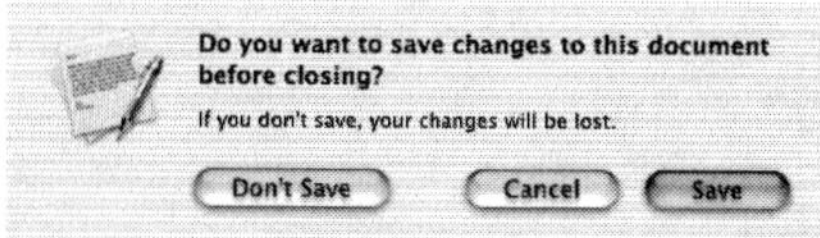

Figure 6 A dialog sheet like this appears when you quit TextEdit with an unsaved document open.

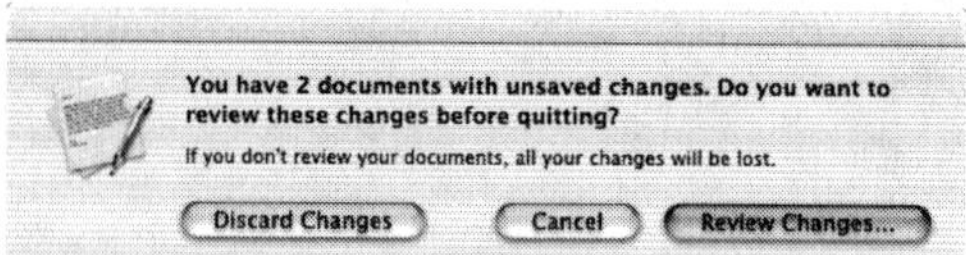

Figure 7 A dialog like this appears when you quit TextEdit with multiple unsaved documents open.

To quit TextEdit

1. Choose TextEdit > Quit TextEdit (**Figure 5**), or press [⌘ Q].
2. If a single unsaved document is open, a dialog sheet like the one in **Figure 6** appears, attached to the document window.
   - ▲ Click Don't Save to quit without saving the document.
   - ▲ Click Cancel or press [Esc] to return to the application without quitting.
   - ▲ Click Save or press [Return] or [Enter] to save the document.

   or

   If multiple unsaved documents are open, a dialog like the one in **Figure 7** appears:
   - ▲ Click Discard Changes to quit TextEdit without saving any of the documents.
   - ▲ Click Cancel or press [Esc] to return to the application without quitting.
   - ▲ Click Review Changes or press [Return] or [Enter] to view each unsaved document with a dialog like the one in **Figure 6** to decide whether you want to save it.

   TextEdit closes all windows and quits.

✔ Tip

- You learn more about saving TextEdit documents later in this chapter.

Entering & Editing Text

You enter text into a TextEdit document by typing it in. Don't worry about making mistakes; you can fix them as you type or when you're finished. This section tells you how.

✔ Tip

- The text entry and editing techniques covered in this section work exactly the same in most word processors, as well as many other Mac OS applications.

To enter text

Type the text you want to enter. It appears at the blinking insertion point (**Figure 8**).

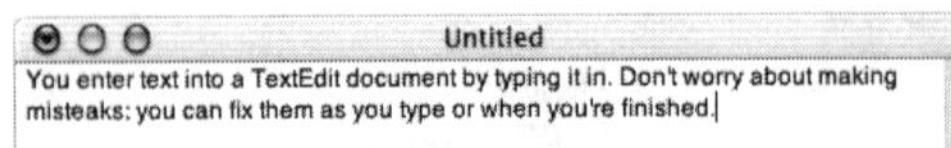

Figure 8 The text you type appears at the blinking insertion point.

✔ Tips

- It is not necessary to press Return at the end of a line. When the text you type reaches the end of the line, it automatically begins a new line. This is called *word wrap* and is a feature of all word processors. By default, in TextEdit, word wrap is determined by the width of the document window.
- The insertion point moves as you type.
- To correct an error as you type, press Delete. This key deletes the character to the left of the insertion point.

Figure 9 Position the mouse pointer...

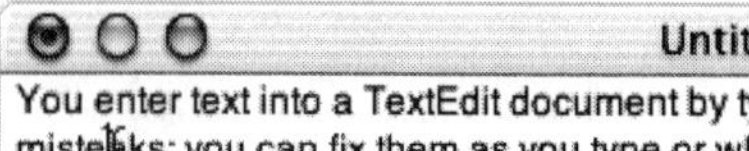

Figure 10 ...and click to move the insertion point.

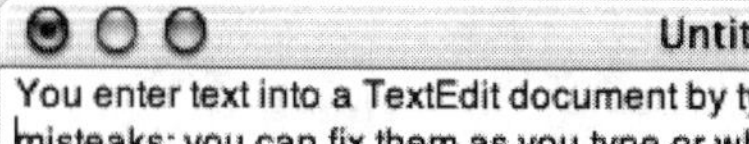

Figure 11 Position the insertion point...

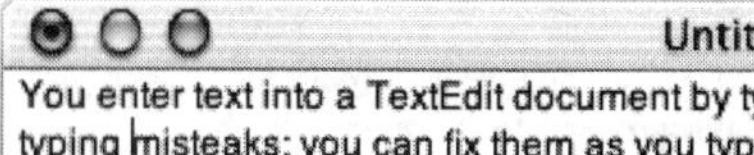

Figure 12 ...and type the text that you want to appear.

To move the insertion point

Press ←, →, ↑, or ↓ to move the insertion point left, right, up, or down one character or line at a time.

or

1. Position the mouse pointer, which looks like an I-beam pointer, where you want the insertion point to appear (**Figure 9**).
2. Click the mouse button once. The insertion point appears at the mouse pointer (**Figure 10**).

✔ Tips

- Since the text you type appears at the insertion point, it's a good idea to know where the insertion point is *before* you start typing.
- When moving the insertion point with the mouse, you must click to complete the move. If you simply point with the I-beam pointer, the insertion point will stay right where it is (**Figure 9**).

To insert text

1. Position the insertion point where you want the text to appear (**Figure 11**).
2. Type the text that you want to insert. The text is inserted at the insertion point (**Figure 12**).

✔ Tip

- Word wrap changes automatically to accommodate inserted text.

To select text by dragging

Drag the I-beam pointer over the text you want to select (**Figure 13**).

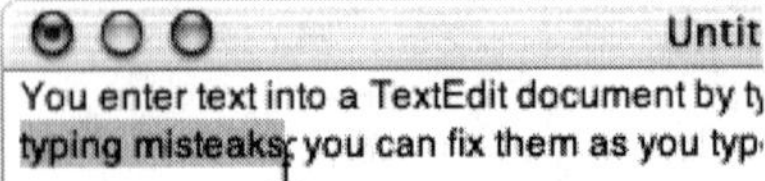

Figure 13 Drag the mouse pointer over the text that you want to select.

To select text with shift-click

1. Position the insertion point at the beginning of the text you want to select (**Figure 14**).
2. Hold down [Shift] and click at the end of the text you want to select. All text between the insertion point's original position and where you clicked becomes selected (**Figure 15**).

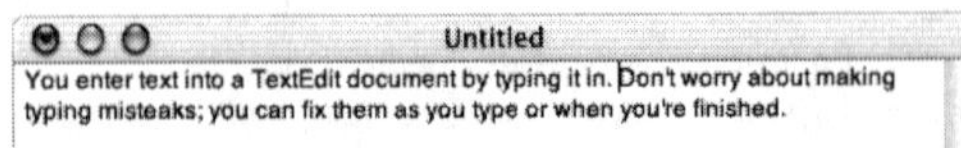

Figure 14 Position the insertion point at the beginning of the text you want to select.

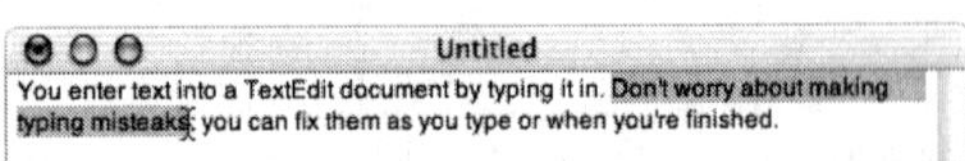

Figure 15 Hold down [Shift] and click at the end of the text you want to select.

✔ Tip

- This is a good way to select large blocks of text. After positioning the insertion point as instructed in step 1, use the scroll bars to scroll to the end of the text you want to select. Then shift-click as instructed in step 2 to make the selection.

To select a single word

Double-click the word (**Figure 16**).

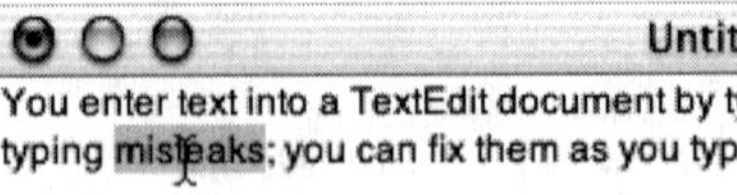

Figure 16 Double-click the word that you want to select.

✔ Tip

- In some applications, double-clicking a word also selects the space after the word.

To select an entire document

To select the entire document, choose Edit > Select All (**Figure 17**) or press [⌘ A].

Edit
Undo Typing ⌘Z
Redo ⇧⌘Z
Cut ⌘X
Copy ⌘C
Paste ⌘V
Delete
Select All ⌘A
Find ▶
Spelling ▶
Speech ▶

Figure 17 The Edit menu.

✔ Tip

- There are other selection techniques in TextEdit and other applications. The techniques on this page work in every application.

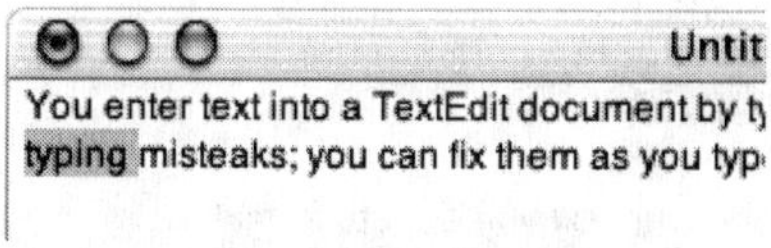

Figure 18 Select the text that you want to delete.

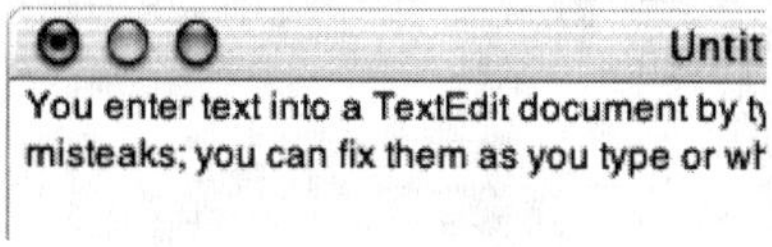

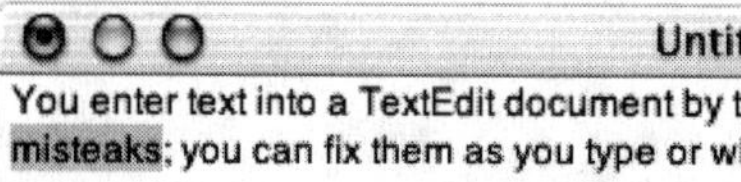

Figure 19 When you press [Delete], the selected text disappears.

Figure 20 Select the text that you want to replace.

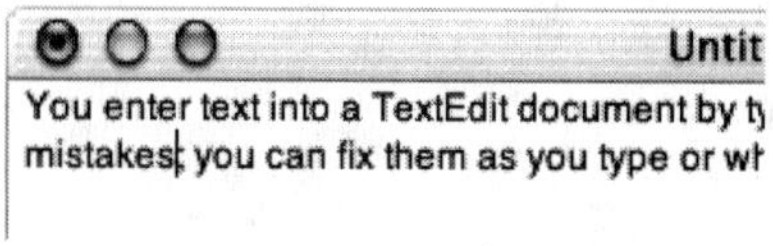

Figure 21 The text you type replaces the selected text.

To delete text

1. Select the text that you want to delete (**Figure 18**).
2. Press [Delete] or [Del]. The selected text disappears (**Figure 19**).

✔ Tip

- You can delete a character to the left of the insertion point by pressing [Delete]. You can delete a character to the right of the insertion point by pressing [Del].

To replace text

1. Select the text that you want to replace (**Figure 20**).
2. Type the new text. The selected text is replaced by what you type (**Figure 21**).

Basic Text Formatting

TextEdit also offers formatting features that you can use to change the appearance of text.

✔ Tip

- This chapter covers the most commonly used formatting options in TextEdit. Explore the other options on your own.

To apply font formatting

1. Select the text to which you want to apply a different font or font size (**Figure 22**).
2. Choose Format > Font > Font Panel (**Figure 23**), or press [⌘ T] to display the Font Panel (**Figure 24**).
3. To change the font, select a font family from the Family list. If the family contains more than one typeface, you can also make a selection from the Typeface list.
4. To change the character size, either enter a new size in the Sizes text entry field or select one of the sizes in the Sizes list.
5. Preview your changes in the document window behind the Font panel (**Figure 25**). Make additional changes as desired.
6. Repeat steps 1 and 3 through 5 for any other text you want to apply formatting to.
7. When you are finished using the Font panel, close it by clicking its close button.

✔ Tips

- Generally speaking, a *font* is a style of typeface.
- The Font panel's Family list displays all fonts that are properly installed in your System. This list may differ from the one illustrated in **Figure 24**.
- The larger the text size, the less text appears on screen or on a printed page.

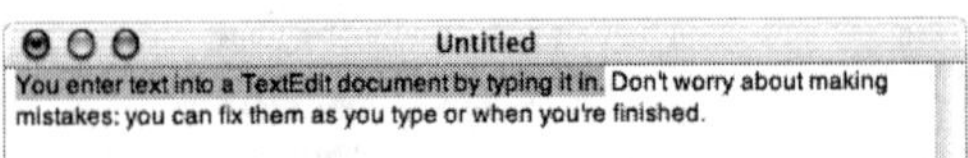

Figure 22 Select the text you want to format.

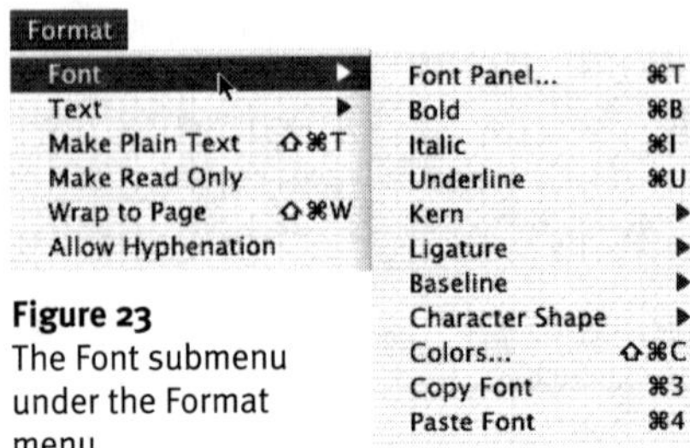

Figure 23 The Font submenu under the Format menu.

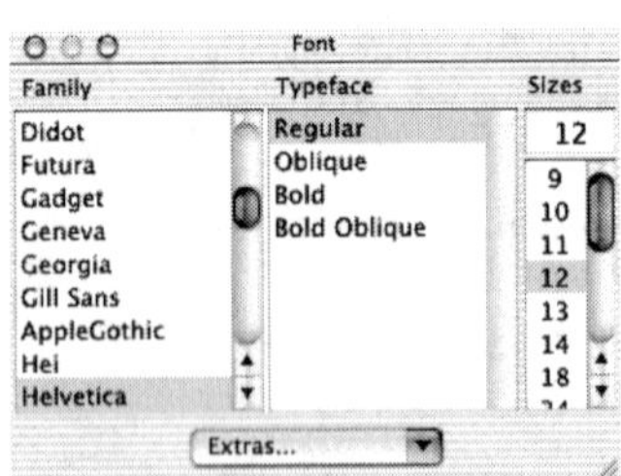

Figure 24 The Font panel.

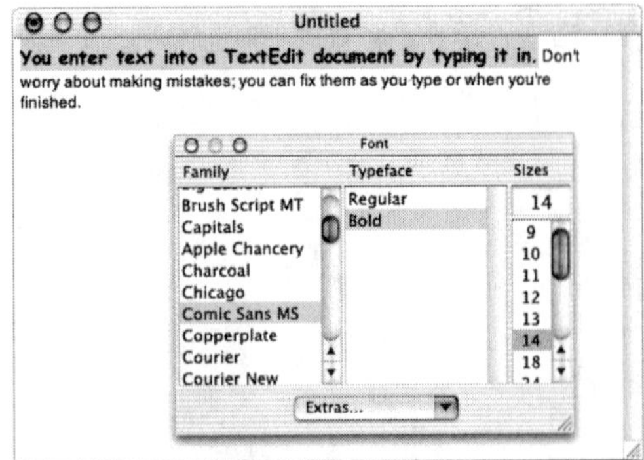

Figure 25 The changes you make in the Font panel are immediately applied to the selected text.

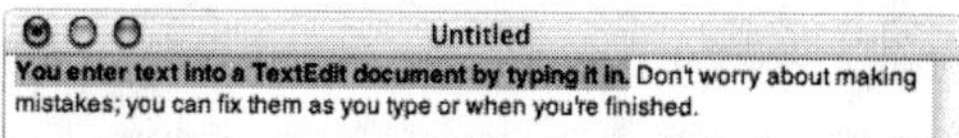

Figure 26 The style you chose is applied.

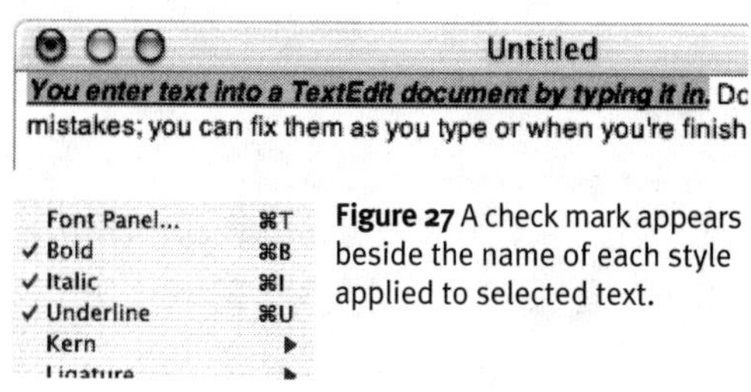

Figure 27 A check mark appears beside the name of each style applied to selected text.

To apply a different font style

1. Select the text you want to apply a different style to (**Figure 22**).
2. Choose a style command from the Font submenu under the Format menu (**Figure 23**) or press its keyboard equivalent. The style options are:
   - ▲ **Bold**, or [⌘ ⌘B], makes text characters appear thicker or darker.
   - ▲ **Italic**, or [⌘ ⌘I], makes text appear slanted.
   - ▲ **Underline**, or [⌘ ⌘U], puts a single underline under text.

   The style you chose is applied to the selected text (**Figure 26**).

✔ Tips

- You can apply more than one style to text (**Figure 27**). Simply select each style you want to apply.
- A check mark appears on the Font submenu beside each style applied to a selection (**Figure 27**).
- To remove an applied style, choose it from the Font submenu again.
- Some styles are automatically applied when you select a specific typeface for a font family in the Font panel (**Figure 25**). Similarly, if you select a typeface in the Font panel, certain style options become unavailable for characters with that typeface applied. For example, if you apply Comic Sans MS Bold font, as shown in **Figure 25**, the Italic option is not available on the Font submenu for that text.

To change paragraph alignment

1. Select the paragraph(s) you want to change the alignment of (**Figure 28**).
2. Choose an alignment option from the Text submenu under the Format menu (**Figure 29**) or press its keyboard equivalent. The alignment options are:
   - ▲ **Align Left**, or [⌘ ⌘][{], aligns text characters against the left side of the window.
   - ▲ **Center**, or [⌘ ⌘][-], centers text characters between the left and right side of the window (**Figure 30**).
   - ▲ **Justify** adjusts the spacing between words so all lines of the paragraph except the last fill the space between the left and right sides of the window.
   - ▲ **Align Right**, or [⌘ ⌘][}], aligns text characters against the right side of the window.

   The alignment option you chose is applied to the selected paragraph(s) (**Figure 30**).

✔ Tip

- Alignment options affect all lines in a paragraph. To begin a new paragraph, position the insertion point where you want the paragraph to begin and press [Return].

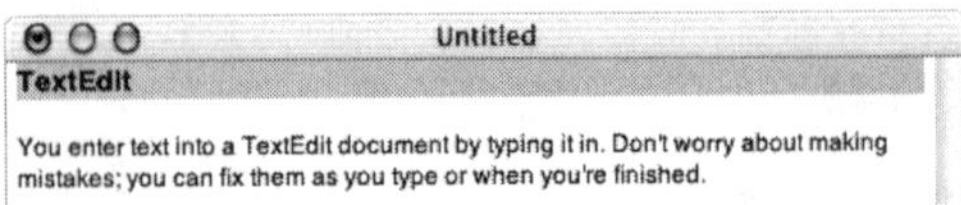

Figure 28 Select the paragraph you want to change the alignment of.

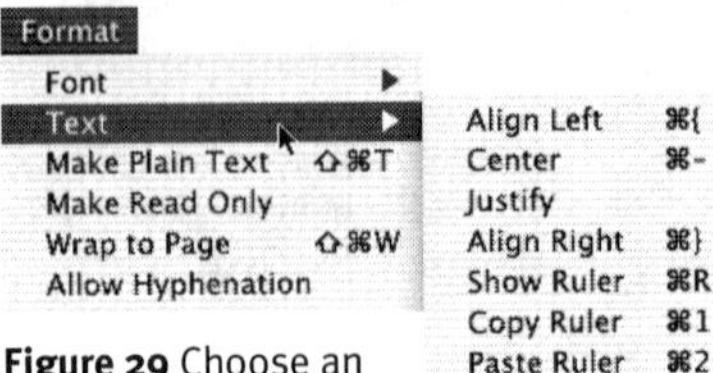

Figure 29 Choose an option from the Text submenu under the Format menu.

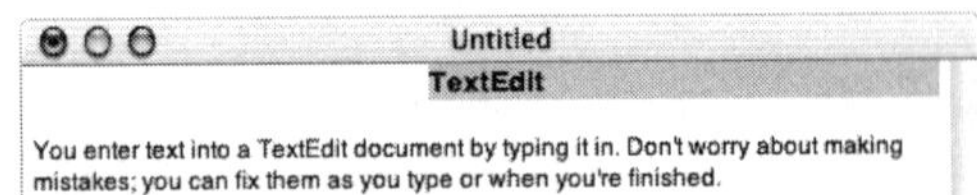

Figure 30 The alignment option you chose is applied.

Changing Alignment

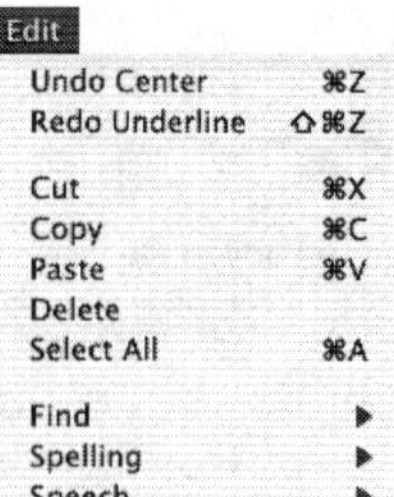

Figure 31 The Edit menu with Undo and Redo commands displayed. If one of these commands were not available, it would be gray.

Undoing & Redoing Actions

The Undo command enables you to reverse your last action, thus offering an easy way to fix errors immediately after you make them. The Redo command, which is available only when your last action was to use the Undo command, reverses the undo action.

✔ Tips

- The Undo and Redo commands are available in most applications and can be found at the top of the Edit menu.
- Unlike most applications, TextEdit supports multiple levels of undo (and redo). That means you can undo (or redo) several actions, in the reverse order that they were performed (or undone).
- The exact wording of the Undo (and Redo) command depends on what was last done (or undone). For example, if the last thing you did was center a paragraph, the Undo command will be Undo Center (**Figure 31**).

To undo the last action

Choose Edit > Undo (**Figure 31**), or press [⌘ ⌘][Z]. The last thing you did is undone.

✔ Tip

- To undo multiple actions, choose Edit > Undo repeatedly.

To redo an action

After using the Undo command, choose Edit > Redo (**Figure 31**), or press [Shift][⌘ ⌘][Z]. The last thing you undid is redone.

✔ Tip

- To redo multiple actions, choose Edit > Redo repeatedly.

Copy, Cut, & Paste

The Copy, Cut, and Paste commands enable you to duplicate or move document contents. Text that is copied or cut is placed on the Clipboard, where it can be viewed if desired and pasted into a document.

✔ Tip

- Almost all Mac OS-compatible applications include the Copy, Cut, and Paste commands on the Edit menu. These commands work very much the same in all applications.

To copy text

1. Select the text that you want to copy (**Figure 32**).
2. Choose Edit > Copy (**Figure 33**), or press [⌘ C].

   The text is copied to the Clipboard so it can be pasted elsewhere. The original remains in the document.

To cut text

1. Select the text that you want to cut (**Figure 32**).
2. Choose Edit > Cut (**Figure 33**), or press [⌘ X].

   The text is copied to the Clipboard so it can be pasted elsewhere. The original is removed from the document.

To paste Clipboard contents

1. Position the insertion point where you want the Clipboard contents to appear (**Figure 34**).
2. Choose Edit > Paste (**Figure 33**), or press [⌘ V].

   The Clipboard's contents are pasted into the document (**Figure 35**).

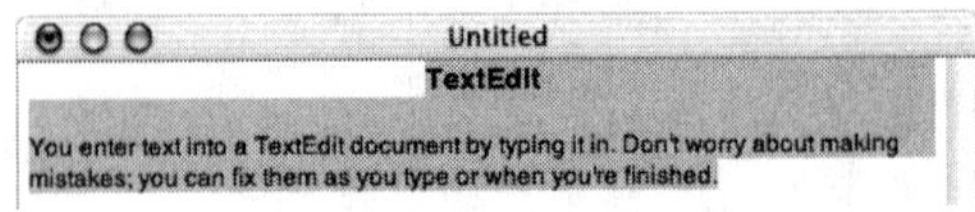

Figure 32 Select the text you want to copy or cut.

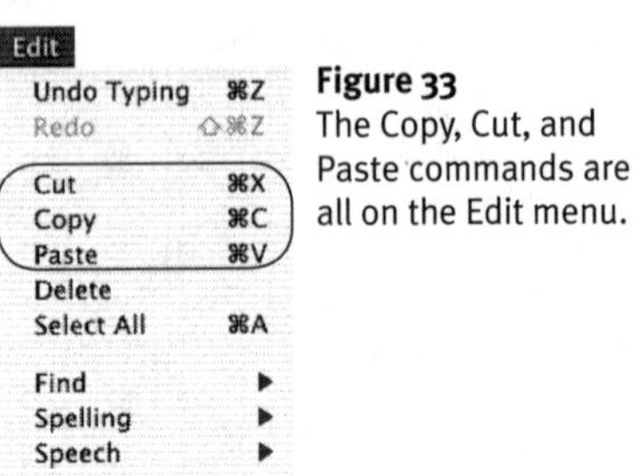

Figure 33 The Copy, Cut, and Paste commands are all on the Edit menu.

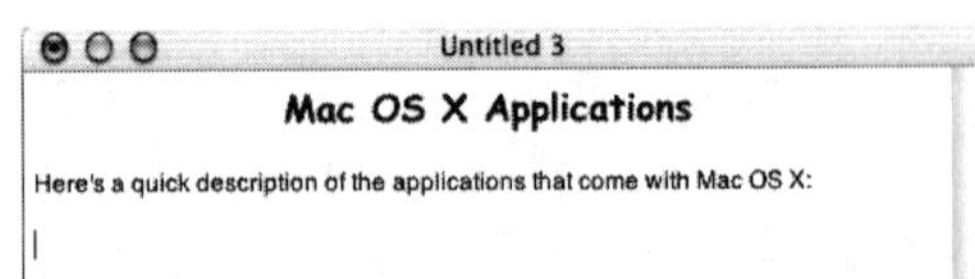

Figure 34 Position the insertion point where you want the contents of the Clipboard to appear.

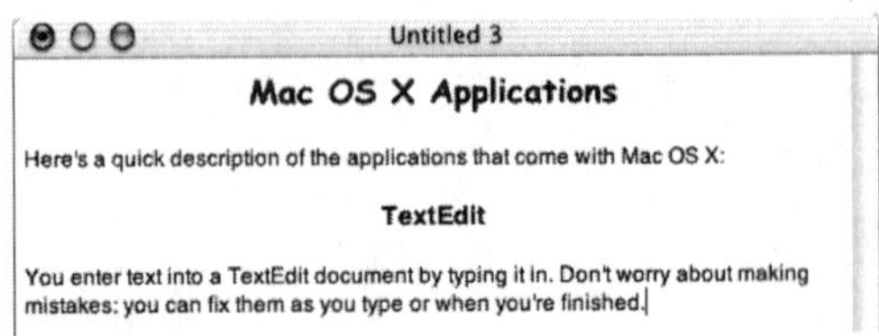

Figure 35 The contents of the Clipboard are pasted into the document.

✔ Tip

- The Clipboard contains only the last item that was copied or cut. Using the Paste command, therefore, pastes in the most recently cut or copied selection.

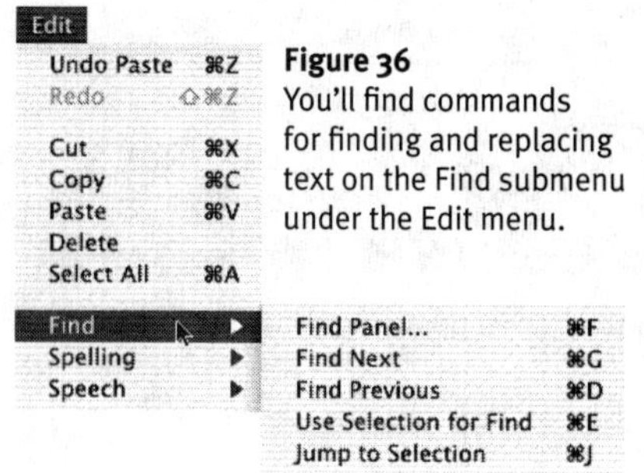

Figure 36
You'll find commands for finding and replacing text on the Find submenu under the Edit menu.

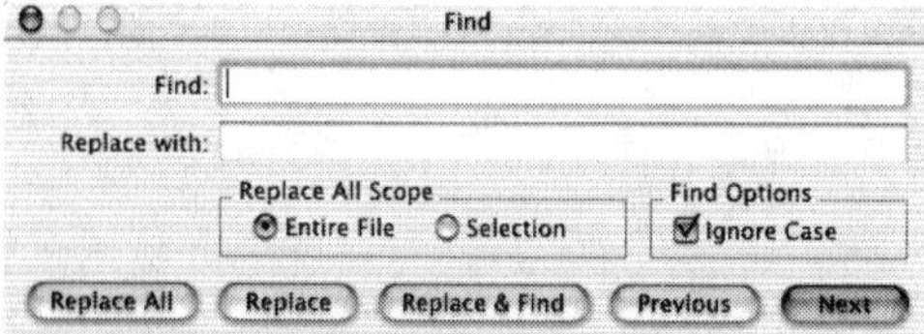

Figure 37 The Find panel.

Find & Replace

TextEdit's find and replace features enable you to quickly locate or replace occurrences of text strings in your document.

✔ Tip

- Most word processing and page layout applications include find and replace features. Although these features are somewhat limited in TextEdit, full-featured applications such as Microsoft Word and Adobe InDesign enable you to search for text, formatting, and other document elements as well as plain text.

To find text

1. Choose Edit > Find > Find Panel (**Figure 36**), or press [⌘ F]. The Find panel appears (**Figure 37**).
2. Enter the text that you want to find in the Find field.
3. If necessary, select one of the options in the Replace All Scope area:
   - **Entire File** searches the entire file.
   - **Selection** searches only selected text.
4. To perform a case-sensitive search, turn off the Ignore Case check box in the Find Options area. With this check box turned off, *word* will not match *Word*.
5. Click Next, or press [Return] or [Enter]. If the text you entered in the Find field is found, it is highlighted in the document.

✔ Tip

- To find subsequent or previous occurrences of the Find field entry, choose Edit > Find > Find Next or Edit > Find > Find Previous (**Figure 36**) or press [⌘ G] or [⌘ D].

To replace text

1. Choose Edit > Find > Find Panel (**Figure 36**), or press ⌘F. The Find panel appears (**Figure 37**).
2. Enter the text that you want to replace in the Find field.
3. Enter the replacement text in the Replace with field (**Figure 38**).
4. If necessary, select one of the options in the Replace All Scope area:
   - ▲ **Entire File** searches the entire file.
   - ▲ **Selection** searches only selected text.
5. To perform a case-sensitive search, turn off the Ignore Case check box in the Find Options area. With this check box turned off, *word* will not match *Word*.
6. Click the buttons at the bottom of the Find pane to find and replace text:
   - ▲ **Replace All** replaces all occurrences of the Find word with the Replace word.
   - ▲ **Replace** replaces the currently selected occurrence of the Find word with the Replace word.
   - ▲ **Replace & Find** replaces the currently selected occurrence of the Find word with the Replace word and then selects the next occurrence of the Find word.
   - ▲ **Previous** selects the previous occurrence of the Find word.
   - ▲ **Next** selects the next occurrence of the Find word.
7. When you're finished replacing text, click the Find panel's close button to dismiss it.

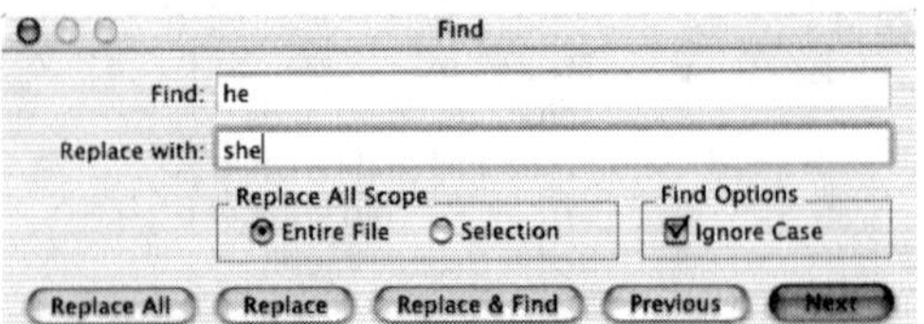

Figure 38 You can set up the Find panel to find and replace text.

✖ Warning!

- Use the Replace All button with care! It will not give you an opportunity to preview and approve any of the replacements it makes.

REPLACING TEXT

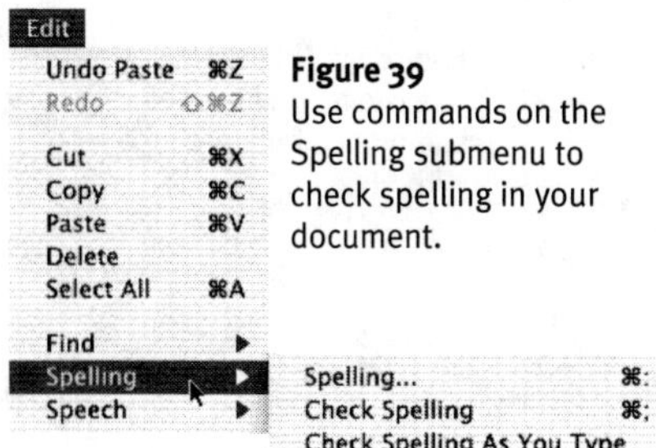

Figure 39 Use commands on the Spelling submenu to check spelling in your document.

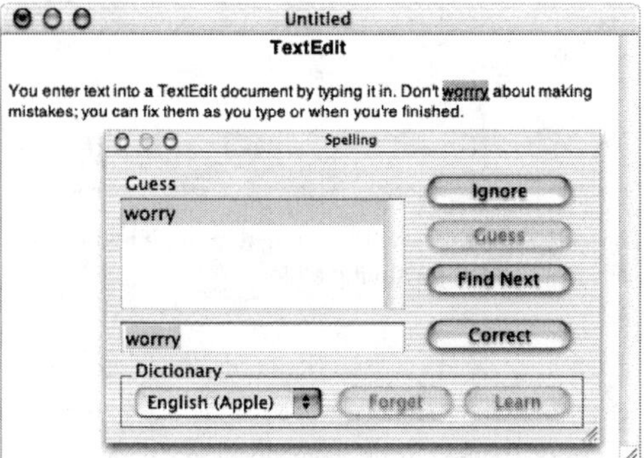

Figure 40 Use the Spelling panel to resolve possible misspelled words.

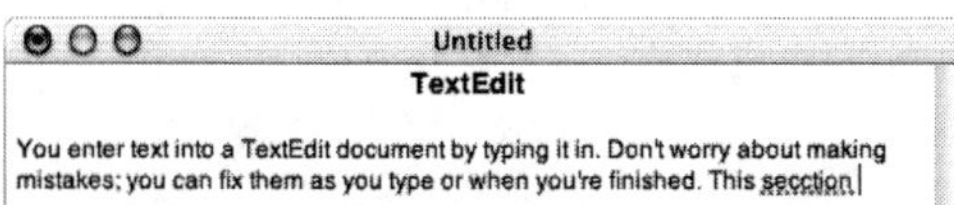

Figure 41 With automatic spelling check enabled, TextEdit underlines possible misspelled words as you type.

Checking Spelling

TextEdit includes a spelling checker that you can use to check spelling in your document.

To check spelling

1. Choose Edit > Spelling > Spelling (**Figure 39**) or press [⌘:] to display the spelling panel and start the spelling check.

   TextEdit selects and underlines the first possible misspelled word it finds. The word appears in a field in the Spelling panel and any suggested corrections appear in the Guess list (**Figure 40**).

2. You have several options:
   - ▲ To replace the word with a guess, select the replacement word and click Correct.
   - ▲ To enter a new spelling for the word, enter it in the field where the incorrect spelling appears and click Correct.
   - ▲ To ignore the word, click Ignore.
   - ▲ To skip the word and continue checking, click Find Next.
   - ▲ To add the word to TextEdit's dictionary, click Learn. TextEdit will never stop at that word again in any document.

3. Repeat step 2 for each word that TextEdit identifies as a possible misspelling.

4. When you're finished checking spelling, click the Spelling panel's close button to dismiss it.

✔ Tip

- You can choose Edit > Spelling > Check Spelling As You Type to have TextEdit check your spelling automatically as you type. With this feature enabled, each time you type a word that isn't in TextEdit's dictionary, a red dotted underline appears beneath it (**Figure 41**).

Saving & Opening Files

When you're finished working with a TextEdit document, you may want to save it. You can then open it another time to review, edit, or print it.

To save a document for the first time

1. Choose File > Save (**Figure 42**), or press [⌘ S].

   or

   Choose File > Save As (**Figure 42**), or press [Shift] [⌘ S].
2. Use the Save As dialog sheet that appears (**Figure 43**) to enter a name and select a location for the file.
3. Click Save, or press [Return] or [Enter].

   The document is saved with the name you entered in the location you specified. The name of the document appears on the document's title bar (**Figure 44**).

✔ Tips

- I explain how to use the Save As dialog in **Chapter 5**.
- There's only one difference between the Save and Save As commands:
  - ▲ The Save command opens the Save As dialog only if the document has never been saved.
  - ▲ The Save As command always opens the Save As dialog.
- By default, TextEdit creates Rich Text Format (RTF) files and appends the *.rtf* extension to the files it saves. This extension does not appear unless the Always show file extensions option is enabled in Finder Preferences. I discuss Finder preferences in **Chapter 4**.

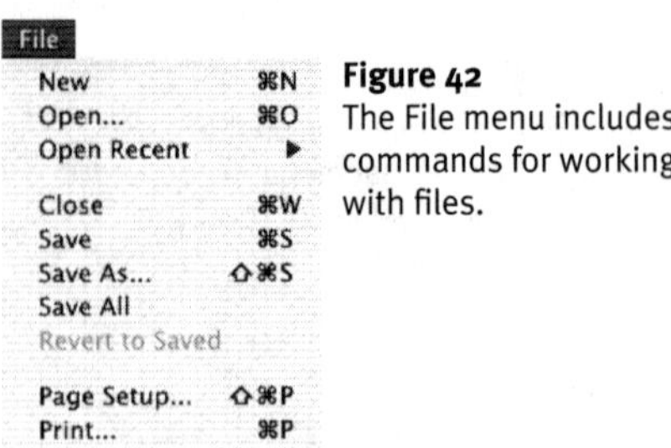

Figure 42 The File menu includes commands for working with files.

Figure 43 Use the Save As dialog to enter a name and select a location for saving a file.

Figure 44 The name of a saved document appears in its title bar.

Saving Documents

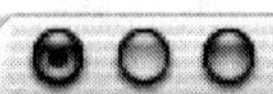

Figure 45 A bullet in the document window's close button...

Window
Close Window
Zoom Window
Minimize Window ⌘M
Bring All to Front
Mac OS Apps
• TextEdit Info

Figure 46 ...or beside its name in the Window menu indicates that the document has unsaved changes.

To save changes to an existing document

Choose File > Save (**Figure 42**), or press ⌘ S.

The document is saved. No dialog appears.

✔ Tips

- TextEdit identifies a document with changes that have not been saved by displaying a bullet in the document window's close button (**Figure 45**) and to the left of the document's name in the Window menu (**Figure 46**).
- It's a good idea to save changes to a document frequently as you work with it. This helps prevent loss of data in the event of a system crash or power outage.

To save an existing document with a new name or in a new location

1. Choose File > Save As (**Figure 42**).
2. Use the Save As dialog that appears (**Figure 43**) to enter a different name or select a different location (or both) for the file.
3. Click Save, or press Return or Enter.

   A copy of the document is saved with the name you entered in the location you specified. The new document name appears in the document's title bar. The original document remains untouched.

✔ Tip

- You can use the Save As command to create a new document based on an existing document—without overwriting the original document with your changes.

To open a document

1. Choose File > Open (**Figure 42**), or press [⌘ ⌘ O].
2. Use the Open dialog that appears (**Figure 47**) to locate and select the document that you want to open.
3. Click Open, or press [Return] or [Enter].

✔ Tip

- I explain how to use the Open dialog in **Chapter 5**.

To close a document

1. Choose File > Close (**Figure 42**), or press [⌘ ⌘ W].
2. If the document contains unsaved changes, a Close dialog like the one in **Figure 6** appears.
   - ▲ Click Don't Save to close the document without saving it.
   - ▲ Click Cancel or press [Esc] to return to the document without closing it.
   - ▲ Click Save or press [Return] or [Enter] to save the document.

The document closes.

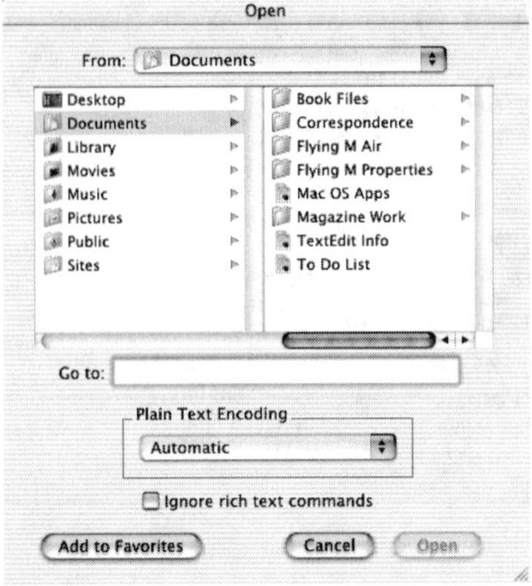

Figure 47 Use the Open dialog to locate and open a file.

Printing

Printing

On a Mac OS system, printing is handled by the operating system rather than the individual applications. You choose the Print command in the application that created the document you want to print. Mac OS steps in, displaying the Print dialog and telling the application how to send information to the printer. There are two main benefits to this:

- If you can print documents created with one application, you can probably print documents created with any application on your computer.
- The Page Setup and Print dialogs, which are generated by Mac OS, look very much the same in every application.

This chapter covers most aspects of printing on a computer running Mac OS X.

To print (an overview)

1. If necessary, add your printer to the Printer List.
2. Open the document that you want to print.
3. If desired, set options in the Page Setup dialog and click OK.
4. Set options in the Print dialog, and click Print.

Printer Drivers

A *printer driver* is software that Mac OS uses to communicate with a specific kind of printer. It contains information about the printer and instructions for using it. You can't open and read a printer driver, but your computer can.

There are basically two kinds of printers:

- A **PostScript** printer uses PostScript technology developed by Adobe Systems. Inside the printer is a *PostScript interpreter*, which can process PostScript language commands to print high-quality text and graphics. Examples of PostScript printers include most Apple LaserWriter printers and Hewlett-Packard LaserJet printers.
- A **non-PostScript** printer relies on the computer to send it all of the instructions it needs for printing text and graphics. It cannot process PostScript commands. Examples of non-PostScript printers include Apple ImageWriters and StyleWriters, Hewlett-Packard DeskJet printers, and most Epson Stylus printers.

A standard installation of Mac OS X installs many commonly used printer drivers. When you buy a printer, it should come with a CD that includes its printer driver software; if your computer does not recognize your printer, you'll need to install this software to use it.

✔ Tips

- If you do not have a printer driver for your printer, you may not be able to print.
- To install a printer driver, follow the instructions that came with its installer or installation disc.
- If you need to install printer driver software for your printer, make sure it is Mac OS X compatible. If your printer did not come with Mac OS X compatible printer software, you may be able to get it from the printer manufacturer's Web site.

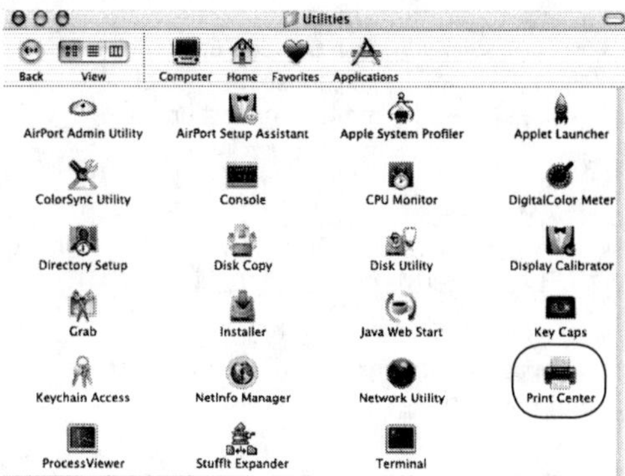

Figure 1 Print Center can be found in the Utilities folder inside the Applications folder.

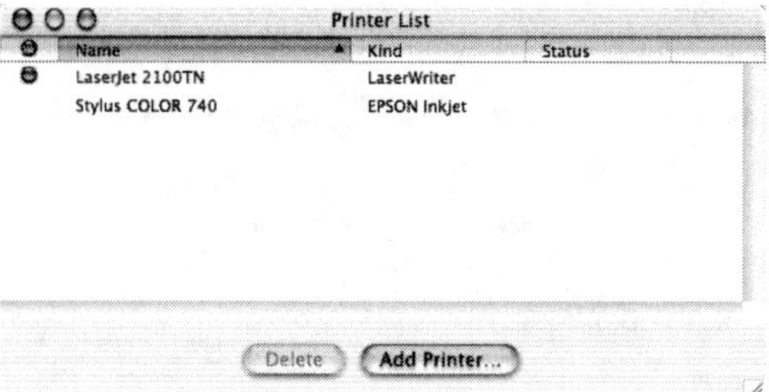

Figure 2 The Printer List window with two printers.

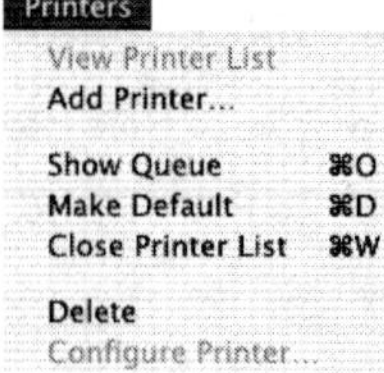

Figure 3 The Printers menu includes commands for working with the Printer List and printers.

Print Center

Print Center (**Figure 1**) is an application that enables you to manage printers and print jobs. It has two main components:

- **Printer List** window (**Figure 2**) lists all of the printers your computer "sees." Use this window to select and configure printers.
- **Printer Queue** window (**Figure 37** and **38**) lists all the print jobs sent to a specific printer. Use this window to check the status of and cancel print jobs, as discussed later in this chapter.

✔ Tip

- Print Center replaces the Chooser and Desktop Printer Utility software that were used for the same functions in Mac OS 9.1 and earlier. Desktop printers are not available in Mac OS X.

To open Print Center

1. Click the Applications icon in the toolbar of any Finder window to open the Applications folder.
2. Open the Utilities folder.
3. Open the Print Center icon (**Figure 1**).

The Printer List window (**Figure 2**) should appear automatically. If it does not, follow the instructions below to display it.

To display the Printer List window

Choose Printers > View Printer List (**Figure 3**).

The Printer List window appears (**Figure 2**).

✔ Tip

- If a question mark appears beside a printer in the Printer List window, you may need to install printer driver software for that printer. Printer drivers are covered on the previous page.

To add a printer

1. Choose Printers > Add Printer (**Figure 3**).

   or

   Click the Add Printer button in the Printer List window (**Figure 2**).

2. A dialog sheet appears. Choose an option from the pop-up menu (**Figure 4**) to indicate the type of printer connection.

3. If you chose AppleTalk, wait while Print Center looks for printers and displays a list of what it finds (**Figure 5**). Select the printer you want to add, and click Add.

   or

   If you chose LPR Printers using IP, enter an IP (or Internet Protocol) address or domain name and set other options in the dialog sheet (**Figure 6**). Then click Add.

   or

   If you chose USB, Print Center displays a list of USB printers connected to the computer (**Figure 7**). Select the printer you want to add, and click Add.

   The printer appears in the Printer List window (**Figure 2**).

✔ Tips

- You only have to add a printer if it does not already appear in the Printer List window (**Figure 2**). This needs to be done only once; Mac OS will remember all printers that you add.

- In step 3, if you chose AppleTalk and your network includes AppleTalk zones, you must select a zone from the pop-up menu that appears in the dialog (**Figure 5**) to see a list of printers.

Figure 4 Use this pop-up menu to choose the type of printer connection.

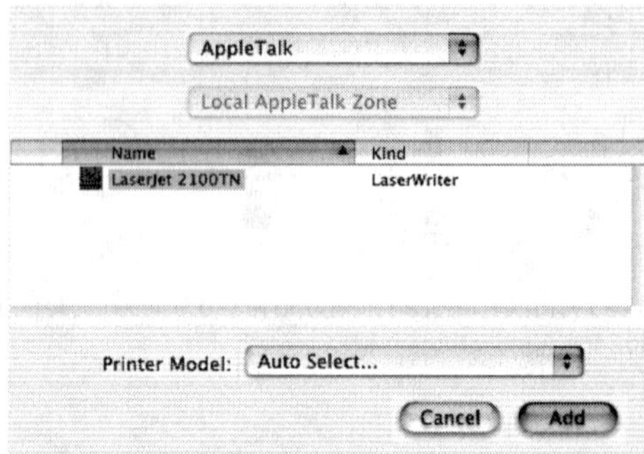

Figure 5 Options for adding an AppleTalk printer,...

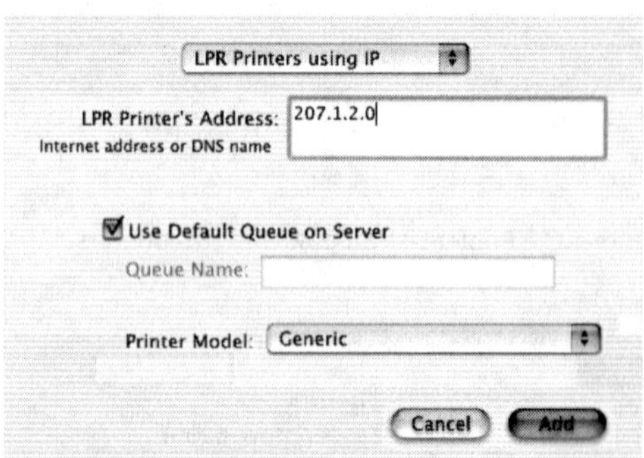

Figure 6 ...an LPR Printer using IP, ...

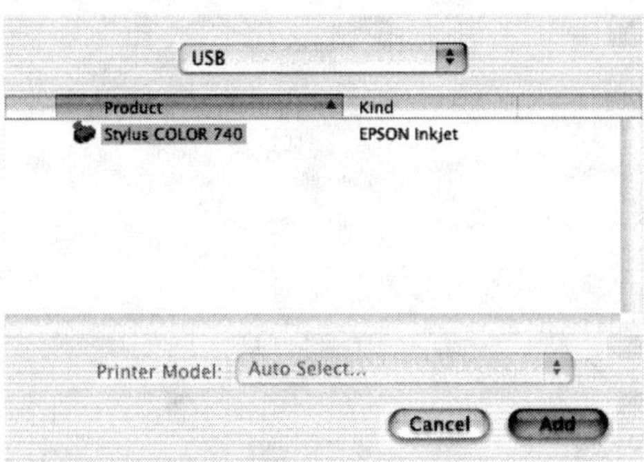

Figure 7 ...and a USB printer.

- If your AppleTalk or USB printer is properly connected but it does not appear in step 3 (**Figures 5** and **7**), you may have to install printer driver software for it. Printer drivers are discussed earlier in this chapter.
- If you're not sure how to set options for an LPR Printer using IP (**Figure 6**), ask your network administrator.

To delete a printer

1. In the Printer List window (**Figure 2**), select the printer you want to delete.
2. Choose Printers > Delete (**Figure 3**).

   or

   Click the Delete button in the Printer List window (**Figure 2**).

   The printer is removed from the list.

To set the default printer

1. In the Printer list window (**Figure 2**), select the printer you want to set as the default.
2. Choose Printers > Make Default (**Figure 3**), or press [⌘ D].

   A colored bullet appears beside the printer you selected, indicating that it is the default printer.

✔ Tip

- The default printer is the one that is selected by default when you open the Print dialog.

The Page Setup Dialog

The Page Setup dialog lets you set page attributes prior to printing, including the printer the document should be formatted for, paper size, orientation, and scale.

To set Page Attributes

1. Choose File > Page Setup (**Figures 8a, 8b,** and **8c**) to display the Page Setup dialog sheet (**Figure 9**).
2. If necessary, choose Page Attributes from the Settings pop-up menu (**Figure 10**).
3. If necessary, select the correct printer from the Format for pop-up menu (**Figure 11**).
4. Select a paper size from the Paper Size pop-up menu (**Figure 12**).
5. Select an Orientation option by clicking it.
6. Enter a scaling percentage in the Scale field.
7. Click OK to save your settings and dismiss the Page Setup dialog.

✔ Tips

- The Format for pop-up menu should list all of the printers that appear in the Print Center's Printer List window (**Figure 2**).
- Options in each of the above steps vary depending on the printer selected from the Format for pop-up menu. Additional options may be available for your printer; check the documentation that came with the printer for details.

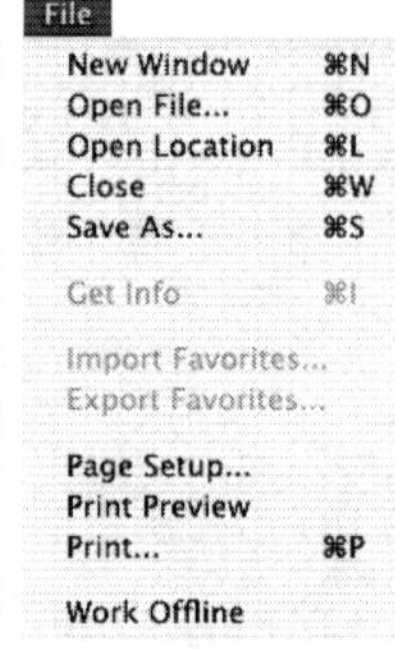

Figures 8a, 8b, & 8c
The Page Setup and Print commands appear on most File menus, including TextEdit (top left), Preview (bottom left), and Internet Explorer (right).

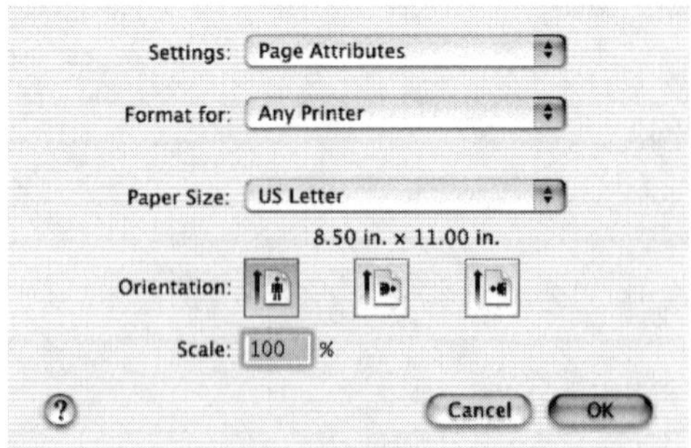

Figure 9 The Page Setup dialog sheet.

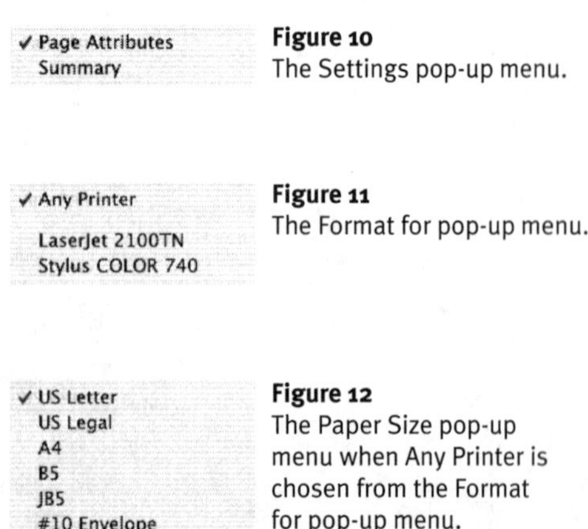

Figure 10
The Settings pop-up menu.

Figure 11
The Format for pop-up menu.

Figure 12
The Paper Size pop-up menu when Any Printer is chosen from the Format for pop-up menu.

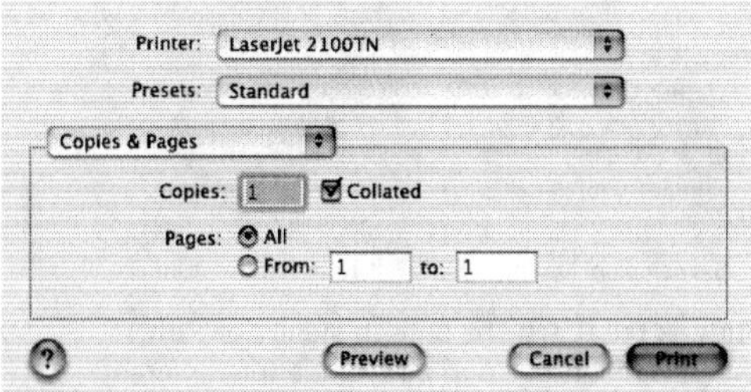

Figure 13 The Copies & Pages pane of the Print dialog.

✓ LaserJet 2100TN
Stylus COLOR 740
Edit Printer List...

Figure 14 The Printer pop-up menu.

The Print Dialog

The Print dialog enables you to set printing options and send the print job to the printer. Like the Page Setup dialog, the Print dialog is a standard dialog, but two things can cause its appearance and options to vary:

- Print options vary depending on the selected printer.
- Additional options may be offered by specific applications.

This section explains how to set the options available for most printers and applications.

✓ Tips

- If your Print dialog includes options that are not covered here, consult the printer's documentation.
- For information about using Print options specific to an application, consult the application's documentation.

To open the Print dialog

Choose File > Print (**Figures 8a**, **8b**, and **8c**), or press ⌘P.

The Copies & Pages pane of the Print dialog appears (**Figure 13**).

To select a printer

In the Print dialog (**Figure 13**) choose a printer from the Printer pop-up menu (**Figure 14**).

✓ Tips

- The Printer pop-up menu (**Figure 14**) includes all printers that appear in Print Center's Printer List window (**Figure 2**).
- Choosing Edit Printer List from the Printer pop-up menu (**Figure 14**) opens Print Center and displays its Printer List window so you can add a printer. Adding printers is covered earlier in this chapter.

To set Copies & Pages options

1. In the Print dialog, choose Copies & Pages from the third pop-up menu (**Figure 15a** or **15b**) to display Copies & Pages options (**Figure 13**).
2. In the Copies field, enter the number of copies of the document to print.
3. To collate multiple copies, turn on the Collated check box.
4. In the Pages area, select either the All radio button to print all pages or enter values in the From and To fields to print specific pages.

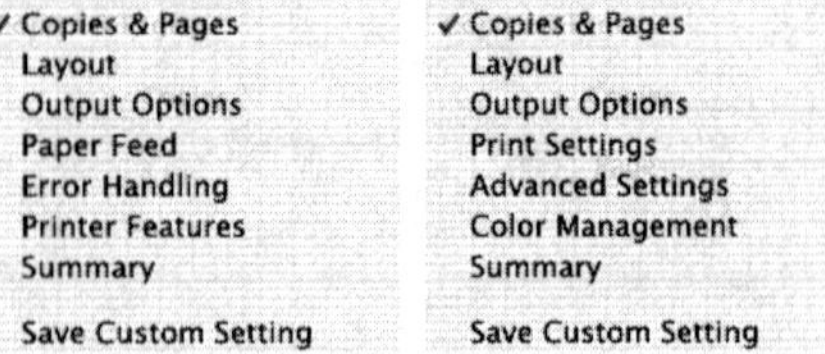

Figures 15a & 15b The pop-up menu beneath the Saved Settings pop-up menu offers different options depending on the printer that is selected. The menu on the left is for a Hewlett-Packard LaserJet printer connected via network and the menu on the right is for an Epson Sylus Color printer connected directly to the computer via USB.

To set Layout options

1. In the Print dialog, choose Layout from the third pop-up menu (**Figure 15a** or **15b**) to display Layout options (**Figure 16**).
2. To set the number of pages that should appear on each sheet of paper, choose an option from the Pages per Sheet pop-up menu (**Figure 17**). The preview area of the dialog changes accordingly (**Figure 18**).
3. To indicate the order in which multiple pages should print on each sheet of paper, select a Layout Direction option. The preview area of the dialog changes accordingly (**Figure 18**).
4. To place a border around each page, choose an option from the Border pop-up menu (**Figure 19**).

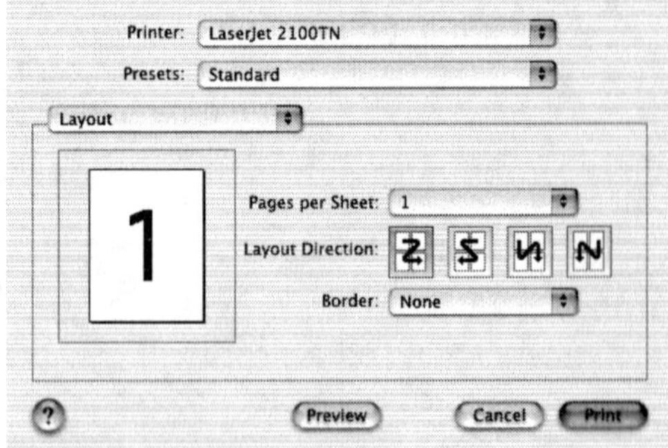

Figure 16 The Layout pane of the Print dialog.

✓ 1
2
4
6
9
16

Figure 17 The Pages per Sheet pop-up menu.

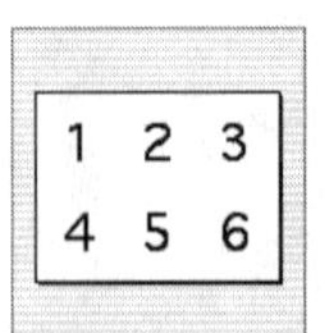

Figure 18 The Preview area indicates the number of pages to be printed per sheet, as well as the page order.

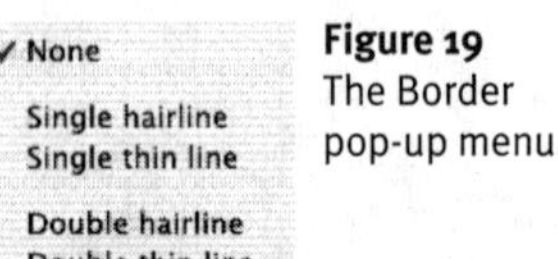

Figure 19 The Border pop-up menu.

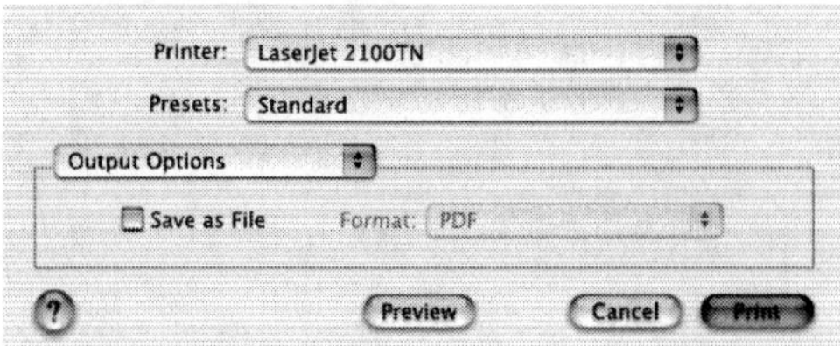

Figure 20 The Output Options pane of the Print dialog.

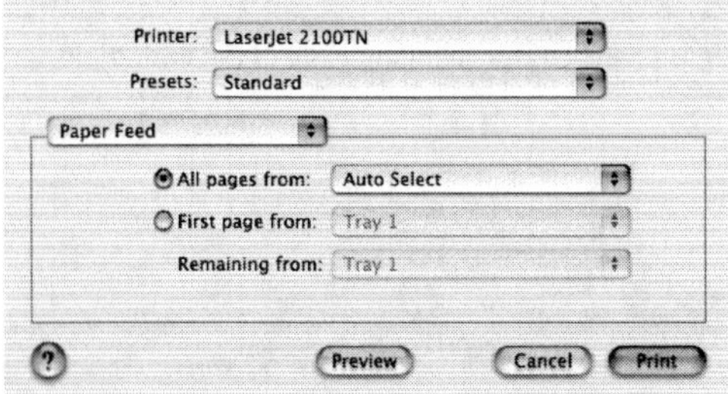

Figure 21 The Paper Feed pane of the Print dialog.

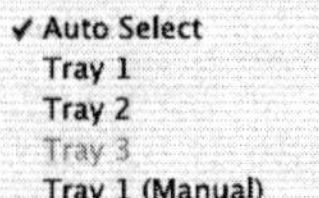

Figure 22 Use this pop-up menu to choose the paper source.

To set Output options

1. In the Print dialog, choose Output Options from the third pop-up menu (**Figure 15a** or **15b**) to display the Output Options pane (**Figure 20**).

2. To save the document as a file (instead of printing it), turn on the Save as File check box, then choose an option from the Format pop-up menu:
   - ▲ **PDF** creates a portable document format (PDF) file that can be read with Preview on Mac OS X or Adobe Acrobat Reader on any computer.
   - ▲ **PostScript** writes PostScript language code to a file that can then be downloaded to and interpreted by a PostScript printer or imagesetter. This is an advanced option that is beyond the needs of most users.

✔ Tip

- When you turn on the Save as File check box, the Print button in the Print dialog turns into a Save button.

To set Paper Feed options

1. In the Print dialog, choose Paper Feed from the third pop-up menu (**Figure 15a**) to display Paper Feed options (**Figure 21**).

2. To specify how paper trays should be used for paper feed, select one of the radio buttons.

3. To specify which paper tray(s) should be used for paper feed, choose options from the pop-up menu(s) (**Figure 22**).

✔ Tip

- The options offered in the Paper Feed pane of the Print dialog (**Figure 21**) vary depending on your printer. The options here are for an HP LaserJet 2100TN printer.

To set Error Handling options

1. In the Print dialog, choose Error Handling from the third pop-up menu (**Figure 15a**) to display Error Handling options (**Figure 23**).
2. To specify how the printer should report PostScript errors, select one of the PostScript™ Errors radio buttons.
3. To specify how the printer should handle an out-of-paper situation for a multiple-tray printer, select one of the Tray Switching radio buttons.

Figure 23 The Error Handling pane of the Print dialog.

✔ Tips

- These options are only available for PostScript printers.
- Tray switching options are only available for printers with multiple paper trays.

To set Printer Features options

1. In the Print dialog, choose Printer Features from the third pop-up menu (**Figure 15a**) to display Printer Features options (**Figure 24**).
2. Click a tab for the group of options you want to set.
3. Set options as desired in the pane.
4. Repeat steps 2 and 3 to set all options to your specifications.

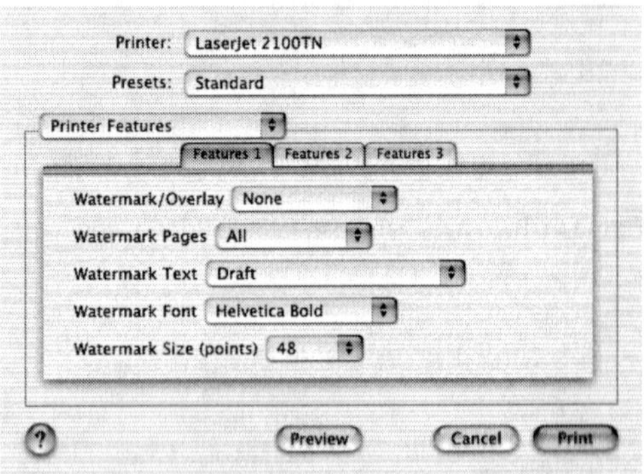

Figure 24 The Printer Features pane of the Print dialog for a LaserJet 2100TN.

✔ Tips

- These options are not available for all printers.
- When available, these options vary greatly from printer to printer. The options shown here are for an HP LaserJet 2100TN printer, which has a variety of watermark and resolution features.

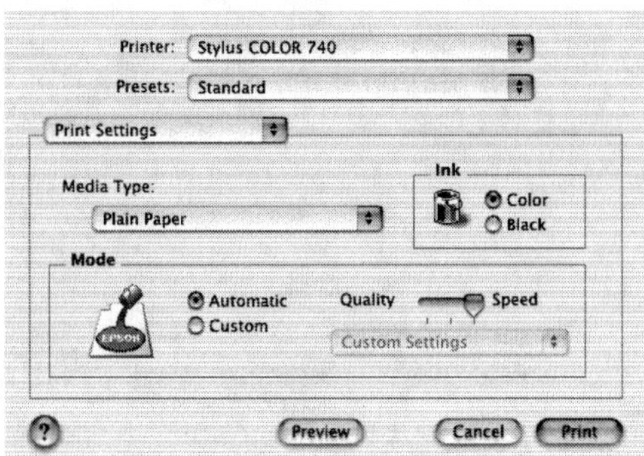

Figure 25 The Print Settings pane of the Print dialog for an Epson Stylus Color printer.

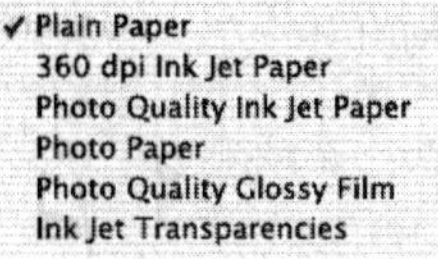

Figure 26 The Media Type pop-up menu for an Epson Stylus Color printer.

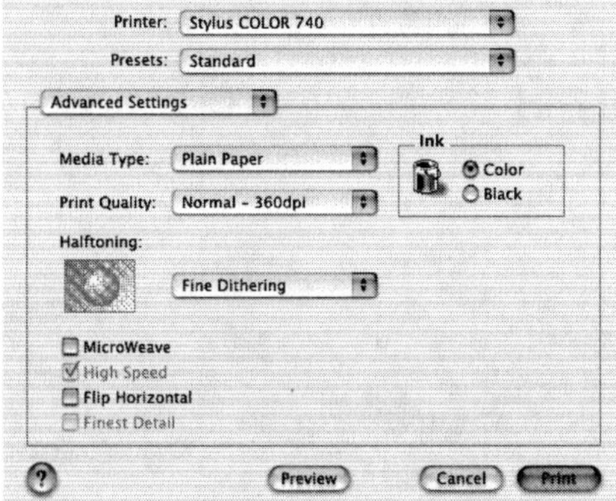

Figure 27 The Advanced Settings pane of the Print dialog for an Epson Stylus Color printer.

To set Print Settings options

1. In the Print dialog, choose Print Settings from the third pop-up menu (**Figure 15b**) to display the Print Settings pane (**Figure 25**).
2. Select the type of paper you will print on from the Media Type pop-up menu (**Figure 26**).
3. For a color printer, select an Ink option.
4. Set Mode options as desired. These options vary from printer to printer; check the documentation that came with your printer for details.

To set Advanced Settings options

1. In the Print dialog, choose Advanced Settings from the third pop-up menu (**Figure 15b**) to display the Advanced Settings pane options (**Figure 27**).
2. Set options as desired. These options vary from printer to printer; check the documentation that came with your printer for details.

To set Color Management options

1. In the Print dialog, choose Color Management from the third pop-up menu (**Figure 15b**) to display Color Management options (**Figure 28**).
2. To indicate the color management method, select one of the radio buttons near the top of the pane. The options in the dialog change depending on the method you select (**Figures 28** and **29**).
3. If you selected Color Controls, set options in the dialog as desired.

✔ Tips

- Color management methods and options are far beyond the scope of this book.
- ColorSync is discussed in *Mac OS X Advanced: Visual QuickPro Guide.*

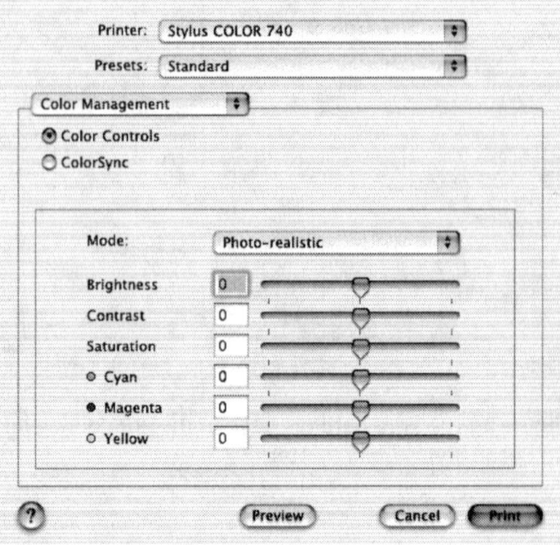

Figure 28 The Color Management pane of the Print dialog with Color Controls selected...

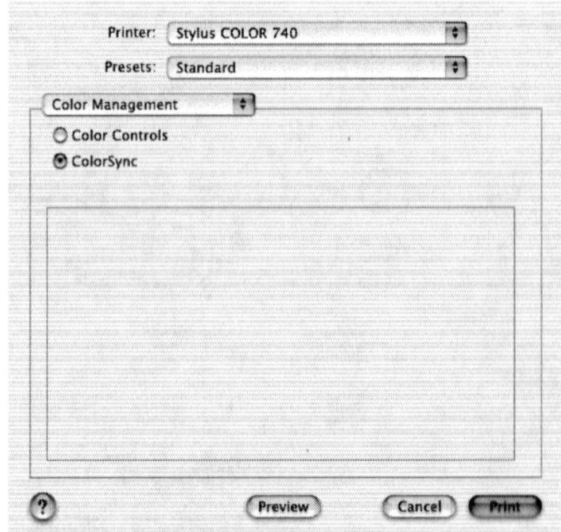

Figure 29 ...and with ColorSync selected.

Standard
✔ Custom

Figure 30 The Presets pop-up menu.

To save settings

In the Print dialog (**Figures 13, 16, 20, 21, 23, 24, 25, 27, 28,** and **29**), choose Save Custom Setting from the third pop-up menu (**Figure 15a** or **15b**).

Custom is automatically selected from the Presets pop-up menu (**Figure 30**).

✔ Tip

- It's a good idea to save settings if you often have to change the Print dialog's settings. This can save time when you need to print.

To use saved settings

In the Print dialog, choose Custom from the Presets pop-up menu (**Figure 30**). All Print dialog settings are restored to what they were the last time you saved settings.

To preview a document

1. In the Print dialog (**Figure 13**), click the Preview button. The Print dialog disappears and Mac OS opens Preview. A moment later, the document appears in a Preview window (**Figure 31**).
2. If necessary, use controls at the bottom of the preview window to scroll from one page to the next.
3. When you're finished previewing the document, you have three options:
   - ▲ Choose File > Print (**Figure 8b**) or press [⌘ P] to display the Print dialog and print the document from Preview.
   - ▲ Choose File > Save as PDF (**Figure 8b**) to display a Save Location dialog (**Figure 32**) and save the document as a PDF file from within Preview.
   - ▲ Choose Preview > Quit Preview (**Figure 33**) or press [⌘ Q] to quit Preview and return to the original document.

✔ Tips

- Preview is covered in **Chapter 6**. The Save Location dialog is covered in **Chapter 5**.
- Some applications, such as Internet Explorer, include a Print Preview command on their File menu (**Figure 8c**).

February 16, 2002

Dear Laura,

I just got my dress for Norb and Missy's wedding. It's a lot nicer than I thought it would be. And fortunately, it fits! I just have to have it taken up. This is the first time in my life that I've ever had to had something shortened—I'm sure you know what I mean.

Although I won't be back in New Jersey for the wedding shower, I'll be back at least a few days before the wedding. I hope we can spend some time together. Perhaps you can take me to your hairdresser to get my hair done before the wedding? I wouldn't mind a manicure, too—if I have any nails left.

Don't tell Ma, but I'm thinking about flying my helicopter to New Jersey for the wedding. The trip would take about a week, but I'd allow myself more time just in case I get stuck somewhere due to weather. I ordered all the charts I need to plan the trip and should be able to make a decision on whether to attempt it later this month. I'm very excited about the possibility of making such a long solo flight. I think it would be a good experience for me.

Well, it's time to get back to work! I'll write more later.

Love,
Maria

Figure 31 The Preview button displays the document in a Preview window. You can use controls at the bottom of the window to scroll from page to page.

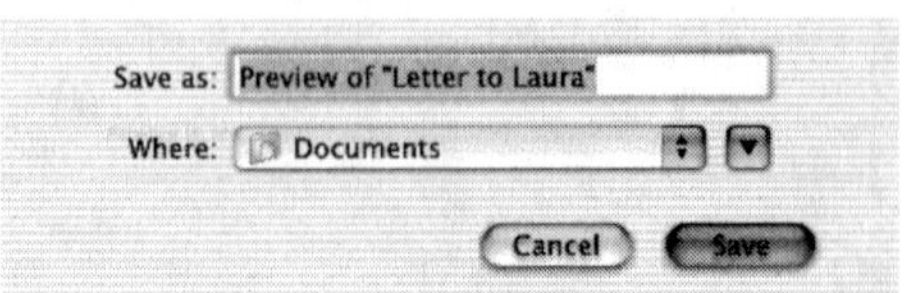

Figure 32 Use a standard Save Location dialog to save the document as a PDF file.

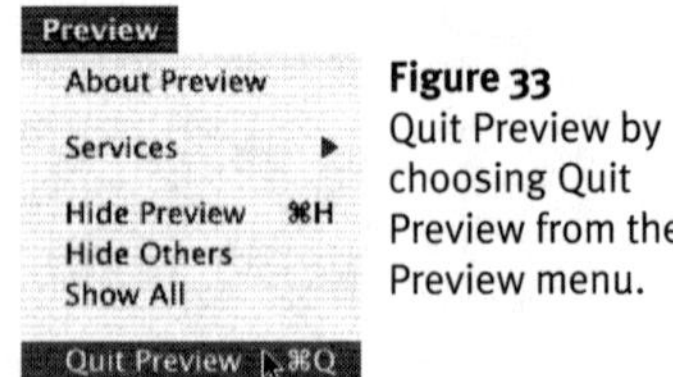

Figure 33 Quit Preview by choosing Quit Preview from the Preview menu.

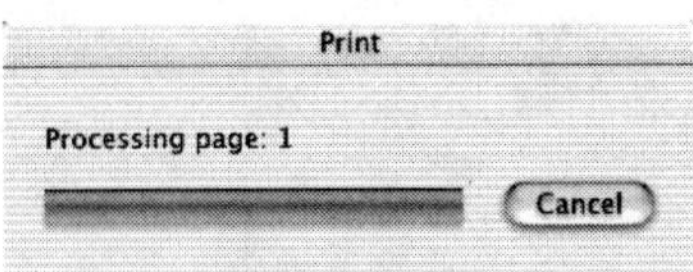

Figure 34 A progress window like this appears as a print job is spooled to the print queue.

Figure 35 When you turn on the Save as File check box, the Print button turns into a Save button.

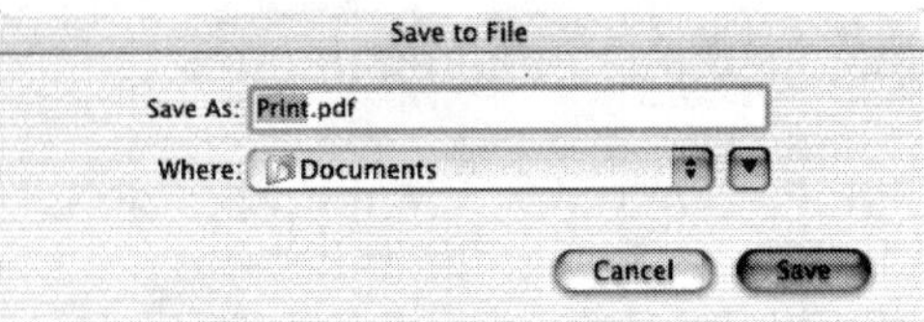

Figure 36 Use this dialog to enter a name, select a location, and Save a document as a file.

To print

In the Print dialog (**Figures 13, 16, 20, 21, 23, 24, 25, 27, 28,** and **29**), click Print.

The print job is sent to the print queue, where it waits for its turn to be printed. A progress window like the one in **Figure 34** appears as it is sent or *spooled*.

✔ Tips

- You can normally cancel a print job as it is being spooled to the print queue or printer by pressing [⌘ .]. Any pages spooled *before* you press [⌘ .], however, may be printed anyway.
- Canceling a print job that has already been spooled to a print queue is discussed later in this chapter.

To save a document as a PDF file

1. In the Output Options pane of the Print dialog (**Figure 20**), turn on the Save as File check box and choose PDF from the Format pop-up menu (**Figure 35**).
2. Set other options in other panes of the Print dialog as desired.
3. Click Save (**Figure 35**).
4. A Save to File dialog like the one in **Figure 36** appears. Use it to enter a name and choose a disk location for the PDF file.

✔ Tip

- Using the Save Location dialog is covered in **Chapter 5**.

Print Queues

As mentioned earlier in this chapter, Print Center can also be used to manage print queues. A *print queue* is a list of documents waiting to be printed. When you click the Print button to send a document to a printer, you're really sending it to the printer's queue, where it waits its turn to be printed.

Print Center's queue windows enable you to check the progress of documents that are printing; to stop printing; and to hold, resume, or cancel a specific print job.

To open a printer's queue window

1. Open Print Center.
2. In the Printer List window (**Figure 2**), double-click the name of the printer for which you want to open the queue.

   or

   In the Printer List window (**Figure 2**) select the name of the printer for which you want to open the queue, and choose Printers > Show Queue (**Figure 3**) or press ⌘O.

   The printer's queue window appears (**Figure 37** or **38**).

✔ Tips

- Instructions for opening Print Center are provided earlier in this chapter.
- When a document is in the print queue, the Print Center icon appears in the Dock (**Figure 39**). Click the icon to open the Print Center.

To stop the print queue

Choose Queue > Stop Queue (**Figure 40**).

Any printing stops and the words "Queue stopped" appear near the top of the queue window (**Figure 41**).

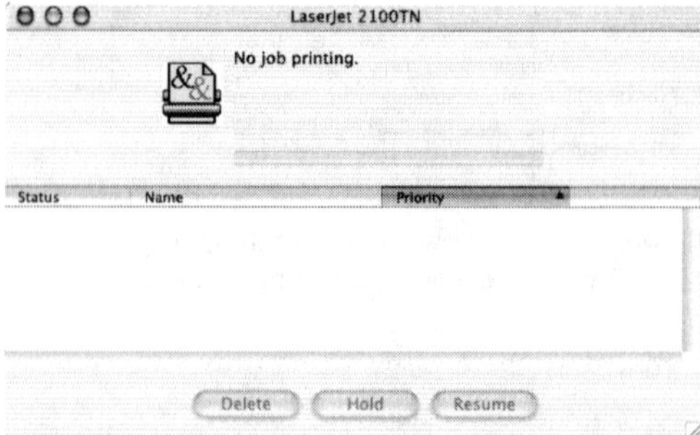

Figure 37 A printer's queue window, with no documents in the queue...

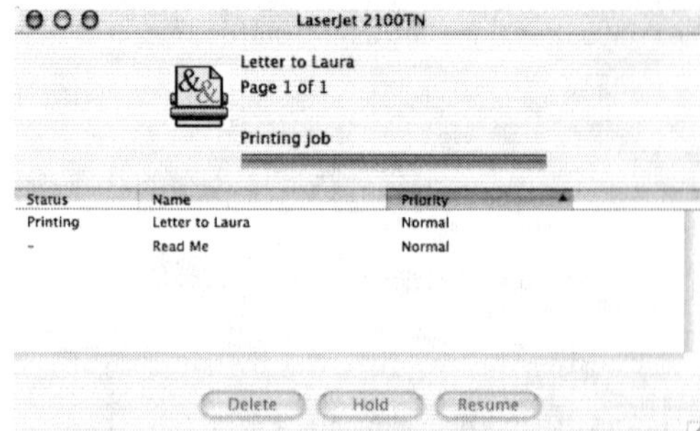

Figure 38 ...and the same printer's queue window with two documents in the queue, one of which is printing.

Figure 39 When print jobs are in a printers queue, the Print Center icon appears in the Dock.

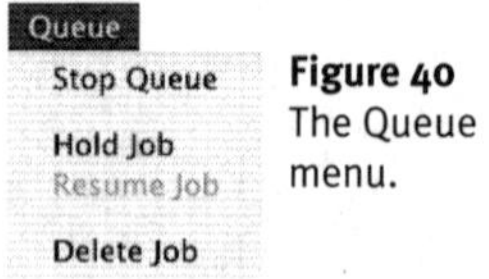

Figure 40 The Queue menu.

Figure 41 The queue status appears near the top of the queue window.

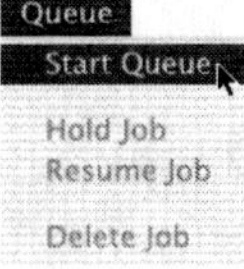

Figure 42 Choose Start Queue from the Queue menu to restart the print queue.

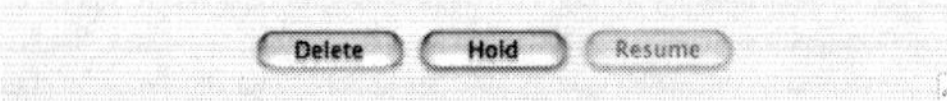

Figure 43 When you select a print job that is not on hold, the Delete and Hold buttons become active.

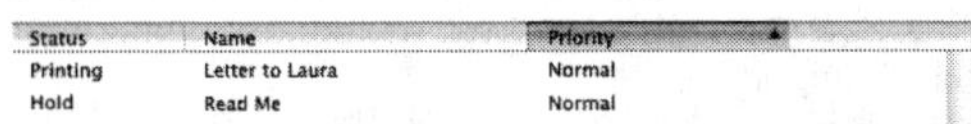

Figure 44 The word "Hold" appears in the status column for any job on hold.

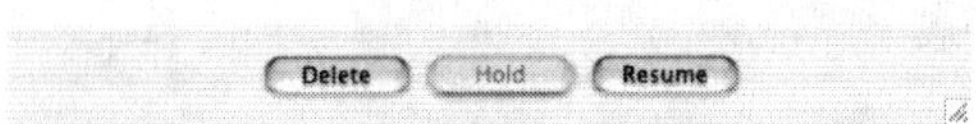

Figure 45 When you select a print job that is on hold, the Resume button becomes active.

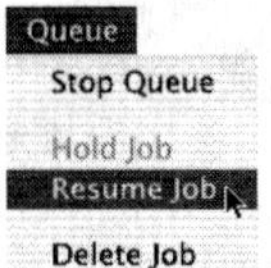

Figure 46 To resume a print job on hold, choose Resume Job from the Queue menu.

To restart the print queue

Choose Queue > Start Queue (**Figure 40**).

The next print job starts printing.

To hold a specific print job

1. In the printer's queue window (**Figure 38**), select the print job you want to hold.
2. Click the Hold button (**Figure 43**).

   or

   Choose Queue > Hold Job (**Figure 40**).

   The word "Hold" appears in the Status column beside the job name in the queue window (**Figure 44**). If the job was printing, printing stops and another job in the queue begins to print.

To resume a specific print job

1. In the printer's queue window (**Figure 38**), select the print job you want to resume.
2. Click the Resume button (**Figure 45**).

   or

   Choose Queue > Resume Job (**Figure 46**).

   The word "Hold" disappears from the Status column beside the job name in the queue window. If no other jobs are printing, the job begins to print.

To cancel a specific print job

1. In the printer's queue window (**Figure 38**), select the print job you want to cancel.
2. Click the Delete button (**Figure 43**).

   or

   Choose Queue > Delete Job (**Figure 40**).

   The job is removed from the print queue. If it was printing, printing stops.

Troubleshooting Printing Problems

When a printing problem occurs, Mac OS can often give you hints to help you figure out why. Here are some examples:

- A dialog like the one in **Figure 47** appears when your printer has a paper jam. Clear the jam.
- A dialog like the one in **Figure 48** appears when your computer can't find the selected printer. Check to make sure the printer is properly connected and turned on.
- A dialog like the one in **Figure 49** appears when your printer is out of paper. Add paper!

When you get one of these error messages, click the Stop Job button and fix the problem (if you can). Then select the document in the queue window (**Figure 50**) and click the Retry button. If the problem is fixed, the document should print.

✔ Tip

- If you have printing problems that Mac OS can't help you identify, check the troubleshooting section of the documentation that came with your printer.

Figure 47 This dialog appeared when the printer got a paper jam.

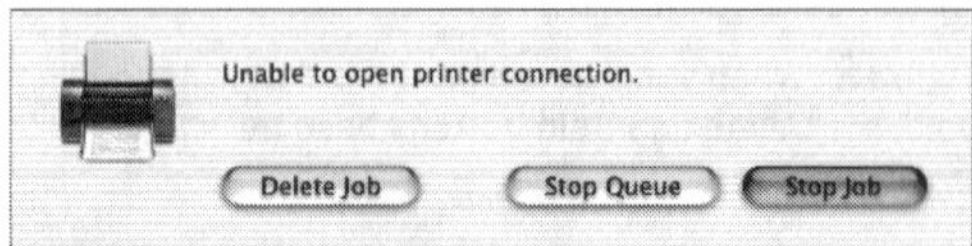

Figure 48 This dialog appeared when the printer wasn't turned on.

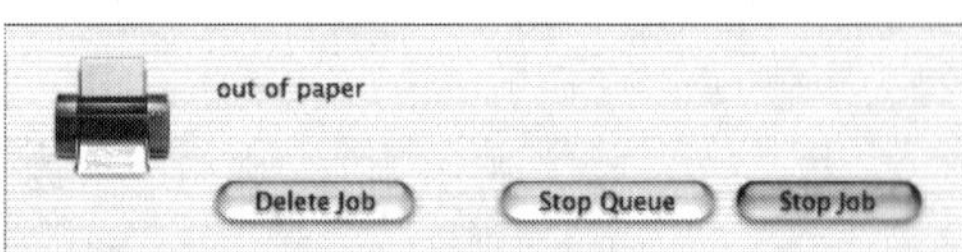

Figure 49 This dialog appeared when the printer ran out of paper.

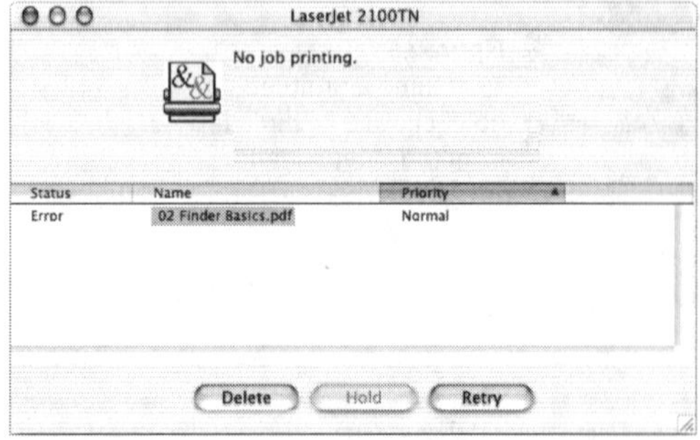

Figure 50 The word "Error" appears in the Status column beside a document that couldn't print. Fix the problem, select the document's name, and click Retry.

Connecting to the Internet

Connecting to the Internet

The *Internet* is a vast, worldwide network of computers that offers information, communication, online shopping, and entertainment for the whole family.

There are two ways to connect to the Internet:

- In a *direct* or *network connection*, your computer has a live network connection to the Internet all the time. This is relatively common for workplace computers on companywide networks. For home use, *DSL*, a type of direct connection, is gaining popularity, although it can be costly.
- In a *modem* or *dial-up connection*, your computer uses its modem to dial in to a server at an *Internet Service Provider* (*ISP*), which gives it access to the Internet. This is a cheaper way to connect, but your access speed is limited by the speed of your modem.

This chapter explains how to configure your system for an Internet connection, connect to the Internet, and use the Internet applications and utilities included with Mac OS X.

✔ Tips

- An ISP is a business that provides access to the Internet for a fee.
- The *World Wide Web* is part of the Internet. The Web and the *Web browser* software you use to access it are covered later in this chapter.

TCP/IP, PPP, & Internet Connect

Your computer accesses the Internet via a TCP/IP connection. *TCP/IP* is a standard Internet *protocol*, or set of rules, for exchanging information.

A TCP/IP connection works like a pipeline. Once established, Internet applications—such as your Web browser and e-mail program—reach through the TCP/IP pipeline to get the information they need. When the information has been sent or received, it stops flowing through the pipeline. But the pipeline is not disconnected.

If you have a direct or network connection to the Internet, the Internet is accessible all the time. But if you connect via modem, you need to use Internet Connect software. This software, which comes with Mac OS, uses PPP to connect to TCP/IP networks via modem. *PPP* is a standard protocol for connecting to networks.

When you connect via modem using Internet Connect, you set up a temporary TCP/IP pipeline. Internet applications are smart enough to automatically use Internet Connect to connect to the Internet when necessary. When you're finished accessing Internet services you should tell Internet Connect to disconnect.

✔ Tip

- Internet Connect is new to Mac OS X. It replaces the Remote Access software found in previous versions of Mac OS.

Manually Setting Internet Configuration Options

If you set up your Internet connection as part of the setup process discussed in **Chapter 1**, your computer should be ready to connect to the Internet and you can skip ahead to the sections that discuss Internet connection software. But if you didn't set up your connection or your Internet connection information has changed since setup, you'll have to do some manual configuration.

Mac OS X includes two System Preferences panels that you can use to manually set up an Internet configuration:

- **Network** enables you to set the server IP address and domain name information, as well as proxy and PPP dialup information.
- **Internet** enables you to set a wide variety of configuration options, including personal, e-mail, Web, and news information.

The following two sections explain the configuration options in these System Preference panels in case you ever need or want to modify your settings.

✔ Tip

- If your Internet configuration is working fine, don't change it! Internet connections follow one of the golden rules of computing: *If it ain't broke, don't fix it.*

Network Preferences

The Network pane of System Preferences enables you to configure your modem or network connection:

- For **modem or network connections**, you can set options to configure your TCP/IP address and proxy information.
- For **modem connections only**, you can set options for your PPP connection to the Internet and your modem.
- For **network connections only**, you can set options for your PPPoE connection to a DSL server and AppleTalk connection to an internal network.

✔ Tips

- A discussion of AppleTalk network connections is beyond the scope of this book. You can learn more about networking in the sequel to this book, *Mac OS X Advanced: Visual QuickPro Guide.*
- *PPPoE*, which stands for *Point to Point Protocol over Ethernet*, is a connection method used by some cable and DSL ISPs.
- Before you set Network preferences, make sure you have all the information you need to properly configure the options. You can get all of the information you need from your ISP or network administrator.

To open Network preferences

1. Choose Apple > System Preferences (**Figure 1**).
2. In the System Preferences window that appears (**Figure 2**), click the Network icon to display the Network pane (**Figure 3**).

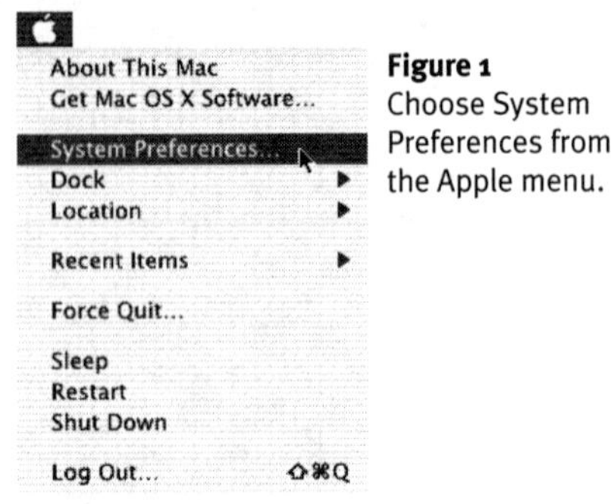

Figure 1 Choose System Preferences from the Apple menu.

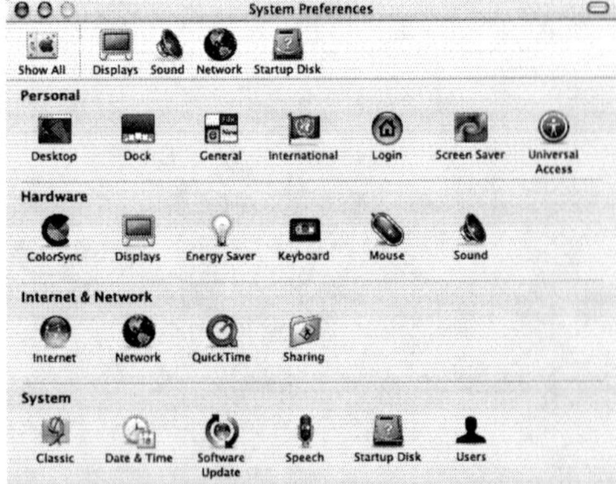

Figure 2 The System Preferences window.

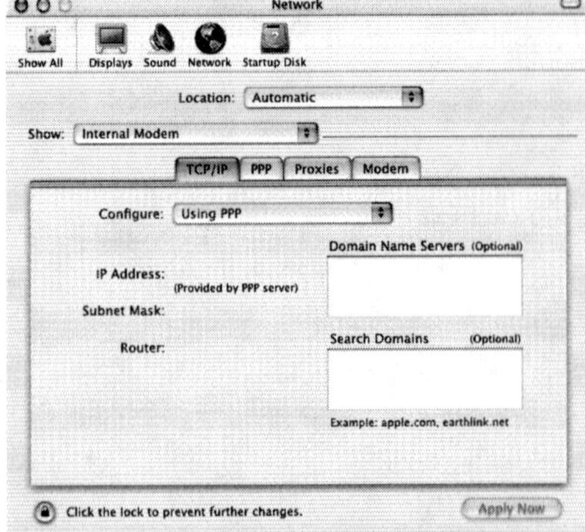

Figure 3 The Network pane of System Preferences with the TCP/IP tab selected for a modem connection.

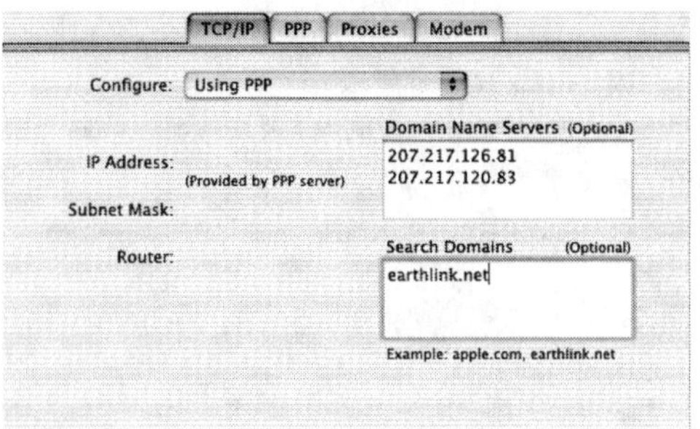

Figure 4 If your ISP has not provided you with a static IP address, the TCP/IP tab might look like this.

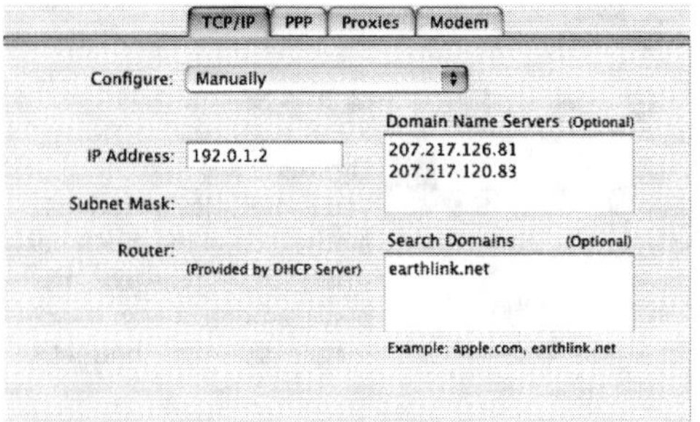

Figure 5 If your ISP has provided you with a static IP address, the TCP/IP tab should include all address information.

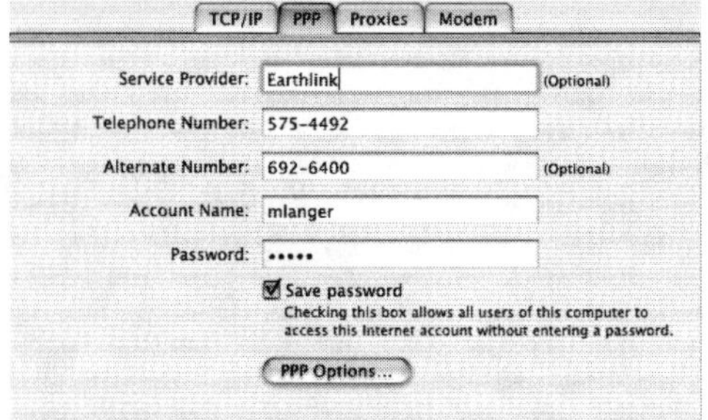

Figure 6 The PPP tab should include all of the information your computer needs to dial in and log on to the ISP's server.

To set up a modem connection

1. In the Network pane of System Preferences (**Figure 3**), choose Modem or Internal Modem from the Show pop-up menu above the tabs.
2. If necessary, click the TCP/IP tab to display its options (**Figure 3**).
3. If your ISP's instructions say that IP address and domain name information will be assigned automatically (i.e., you have a *dynamic* IP address), choose Using PPP from the Configure pop-up menu in the TCP/IP pane. Then enter the domain information in the fields. **Figure 4** shows an example. (This is the most commonly used option for dial-up connections to ISPs.)

   or

   If your ISP provided a *static* IP address and domain name server information for your connection, choose Manually from the Configure pop-up menu in the TCP/IP pane and enter the information provided in each of the fields that appear. **Figure 5** shows an example.
4. Click the PPP tab to display its options.
5. Enter the dialup information provided by your ISP. **Figure 6** shows an example.
6. Click the Modem tab to display its options (**Figure 7**).
7. Choose your modem type from the Modem pop-up menu.
8. To minimize errors and speed up data transfer, turn on the Enable error correction and compression in modem check box.

Continued on next page...

Continued from previous page.

9. Select a Sound radio button:
   - ▲ **On** plays dialing and connection sounds through the modem or computer speaker.
   - ▲ **Off** dials and connects silently.
10. Select a dialing radio button:
    - ▲ **Tone** enables you to dial with touch-tone dialing.
    - ▲ **Pulse** enables you to dial with pulse dialing. Select this option only if touchtone dialing is not available on your telephone line.
11. To instruct your computer to wait until it "hears" a dial tone before it dials, turn on the Wait for dial tone before dialing check box. This, however, can prevent the computer from dialing if you have an unusual dial tone.
12. To include a modem status icon and menu in the menu bar (**Figures 8** and **9**), turn on the Show modem status in menu bar check box.
13. Click Apply Now to save your changes to Network preferences.

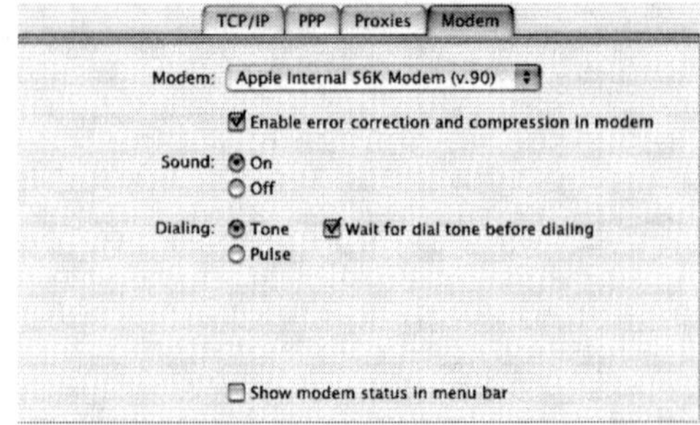

Figure 7 The Modem tab enables you to set options for your modem.

Figures 8 & 9 You can display a modem status icon in the menu bar (top). Clicking the icon displays a menu of commands for accessing the Internet.

✔ Tips

- Do not use the settings illustrated here. Use the settings provided by your ISP.
- In step 5, if you turn on the Save password check box, you won't have to enter your password when you connect to the Internet. Be aware, however, that anyone who accesses your computer with your login will also be able to connect to the Internet with your account.
- The Modem menu in step 7 includes dozens of modem makes and models, so your modem should be listed. If it isn't, choose another model from the same manufacturer or, if the manufacturer isn't listed, choose one of the Hayes models.
- The Enable error correction and compression in modem option in step 8 is not available for all modems.
- In step 9, you may want to keep modem sounds on until you're sure you can connect. This enables you to hear telephone company error recordings that can help you troubleshoot connection problems. You can always turn sound off later.

To set up a network connection

1. In the Network panel of System Preferences, choose the network option from the Configure pop-up menu above the tabs. This option will probably be labeled "Built-in Ethernet," but it could have another name.
2. If necessary, click the TCP/IP tab to display its options.
3. Choose one of the options from the Configure pop-up menu in the TCP/IP tab (**Figure 10**). The option you select determines the appearance of the rest of the tab—**Figures 11** through **14** show examples.
4. Enter the appropriate IP addresses and domain names in the fields.
5. If you have a DSL connection via PPPoE, click the PPPoE tab to display its options. Turn on the Connect using PPPoE check box and enter the connection information provided by your ISP. **Figure 15** shows an example.
6. Click Apply Now to save your changes to Network preferences.

Figure 10 The Configure menu in the TCP/IP pane for a network connection offers four options.

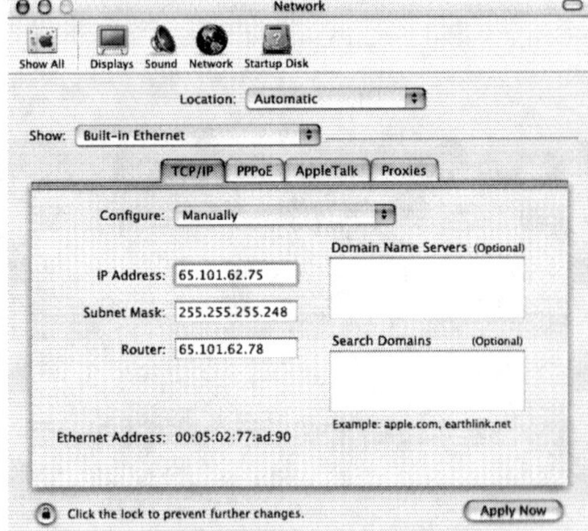

Figure 11 Examples of various configurations for a network TCP/IP connection: manual,...

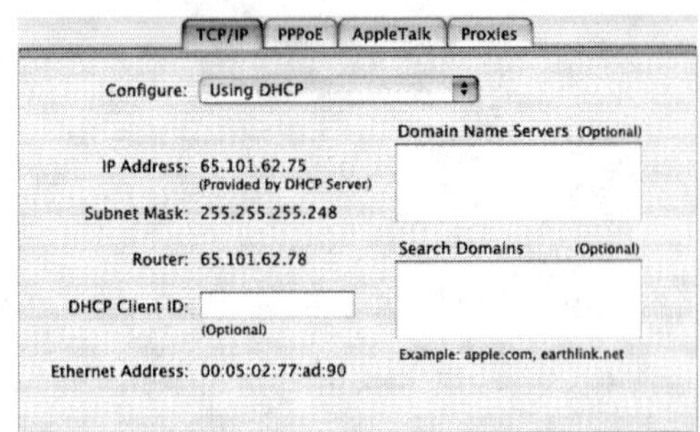

Figure 12 ...DHCP, ...

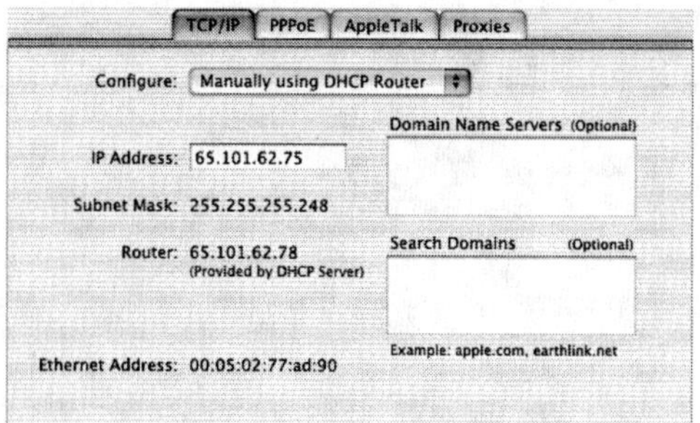

Figure 13 ...DHCP with a fixed IP address,...

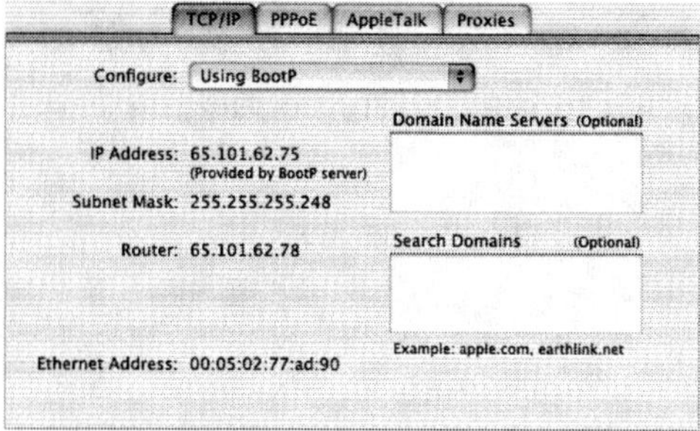

Figure 14 ...and using BootP.

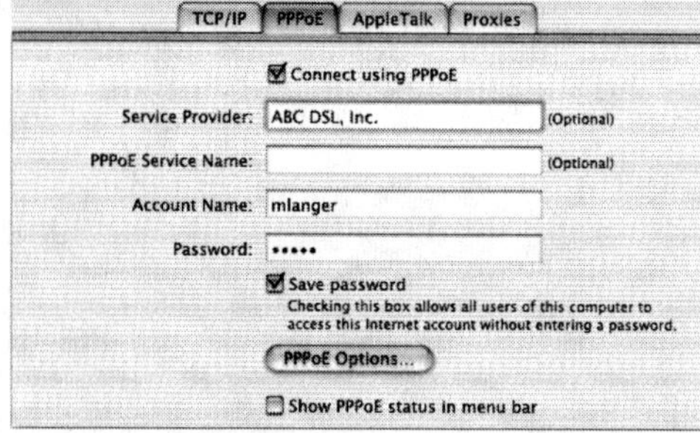

Figure 15 You can use the PPPoE tab to set up a PPPoE connection to a DSL server.

✔ Tips

- Do not use the settings illustrated here. Use the settings provided by your ISP or network administrator.
- If you're not sure which option to choose in step 3, ask your network administrator.
- In step 5, if you turn on the Save password check box, you won't have to enter your password when you connect to the Internet. Be aware, however, that anyone who accesses your computer with your login will also be able to connect to the Internet with your account.

To set proxy options

1. In the Network pane of System Preferences, click the Proxies tab to display its options (**Figure 16**).
2. Turn on the check box beside each proxy option you need to set up. Then enter appropriate information for each one.
3. Click Apply Now to save your changes to Network preferences.

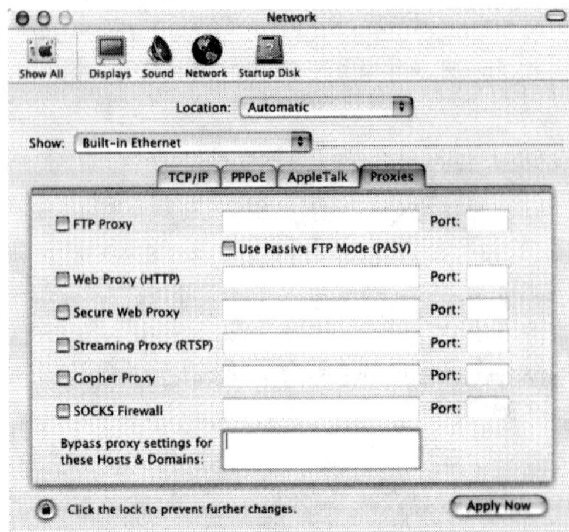

Figure 16 The Proxies tab of the Network preferences pane.

✔ Tips

- Proxies are most often required for network connections; they are seldom required for dialup connections.
- Do not change settings in the Proxies tab of Network preferences unless instructed by your ISP or network administrator. Setting invalid values may prevent you from connecting to the Internet.
- Proxies tab options are the same for modems as for network connections.

Internet Preferences

The Internet pane of System Preferences includes tabs you can use to set options for accessing Internet features:

- **iTools** enables you to enter your iTools member name and password so you can access iTools features on Apple's Web site. iTools is discussed in **Appendix B**.
- **Email** enables you to set your default e-mail reader application, e-mail address, and e-mail server information.
- **Web** enables you to set your default Web browser, home page, search page, and file download location.
- **News** enables you to set your default news reader application, news server information, and connection information.

✔ Tip

- Internet preferences also enables you to set options for iTools, which is discussed in **Appendix B**.

To open Internet preferences

1. Choose Apple > System Preferences (**Figure 1**).
2. In the System Preferences window that appears (**Figure 2**), click the Internet icon to display its options (**Figures 17**, **18**, and **19**).

To set Email options

1. In the Internet pane of System Preferences, click the Email tab to display its options (**Figure 17**).
2. To specify your e-mail application, choose an option from the Default Email Reader pop-up menu. The default selection is Mail, which is discussed in this chapter, but you can choose any e-mail program that is listed or choose Select to use an Open dialog to locate and select the program you want to use.
3. Fill in the fields with address and connection information for your e-mail address. This information should have been provided by your ISP or network administrator.

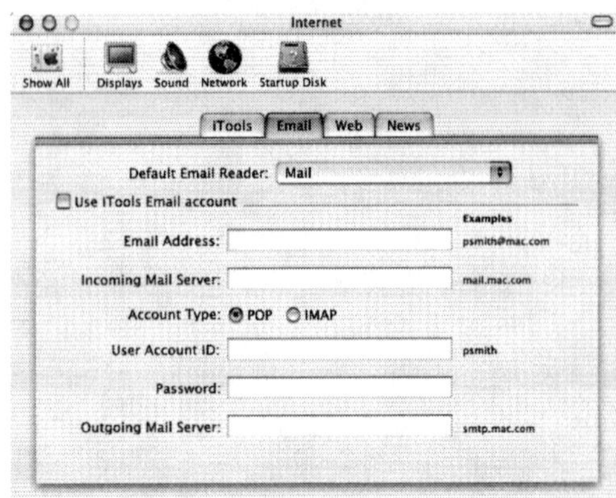

Figure 17 The Internet pane of System Preferences for Email, ...

✔ Tip

- If you turn on the Use iTools Email account check box, all other options are filled in and you can skip step 3. iTools is discussed in **Appendix B**.

To set Web options

1. In the Internet pane of System Preferences, click the Web tab to display its options (**Figure 18**).
2. To specify your Web browser application, choose an option from the Default Web Browser pop-up menu. The default option is Internet Explorer, which is discussed in this chapter, but you can choose any Web browser that is listed or choose Select to use an Open dialog to locate and select the program you want to use.
3. Fill in the fields with URLs for your preferred home page, search page, and file download location.

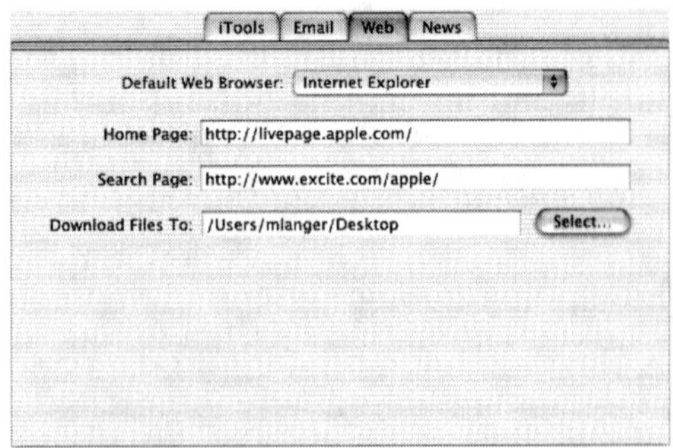

Figure 18 ...Web, ...

✔ Tip

- *URL* is defined and discussed later in this chapter.

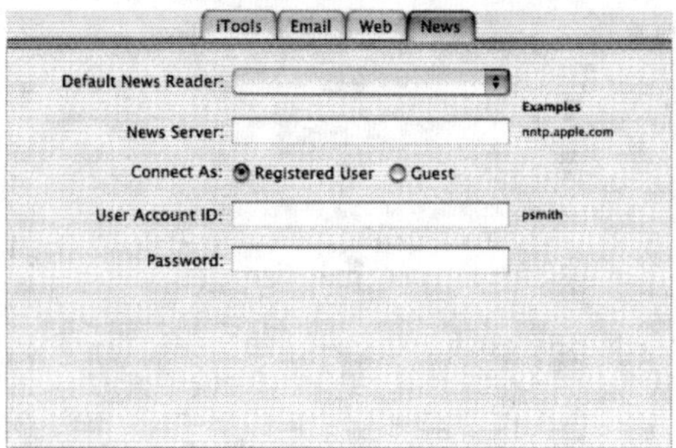

Figure 19 ...and News.

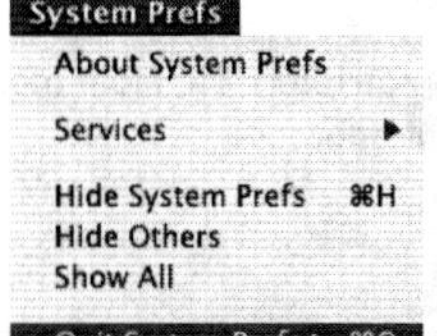

Figure 20 When you quit System Preferences, all of your Internet Preference settings are saved.

To set News options

1. In the Internet pane of System Preferences, click the News tab to display its options (**Figure 19**).
2. To specify your news reader application, choose an option from the Default News Reader pop-up menu or choose Select to use an Open dialog to locate and select the program you want to use.
3. Fill in the fields with server and connection information to access news groups.

✔ Tip

- Outlook Express may be the only option on the Default News Reader pop-up menu in step 2. This is a Classic application that comes with Mac OS 9.x and is not covered in this book.

To save Internet preferences

Choose System Prefs > Quit System Prefs (**Figure 20**), or press [⌘ Q].

The System Preferences application quits, and all of your settings are saved.

Connecting to an ISP

You can establish a PPP connection to your ISP by using Internet Connect to dial in.

✔ Tip

- If you have a network connection to the Internet, you are always connected.

To connect to an ISP

1. Open the Internet Connect icon in the Applications folder (**Figure 21**).
2. Check the settings in the main Internet Connect window that appears (**Figure 22**).
3. Click the Connect button. Internet Connect dials your modem. It displays the connection status in its Status area (**Figure 23**).

   When Internet Connect has successfully connected, the Connect button turns into a Disconnect button and the Status area fills with connection information (**Figure 24**).

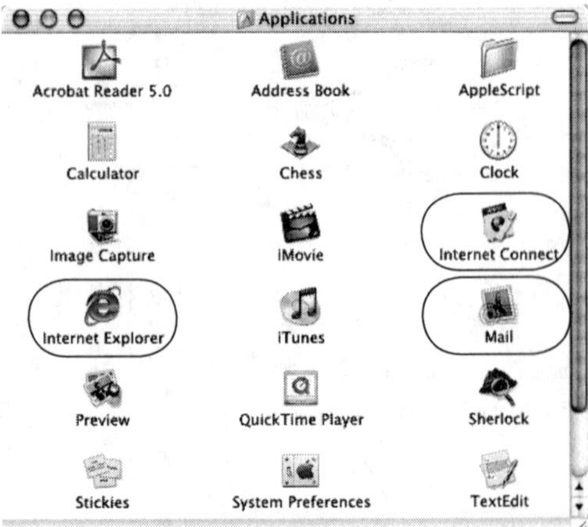

Figure 21 The Applications folder includes a number of applications for accessing the Internet..

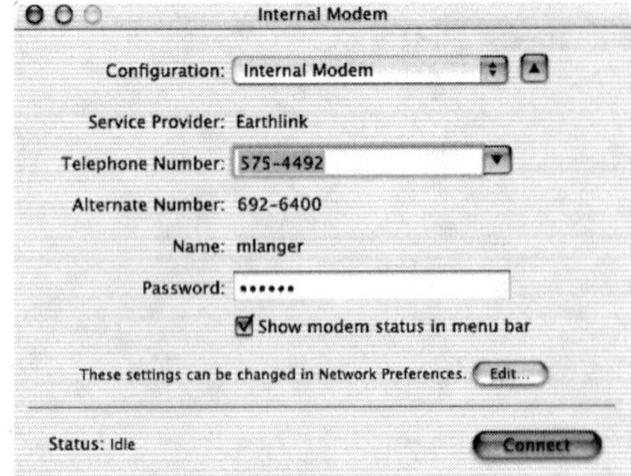

Figure 22 Internet Connect's main window.

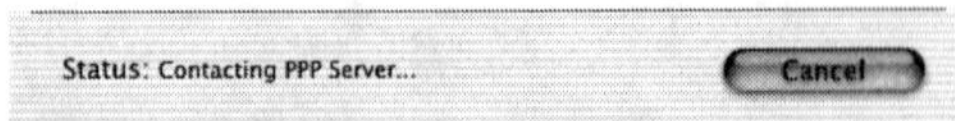

Figure 23 The Status area displays connection status information while you are connecting...

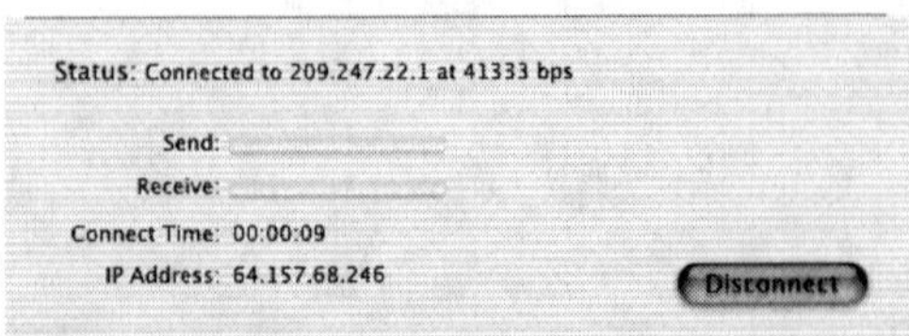

Figure 24 ...and after you have connected.

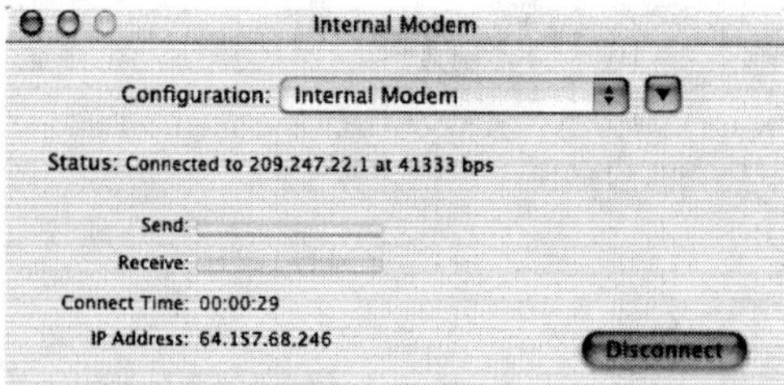

Figure 25 You can collapse Internet Connection's window to show only connection status.

✔ Tips

- If the main Internet Connect window does not display your configuration settings as shown in **Figure 22**, click the triangle beside the Configuration pop-up menu. This will expand the window to show all settings (**Figure 22**).
- The settings that appear in the Internet Connect window (**Figure 22**) should reflect settings you made in the PPP tab of the Network preferences pane (**Figure 6**). If you need to make changes, click the Edit button and follow the instructions provided earlier in this chapter.
- You can click the triangle beside the Configuration pop-up menu to collapse the window and display only the status area (**Figure 25**).
- Internet Connect does not have to be open while you are connected to the Internet.

To disconnect from an ISP

1. Open or switch to Internet Connect (**Figures 22** and **25**).
2. Click the Disconnect button (**Figures 24** and **25**). The connection is terminated.

Internet Applications

Mac OS X includes two applications for accessing the Internet:

- **Mail** is an Apple program that enables you to send and receive e-mail messages.
- **Internet Explorer** is a Microsoft program that enables you to browse Web sites and download files from FTP sites.

This section provides brief instructions for using these two programs. You can explore the other features of these programs on your own.

✔ Tips

- Mail and Internet Explorer are set as the default e-mail and Web browser programs. If you prefer to use other applications, be sure to change the appropriate settings in the Internet preferences pane, as discussed earlier in this chapter.
- Mac OS 9.x, which is bundled with Mac OS X to handle Classic applications, includes Outlook Express, an e-mail application and Netscape Communicator, a Web browser.

To open Mail

Use one of the following techniques:

- Open the Mail icon in the Applications folder (**Figure 21**).
- Click the Mail icon in the Dock (**Figure 26**).

To open Internet Explorer

Use one of the following techniques:

- Open the Internet Explorer icon in the Applications folder (**Figure 21**).
- Click the Explorer icon in the Dock (**Figure 26**).

Figure 26 You can open both Mail and Internet Explorer by clicking their icons in the Dock.

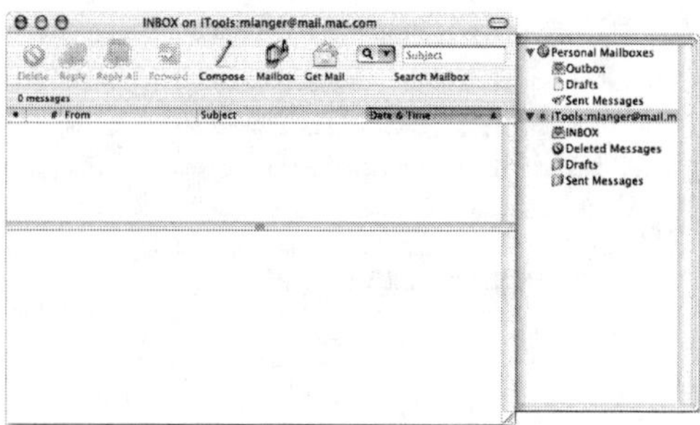

Figure 27 The Mail main window with the Mailbox drawer displayed.

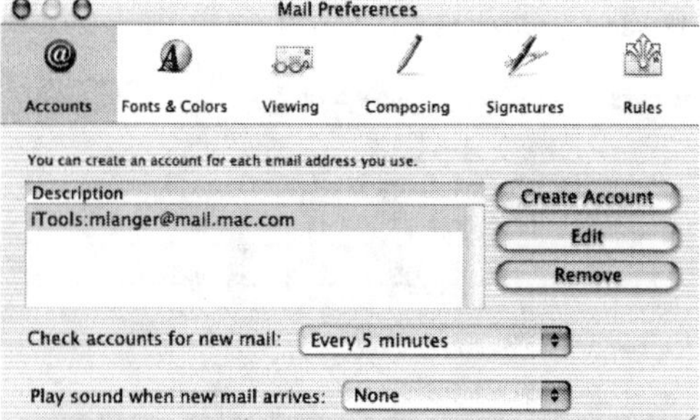

Figure 28 The Account pane of the Mail Preferences window.

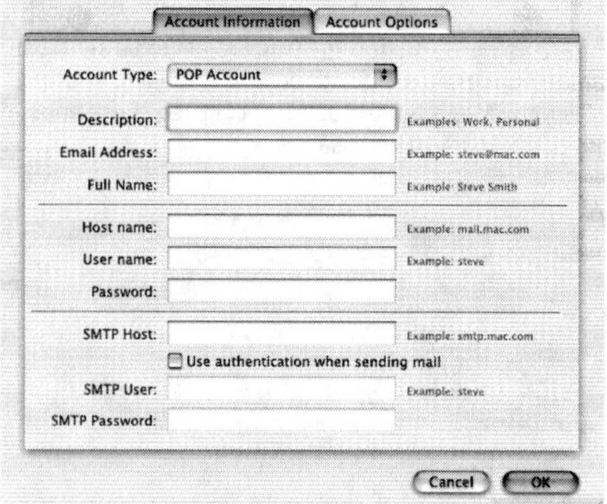

Figure 29 The Account Information pane enables you to enter basic information for your e-mail account.

Figure 30 The account you added appears in the list.

Mail

Mail (**Figure 27**) is an e-mail application from Apple Computer, Inc. It enables you to send and receive e-mail messages using your Internet e-mail account.

This section provides enough information about Mail to get you started sending and receiving e-mail messages.

To set up an e-mail account

1. Choose Mail > Preferences.
2. In the Mail Preferences window that appears, click the Accounts button to display its options (**Figure 28**).
3. Click the Create Account button.
4. In the Account Information pane of the dialog that appears (**Figure 29**), enter the account and server information for the e-mail account.
5. Click OK to save your settings and dismiss the dialog. The account appears in the Mail Preferences window (**Figure 30**).
6. Click the Mail Preferences window's close button to dismiss it.

✔ Tips

- Your e-mail account may have already been set up for you based on information you provided in the Mac OS X configuration process, which was discussed in **Chapter 1**.
- You only have to set up an e-mail account once.
- Your ISP or network administrator can provide most of the information you need to set up an e-mail account.

To create & send a message

1. Click the Compose button at the top of the Mail main window (**Figure 27**). The New Message window appears (**Figure 31**).
2. Enter the e-mail address of the message recipient in the To field, and press Tab twice.
3. Enter a subject for the message in the Subject field, and press Tab.
4. Type your message into the large box at the bottom of the window. When you are finished, the window might look like the one in **Figure 32**.
5. Click the Send button near the top of the window. The message window closes and Mail sends the message.

✔ Tips

- You can use the Address Book application to maintain a directory of the people you write to. Select the name of the person in the Address Book list (**Figure 33**) and click the Send Mail button to launch Mail and display a preaddressed New Message form. Address Book is covered in **Chapter 6**.
- If you have a modem connection to the Internet, you must connect before you can send a message.

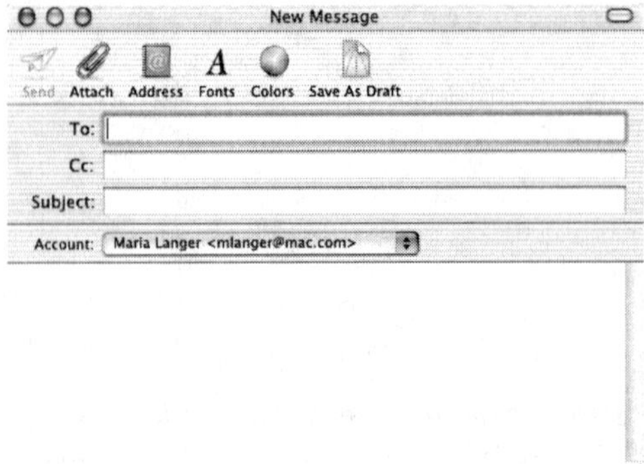

Figure 31 Clicking the Compose button opens a New Message window like this one.

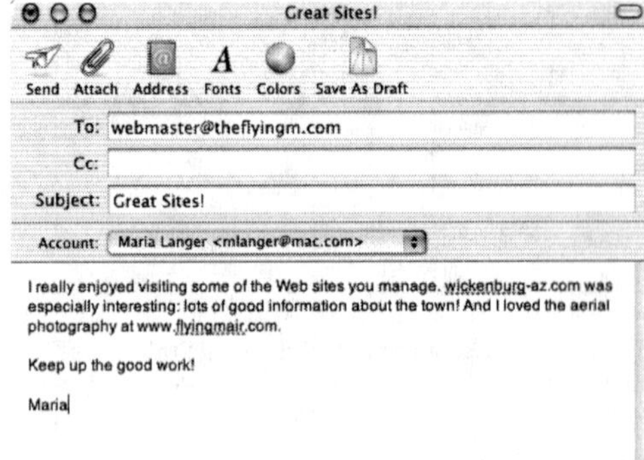

Figure 32 Here's a short message ready to be sent. The dashed underlines indicate potential spelling errors caught by Mail's built-in spelling checker; these lines aren't sent with the messages.

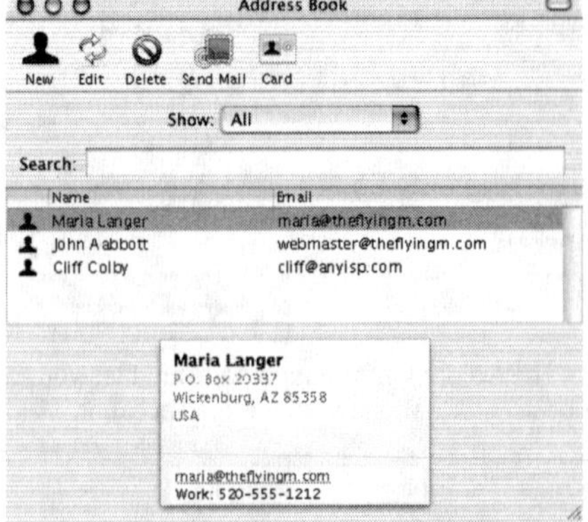

Figure 33 You can use Mail to send an e-mail message to someone in your Address Book by selecting the person's name and clicking the Send Mail button.

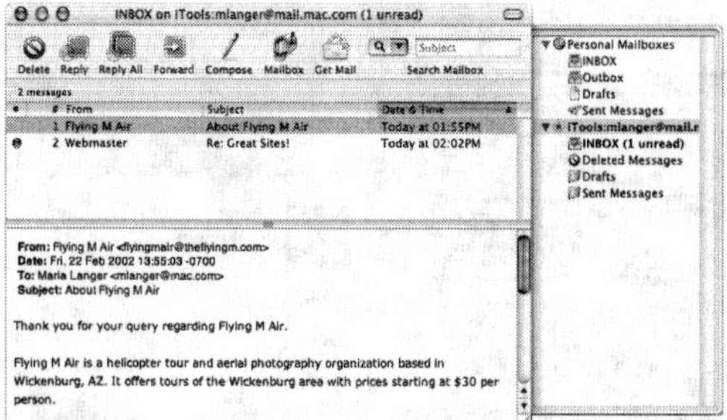

Figure 34 Incoming messages appear in the Inbox. Select a message to display it in the window.

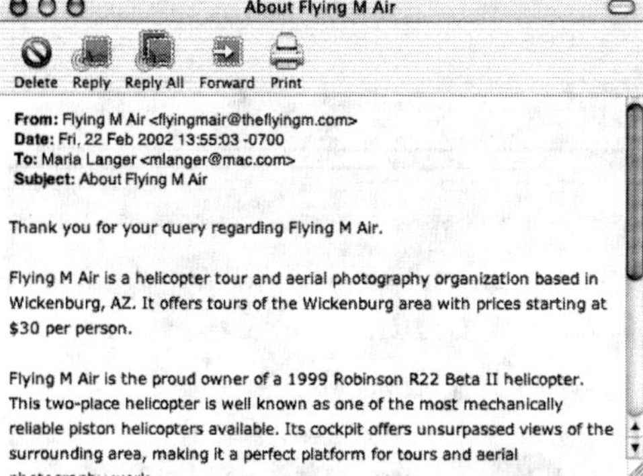

Figure 35 Double-click a message to open it in its own window.

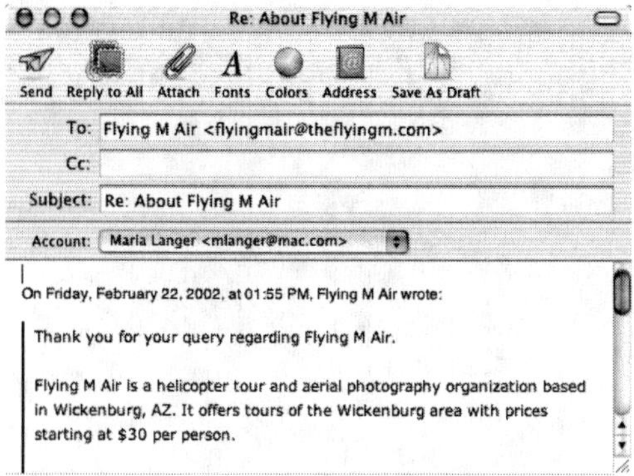

Figure 36 When you click the Reply button, a preaddressed message window appears.

To retrieve e-mail messages

1. If necessary, select the account or mailbox you want to retrieve mail for.
2. Click the Get Mail button at the top of the main window (**Figure 27**).
3. Mail connects to your e-mail server and downloads messages waiting for you. Incoming messages appear in a list when you select the Inbox icon for the account in the Mailbox drawer (**Figure 34**).

✔ Tips

- You can toggle the display of the Mailbox drawer by clicking the Mailbox button in the main Mail window (**Figure 34**).
- You can view the contents of the Inbox or other mail folders by clicking icons in the Mailbox drawer (**Figure 34**).

To read a message

1. Click the message that you want to read. It appears in the bottom half of the main Mail window (**Figure 34**).
2. Read the message.

✔ Tips

- You can also double-click a message to display it in its own message window (**Figure 35**).
- To reply to the message, click Reply. A preaddressed message window with the entire message quoted appears (**Figure 36**). Type your reply, and click Send.
- To forward the message to another e-mail address, click Forward. A message window containing a copy of the message appears. Enter the e-mail address for the recipient in the To field, and click Send.

Internet Explorer

Internet Explorer is a popular Web browser application from Microsoft. It enables you to view, or *browse*, pages on the World Wide Web.

A Web *page* is a window full of formatted text and graphics (**Figures 37** and **38**). You move from page to page by clicking text or graphic links or by opening *URLs* (*uniform resource locators*) for specific Web pages. These two methods of navigating the World Wide Web can open a whole world of useful or interesting information.

Figure 37 When you launch Internet Explorer, it displays the default home page.

✔ Tips

- The version of Internet Explorer included with Mac OS X is Mac OS X compatible. (Older versions run under the Classic environment only.) It has been customized to start with a specific home page and offers buttons with links to Apple and Microsoft pages.
- You can easily identify a link by pointing to it; the mouse pointer turns into a pointing finger and the link destination appears in the status bar at the bottom of the window (**Figure 37**).

Figure 38 Clicking the link in **Figure 37** displays this page.

To follow a link

1. Position the mouse pointer on a text or graphic link. The mouse pointer turns into a pointing finger (**Figure 37**).
2. Click. After a moment, the page or other location for the link you clicked will appear (**Figure 38**).

Figure 39 Enter the URL in the Address field at the top of the Internet Explorer window, and press Enter.

Figure 40 The Add Page to Favorites command adds the currently displayed page to the Favorites menu,...

Figure 41 ...as shown here.

To view a specific URL

Enter the URL in the Address field near the top of the Internet Explorer window (**Figure 39**), and press Return or Enter.

To return to the home page

Click the Home button at the top of the Internet Explorer window (**Figure 39**).

✔ Tip

- You can change the default home page by specifying a different page's URL in the Web tab of the Internet preferences pane (**Figure 18**). The page you specify will load each time you launch Internet Explorer. The Internet pane is discussed earlier in this chapter.

To save a page as a favorite

1. Display the Web page that you want to save as a favorite.
2. Choose Favorites > Add Page to Favorites (**Figure 40**), or press ⌘ D.

   The name of the page is added to the Favorites menu (**Figure 41**).

✔ Tips

- Once a page has been added to the Favorites menu, you can display it by selecting its name from the menu.
- Favorites are also referred to as *bookmarks*.

Using Sherlock

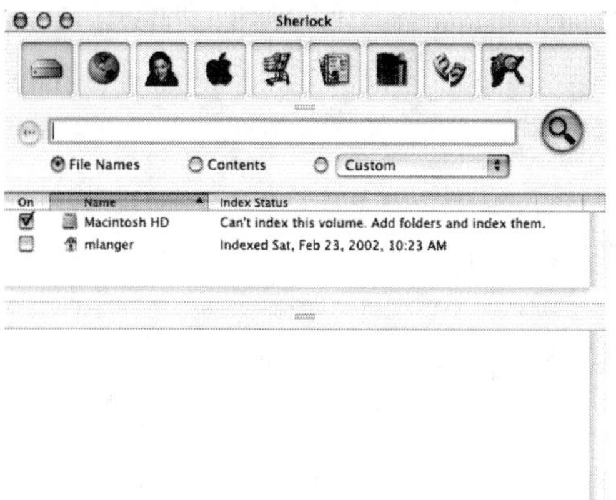

Figure 1 Sherlock enables you to search for files on mounted disks and information on the Internet.

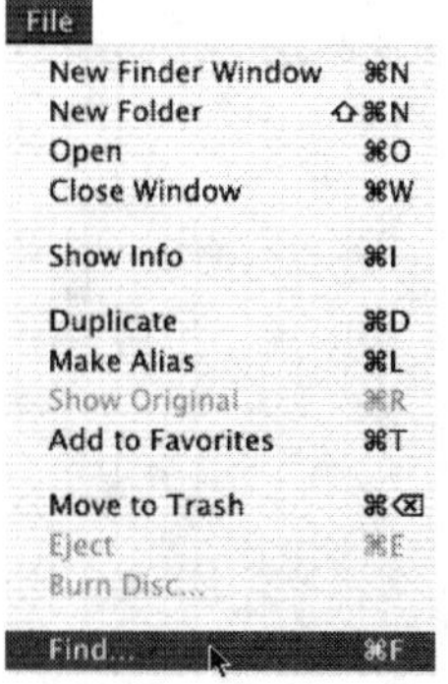

Figure 2 You can launch Sherlock by choosing Find from the Finder's File menu, ...

Figure 3 ...by clicking the Sherlock icon in the Dock, ...

Sherlock

Figure 4 ...or by double-clicking the Sherlock icon in the Applications folder.

Sherlock

Sherlock (**Figure 1**) is Apple's powerful search utility. It enables you to perform the following searches:

- Search your internal hard disk and other mounted volumes for files based on file name, content, or other criteria.
- Search the Internet for information found on Web sites all over the world, including contact information for people you know and merchandise available from online vendors.

This chapter explain show to use Sherlock's search features as well as how to customize Sherlock so it works the way you want it to.

✔ Tips

- **Chapter 3** tells you more about mounted disks and volumes.
- Internet access is required to use Sherlock to search the Internet. **Chapter 9** covers accessing the Internet.

To launch Sherlock

Use one of these techniques:

- Choose File > Find (**Figure 2**), or press [⌘ ⌘][F].
- Click the Sherlock icon in the Dock (**Figure 3**).
- Double-click the Sherlock icon in the Applications folder (**Figure 4**).

Channels

Sherlock's interface includes a feature called *channels*, which enables you to organize search sites based on the types of information they can find for you. Sherlock comes preconfigured with nine channels:

- **Files** (⌘F) is for searching mounted volumes and folders for files. It is the only channel that does not require Internet access to use.
- **Internet** (⌘K) is for searching the Internet for general information.
- **People** (⌘J) is for searching the Internet for the e-mail addresses and other contact information of people you know.
- **Apple** is for searching Apple computer for product and technical information.
- **Shopping** is for searching online stores for items you may want to purchase.
- **News** is for searching news and information sites for news articles.
- **Reference** is for searching reference libraries for information.
- **Entertainment** is for searching for information from the world of entertainment.
- **My Channel** is an empty channel you can use to organize your own search sites.

To switch to a specific channel

Click the icon for the channel at the top of the Sherlock window (**Figure 5**).

or

Choose the name of the channel from the Channels menu (**Figure 6**).

Figure 5 Buttons for Sherlock's default channels appear at the top of the Sherlock window.

Figure 6 You can switch to a channel by choosing its name from the Channels menu.

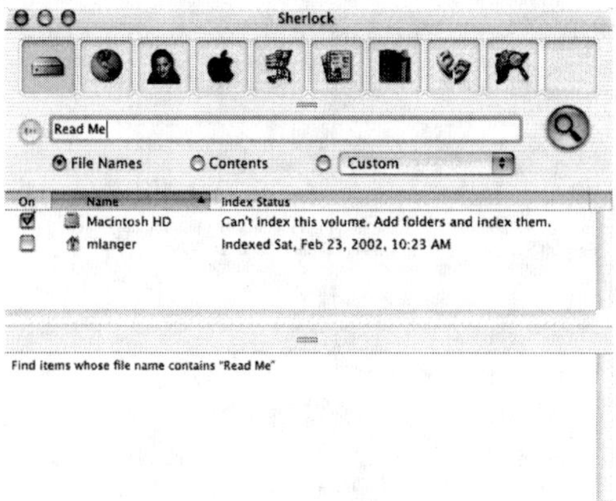

Figure 7 Here's an example of search criteria for searching by name...

Figure 8 ...and here's what the search results might look like.

Finding Files

Sherlock enables you to search your internal hard disk, user folders, or other mounted volumes, including CD-ROM, floppy, Zip, and networked disks, for files based on a variety of search criteria:

- **File Names** enables you to search for files based on all or part of the file name.
- **Contents** enables you to search for files based on any part of the document's contents.
- **Custom** criteria enables you to search for files based on any combination of criteria, including file name, contents, and other file attributes.

✔ Tip

- File attributes are covered in greater detail later in this section.

To find files by name

1. Click the Files channel button at the top of the Sherlock window (**Figure 5**) or press [⌘F] to display Sherlock's Files channel (**Figure 1**).
2. Select the File Names radio button.
3. Enter all or part of the name of the file you want to find in the text field near the top of the window (**Figure 7**).
4. Turn on the check box beside each disk or folder you want to search.
5. Click the magnifying glass button to begin the search. Sherlock searches the specified disks, displaying its status while it works. The search results appear in the bottom half of the window (**Figure 8**).

To find files by content

1. Click the Files channel button at the top of the Sherlock window (**Figure 5**) or press ⌘ ⌘F to display Sherlock's Files channel (**Figure 1**).
2. Select the Contents radio button.
3. Enter the text you are searching for within the file's contents in the text field near the top of the window (**Figure 9**).
4. Turn on the check box beside each disk or folder you want to search. If all of the checked items have been recently indexed (as noted beside the item name), skip ahead to step 8.
5. If a disk or folder you want to search has not been recently indexed, select it and choose Find > Index Now (**Figure 10**).
6. Wait while the item is indexed. Information about indexing progress appears beside the item name while Sherlock works (**Figure 11**). When it is finished, the item's Index Status changes to reflect the recent indexing.
7. Repeat steps 5 and 6 for every disk or folder you want to index.
8. Click the magnifying glass button to begin the search. Sherlock searches the specified disks, displaying its status while it works. The search results appear in the bottom half of the window (**Figure 12**).

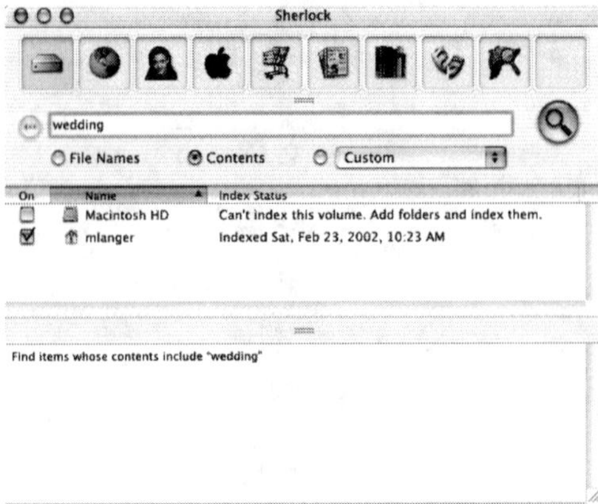

Figure 9 Here's the criteria set up for searching by content.

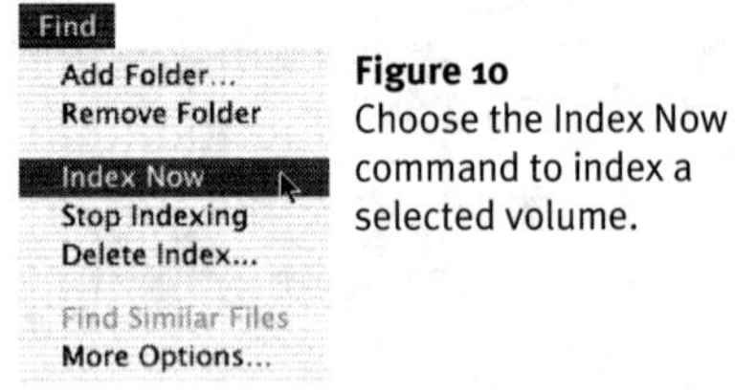

Figure 10 Choose the Index Now command to index a selected volume.

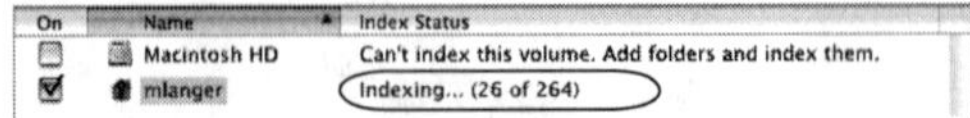

Figure 11 Indexing progress is displayed beside the volume name in Sherlock's window.

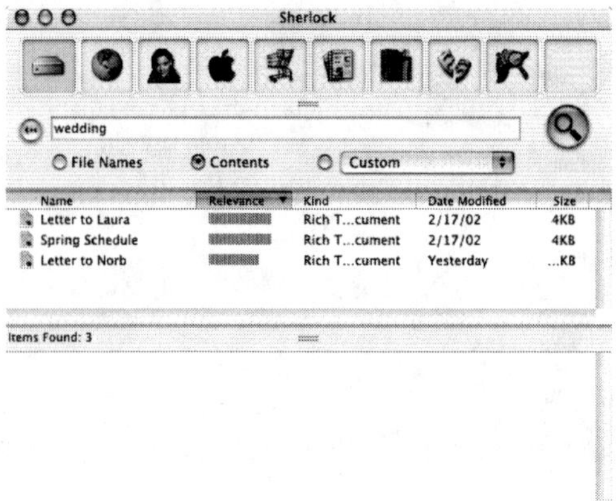

Figure 12 The search results appear in the bottom half of the Sherlock window.

✔ Tips

- The Find by Content feature searches the index, not the actual files. Therefore, it cannot find files that match criteria if the files were created or modified after the index was last updated.
- Not all volumes can be indexed. For example, you may not be able to index your entire internal hard disk (named *Macintosh HD* in **Figure 9**). I explain how to add and index folders later in this chapter.
- To index a server disk, you must be the server's administrator. To index a user folder, you must be the folder's owner.
- The amount of time it takes to index a disk or folder depends on how many items it contains. For large hard disks and CD-ROM discs, indexing can take ten minutes or longer.
- Options for automatically indexing disks and folders are discussed later in this chapter.
- When displaying the results of a search by content, Sherlock includes a Relevance column (**Figure 12**) that indicates how many times the search criteria appeared in the content of the file. Found files are sorted by relevance, so the most likely matches appear at the top of the list.

To find files by custom criteria

✓ Custom
Applications
Larger than 1MB
Modified today
Modified yesterday
Edit...

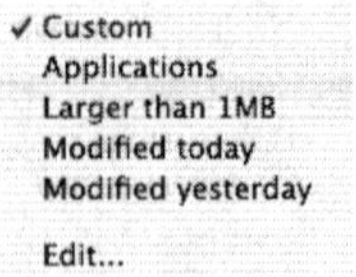

Figure 13
The Custom pop-up menu enables you to choose from predefined searches or create your own custom search.

1. Click the Files channel button at the top of the Sherlock window (**Figure 5**) or press ⌘F to display Sherlock's Files channel (**Figure 1**).
2. Select the radio button beside the Custom pop-up menu.
3. Choose Edit from the Custom pop-up menu (**Figure 13**).
4. In the More Search Options dialog that appears (**Figure 14**), turn on check boxes and enter search criteria for the attributes you want to use to search for files. Here are your options:
   - ▲ **File name** is the name of the file. Choose an option from the pop-up menu (**Figure 15**), and enter all or part of the file name beside it.
   - ▲ **Content includes** enables you to specify text to find within a file's contents. Enter the text in the text field. (The volume must be indexed to find by content; see the section titled "To find files by content" for details.)
   - ▲ **Date created** is the date the file was created. Choose an option from the pop-up menu (**Figure 16**), and enter a date beside it.
   - ▲ **Date modified** is the date the file was last changed. Choose an option from the pop-up menu (**Figure 16**), and enter a date beside it.
   - ▲ **Size** is the size of the file in kilobytes (KB). Choose an option from the pop-up menu (**Figure 17**), and enter a size value beside it.
   - ▲ **Kind** is the type of file. Choose an option from the first pop-up menu (**Figure 18**), and then choose a type from the pop-up menu beside it (**Figure 19**). (**Chapter 2** covers file types.)

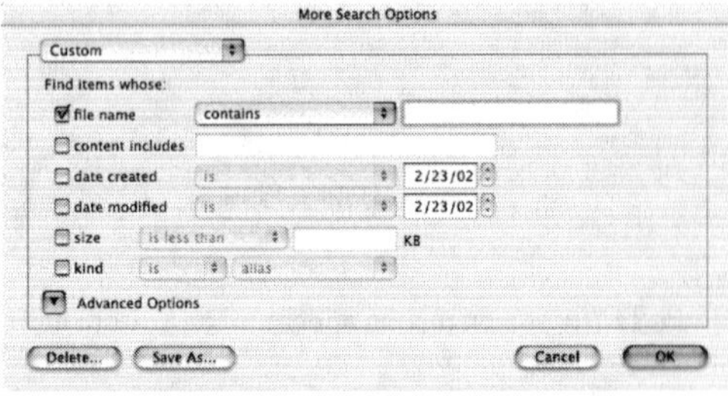

Figure 14 Use the More Search Options dialog to set up custom search criteria.

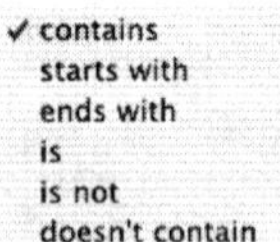

Figure 15
Use this pop-up menu to specify how a file's name should match your entry.

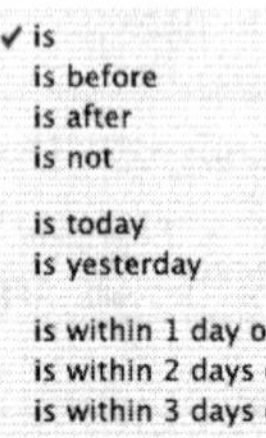

Figure 16
Use a pop-up menu like this one to specify how a date you enter should match the creation or modification date of a file.

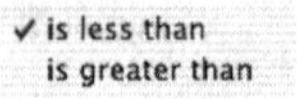

✓ is less than
is greater than

Figure 17 Use this pop-up menu to specify how size should match your criteria.

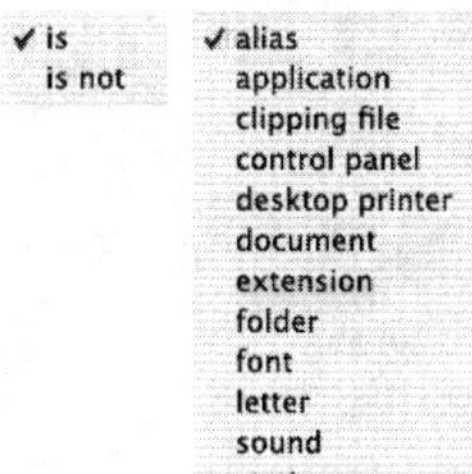

Figures 18 & 19 To specify a kind of document, choose an option from these two pop-up menus.

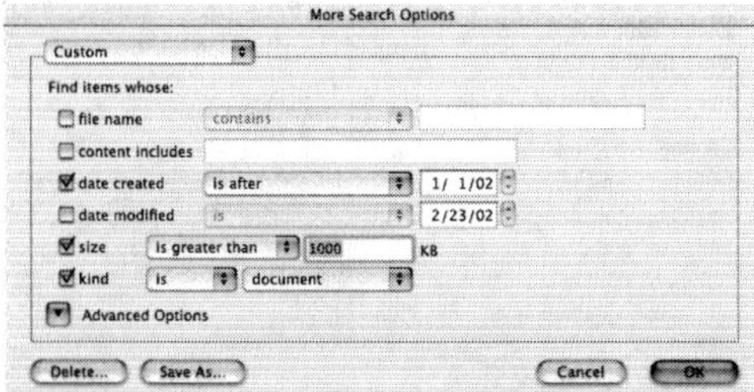

Figure 20 Here's what the More Search Options dialog looks like with some criteria set,...

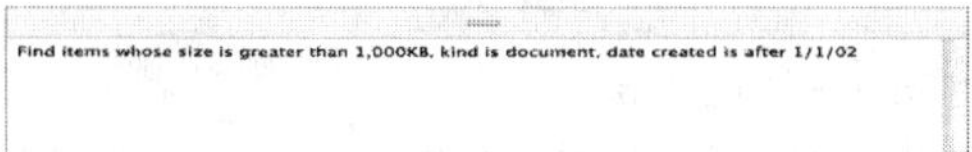

Figure 21 ...here's what the same criteria looks like in the bottom of the Sherlock window,...

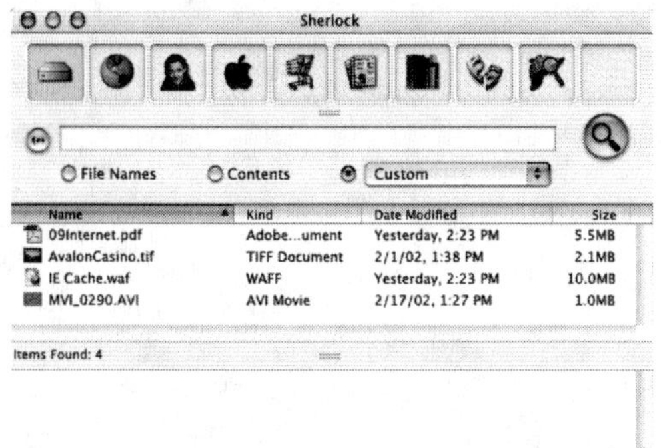

Figure 22 ...and here's what the items found list might look like for that criteria.

5. When you are finished setting up search criteria (**Figure 20**), click OK to return to the Sherlock window. The criteria appears in the bottom of the window (**Figure 21**).
6. Turn on the check box beside each disk or folder you want to search.
7. Click the magnifying glass button to begin the search. Sherlock searches the specified disks, displaying its status while it works. The search results appear in the bottom half of the window (**Figure 22**).

✓ Tips

- The Custom pop-up menu in the Sherlock window includes other predefined custom search options (**Figure 13**). Choose an option and click Sherlock's magnifying glass button to perform the search.
- Sherlock finds files that match *all* search criteria in the More Search Options dialog (**Figure 20**). The more criteria you include, the fewer files you will find.
- Clicking the Advanced Options button in the More Search Options dialog expands the dialog to offer additional options for setting search criteria (**Figure 23**). These options are technical in nature and far beyond the scope of this book.

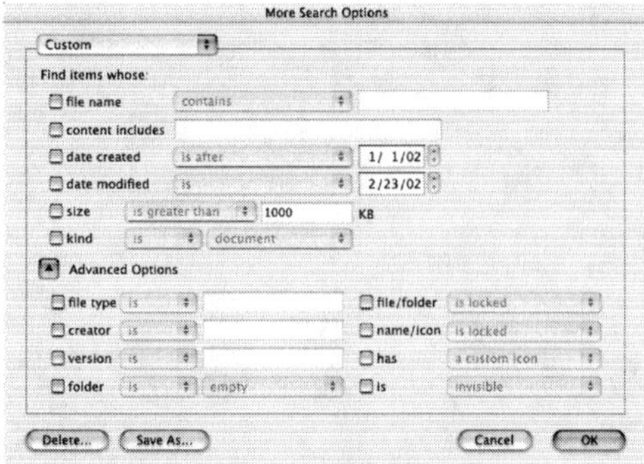

Figure 23 Clicking the triangle beside Advanced Options expands the dialog to offer more options.

To save custom criteria

1. Follow steps 1 through 4 in the section titled "To find files by custom criteria" to set up criteria in Sherlock's More Search Options dialog (**Figure 20**).
2. Click Save.
3. Enter a name for the set of search criteria in the Save Custom Settings dialog that appears (**Figure 24**).
4. Click Save to save the settings and return to the Sherlock window.

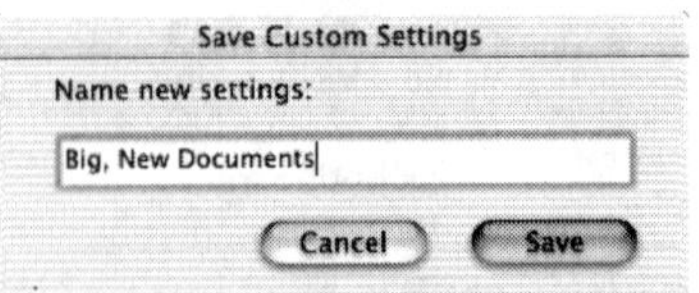

Figure 24 Use this dialog to name and save a set of custom search criteria so you can use it again and again.

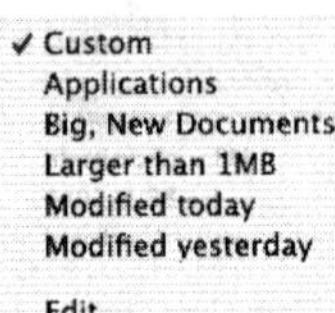

Figure 25 When you save custom search criteria, its name appears in the Custom pop-up menu in the Sherlock window.

✔ Tips

- Once you've saved custom search criteria, you can use it any time by choosing its name from the Custom pop-up menu in the Sherlock window (**Figure 25**).
- You can remove a set of custom search criteria by clicking Delete in the More Search Options dialog (**Figure 20**). Select the criteria set you want to delete in the Delete Custom Search Settings dialog that appears (**Figure 26**), and click Delete.

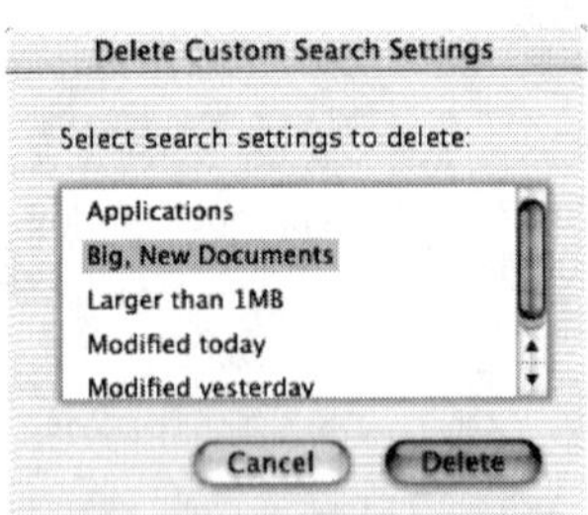

Figure 26 Use this dialog to delete sets of custom search criteria you no longer use.

Figure 27 When you select an item, the complete path to its location appears in Sherlock's window.

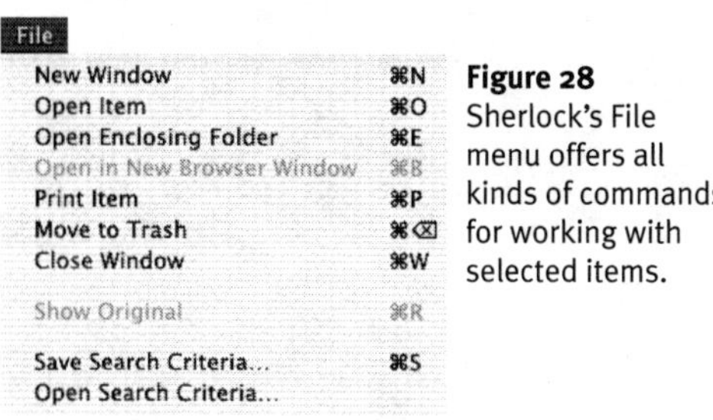

Figure 28 Sherlock's File menu offers all kinds of commands for working with selected items.

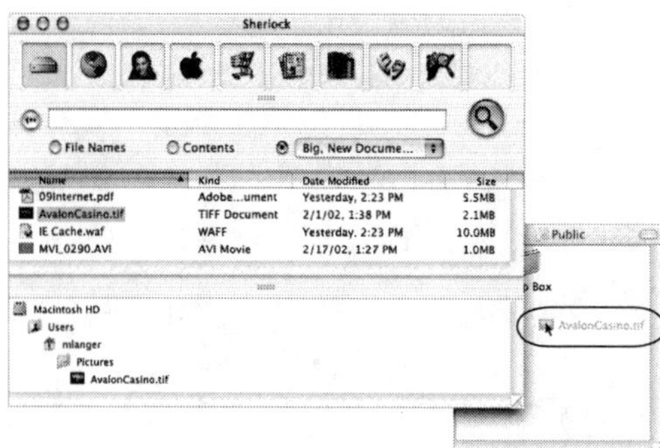

Figure 29 You can move an item by dragging it from the Sherlock window to a new place on disk.

Figure 30 When you release the item, its path changes.

To work with the list of items found

1. Scroll through the list of items found (**Figures 8**, **12**, and **22**) to locate an item that interests you.
2. Click the item to select it (**Figure 27**), then:
   - ▲ To see where the item is located, consult the bottom part of the window for the complete path to its location (**Figure 27**).
   - ▲ To open the item, double-click it, choose File > Open Item (**Figure 28**), or press ⌘O.
   - ▲ To open the folder in which the item is stored, choose File > Open Enclosing Folder (**Figure 28**) or press ⌘E.
   - ▲ To print the item (if it is a printable file), choose File > Print Item (**Figure 28**) or press ⌘P. (**Chapter 8** covers printing.)
   - ▲ To move the item, drag it from the Sherlock window to a disk, folder, or Finder window (**Figure 29**). When you release the mouse button, the item still appears in the Sherlock window, but its path at the bottom of the window changes (**Figure 30**).
   - ▲ To delete the item, drag it from the Sherlock window to the Trash, choose File > Move to Trash (**Figure 28**), or press ⌘ Delete. The item still appears in the Sherlock window, but its path at the bottom of the window shows that it is in the Trash.
   - ▲ To view the original for the item (if it is an alias), choose File > Show Original or press ⌘R. (**Chapter 4** covers aliases.)

Continued on next page...

Continued from previous page.

- ▲ To find files that are similar to the item, choose Find > Find Similar Files (**Figure 31**). Sherlock performs another find based on the selected file's contents and attributes and displays the results in its window.

Figure 31
The Find menu includes the Find Similar Files command, which searches for files based on the contents or attributes of the selected file.

✔ Tips

- To select more than one found item at a time, hold down [⌘] while clicking each one. The paths for the items do not appear at the bottom of the Sherlock window when more than one item is selected.
- You can sort the items found list in the Sherlock window (**Figure 27**) by clicking one of its column headings. To reverse the sort order, just click the same column heading again.
- To remove the items found list so you can perform a new search, click the Files channel button at the top of the Sherlock window (**Figure 5**).
- To open a separate Sherlock window to perform a new search (without disturbing the items found list), choose File > New Window (**Figure 28**) or press [⌘][N].

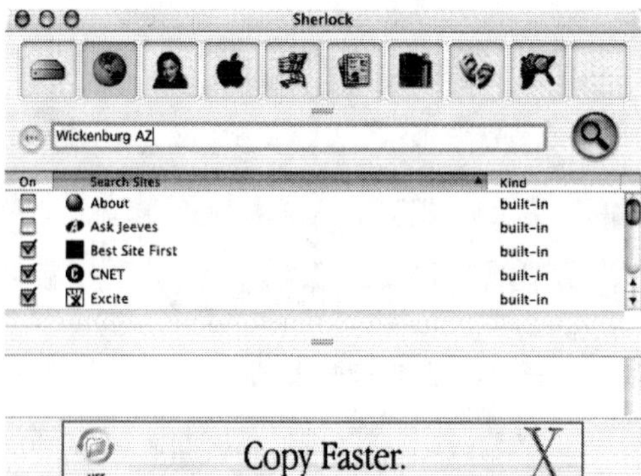

Figure 32 Use Sherlock's Internet channel to search the Internet for information.

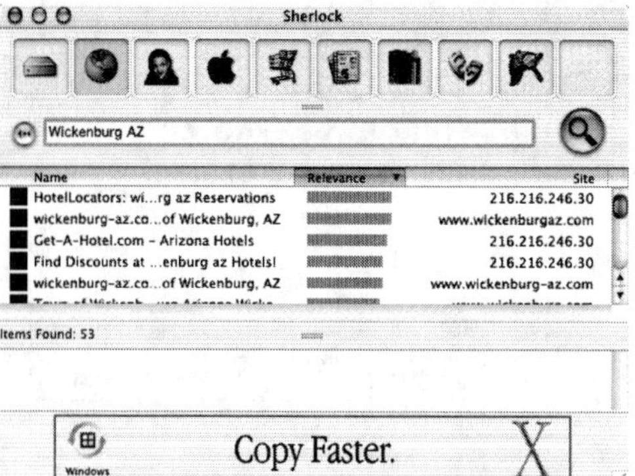

Figure 33 Sherlock displays matches, in order of relevance, in its window.

✔ Tips

- When entering words in step 2, enter at least two or three words you expect to find in documents about the topic you area searching for. This helps narrow down the search, resulting in more useful matches.
- The more search sites you select the longer the search will take.
- Ads appear at the bottom of the Sherlock window. Click an ad to open a corresponding Web page in your Web browser.

Searching the Internet

If you have Internet access, you can use Sherlock to search for Web pages with information about topics that interest you. Unlike most other Internet search engines, Sherlock can search multiple directories (or *search sites*) at once. Best of all, you don't need to know special search syntax. Just enter a search word or phrase in plain English, select the search sites you want to use, and put Sherlock to work. It displays matches in order of relevance, so the most likely matches appear first.

To search the Internet

1. Click the button for one of the Internet search channels:
   - ▲ **Internet** (⌘ J) is a general purpose search channel, good for finding Web pages that cover specific topics.
   - ▲ **Apple** is best for searching for Apple-related information, including products and how-to instructions.
   - ▲ **News** is best for finding news stories from news Web sites.
   - ▲ **Reference** is good for finding articles about specific topics on reference sites.
   - ▲ **Entertainment** is good for finding information about movies, music, and your favorite entertainment artists.
2. Enter a search word or phrase in the text field near the top of the window (**Figure 32**).
3. Turn on the check box beside each search site you want to use to search.
4. Click the magnifying glass button to begin the search. Sherlock searches the Internet, displaying its status while it works.
5. After a moment, the matches begin to appear. You can begin working with matches immediately or wait until Sherlock has finished searching (**Figure 33**).

To work with the items found list of Web pages

1. Scroll through the list of items found (**Figure 33**) to locate an item that interests you.

2. Click the item to select it (**Figure 34**), then:

   ▲ To learn more about the item, consult the information that appears beneath the items found list (**Figure 34**).

   ▲ To open the item's Web page, double-click it, choose File > Open, or press [⌘][O]. Your Web browser launches and displays the item in its window (**Figure 35**).

✔ Tips

- To open a Web page in new Web browser window (rather than in the currently open Web browser window), choose File > Open in New Browser Window or press [⌘][B].
- You can sort the items found list in the Sherlock window (**Figure 33**) by clicking one of its column headings. To reverse the sort order, just click the same column heading again.
- To remove the items found list so you can perform a new search, click a button for one of the Internet search channels at the top of the Sherlock window (**Figure 5**).
- To open a separate Sherlock window to perform a new search (without disturbing the items found list), choose File > New Window (**Figure 28**) or press [⌘][N].

Figure 34 Select a Web page to display information about it.

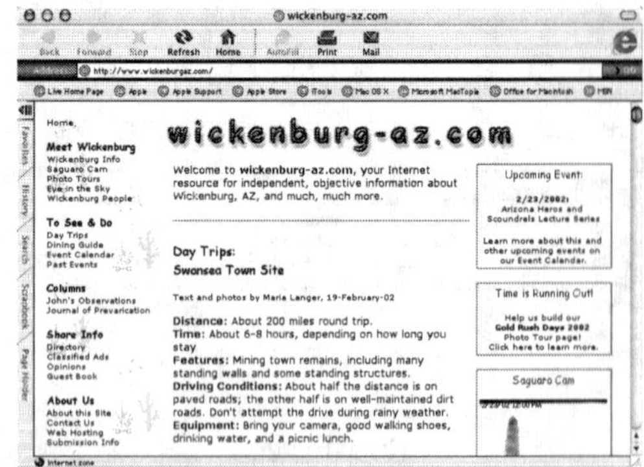

Figure 35 Double-clicking the name of a Web page displays the page in your Web browser window. Here's my favorite Web site for my favorite western town.

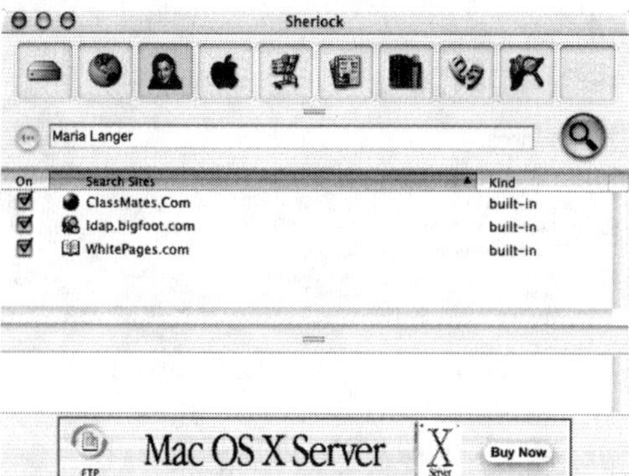

Figure 36 Use Sherlock to search for people you know.

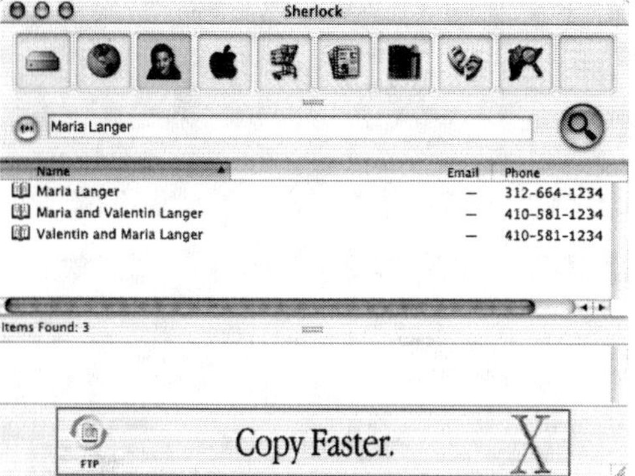

Figure 37 Sherlock displays a list of all matches for the name you entered. (Please do not dial these phone numbers; they're not real!)

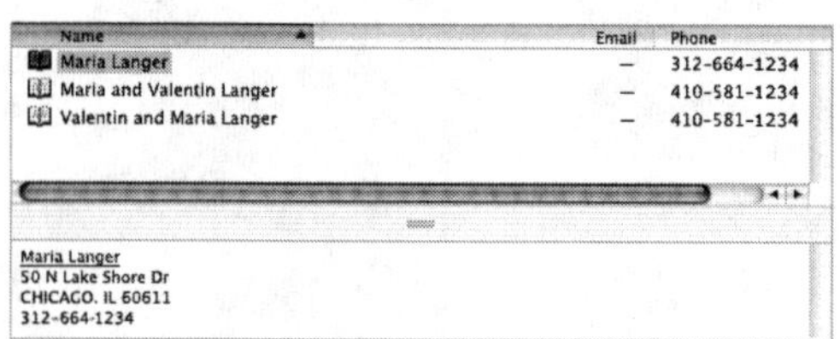

Figure 38 Click an item to see its details in the bottom of the window. (Please do not bother this person; she is not me!)

Searching for People

If you have Internet access, you can use Sherlock to find the contact information for people you know. This feature searches the entries in several popular e-mail directories to find matches.

To search for a person

1. Click the People channel button at the top of the Sherlock window (**Figure 5**) or press [⌘][J] to display Sherlock's People channel.
2. Enter the complete name for the person in the text field near the top of the window (**Figure 36**).
3. Turn on the check box beside each search site you want to use to search.
4. Click the magnifying glass button to begin the search. Sherlock searches the directories you selected, displaying its status while it works.
5. After a moment, the matches begin to appear. You can begin working with matches immediately or wait until Sherlock has finished searching (**Figure 37**).
6. To get all the information about a matched item, click it once. The information appears in the area beneath the list (**Figure 38**).

✔ Tip

- Although Sherlock can find people, the search sites it uses may not have complete or up-to-date data. For example, although Sherlock found 3 matches for "Maria Langer," none of them is for me.

Shopping Online

If you have Internet access, you can also use Sherlock to find products that you can buy online. This feature can search various online retailers and auctions.

To search for a product

1. Click the Shopping channel button at the top of the Sherlock window (**Figure 5**) to display Sherlock's Shopping channel.
2. Enter the name or some key words for the product you want to find in the text field near the top of the window (**Figure 39**).
3. Turn on the check boxes beside each search site where you want to shop.
4. Click the magnifying glass button to begin the search. Sherlock searches the online stores you selected, displaying its status while it works.
5. After a moment, the matches begin to appear. You can begin working with matches immediately or wait until Sherlock has finished searching (**Figure 40**).
6. To get all the information about a matched item, click it once. The information appears in the area beneath the list (**Figure 40**).
7. To learn more about the item or buy it, double-click it. This launches your Web browser and displays the page on the Web site where the item is offered for sale.

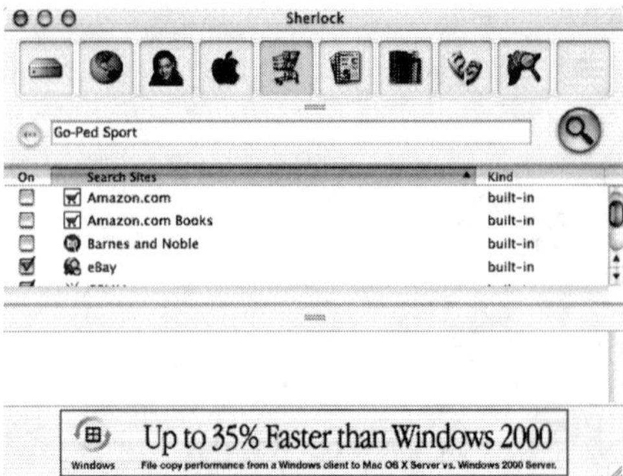

Figure 39 Use Sherlock to shop online.

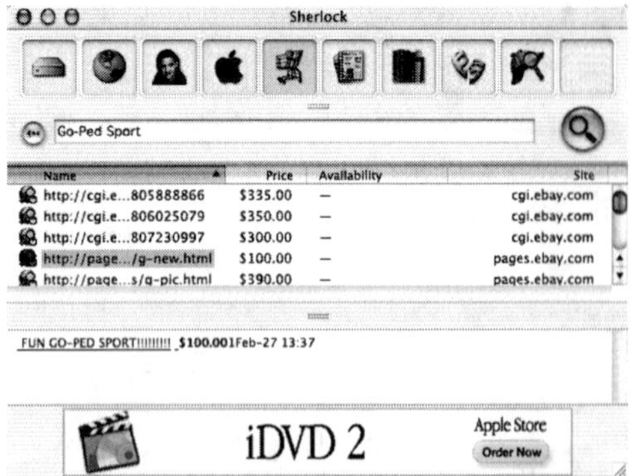

Figure 40 Select one of the matches to get more information about it, along with a clickable link to the Web site where it's available for sale.

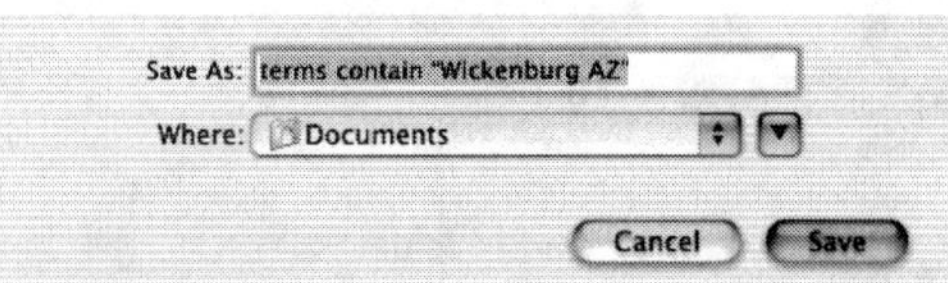

Figure 41 Use a standard Save Location dialog to save search criteria as a file on disk.

Figure 42 A Sherlock search file's icon looks like this.

Figure 43 You can open a search file from within Sherlock, using a standard Open dialog.

Saving Searches

Sherlock enables you to save search files with the details of frequently used searches. This makes it possible to repeat a search by simply opening a Sherlock search file icon.

To save a search

1. Use Sherlock as described throughout this chapter to set up search criteria and perform a search.
2. Choose File > Save Search Criteria (**Figure 28**), or press ⌘S.
3. Use the Save Location dialog sheet that appears (**Figure 41**) to select a disk location and enter a name for the search file.
4. Click Save. The search criteria is saved as a file on disk.

To use a saved search

Double-click the icon for a saved search file (**Figure 42**).

or

1. Choose File > Open Search Criteria (**Figure 28**).
2. Use the Open dialog sheet that appears (**Figure 43**) to locate, select, and open the saved search criteria file.

Sherlock performs the search, displaying the results in its window.

Customizing Sherlock

There are a number of things you can do to customize the way Sherlock works for you. This section explores some of the most useful ones.

To add a folder to the Files channel

1. Click the Files channel button at the top of the Sherlock window (**Figure 5**) or press [⌘ F] to display Sherlock's Files channel (**Figure 1**).
2. Choose Find > Add Folder (**Figure 44**).
3. Use the Open dialog sheet that appears to select the folder you want to add (**Figure 45**).
4. Click Add. The folder is added to Sherlock's list of disks and folders (**Figure 46**), and if automatic indexing is enabled, Sherlock indexes the folder.

✔ Tips

- Adding folders to the Files channel makes it easy to search specific folders without searching an entire disk.
- Automatic indexing options are covered later in this chapter.

Figure 44 Use the Add Folder command to add a folder to the Files channel.

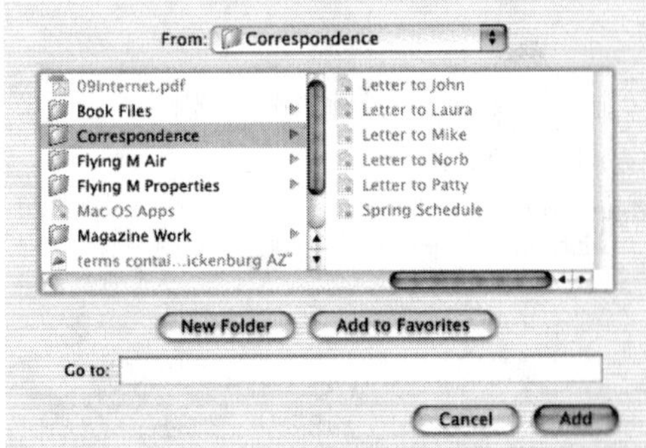

Figure 45 Choose the folder you want to add.

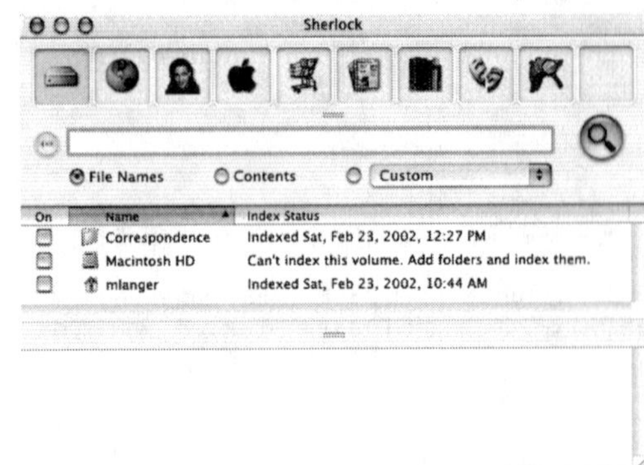

Figure 46 The added folder appears with the rest of the disks and folders in Sherlock's Files channel.

Automatically Indexing Volumes

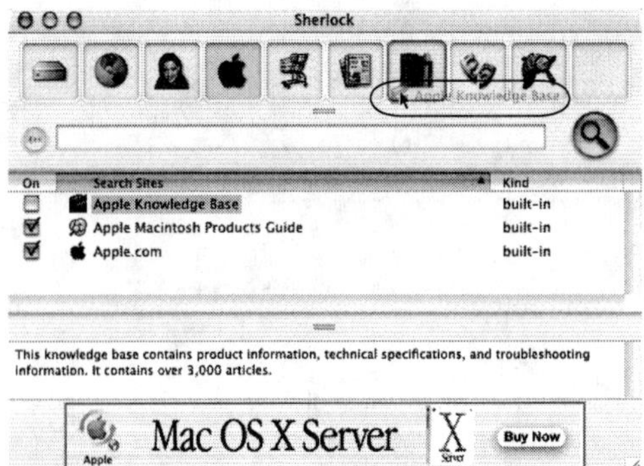

Figure 47 Drag a search site from the channel's window to a channel button.

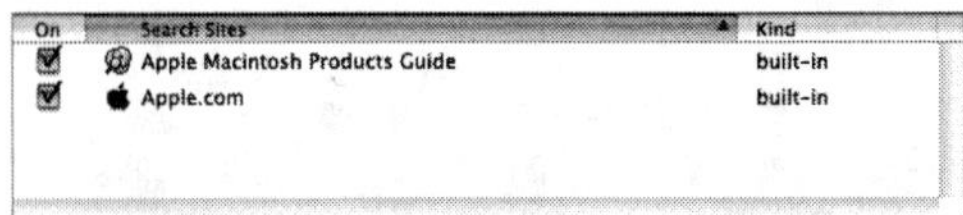

Figure 48 The search site moves from the source channel's list...

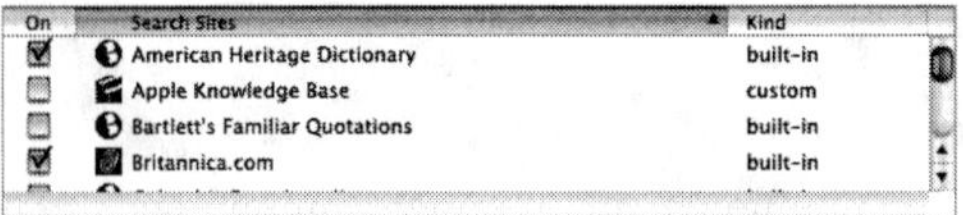

Figure 49 ...to the destination channel's list.

To move or copy Internet search sites from one channel to another

1. Display the channel containing the search site you want to move.
2. Drag the search site name from the list of search sites to the button for the channel you want to move it to (**Figure 47**).

   or

   Hold down Option while dragging the search site name from the list of search sites to the button for the channel you want to copy it to.
3. Release the mouse button. The search site moves (**Figures 48** and **49**) or is copied.

✔ Tips

- Search site files are also referred to as *Sherlock plug-ins.*
- Moving or copying search sites helps you organize them so they're easier to find and use.
- You can use these techniques to add search sites to a new channel. I explain how to create a new channel on the next page.
- Sherlock automatically downloads and installs new search sites when it connects to the Internet. Search sites are installed in the appropriate channel(s), but you can move or copy them as desired by following the above instructions.

To create a new channel

1. Choose Channel > New Channel (**Figure 6**) to display the New Channel dialog (**Figure 50**).
2. Enter a name for the channel in the Name the Channel box.
3. Choose an icon for the Channel by clicking the up or down arrow in the Icon area.
4. Choose the type of channel from the Channel type pop-up menu (**Figure 51**).
5. Click OK. The new, empty channel is added (**Figure 52**).
6. Follow the instructions in the section titled "To move or copy a search site from one channel to another" on the previous page to add search sites to the new channel.

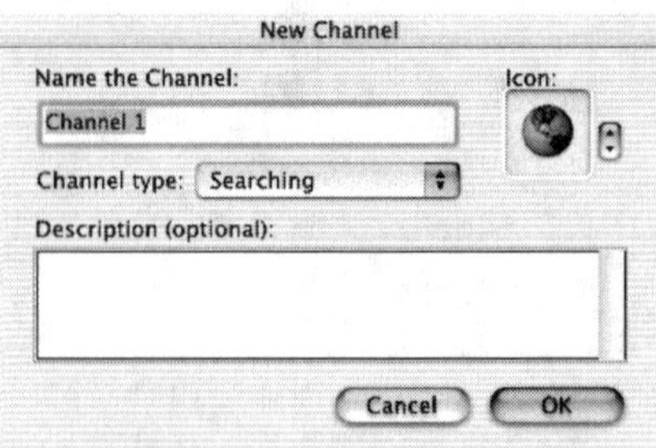

Figure 50 The New Channel dialog.

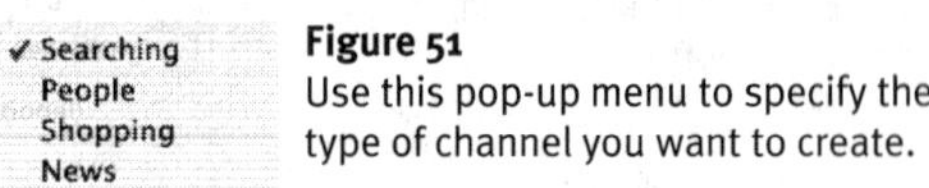

Figure 51
Use this pop-up menu to specify the type of channel you want to create.

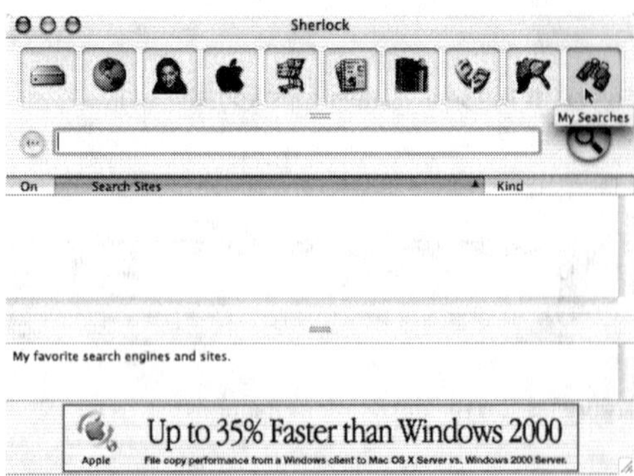

Figure 52 A new channel starts out empty.

✔ Tips

- You can create custom channels to organize your favorite search sites and make it easier to perform searches.
- The type of channel you choose in step 4 determines the channel's general interface and functionality.
- When you point to a channel, its name appears in a Help Tag beneath it (**Figure 52**).

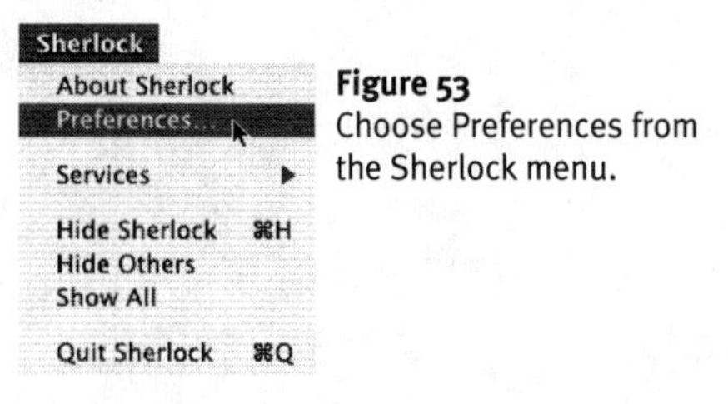

Figure 53 Choose Preferences from the Sherlock menu.

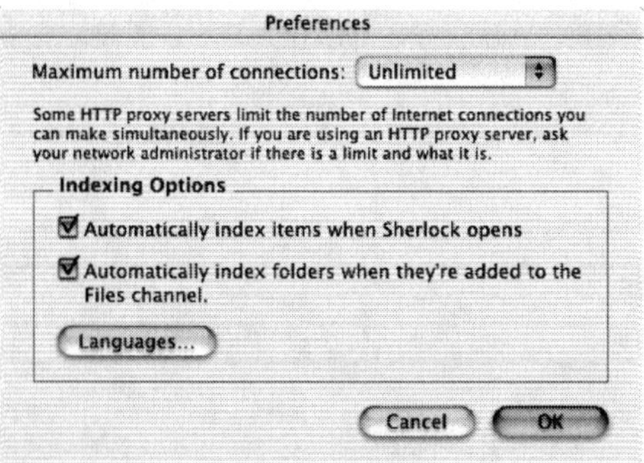

Figure 54 Use the Preferences dialog to set indexing options. These are the default settings.

To set automatic indexing options

1. Choose Sherlock > Preferences (**Figure 53**) to display the Preferences dialog (**Figure 54**).
2. Toggle check boxes to set the indexing options:
   - ▲ **Automatically index items when Sherlock opens** tells Sherlock to automatically index disks and folders when you launch it.
   - ▲ **Automatically index folders when they're added to the Files channel** tells Sherlock to automatically index a folder when you add it to the Files channel list of disks and folders.
3. Click OK.

✔ Tip

- You may want to turn automatic indexing off if the Files channel includes seldom-searched disks or folders with many files. Just remember to manually index items before you use the search by content feature to search them.

Using Mac OS i-Applications

11

Using Mac OS X i-Applications

Desperate for a short chapter title, I coined the term *i-Applications* to apply to a number of additional applications that are available to Mac OS X users:

- **iTunes** enables you to play CDs, record music from CD to your hard disk, burn music CDs, or download music to MP3 players.
- **iPhoto** enables you to store, organize, and share digital photos.
- **iMovie** enables you to create your own movies, complete with transitional effects, subtitles, and voiceovers, from digital video clips.
- **iDVD** enables you to take movies created with iMovie and burn DVDs.

This chapter covers the basics of each of these applications—just enough information to help you explore them on your own.

✔ Tip

- Peachpit Press offers a number of titles in its *Visual QuickStart Guide* and *Little Book* series that cover each of these programs. To get the most out of a specific application, I highly recommend that you obtain one of these books. You can learn more on the Peachpit Press Web site, `www.peachpit.com`.

Obtaining the Latest Versions

Some of the i-Apps—for example, iTunes and iMovie—are installed automatically as part of a Mac OS X installation. Others must be downloaded from the Apple Web site. Either way, it's a good idea to make sure you have the latest version.

✔ Tip

- You need an Internet connection to update or download the applications covered in this chapter.

To update using Software Update

1. Choose Apple > System Preferences (**Figure 1**) to display the System Preferences window.
2. Click the Software Update icon in the System row to display the Software Update pane (**Figure 2**).
3. Click Update Now. Software update connects to the Internet and checks for available updates.

   If Software Update finds updates, it displays them in a window like the one in **Figure** 3. Continue following instructions with step 4.

   or

   If Software Update does not find updates, it tells you. Choose System Prefs > Quit System Prefs or press ⌘Q to dismiss the Software Update pane. Skip the remaining steps below.
4. Turn on the check box beside each update you want to download.

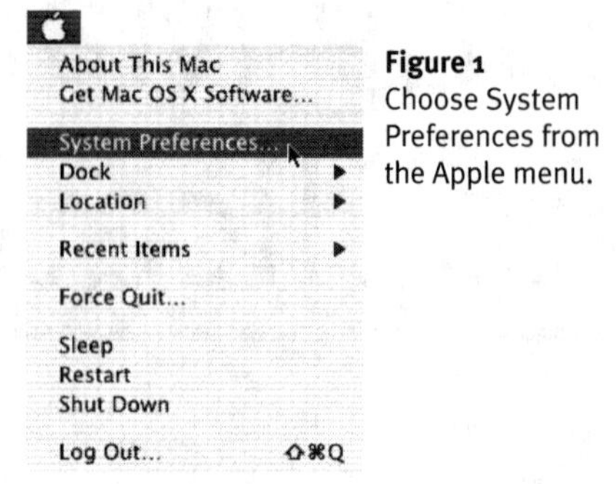

Figure 1 Choose System Preferences from the Apple menu.

Figure 2 The Software Update preferences pane.

Updating with Software Update

Figure 3 Software Update lists the updates available for your computer. In this example, it listed a bunch of language updates I don't need, but if an update was available for one of the i-Apps, it would be listed here.

5. Click Install. Software Updates downloads the updater files you selected and installs them.

6. If Software Update prompts you to restart your computer, do so.

   or

   Choose Software Update > Quit Software Update or press ⌘ Q to quit the Software Update application. Then choose System Prefs > Quit system Prefs or press ⌘ Q to quit System Preferences.

✔ Tips

- Software Update only updates Apple and related software that is already installed on your computer. For example, I have iDVD installed on my G4, but not on my iMac. Software Update offered to update iDVD on my G4 but never listed the update in the Software Update window on my iMac.
- As shown in **Figure 3**, Software Update may offer to download updates you don't need. You can safely quit Software Update without installing unnecessay updates.
- It's a good idea to run Software Update regularly and download updates to Mac OS X and its applications. I tell you more about Software Update in **Chapter 1** and in *Mac OS X Advanced: Visual QuickStart Guide*.

To download the latest version of other i-Apps

1. Launch Internet Explorer or your preferred Web browser software and use it to view one of the following URLs:
   - ▲ For iTunes, visit `www.apple.com/itunes/` (**Figure 4**).
   - ▲ For iPhoto, visit `www.apple.com/iphoto/`.
   - ▲ For iMovie, visit `www.apple.com/imovie/`.
   - ▲ For iDVD, visit `www.apple.com/idvd/` (**Figure 5**).
2. Follow the links on the page to download the latest version of the software you need. Follow any instructions that appear in the Web browser window. You may be prompted to enter information, including your name and e-mail address before you can download software.
3. When you are finished downloading software, choose Explorer > Quit Explorer or press [⌘ Q].

✔ Tips

- I explain how to use Internet Explorer in **Chapter 9**.
- After step 2, you can watch the progress of the download in the Download Manager window (**Figure 6**). In Internet Explorer, choose Window > Download Manager to view this window if it does not appear automatically.
- The Web site for a specific application can provide additional information about the program's use and hardware compatibility. It's a good idea to read the information on an application's Web site, especially if you have trouble using the application with your hardware.

Figures 4 & 5 Here's the home page for iTunes (above) and iDVD (below). Both offer links for downloading software.

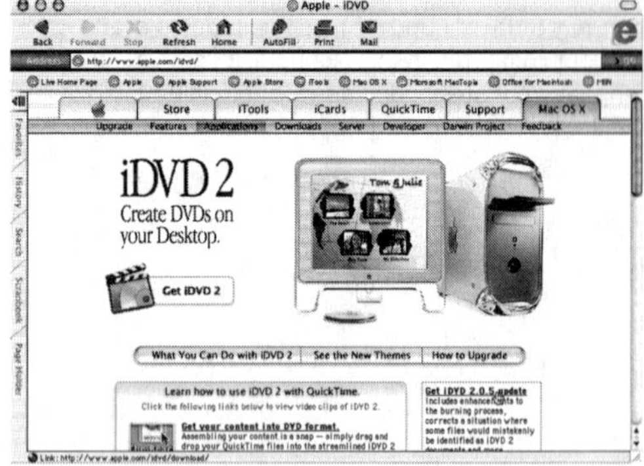

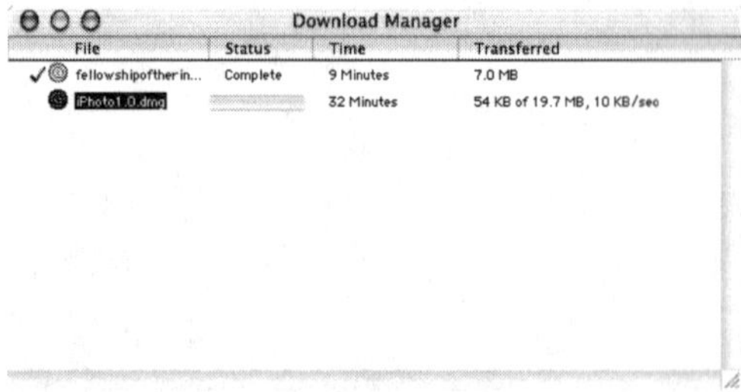

Figure 6 The Download Manager window displays the progress of downloads from Web sites.

Figures 7 & 8 A downloaded file can appear as a disk image file (left) which is mounted as a disk (right) when you double-click it.

iPhoto.mpkg

Figure 9 Your goal is to find the installer file, which may look like this.

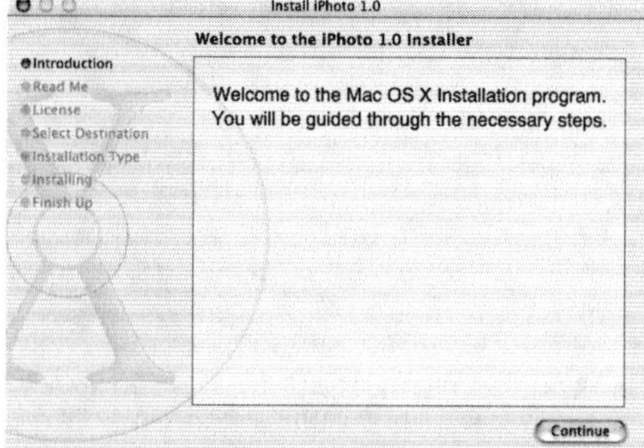

Figure 10 The main installer window guides you through the installation process.

To install downloaded software

1. Double-click the icon for the downloaded software. One of three things will happen:
   - ▲ If the icon is for an installer (**Figure 9**), the installer launches. Skip ahead to step 5.
   - ▲ If the icon is for a disk image file (**Figure 7**), Mac OS X launches Disk-Copy. Skip ahead to step 3.
   - ▲ If the icon is for a compressed file, Mac OS X launches StuffIt Expander to open the file. Continue following instructions with step 2.
2. StuffIt Expander decompresses the file and displays its icon with the downloaded file's icon. Double-click the icon. One of two things will happen.
   - ▲ If the icon is for an installer (**Figure 9**), the installer launches. Skip ahead to step 5.
   - ▲ If the icon is for a folder, the folder opens. Skip ahead to step 4.
   - ▲ If the icon is for a disk image file (**Figure 7**), Mac OS X launches Disk-Copy to mount the image as a file on disk. Continue following instructions with step 3.
3. DiskCopy mounts the image file as a disk. Its icon appears on the desktop (**Figure 8**). Double-click it to open it.
4. In the Finder window, locate the installer icon for the software. (You may have to open multiple folders to find it.) Double-click the installer icon (**Figure 9**) to launch it.
5. In the main installer window (**Figure 10**), read the instructions that appear onscreen and click the Continue button to step through the installation process.

Continued on next page...

Continued from previous page.

6. At the end of the installation process, the installer tells you it has finished. Click Close (**Figure 11**) to quit the installer or Restart (if displayed) to restart your computer.

✔ Tips

- By default, your Web browser should be configured to download software to the desktop. If you have changed this configuration to a different folder on disk, you must look for the downloaded files in that location. I explain how to change Web settings, including file download location, in **Chapter 9**.
- You may be prompted to agree to a license agreement somewhere in the installation process. If you do not click Agree, you cannot install the software.
- The main installer window may tell you that you need an Administrator password to install the software (**Figure 12**). Click the lock icon near the bottom of the window, and then enter an administrator Name and Password in the Authenticate dialog that appears (**Figure 13**). Click OK to continue the installation.
- The installer varies from one application to another, so its impossible to cover all variables here. The process, however, is relatively self-explanatory and easy to complete.
- You can delete the downloaded file after the application has been successfully installed.
- The instructions in this section apply to most Mac OS X software you download from the Web—not just Apple software.
- An application's installer normally installs Mac OS X software into the Applications folder on your hard disk.

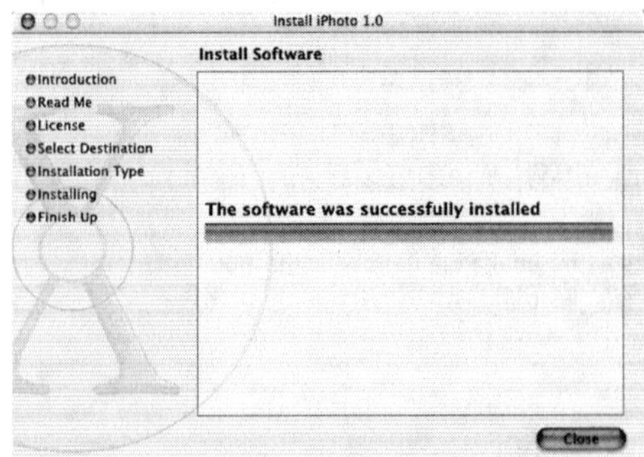

Figure 11 The Installer tells you when it's finished working.

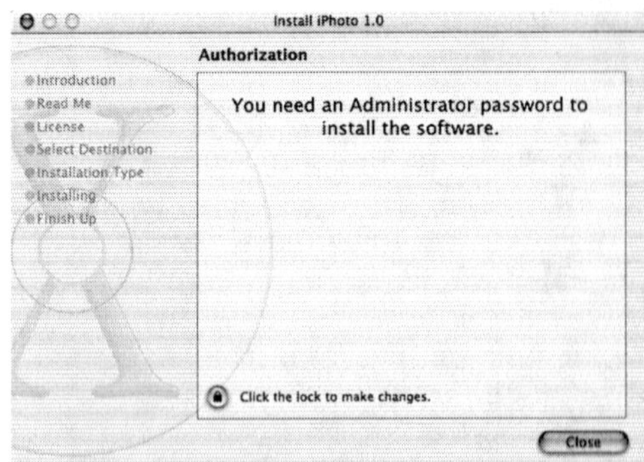

Figure 12 When you first launch the installer, it may tell you that you need an Adminstrator password to install the software.

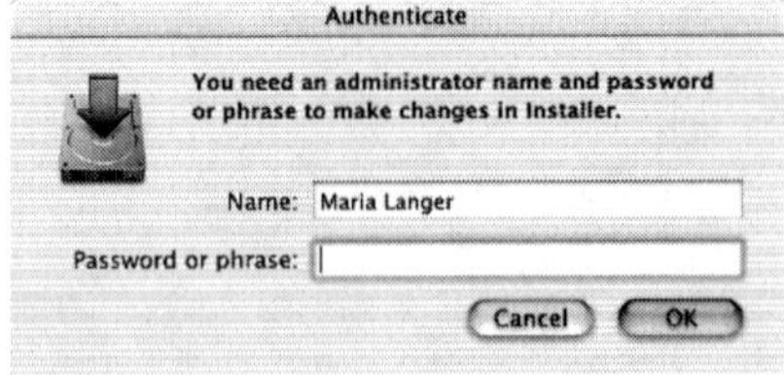

Figure 13 Enter an administrator Name and Password in this dialog.

Installing Downloaded Software

iTunes

Figure 14
The iTunes icon.

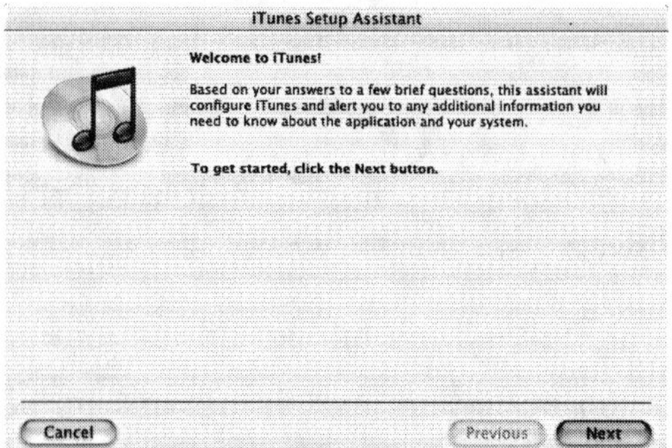

Figure 15 The first screen of the iTunes Setup Assistant.

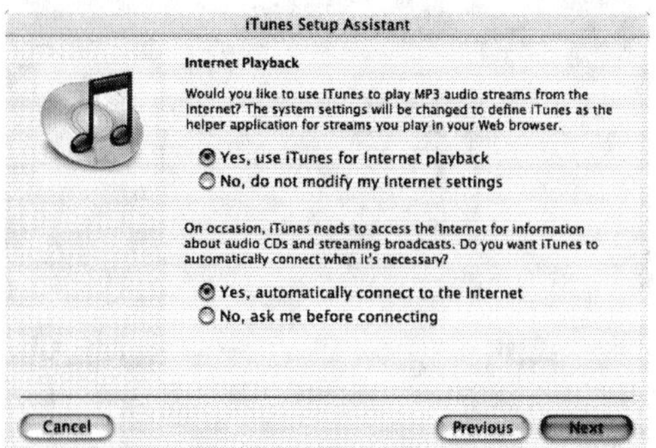

Figure 16 Set options for Internet playback in this screen.

iTunes

iTunes is a computer-based "jukebox" that enables you to do several things:

- Play MP3 format audio files.
- Record music from audio CDs on your Macintosh as MP3 files.
- Create custom CDs of your favorite music.
- Listen to Internet-based radio stations.

The next few pages explain how you can use iTunes to record and play MP3 music, copy MP3 files to an MP3 player, and burn audio CDs.

✔ Tips

- MP3 is a standard format for audio files.
- Your computer must have a CD-R drive or SuperDrive to burn CDs.

To set up iTunes

1. Double-click the iTunes icon (**Figure 14**).
2. If a license agreement window appears, click Agree.
3. The iTunes Setup Assistant window appears (**Figure 15**). Read the welcome message and click Next.
4. In the Internet Playback window (**Figure 16**), set options as desired:
   - Select an Internet playback option. **Yes, use iTunes for Internet playback** instructs your computer to change your Web browser helper settings to use iTunes for all MP3 audio playback. **No, do not modify my Internet settings** does not change your Web browser's helper settings.

Continued on next page...

Continued from previous page.

- ▲ Select an Internet connection option. **Yes, automatically connect to the Internet** tells iTunes that it's okay to connect to the Internet anytime it needs to. **No, ask me before connecting** tells iTunes to display a dialog that asks your permission before connecting to the Internet.

5. Click Next.
6. In the Find MP3 files window (**Figure 17**), select an option:
   - ▲ **Yes, find any MP3 files I have on my hard disk(s)** tells iTunes to search your hard disk for MP3 files and add them to you music library.
   - ▲ **No, I'll add them myself later** tells iTunes not to look for MP3 files.
7. Click Done.

   iTunes completes its configuration and displays the iTunes main window. If you instructed iTunes to find MP3 files and it found some, those files are displayed in the window (**Figure 18**).

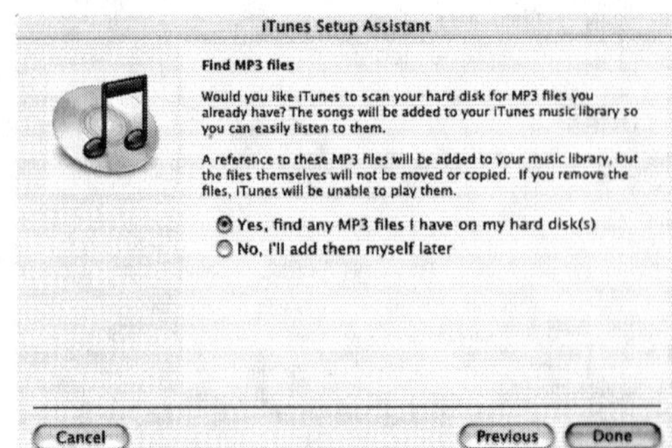

Figure 17 The Find MP3 files window.

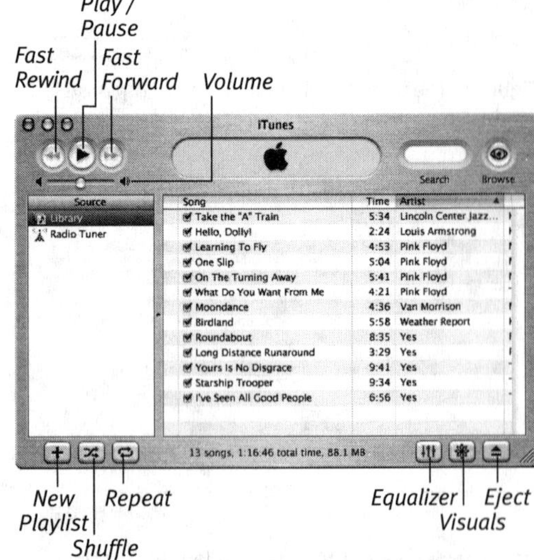

Figure 18 iTunes' main window. (This is the kind of music an oldtimer like me listens to.)

Figure 19 When you insert a CD, it appears in the Source list.

Figure 20 iTunes shows import progress at the top of its window.

File
New Playlist ⌘N
New Playlist From Selection ⇧⌘N
Add to Library...
Close Window ⌘W
Update iPod
Get Info ⌘I
Show Song File ⌘R
Shop for iTunes Products...

Figure 21 iTunes' File menu.

Figure 22 Use the Choose Object dialog to select songs on disk to add to iTunes' library.

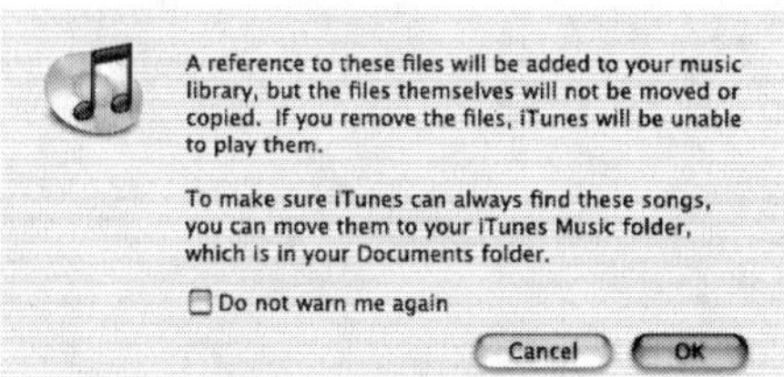

Figure 23 This dialog appears when you add a song.

To add songs from an audio CD to the Library

1. Insert an audio CD in your CD drive. After a moment, the CD's name appears in the Source list and a list of the tracks on it appears in the Song list (**Figure 19**).
2. Turn on the check box beside each song you want to add to the Library. (They should already all be turned on.)
3. Click the Import button. iTunes begins importing the first song. The status area provides progress information (**Figure 20**). The song may play while it is imported.

✔ Tips

- Sometime during step 1, iTunes may ask your permission to connect to the Internet. It must do this to retrieve information about the songs on the CD.
- You can specify whether a song plays while it is imported by setting iTunes preferences. Choose iTunes > Preferences to get started.
- When iTunes is finished importing songs, it plays a sound. In most cases, iTunes will finish importing songs from a CD before it finishes playing them.

To add songs on disk to the Library

1. Choose File > Add to Library (**Figure 21**).
2. Use the Choose Object dialog that appears (**Figure 22**) to locate and select the MP3 file you want to add.
3. Click Choose.
4. A dialog like the one in **Figure 23** appears. It explains that although a reference to the file will be added to your library, the file will not be copied. Click OK.

   The song is added to the Library list.

To play music from iTunes

1. Select the Library or playlist in the Source list that includes the song(s) you want to play.
2. If you want to play a specific song, select the song you want to play.
3. Click the Play button (**Figure 18**), choose Controls > Play (**Figure 24**), or press Spacebar. The songs in the playlist or the song you selected plays.

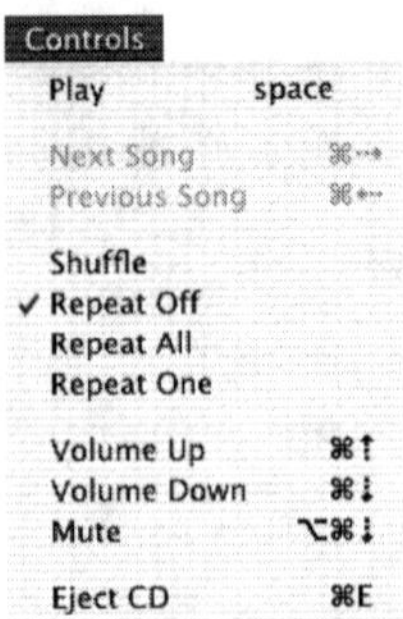

Figure 24
The Controls menu includes commands for controlling play, play order, and volume.

Tips

- In step 2, you can select multiple songs my holding down ⌘ while selecting each song. Then, when you start play, the songs you selected are played first.
- If you selected one or more specific songs, when the songs are finished playing, the next song in the list automatically begins playing.
- You can use the Shuffle and Repeat buttons or commands to play songs in random order or repeat songs.
- If you often play music from iTunes while you work (as I do), I highly recommend connecting stereo speakers to your Macintosh. The sound out of the built-in speakers of some Mac models (like my Strawberry iMac) can be worse than the sound out of an old AM radio with weak batteries.

To pause play

Click the Stop button, choose Controls > Pause, or press Spacebar.

Figure 25 Clicking the New Playlist button creates a new, untitled playlist.

Figure 26 To give the library a name, simply type it in and press Enter.

Figure 27 To add songs to a playlist, drag them from the song list to the playlist name.

To create a playlist

1. Click the New Playlist button (**Figure 18**), choose File > New Playlist (**Figure 21**), or press ⌘N.
2. A new untitled playlist appears in the Source list (**Figure 25**). Type a name for the list, and press Enter (**Figure 26**).

To add songs to a playlist

1. If necessary, select Library in the source window to display all MP3 files.
2. Drag a song you want to include in the new playlist from the Song list to the new playlist name in the Source list (**Figure 27**).
3. Repeat step 4 for each song you want to add to the playlist.
4. When you're finished adding songs, click the playlist name. The songs appear in the list. You can play them by following the above instructions.

✔ Tips

- In step 2, you can select and drag multiple songs. Hold down ⌘ while selecting songs to select more than one, then drag any one of them.
- You can change the order of songs in a playlist by dragging them up or down.
- You can sort songs in a playlist by clicking a column heading. Clicking once sorts in ascending order; clicking twice sorts in descending order.

To remove a song from a playlist

1. Select the song you want to remove.
2. Press Delete. The song is removed from the playlist.

To copy songs to an MP3 player

1. Using the USB or Firewire cable that came with your MP3 player, connect the player to your Macintosh and turn it on.
2. If iTunes is not already running, launch it.

   After a moment, the MP3 player should appear in the Source list (**Figure 28**).
3. Drag the song(s) you want to copy to the MP3 player from the song list to the MP3 player in the Source list (**Figure 29**). The status area indicates that the song is being copied (**Figure 30**).
4. Repeat step 3 for each song you want to copy.
5. When you are finished copying songs, you can disconnect your MP3 player and use it to play the songs you copied.

✔ Tips

- If iTunes was already running when you connected your MP3 player and it did not list the MP3 player in the Source list, quit iTunes and relaunch it. If it still doesn't appear, your MP3 player may not be compatible with iTunes. Check the iTunes Web site for assistance: `www.apple.com/itunes/`.
- In step 3, you can select and drag multiple songs. Hold down ⌘ while selecting songs to select more than one, then drag any one of them.
- The number of songs you can copy to an MP3 player is limited by the amount of memory in the player and the size of the songs.

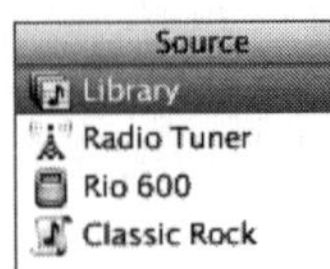

Figure 28
Your MP3 player should appear in the Source list, like my Rio 600 does.

Figure 29 Drag the song from the song list to the MP3 player.

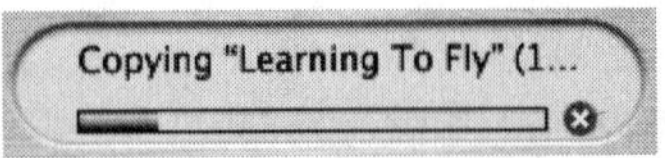

Figure 30 The status area confirms that the song is being copied.

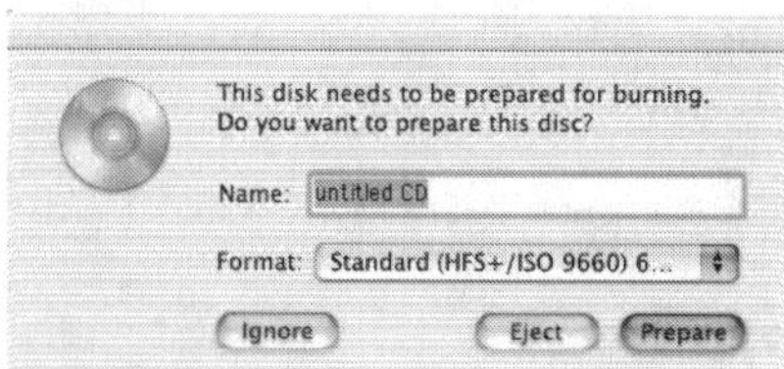

Figure 31 When you insert a blank CD, Mac OS X wants to prepare it for use.

Figure 32 Be sure to choose iTunes (Audio) from the Format pop-up menu.

Figure 33 Select the Playlist you want to burn to CD and click the Burn CD button.

Figure 34 iTunes prompts you to click the Burn CD button again.

Figure 35 Burning progress appears at the top of the iTunes window.

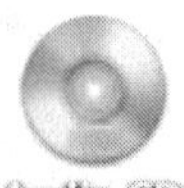

Figure 36 When the CD is finished, its icon appears on the desktop.

To burn an audio CD

1. Create a playlist that contains the songs you want to include on the CD.
2. Insert a blank CD in your computer's CD-R drive or SuperDrive. A dialog like the one in **Figure 31** appears.
3. Enter a name for the CD in the Name box.
4. Choose iTunes (Audio) from the Format pop-up menu (**Figure 32**).
5. Click Prepare.
6. iTunes' main window appears (**Figure 33**). Select the playlist that you want to burn to CD and click the Burn CD button.
7. The Burn CD button changes to a black and yellow symbol and the status area tells you to click the Burn CD button (**Figure 34**). Click it again.
8. Wait while iTunes prepares and burns the CD. This could take a while; the progess appears in the status window at the top of the iTunes window (**Figure 35**).You can switch to and work with other applications while you wait.
9. When iTunes is finished burning the CD, it makes a sound. The icon for the CD appears on your desktop (**Figure 36**).

✓ Tips

- Your computer must have a compatible CD-R drive or SuperDrive to burn audio CDs. You can find a list of compatible devices on the iTunes Web site, `www.apple.com/itunes/`.
- I explain how to create a playlist earlier in this section.
- Do not cancel the disc burning process after it has begun. Doing so can render the CD unusable.

iPhoto

iPhoto is a computer-based photo storage system that enables you to do several things:

- Import photos from a digital camera or disk.
- Organize photos by name, keywords, and other criteria.
- Edit photos to crop them and remove red-eye.
- Create a book full of photos.
- Share photos with others by printing, exporting, or building Web pages.

The next few pages explain the basics of iPhoto to import, organize, and share photos.

Figure 37 The iPhoto icon.

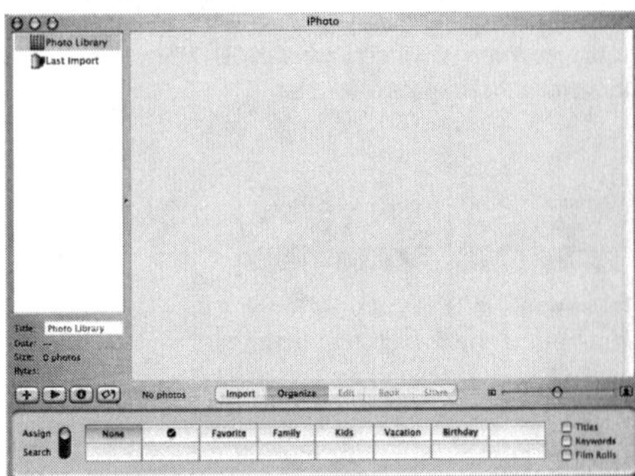

Figure 38 iPhoto's main window.

✔ Tips

- To import photos from a digital camera, you must have a digital camera that is compatible with iPhoto.
- You can also use Image Capture to import photos from a digital camera. I tell you about Image Capture in **Chapter 6**.
- iPhoto can only import still pictures. To import video (AVI) pictures from a digital camera, use Image Capture, which is covered in **Chapter 6**. To import movies from a digital video camera, use iMovie, which is covered later in this chapter.
- As this book went to press, iPhoto was not included in a standard mac OS X 10.1 installation. If iPhoto is not in your Applications folder, you can download it from Apple's Web site at `www.apple.com/iphoto/`. I explain how earlier in this chapter.

To launch iPhoto

Open the iPhoto icon (**Figure 37**) in your Applications folder. iPhoto's main window appears (**Figure 38**).

To set iPhoto to automatically launch when you connect a digital camera

The first time you launch iPhoto, a dialog like the one in **Figure 39** appears. Click Yes.

or

1. Open the Image Capture icon in the Applications folder (**Figure 40**) to display the Image Capture window (**Figure 41**).
2. Choose iPhoto from the Hot Plug Action pop-up menu (**Figure 42**).

   or

   Choose Other from the Hot Plug Action pop-up menu (**Figure 42**). Then use the dialog sheet that appears (**Figure 43**) to locate and select iPhoto. Click OK.
3. Choose Image Capture > Quit Image capture or press ⌘Q to quit Image Capture.

✔ Tips

- Wondering why you have to change a setting in Image Capture to get iPhoto to launch automatically? It's because Image Capture normally launches automatically when you attach a digital camera. Changing the setting in Image Capture tells Mac OS X to use iPhoto instead.
- To prevent iPhoto from launching when you attach a digital camera, follow the numbered steps above, but choose an application other than iPhoto from the Hot Plug Action pop-up menu (**Figure 42**).

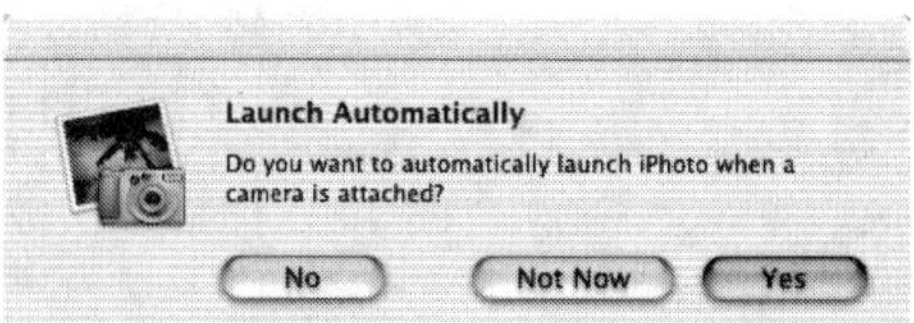

Figure 39 The first time you open iPhoto, it asks if you want to automatically launch it when you connect a camera.

Figure 40 The Image Capture icon.

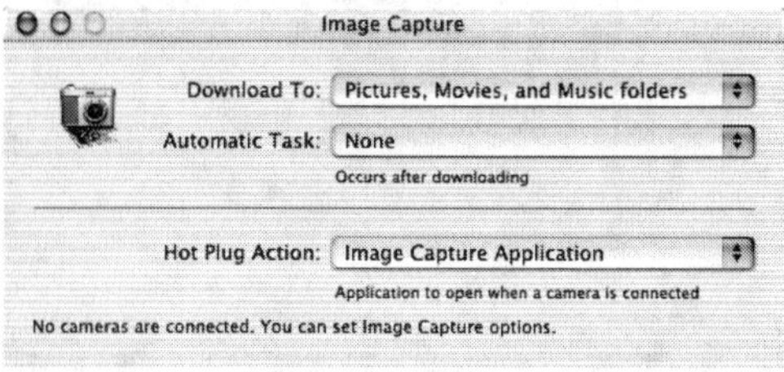

Figure 41 Image Capture's main window.

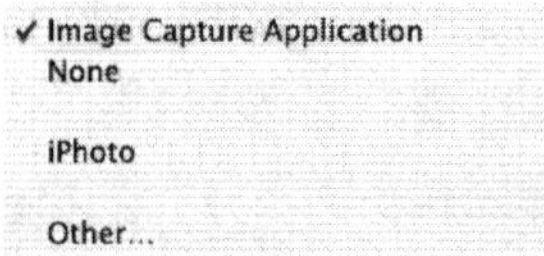

Figure 42 The Hot Plug Action pop-up menu.

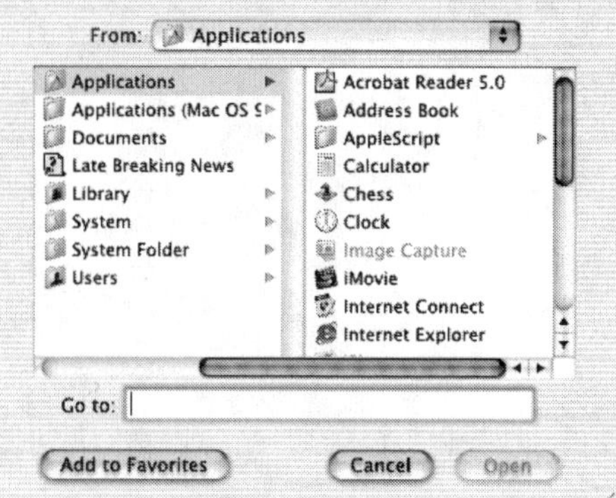

Figure 43 Use this dialog to locate, select, and open iPhoto.

To import photos from a camera

1. Using the USB or Firewire cable that came with your digital camera, connect the camera to your Macintosh and turn on the camera.
2. If iPhoto does not automatically launch, open it as discussed on the previous page. Make sure the Import button near the bottom of the window is selected.
3. iPhoto "sees" your camera and displays information about it in the lower-left corner of the window (**Figure 44**). Click the Import button at the lower-right corner of the window.

   iPhoto imports the photos. Its progress appears in the bottom of the window (**Figure 45**). When it's finished, thumbnails of the images appear in the iPhoto window (**Figure 46**).

✔ Tips

- If iPhoto does not "see" your camera, it may not be compatible with iPhoto. Check Apple's iPhoto Web site for more information, `www.apple.com/iphoto/`.
- To have iPhoto automatically erase all photos it downloads, turn on the Erase Contents after transfer check box.
- When the import is complete, you can disconnect and turn off your camera.
- iPhoto also recognizes photo CDs, including Kodak PictureCD discs. If set to automatically launch when a camera is attached, it will also automatically launch when you insert a photo CD. Follow step 3 above to import the images.

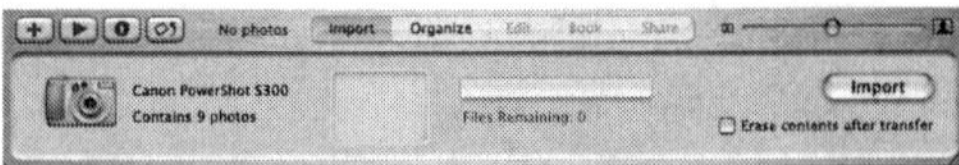

Figure 44 iPhoto "sees" your camera and tells you how many pictures are on it.

Figure 45 iPhoto reports its progress at the bottom of the window. (Thank heaven this is just a thumbnail image.)

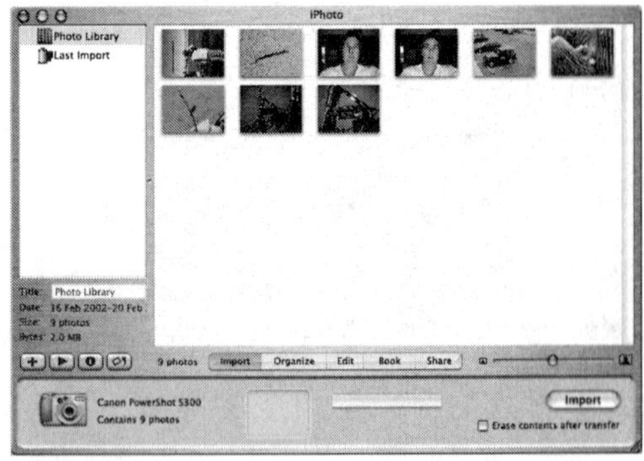

Figure 46 iPhoto displays thumbnail images of the photos it has imported.

Importing Photos from a Camera

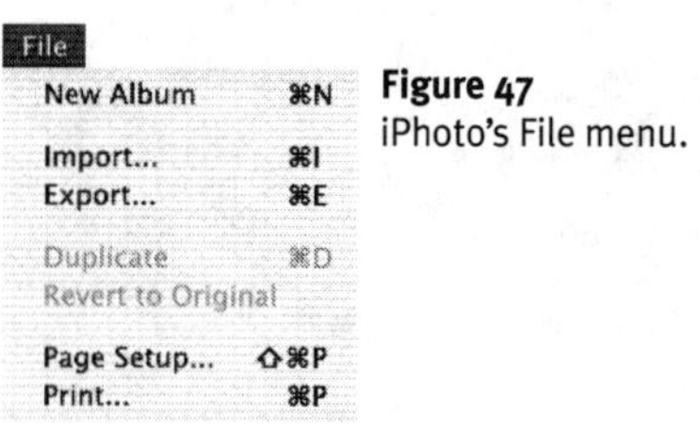

Figure 47 iPhoto's File menu.

Figure 48 The Import Photos dialog.

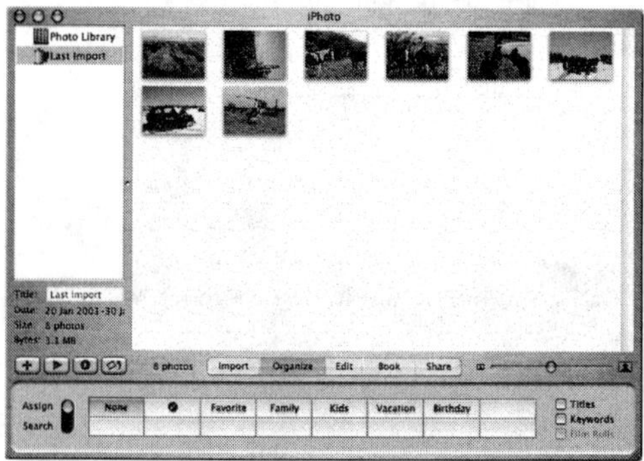

Figure 49 The most recently imported photos appear in the window as thumbnails when you select Last Import in the album list.

To import images from disk

1. Choose File > Import (**Figure 47**).
2. Use the Import Photos dialog that appears (**Figure 48**) to locate the photo(s) you want to import.
3. To import only one photo, select the name of the photo and click Open.

   or

   To import multiple photos, hold down [⌘] while selecting the name of each photo you want to import. Then click Open.

   or

   To import all photos in a folder, select the name of the folder and click Open.

   iPhoto imports the photo(s). It displays its progress in the bottom of its window. When it's finished, the photos appear in the main window.

✔ Tip

- You may find this technique useful to add scanned photos and images to iPhoto.

To review the most recently imported files

Click Last Import in the album list. The most recently imported images appear as thumbnails in the main window (**Figure 49**).

Importing Images from Disk

To create an album

1. Click the New Album button at the bottom of the album list (**Figure 50**).

   or

   Choose File > New Album (**Figure 47**), or press ⌘N.
2. Enter a name for the album in the New Album dialog (**Figure 51**).
3. ClickOK.

   The album appears in the album list (**Figure 52**).

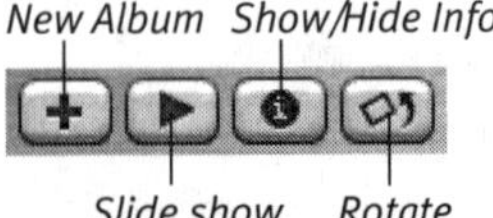

Figure 50 Buttons at the bottom of the album list.

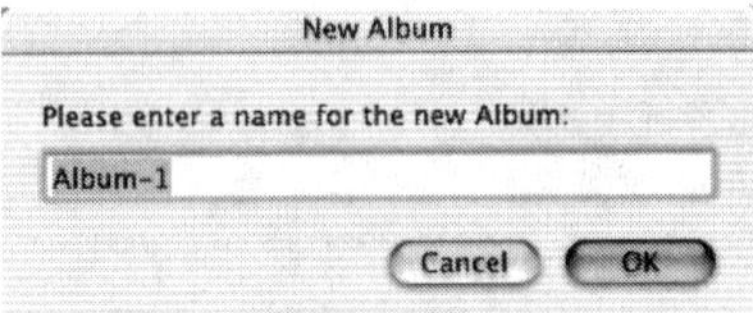

Figure 51 The New Album dialog.

To add photos to an album

1. In the album list, select Photo Library or the name of the album containing the photos you want to add.
2. Drag the thumbnail image from the main window to the name of the photo album you want to add the image to (**Figure 53**). When you release the mouse button, the image is added to the album.

Figure 52 The new album is added to the album list.

Figure 53 Drag a thumbnail image to the photo album.

✔ Tip

- You can select and drag multiple images at once. Hold down ⌘ while selecting each image, then drag any one image to the album name. All selected images are added to the album.

To remove photos from an album

1. Select the thumbnail for the image you want to remove.
2. Press Delete. The photo disappears.

✔ Tip

- If you try to remove a photo from the Photo Library or Last Import album, a dialog like the one in **Figure 54** appears. Clicking OK deletes the photo from iPhoto and your hard drive.

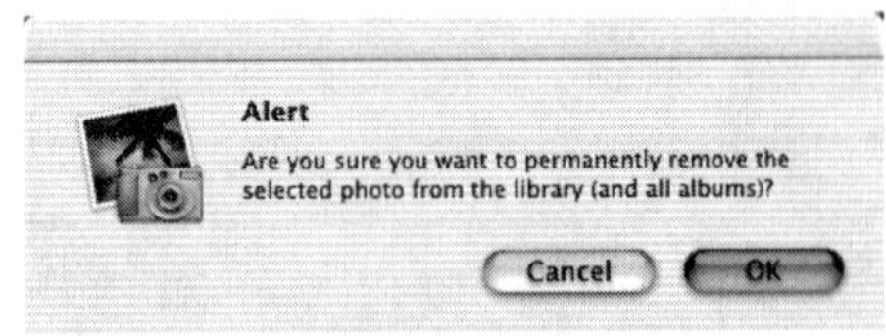

Figure 54 Clicking OK in this dialog removes the photo from your computer.

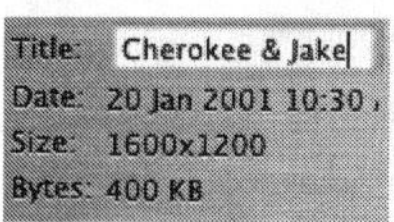

Figure 55 Enter a title for the photo in the Title box.

Figure 56 Click as many keywords as you like to assign them to the selected photo.

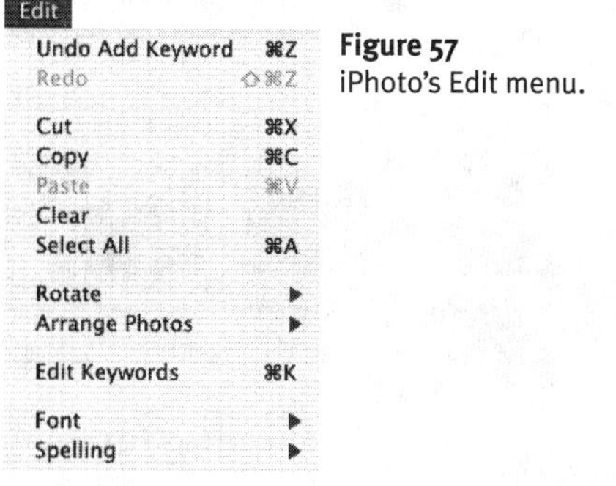

Figure 57 iPhoto's Edit menu.

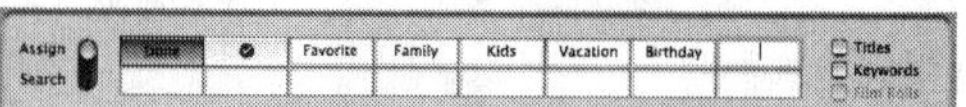

Figure 58 You can edit keywords by making changes to the keywords at the bottom of the window.

To enter a title for a photo

1. If necessary, click the Organize button near the bottom of the iPhoto window.
2. Select the album containing the photo you want to enter a title for.
3. Select the thumbnail for the photo.
4. Enter a title for the photo in the Title box beneath the album list (**Figure 55**) and press [Enter].

✔ Tips

- If the Title box does not appear beneath the album list, click the Show/Hide Info button (**Figure 50**) until it does.
- If desired, you can give two or more photos in the same album the same title.

To assign keywords to a photo

1. If necessary, click the Organize button near the bottom of the iPhoto window.
2. Make sure the Assign/Search button in the bottom left corner is set to Assign.
3. Select the album containing the photo you want to assign keywords to.
4. Select the thumbnail for the photo.
5. Click the keywords you want to assign to the photo (**Figure 56**). You can assign as many as you like.

✔ Tips

- To edit keywords, choose Edit > Edit Keywords (**Figure 57**) or press [⌘][K], and make changes in the keyword boxes at the bottom of the window (**Figure 58**). When you are finished, choose Edit > Done Editing Keywords or or press [⌘][K].
- To remove keywords from a photo, follow the above steps, but in step 5, click the None keyword.

To change the size of thumbnail images

Move the size slider to the left or right:

- Move the slider to the left to make the thumbnails smaller.
- Move the slider to the right to make the thumbnails larger (**Figure 59**).

✔ Tip

- Changes to the thumbnail size affect all albums, not just the one that is selected when you make the change.

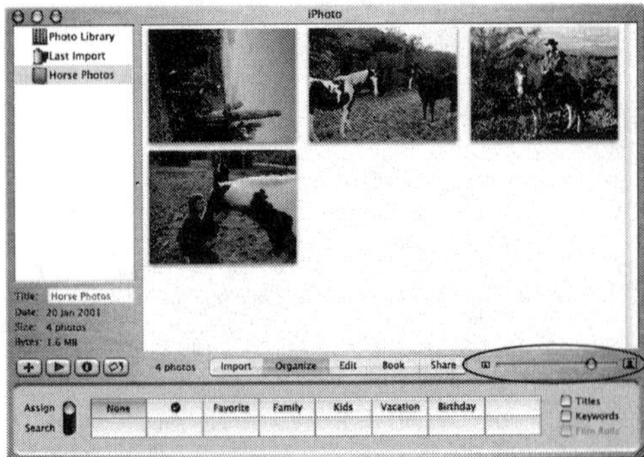

Figure 59 Drag the size slider to the right to make the thumbnails larger.

To show titles or keywords with thumbnails

To display photo titles beneath thumbnails (**Figure 60**), turn on the Titles check box in the bottom right corner of the window.

or

To display photo keywords to the right of thumbnails (**Figure 60**), turn on the Keywords check box in the bottom right corner of the window.

✔ Tips

- As shown in **Figure 60**, you can display titles and keywords for photos.
- Changes to the Titles and Keywords check boxes affect all albums, not just the one that is selected when you make the change.

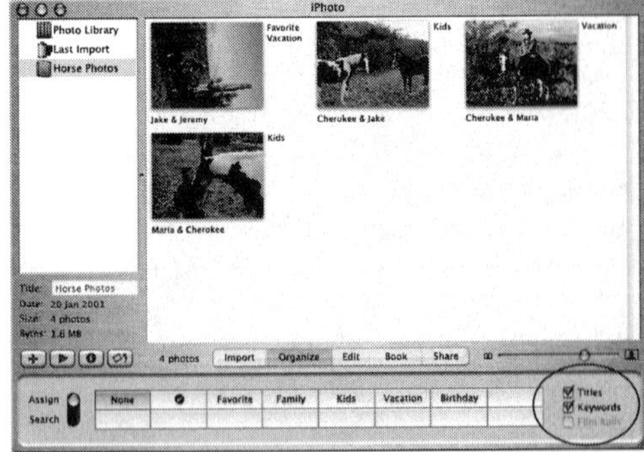

Figure 60 You can display photo titles and keywords for each thumbnail image. (And yes, my horses *are* my kids.)

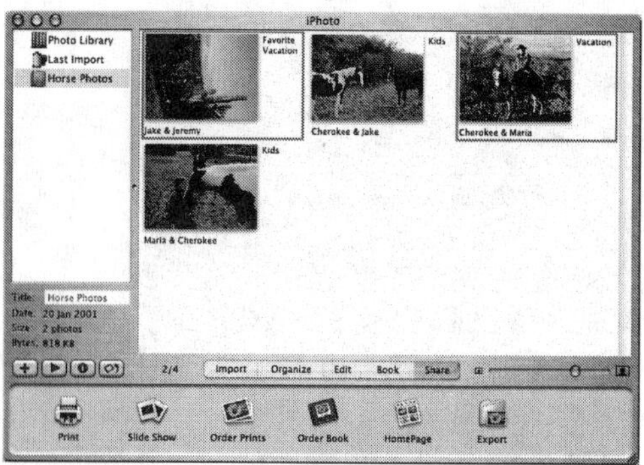

Figure 61 Select the photos you want to print.

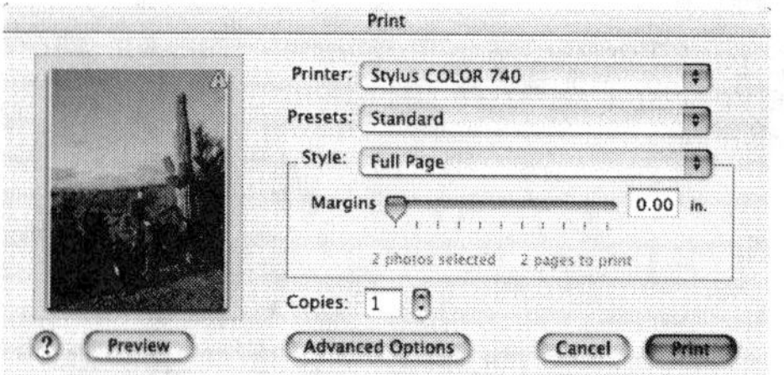

Figure 62 The Print dialog with the default Style option—Full Page—chosen.

Contact Sheet
✓ Full Page
Greeting Card
Standard Prints

Figure 63 The Style pop-up menu.

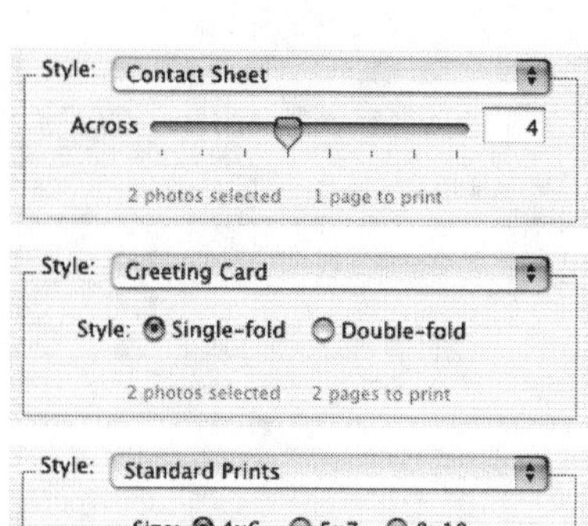

Figures 64, 65, & 66 The Print dialog offers different options for the Contact Sheet (top), Greeting Card (middle), and Standard Prints (bottom) styles.

To print photos

1. If necessary, click the Share button near the bottom of the iPhoto window.
2. Select the photos you want to print. To select more than one photo (**Figure 61**), hold down [⌘] while clicking each photo.
3. Click the Print button, choose File > Print (**Figure 47**), or press [⌘][P] to display the Print dialog (**Figure 62**).
4. Choose the printer you want to use from the Printer pop-up menu.
5. Choose a style from the Style pop-up menu (**Figure 63**):
   - ▲ **Contact Sheet** prints multiple photos on each page. With this option chosen, the slider changes the number of photos across each page, thus changing the size of each photo (**Figure 64**).
   - ▲ **Full Page** prints one photo on each page. With this option chosen, the slider adjusts the size of the page's margins (**Figure 62**).
   - ▲ **Greeting Card** prints one photo on each page. With this option chosen, you can use radio buttons to specify whether you want a single-fold or double-fold card (**Figure 65**).
   - ▲ **Standard Prints** prints one photo on each page. With this option chosen, you can specify whether you want 4x6, 5x7, or 8x10 prints (**Figure 66**).
6. Click Print. The photos are printed to your specifications.

✔ Tips

- The Preview area of the Print dialog changes when you change Style settings.
- I tell you more about printing in **Chapter 8**.

To display a slide show

1. If necessary, click the Share button near the bottom of the iPhoto window.
2. Select the photos you want to include in the slide show. To select more than one photo, hold down [⌘] while clicking each photo.
3. Click the Slide Show button to display the Slide Show Settings dialog (**Figure 67**).
4. Enter a value in the Play each slide for box to determine how long each slide should appear onscreen.
5. Toggle the Repeat slide show check box to indicate whether the slide show should repeat after all photos have been displayed once.
6. Choose an option from the Music pop-up menu (**Figure 68**). None puts the slide show in silent mode.
7. Click OK.

   If you selected music for the slide show, the music begins. The first photo fades in, remains on screen, then fades out to be replaced with the next photo.
8. To end the slide show, press [Esc].

✔ Tips

- You can display a slide show quickly using the default settings by clicking the Slide Show button at the bottom of the album list (**Figure 50**).
- If any of your photos have vertical orientation (like the first one in **Figure 61**) use the Rotate button at the bottom of the album list (**Figure 50**) to correct its orientation before including it in a slide show. (Unless, of course, you prefer to tilt your head when that photo appears.)

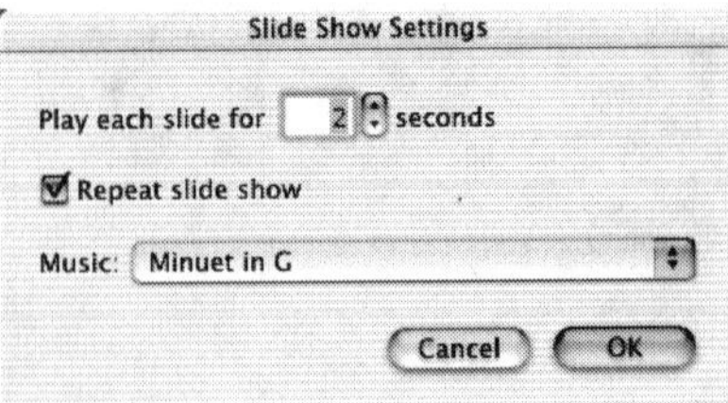

Figure 67 The Slide Show Settings dialog.

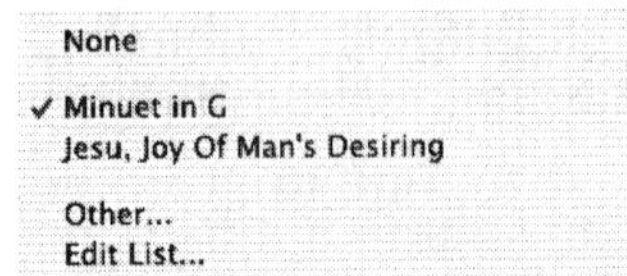

Figure 68 The Music pop-up menu enables you to select a tune or omit music.

Displaying a Slide Show

iMovie

iMovie is a like a director's editing studio right inside your Mac. It can do several things:

- Import movie clips from a digital video camera into your computer.
- Edit clips for length and content.
- Add titles, special transitional effects, music, and voiceovers.
- Combine the clips to make a movie.
- Export the completed movie to a file on disk or to a video camera.

The next few pages provide some basic information about using iMovie to import, edit, and combine movie clips, as well as how to save a finished movie as a QuickTime movie.

✔ Tip

- To import movie clips from a digital video camera, you must have a video camera that can be connected to your computer via Firewire cable and is compatible with iMovie. You can learn more about camera compatibility at Apple's iMovie Web site, `www.apple.com/imovie/`.

To launch iMovie

Figure 69 The iMovie application icon.

1. Open the iMovie icon (**Figure 69**) in your Applications folder.

   If you have already used iMovie to work with movie clips, it opens and displays its windows for the last movie you worked on. Skip the remaining steps.

2. If this is the first time you're running iMovie, an intro window like the one in **Figure 70** appears. Click New Project.

3. Use the Create New Project window that appears (**Figure 71**) to enter a name and select a location for your movie files. Then click Create.

   iMovie's empty windows appear (**Figure 72**).

✔ Tips

- iMovie documents are called *movie projects*. A movie project contains all the information necessary to create your movie.
- When you create a movie project, iMovie creates a folder that contains all of the movie clips and other files for that project.
- If you have already created a movie project and want to start a new one, choose File > New Project (**Figure 73**), or press [⌘N]. Then follow step 3 above to name and save your new project.
- To work with an existing movie project, either click Open Project in the intro window (**Figure 70**) or choose File > Open Project (**Figure 73**). Then use the dialog that appears to locate and open your movie project file.

Figure 70 This iMovie introduction screen appears when you first launch iMovie.

Figure 71 Use this dialog to enter a name and select a disk location for your movie project.

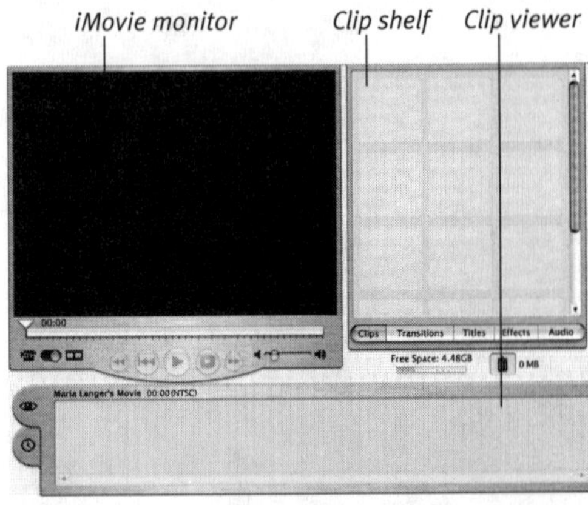

Figure 72 iMovie's interface includes three main windows.

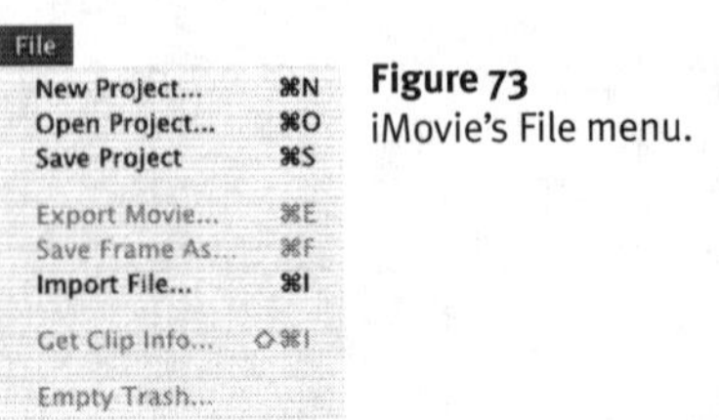

Figure 73 iMovie's File menu.

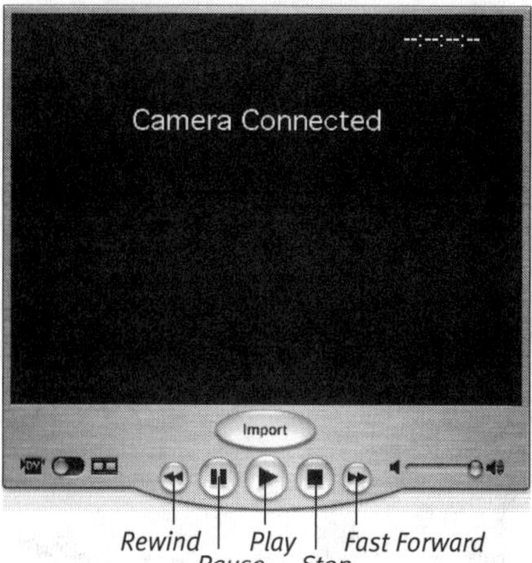

Figure 74 When iMovie "sees" your digital video camera, it tells you.

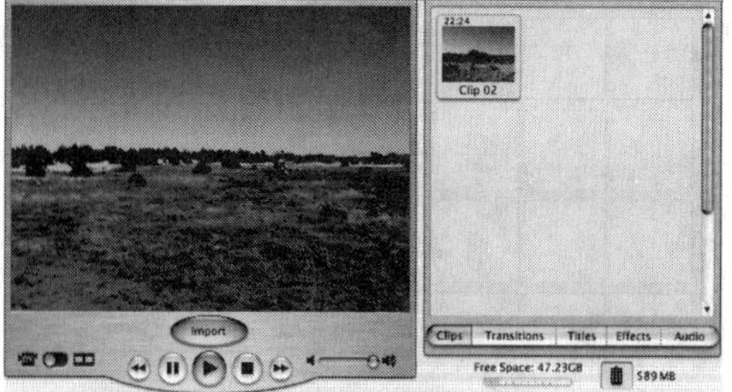

Figure 75 iMovie begins importing clips.

Figure 76 Each clip appears in the clip

To import movie clips

1. Using a Firewire cable, connect your digital video camera to your Macintosh and turn the camera on. If necessary, set the camera to its VCR or Play mode and rewind to the beginning of the first clip you want to import.
2. If you haven't already done so, launch iMovie.
3. Click the DV button at the bottom of the iMovie monitor. The iMovie monitor turns blue and the words *Camera Connected* appear (**Figure 74**).
4. Click the Import button. iMovie starts the camera and begins importing movie clips. The video for each clip appears in the iMovie monitor while each clip appears in the clip shelf (**Figures 75** and **76**).
5. When you're finished importing clips, click the Stop button at the bottom of the iMovie monitor window. The camera stops.

✔ Tips

- If iMovie does not "see" your camera (**Figure 74**), it may not be compatible. You can learn more at `www.apple.com/imovie/`.
- iMovie can separate clips based on when the camera was stopped or paused during recording. It calculates the total time for each clip and displays it with the clip in the clip shelf (**Figure 76**).
- The free space indicator beneath the clip shelf shows how the video import consumes your hard disk space (**Figures 75** and **76**).
- When you're finished importing clips, you can disconnect and turn off your camera.

To review & edit movie clips

1. In the clip shelf, click to select the clip you want to review and edit. the first frame of the clip appears in the iMovie monitor (**Figure 77**).
2. To play the clip, click the Play button at the bottom of the iMovie monitor (**Figure 78**). As the movie plays, the playhead triangle moves along the blue scrubber bar to track the play progress. You can also manually drag the playhead to view a specific frame.
3. To select a portion of the movie, drag the playhead to the beginning of the portion you want to select, hold down s, and drag the playhead to the end of the portion you want to select. The scrubber bar turns yellow between beginning and ending points (**Figure 79**).
4. Edit the clip using commands on the Edit menu (**Figure 80**):
   - ▲ To cut or copy a clip selection, choose Edit > Cut (⌘X) or Edit > Copy (⌘C).
   - ▲ To paste a clip selection from the clipboard into the clip at the playhead point, choose Edit > Paste (⌘V).
   - ▲ To remove all of the clip except the selection, choose Edit > Crop (⌘K).
   - ▲ To cut the clip into two separate clips split at the playhead, choose Edit > Split Video Clip at Playhead (⌘T).
   - ▲ To create a still video clip of the image in the iMovie monitor, choose Edit > Create Still Clip (Shift⌘S).

✔ Tip

- You can use other controls at the bottom of the iMovie monitor (**Figure 78**) to control movie play. Experiment with them on your own.

Figure 77 Select the clip you want to edit. (This is John.)

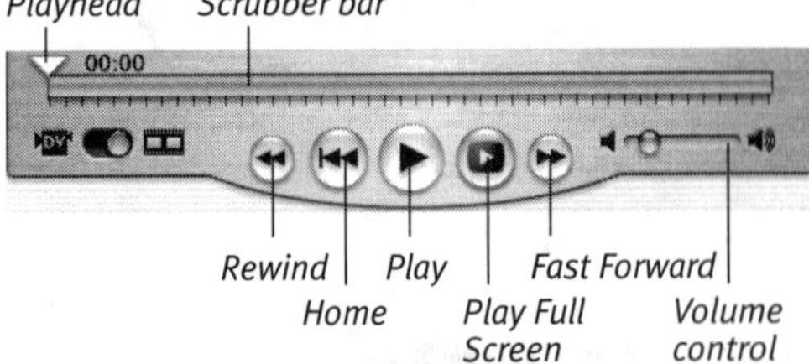

Figure 78 The controls at the bottom of the iMovie monitor when a clip is selected for playing or editing.

Figure 79 The scrubber bar turns yellow to indicate the portion of the clip that is selected.

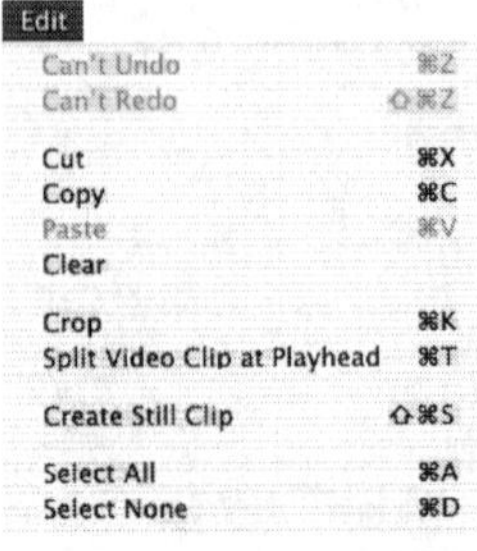

Figure 80 iMovie's Edit menu when a portion of a clip is selected.

Figure 81 Drag a clip from the clip shelf to the clip viewer.

Figure 82 The clip is moved from the clip shelf to the clip viewer.

Figure 83 Multiple clips in the clip viewer.

To delete a clip

1. In the clip shelf, click to select the clip you want to delete.
2. Press Delete. The clip is removed from the movie project.

✔ Tip

- When you delete a clip, it is no longer available for use in the movie project.

To add clips to a movie

1. Drag the clip you want to add from the clip shelf to the clip viewer (**Figure 81**) When you release the mouse button, the clip appears in the clip viewer (**Figure 82**).
2. Repeat step 1 until all clips you want to include in the movie have been added to the clip viewer (**Figure 83**).

✔ Tip

- To remove a clip from the clip viewer without deleting it from the movie project, drag it back to the clip shelf.

To add transitions between clips

1. Click the Transitions button at the bottom of the clip shelf to display the Transitions pane (**Figure 84**).
2. Click to select the transition you want to use. A preview of the transition appears in the Preview area at the top of the Transitions pane (**Figure 85**).
3. Use the slider to set the speed of the transition. The Preview area shows the results of your change.
4. Drag the transition into position in the clip viewer (**Figure 86**). When you release the mouse button, it appears in the clip viewer (**Figure 87**).
5. Repeat steps 2 through 4 for each transition you want to add. **Figure 88** shows what the clip viewer window might look like with several transitions added.

✔ Tip

- Transition effects enable you to make smoother changes from one movie scene to another.

To preview a movie

1. Choose Edit > Select None (**Figure 80**), or press ⌘D.
2. Click the Play button at the bottom of the the iMovie monitor (**Figure 78**).

   The movie plays in the iMovie monitor window, from the beginning to the end.

✔ Tip

- To play only part of a movie, in the clip viewer, select the clips and transitions you want to play. You can hold down ⌘ while clicking each item to select more than one. Then click the Play button.

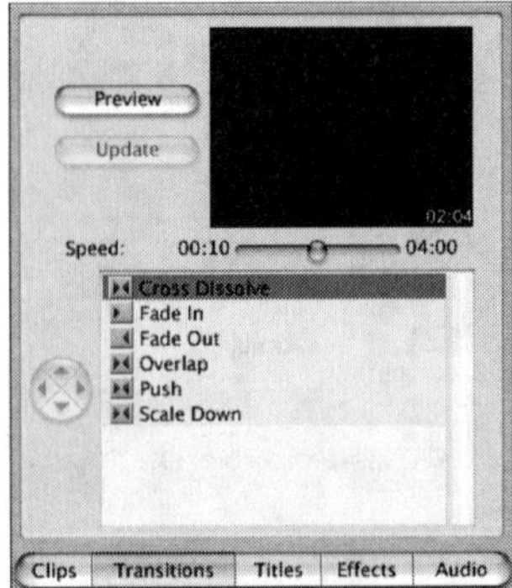

Figure 84 The Transition pane.

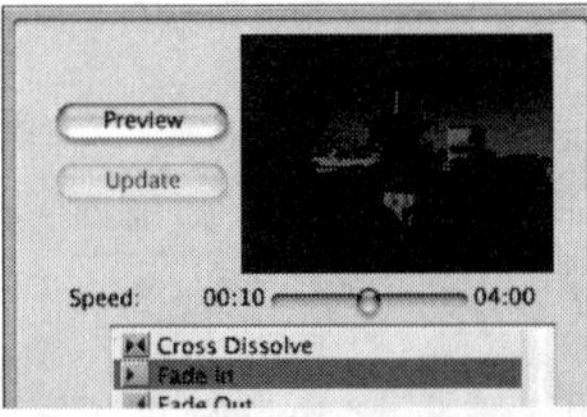

Figure 85 When you select a transition, you can watch a preview in the top of the Transition pane.

Figure 86 Drag the transition into position in the clip viewer.

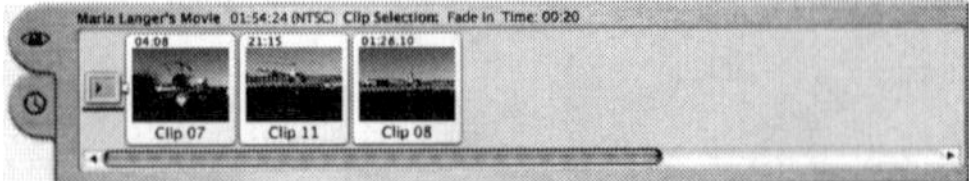

Figure 87 The transition appears in the clip viewer.

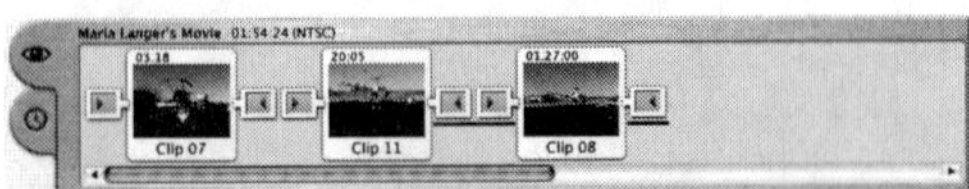

Figure 88 Here's an example with several transitions added to the clip viewer.

Figure 89 Choose Export Movie from the File menu.

✓ To Camera
To QuickTime™
For iDVD

Figure 90 The Export pop-up menu offers three options.

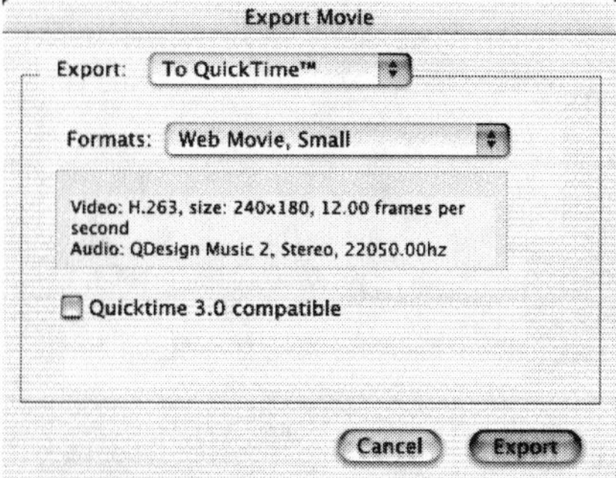

Figure 91 The Export Movie dialog with QuickTime export options displayed.

✓ Web Movie, Small
Email Movie, Small
Streaming Web Movie, Small
CD-ROM Movie, Medium
Full Quality, Large
Expert...

Figure 92 The Formats pop-up menu enables you to choose a format appropriate for how you plan to use the movie.

Figure 93 Use this dialog to save the movie.

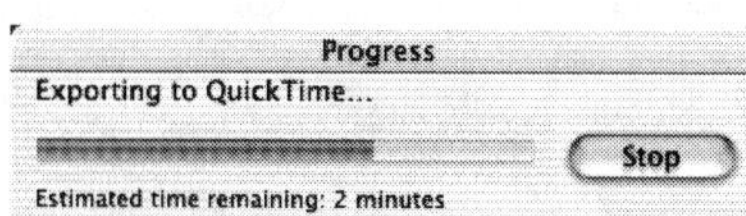

Figure 94 A Progess dialog like this one appears while the movie is being exported.

To export a movie project as a QuickTime movie

1. Choose File > Export Movie (**Figure 89**), or press ⌘E.
2. In the Export Movie dialog that appears, choose To QuickTime™ from the Export pop-up menu (**Figure 90**) to display QuickTime export options (**Figure 91**).
3. Choose an appropriate option from the Formats pop-up menu (**Figure 92**).
4. To make the movie compatible with QuickTime version 3, turn on the QuickTime 3.0 compatible check box.
5. Click Export.
6. Use the Export QuickTime™ Movie dialog that appears (**Figure 93**) to enter a name and select a disk location for the movie. Then click Save.

   iMovie exports the movie. As it works, a Progress dialog like the one in **Figure 94** appears. When the Progress dialog disappears, the export is finished.

✓ Tip

- Once you have exported your movie project as a QuickTime movie, you can open and view it in QuickTime Player (**Figure 95**). Simply double-click the movie's icon. I tell you more about QuickTime Player in **Chapter 6**.

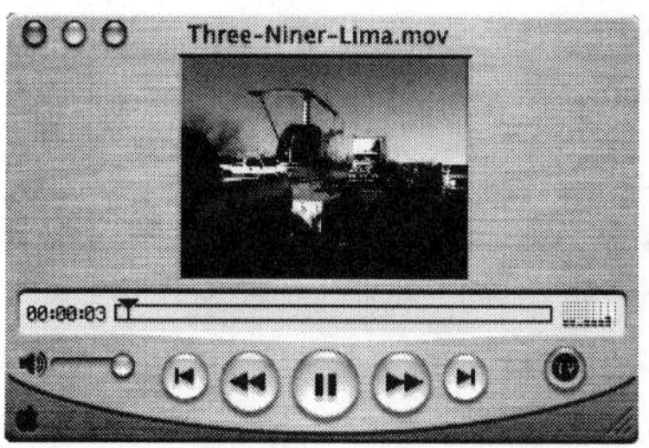

Figure 95 A movie viewed with QuickTime Player.

To export a movie project for use with iDVD

1. Choose File > Export Movie (**Figure 89**), or press [⌘ ⌘][E].
2. In the Export Movie dialog that appears, choose For iDVD from the Export pop-up menu (**Figure 90**) to display iDVD export settings (**Figure 96**).
3. Click Export.
4. Use the Export QuickTime™ Movie dialog that appears (**Figure 93**) to enter a name and select a disk location for the movie. Then click Save.

   iMovie exports the movie. As it works, a Progress dialog like the one in **Figure 94** appears. When the Progress dialog disappears, the export is finished.

✔ Tips

- Movies exported for iDVD are exported as QuickTime movies with specific settings that work with iDVD.
- I explain how to use iDVD next.

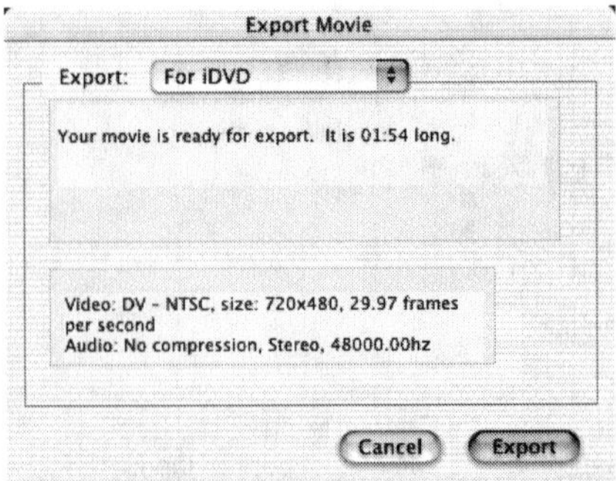

Figure 96 The Export Movie dialog with For iDVD chosen from the Export pop-up menu.

iDVD

iDVD gives you the ability to create DVD discs. It enables you to do the following:

- Add movies created with iMovie.
- Add slideshows of still pictures, with or without a soundtrack.
- Create professional-looking menus that include motion and sound.
- Preview and burn a DVD.

On the next few pages, I explain how to get started using iDVD, including how to choose a menu theme, add movies and slide shows, preview your DVD, and burn a DVD disc.

✔ Tips

- To use iDVD and burn DVD discs, your Macintosh must have a SuperDrive or be connected to compatible DVD writer hardware.
- You can learn more about the system requirements for iDVD at Apple's iDVD Web site, `www.apple.com/idvd/`.

To prepare & organize media for use with iDVD

1. In the Finder, create a folder to store all media that will be used in your DVD.
2. Drag or save media files to the folder you created.

✔ Tips

- iDVD can work with the following types of media:
  - ▲ **Movies** should be saved as digital video movies in QuickTime format. You can use iMovie's export command to save movies for iDVD as discussed earlier in this chapter.
  - ▲ **Pictures** should be sized at 640 x 480 pixels and saved in JPEG (.jpg) or TIFF (.tif or .tiff) format. iPhoto can export to both of these formats.
  - ▲ **Sounds** should be saved in QuickTime, AIFF, or MP3 format. iTunes can save music in MP3 format, as discussed earlier in this chapter.
- Although you don't have to organize iDVD media in advance, it'll make creating your DVD easier if you do.
- You can further organize your iDVD media by including folders within the folders. **Figure 97** shows an example.

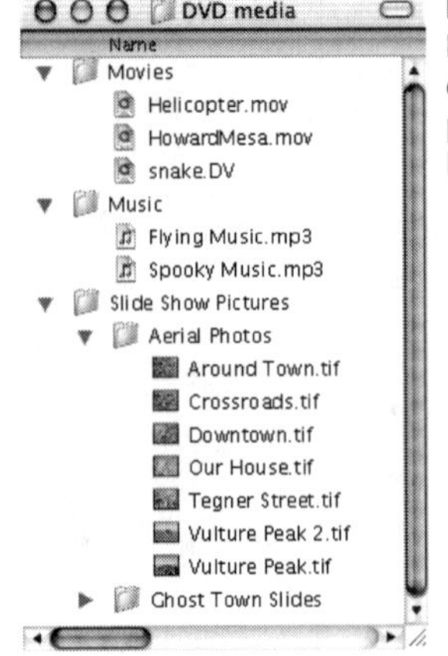

Figure 97 Here's an example of media organized prior to creating a DVD.

Figure 98 The iDVD application icon.

Figure 99 iDVD's welcome window.

Figure 100 Use this dialog to name and save your iDVD project.

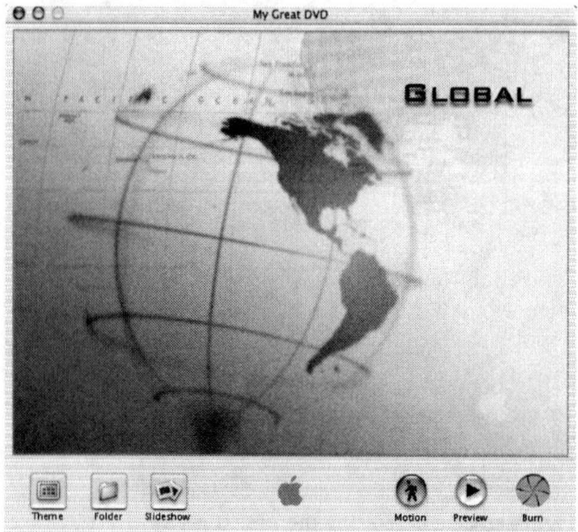

Figure 101 iDVD's default menu window displays a theme.

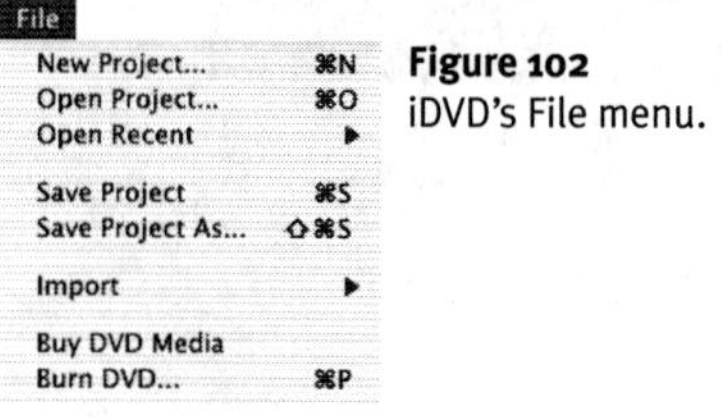

Figure 102 iDVD's File menu.

To launch iDVD

1. Open the iDVD icon (**Figure 98**) in your Applications folder. (It may be inside the iDVD 2 folder).

   If you have already used iDVD, it opens and displays its windows for the last DVD you worked on. Skip the remaining steps.

2. If this is the first time you're running iDVD, an intro window like the one in **Figure 99** appears. Click New Project.

3. Use the Save New Project As window that appears (**Figure 100**) to enter a name and select a location for your iDVD project file. Then click Create.

   iDVD's menu window appears (**Figure 101**).

✔ Tips

- iDVD documents are called *iDVD projects*.
- If you have already created an iDVD project and want to start a new one, choose File > New Project (**Figure 102**), or press [⌘ N]. Then follow step 3 above to name and save your new project.
- To work with an existing iDVD project, either click Open Project in the intro window (**Figure 99**) or choose File > Open Project (**Figure 102**). Then use the dialog that appears to locate and open your iDVD project file.

To choose a theme

1. Click the Theme button at the bottom of the iDVD window (**Figure 101**) to slide out the Theme drawer.
2. If necessary, click the Theme tab to display its options (**Figure 103**).
3. Click the preview for the theme you want to use for your DVD. The menu window changes to display your selected theme (**Figure 104**).

✔ Tip

- Some themes include animation and sound. If you find this distracting as you work, click the motion button at the bottom of the menu window to quiet things down.

To rename the main menu

1. Select the main menu text (**Figure 105**).
2. Enter the text you want to appear in the main menu (**Figure 106**) and press Return.

✔ Tip

- You can use this technique to change any menu text, including the text that appears under buttons.

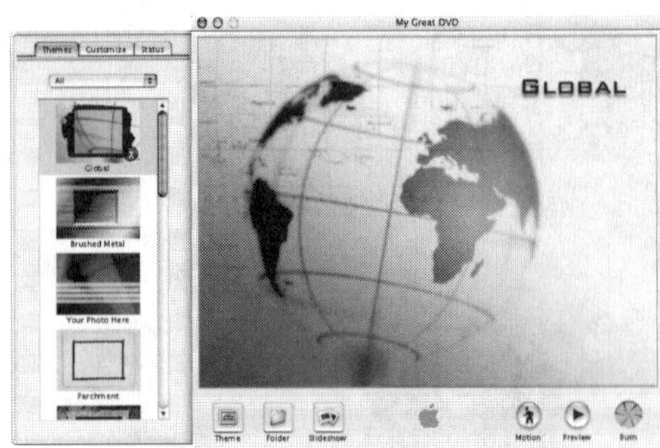

Figure 103 When you click the Theme button, the Theme drawer slides out.

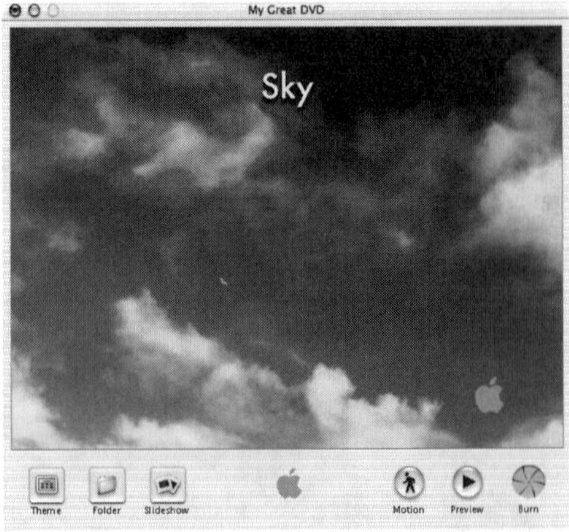

Figure 104 The theme you select is applied to the menu window.

Figure 105 & 106 Editing menu text is as simple as selecting it (above), typing in new text (below), and pressing Return.

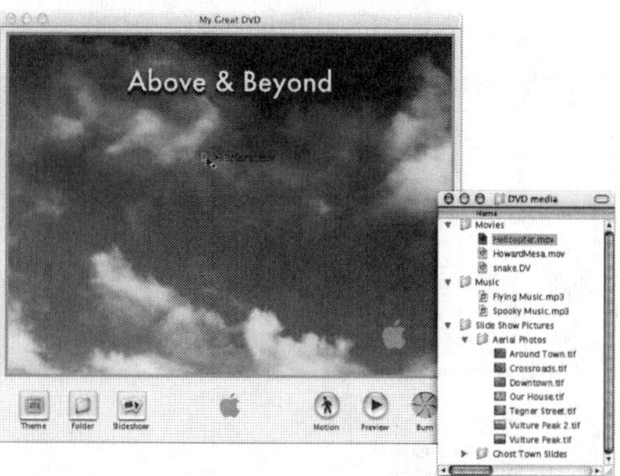

Figure 107 Drag the icon for the movie you want to add from the Finder window to iDVD's menu window.

Figure 108 A button for the movie appears.

Figure 109 When you click the Slide Show button, a button for your slide show appears in the menu window.

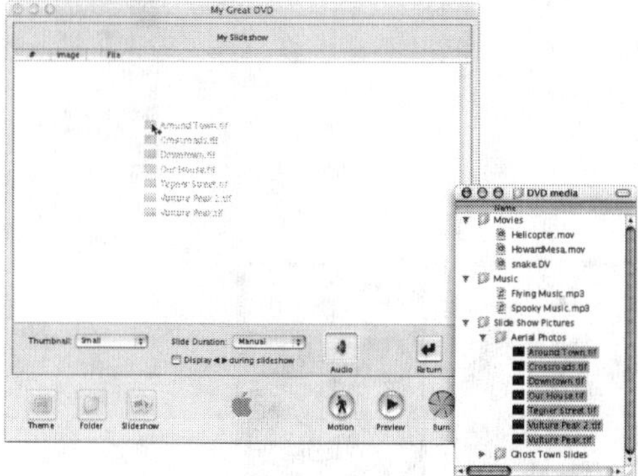

Figure 110 Drag the icons for the pictures you want in your slide show from the Finder window to iDVD's slide show window.

To add a movie

Drag the icon for the movie from the Finder window to iDVD's menu window (**Figure 107**).

When you release the mouse button, the movie appears as a button in the menu window (**Figure 108**).

To add a slide show

1. Click the Slide Show button at the bottom of the menu window.
2. A slide show button appears in the menu window (**Figure 109**). Double-click it to open the slide show window.
3. Drag the icons for the pictures you want to include in the slide show from the Finder window to iDVD's slide show window (**Figure 110**).

   When you release the mouse button, thumbnails of the images appear in the slide show window (**Figure 111**).
4. Click the Return button to return to the main menu window.

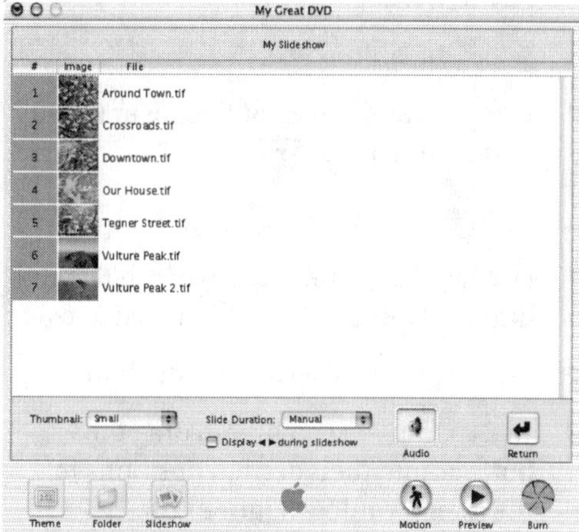

Figure 111 Thumbnails for the images appear in the slide show window.

To customize the appearance of buttons

1. If the Themes drawer is not already showing, click the Themes button to display it.
2. Click the Customize tab to display its options (**Figure 112**).
3. Make changes to settings in the Button area as desired:
   - ▲ Choose a shape from the button shape pop-up menu (**Figure 113**).
   - ▲ Choose a text position from the Position pop-up menu (**Figure 114**).
   - ▲ Choose a text typeface from the Font pop-up menu. (This menu lists all of the fonts properly installed in your system.)
   - ▲ Choose a text color from the Color pop-up menu (**Figure 115**).
   - ▲ Use the slider to change the size of the text.

   Your changes take affect immediately (**Figure 120**).

To rename a button

1. Select the button text.
2. Enter the text you want to appear in the button and press Return.

To move buttons

1. Display the Customize tab of the Themes drawer (**Figure 112**) as instructed above.
2. Select the Freely position radio button.
3. Use your mouse pointer to drag the buttons into their desired positions in the menu window (**Figure 120**).

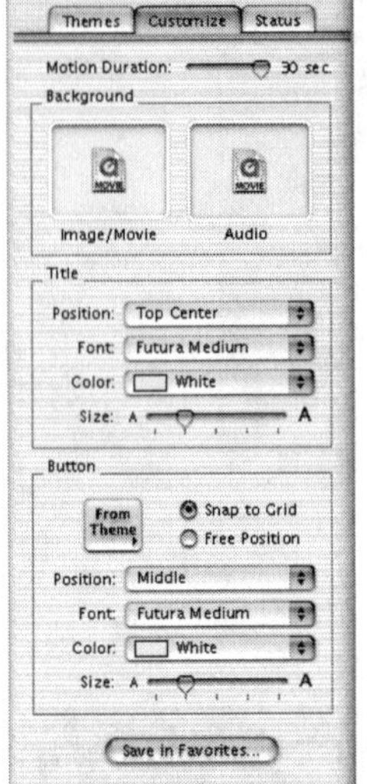

Figure 112 The Customize tab of the Themes drawer.

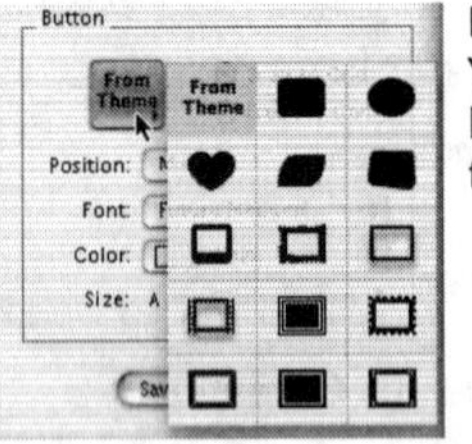

Figure 113 You can choose a button shape from this pop-up menu.

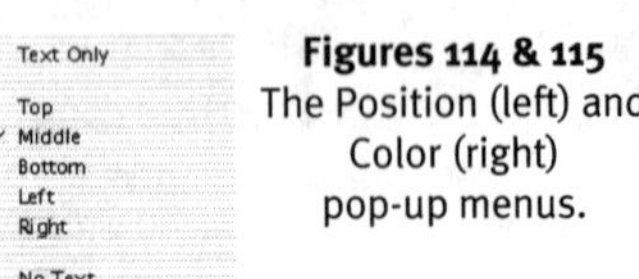

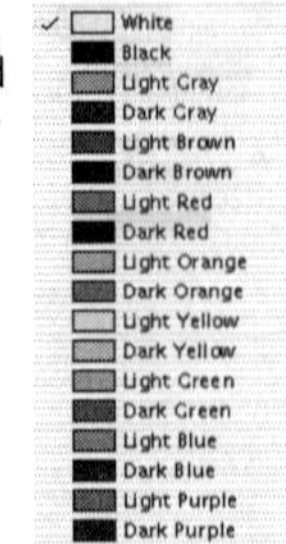

Figures 114 & 115 The Position (left) and Color (right) pop-up menus.

Figures 116 & 117 Select the movie's button to display the slider (left), then slide the tab until the image you want to appear is displayed (right).

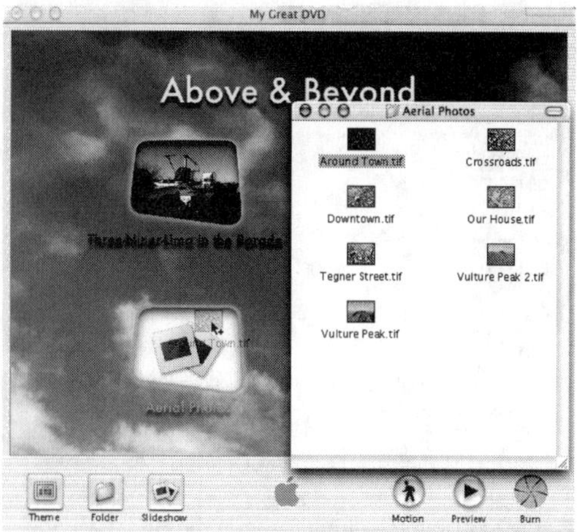

Figure 118 Drag the image from the Finder window to the button on which you want it to appear.

Figure 119 The image appears on the button.

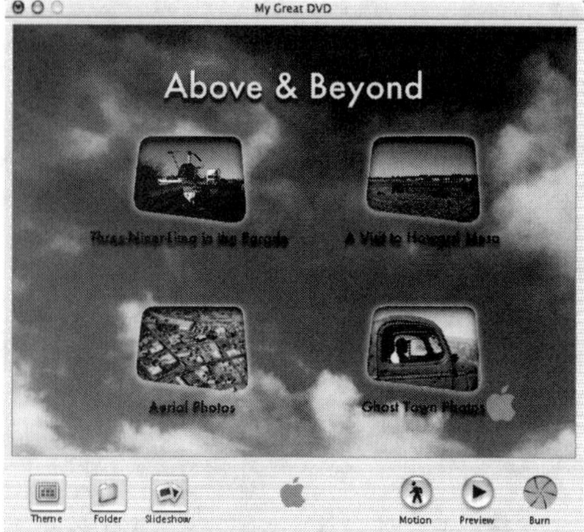

Figure 120 Here's an example of a menu customized using techniques on these two pages.

To display a specific frame on a movie button

1. If necessary, follow the instructions on the previous page to choose a button shape that displays an image.
2. Click the movie's button. A slider appears above it (**Figure 116**).
3. Drag the slider until the frame you want to appear is displayed (**Figures 117** and **120**).

✔ Tip

- To display a still image rather than a looping animation from the movie, turn off the Movie checkbox (**Figure 116** or **117**).

To display a specific image on a slideshow button

1. If necessary, follow the instructions on the previous page to choose a button shape that displays an image.
2. Drag the icon for the picture you want to display on the button from the Finder window to the button (**Figure 118**).

   When you release the mouse button, the picture appears on the button (**Figures 119** and **120**).

To add music to a slide show

1. Double-click the button for the slide show to which you want to add music to open the slide show window.
2. Drag the icon for the music file from the Finder window to the Audio well in the Slide Show window (**Figure 121**).

   When you release the mouse button, the icon for the audio file appears in the Audio well and the Slide Duration pop-up menu is set to Fit To Audio (**Figure 122**).
3. Click the Return button to return to the menu window.

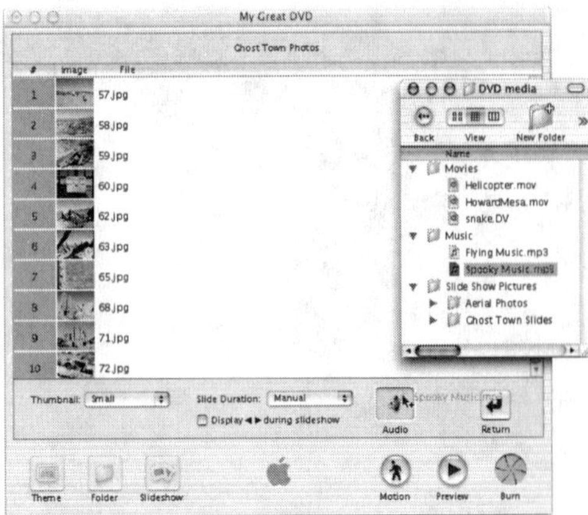

Figure 121 Drag the audio file from the Finder window to the Audio well in the slide show window.

Audio well

Figure 122 An icon for the audio file appears in the Audio well.

To preview the DVD

1. Click the Preview button at the bottom of the menu window.
2. A DVD player control appears and one of the buttons becomes selected (**Figure 123**). Click buttons on the control to simulate running the DVD from a DVD player.
3. When you are finished trying out the DVD, click the Preview button again to return to editing mode.

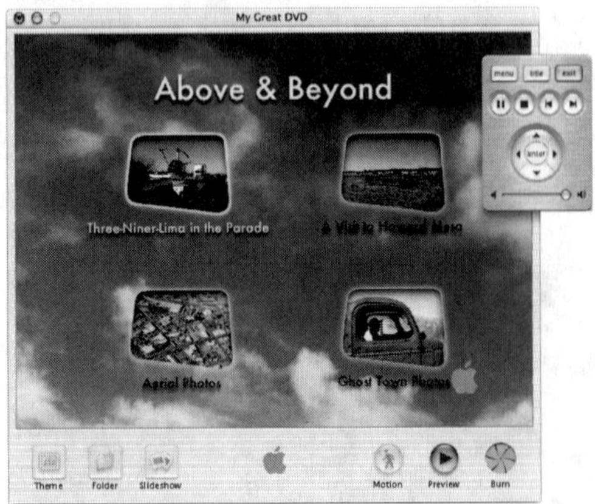

Figure 123 The Preview feature simulates a DVD player.

✔ Tip

- You can also use the arrow keys and [Return] to select and choose DVD menu items while Previewing a DVD.

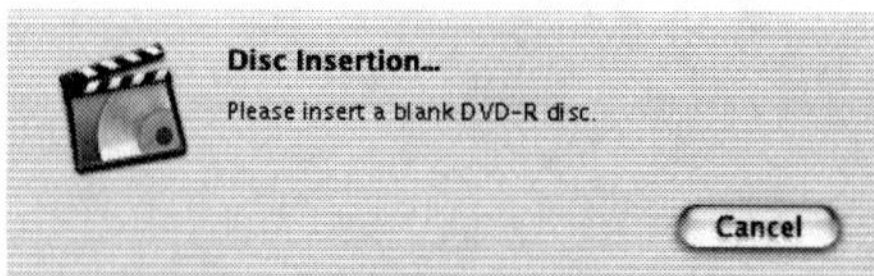

Figure 124 A dialog like this prompts you to insert a blank DVD-R disc.

To burn a DVD disc

1. If you disabled the Motion feature while you worked with iDVD, click the Motion button to enable it.
2. Click the Burn button at the bottom of the menu window.
3. The burn button pulsates black and yellow. Click it again.
4. A dialog appears, telling you to insert a blank DVD-R disc (**Figure 124**). Insert the disk and close the disk tray.
5. After a moment, the dialog is replaced with a progress dialog. It tells you what iDVD is doing and how much time the operation will take. Wait until the disc burning process is complete.
6. When the process is complete, the DVD disc is ejected. A dialog appears, telling you to insert a blank DVD-R disc if you want to create another DVD. Click Done.

✔ Tip

- If you cancel the disc burning process before it is finished, the disc may be rendered unusable.

AppleScript Basics

12

AppleScript

AppleScript is the scripting language that comes with Mac OS X. It enables you to automate tasks and extend the functionality of Mac OS X.

You use AppleScript's Script Editor application to write small programs or *scripts* that include specially worded *statements*. When you run a script, the script can send instructions to the operating system or applications and receive messages in return.

For example, say that at the end of each working day, you back up the contents of a specific folder to a network disk before you shut down your computer. The folder is large and the network can be slow, so you often have to wait ten minutes or more to shut down the computer when the backup is finished. You can write a script that mounts the network drive, backs up the folder, and shuts down your computer automatically. You simply run the script, turn out the lights, and go home. AppleScript does the rest.

As with most programming languages, AppleScript can be extremely complex—far too complex to fully cover in this book. In this chapter, I'll provide some basic information about using Script Editor, examining the example scripts that come with Mac OS X, and using Script Runner. This introduction should be enough to help you decide whether you want to fully explore the world of AppleScript programming.

✔ Tips

- AppleScript statements are converted by Mac OS into *Apple events*—messages that can be understood by the operating system and applications.
- You can find a lot more information about AppleScript, including tutorials, sample scripts, and a reference manual, at Apple's AppleScript Web site, `www.apple.com/applescript/`.
- Peachpit Press offers a number of books that cover AppleScript. Check its Web site, `www.peachpit.com`, for a complete list of titles.

AppleScript Files

There are three types of AppleScript files (**Figure 1**):

- **Script text files** are text files containing AppleScript statements. They can be opened with Script Editor or any text editor applicaton and can be run from within Script Editor. Double-clicking a script text file icon launches Script Editor or the text editing application in which it was created.
- **Compiled scripts** are completed scripts that can be launched from an application's script menu or the Applet Launcher. Double-clicking a compiled script icon launches Script Editor.
- **Applets** or **script applications** are full-fledged applications that can be launched by double-clicking their icons.

✔ Tip

- In most cases, you will create compiled scripts.

Figure 1 An AppleScript file as a script text file (left), an applet (middle) and a compiled script (right).

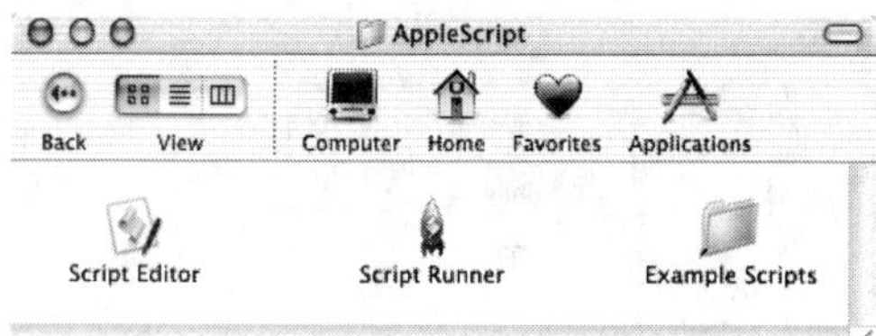

Figure 2 The contents of the AppleScript folder.

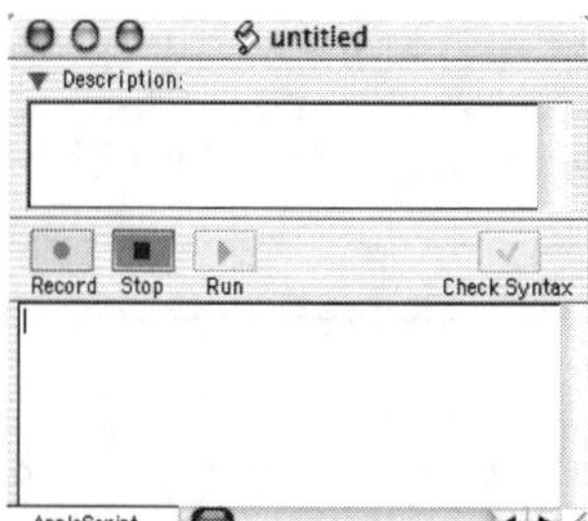

Figure 3 A new, untitled Script Editor window.

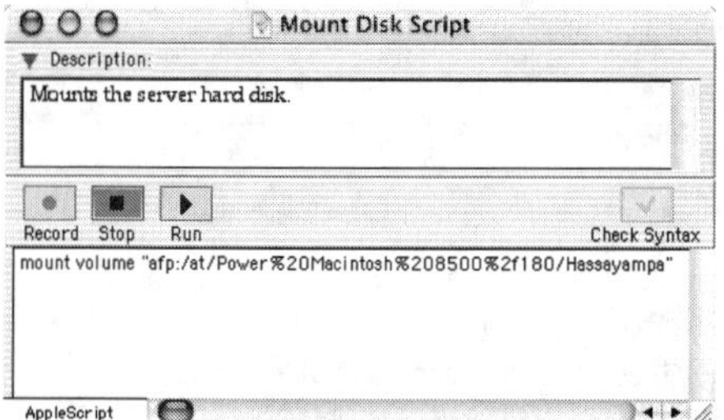

Figure 4 An extremely simple script in a Script Editor window.

Script Editor

Script Editor is an application you can use to write AppleScript scripts. It has a number of features that make it an extremely useful tool for script writing:

- The Script Editor window can automatically format script statements so they're easy to read.
- The syntax checker can examine your script statements and identify any syntax errors that would prevent the script from running or compiling.
- The Open Dictionary command makes it possible t view an application's dictionary of AppleScript commands and classes.
- The record script feature (when it works) can record actions as script steps.
- The Save and Save As commands enable you to save scripts as script text files, compiled scripts, and applets.

✔ Tip

- As this book went to press, AppleScript 1.8.1 did not support recording scripts in the Mac OS X 10.1.3 Finder. In fact, I couldn't find any application it would work with.

To launch Script Editor

Open the Script Editor icon in the AppleScript folder in your Applications folder (**Figure 2**). An untitled Script Editor window appears (**Figure 3**).

or

Open the icon for a compiled script (**Figure 1**, right). The script appears in a Script Editor window (**Figure 4**).

To write a script

1. If necessary, choose File > New Script (**Figure 5**)or press [⌘ ⌘N] to open an empty Script Editor window (**Figure 3**).
2. If desired, type a description for the script in the Description box.
3. Type the script steps in the bottom half of the window. Be sure to press [Return] after each line. **Figure 6** shows an example of another simple script.

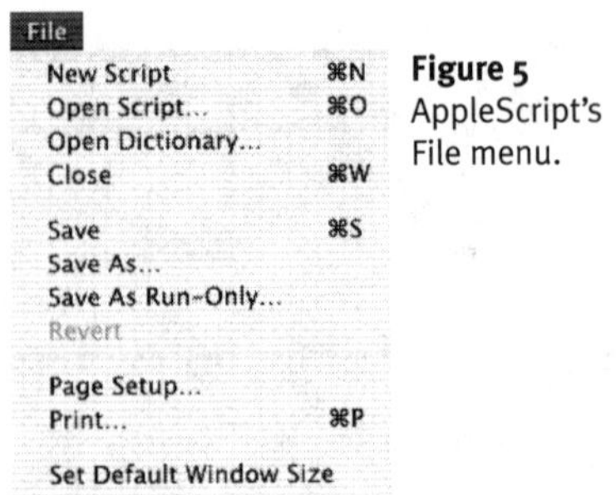

Figure 5 AppleScript's File menu.

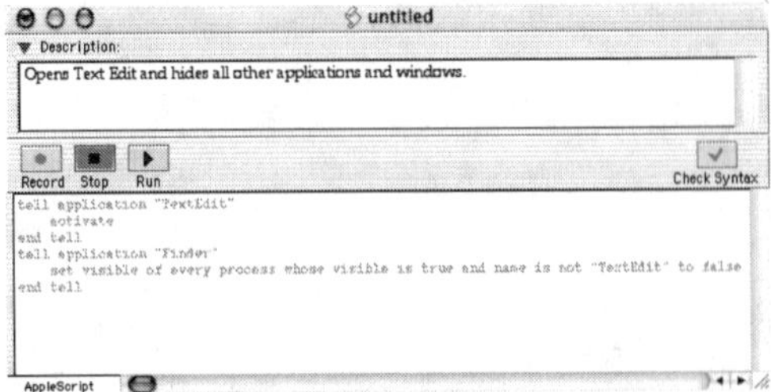

Figure 6 Another simple script.

To check the syntax for a script

Click the Check Syntax button in the script window (**Figure 6**).

If your script's syntax is error-free, Script Editor formats and color-codes your statements (**Figure 7**).

or

If Script Editor finds a problem with your script, it displays a dialog that describes the problem and indicates where it is in the script by selecting it (**Figure 8**). Click Cancel to dismiss the dialog and fix the problem.

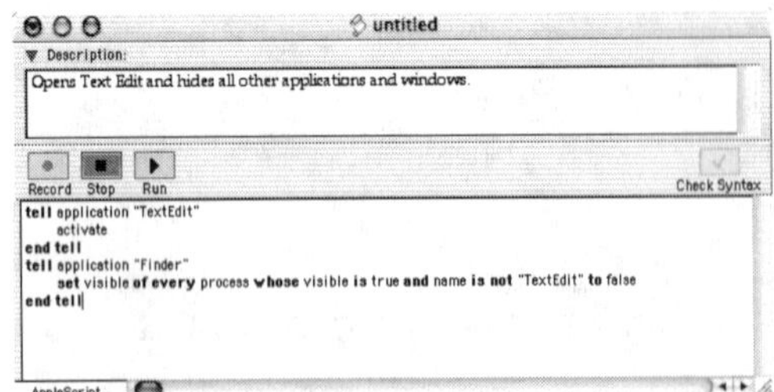

Figure 7 If your script's syntax is okay, Script Editor formats it for you, making it easier to read.

✔ Tips

- The syntax checker attempts to *compile* the script, which translates it into *code* that can be read and understood by your computer. (Compiled code does not appear on screen.) If the script cannot be compiled, a syntax error results.
- Unfortunately, even if you write a script without any syntax errors, the script is not guaranteed to work. The only way to make sure a script works is to run it.

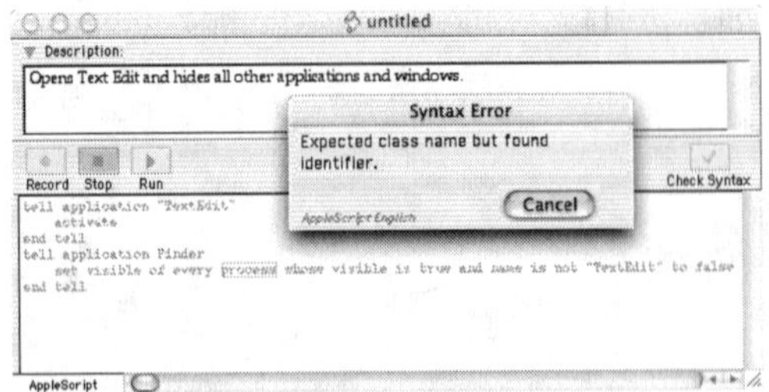

Figure 8 If your script's syntax has a problem, Script Editor displays a cryptic note to explain what it is. In this example, Script Editor had a problem with the word *process* in the second to the last line. But the problem was a direct result of me removing the double quote characters from around the word *Finder* in the previous line. As you can imagine, writing and debugging scripts requires a good knowledge of AppleScript!

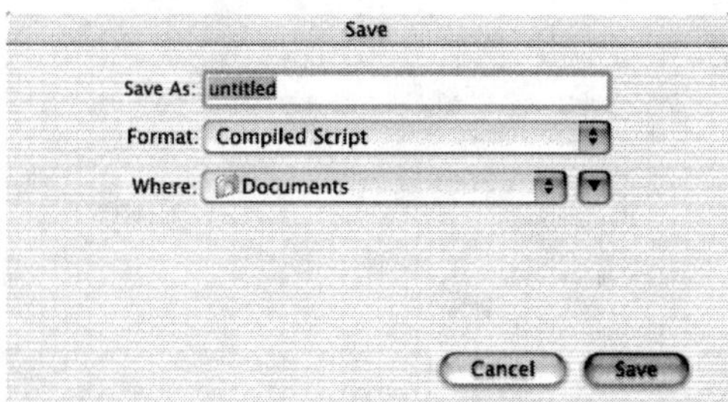

Figure 9 The Save dialog includes a menu you can use to set the format of the file you are saving.

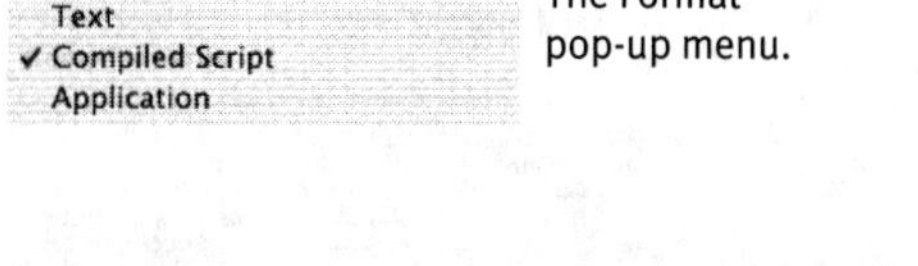

Figure 10 The Format pop-up menu.

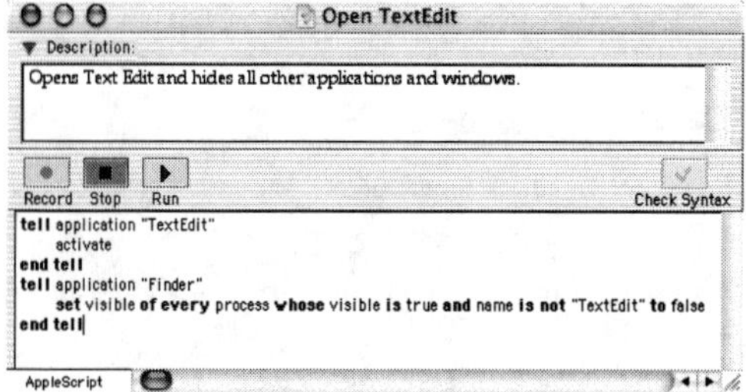

Figure 11 The name of the script file appears in the title bar.

Figure 12 An example of an error message.

To save a script

1. Choose File > Save or press [⌘ S] to display the Save dialog (**Figure 9**).
2. Enter a script name in the Save As box.
3. Choose a file format from the Format pop-up menu (**Figure 10**).
4. Use the Where part of the dialog to select a location in which to save the file.
5. Click Save. The file is saved on disk. The script name appears in the title bar of the Script Editor window (**Figure 11**).

✓ Tips

- You cannot save a script if it will not compile. Check the script syntax before attempting to save the file; I explain how on the previous page.
- If you're not sure what to choose in step 3, choose Compiled Script.
- It's a good idea to save a script before trying to run it for the first time.
- Using the Save Location dialog is covered in **Chapter 5**.

To run a script

Do one of the following:

- ◆ To run a compiled script from within Script Editor, click the Run button in the Script Editor window (**Figure 11**).
- ◆ To run an applet from the Finder, double-click the icon for the applet (**Figure 1**, middle).

If the script is valid, it performs all script commands.

or

If the script is not valid, an error message appears (**Figure 12**). Click Stop to stop the script.

AppleScript Dictionaries

Scriptable applications include *AppleScript dictionaries*, which list and provide syntax information for valid AppleScript commands and classes. These dictionaries are a valuable reference for anyone who wants to write scripts.

An AppleScript dictionary is organized into *suites*. Each suite includes a number of related *commands* and *classes*. Commands are like verbs—they tell an application to do something. Classes are types of objects that a command can be performed on. For example, in TextEdit's Standard Suite, *close* is a command that can be performed on an object such as *window*.

Figures 14 and **15** show examples of AppleScript Dictionaries for two applications: Finder and TextEdit. In each illustration, the first suite is selected to display all commands and classes in that suite. On the left side of the window, suite names appear in bold text, commands appear in normal text, and classes appear in italic text.

✔ Tip

- Although dictionaries are helpful for learning valid AppleScript commands, they are not sufficient for teaching a beginner how to write scripts.

To consult an application's AppleScript dictionary

1. Choose File > Open Dictionary.
2. In the Open Dictionary dialog that appears (**Figure 13**), select a dictionary and click Open. The dictionary opens in its own window (**Figures 14** and **15**).
3. Click the name of a suite, command, or class to display its information in the right side of the window.

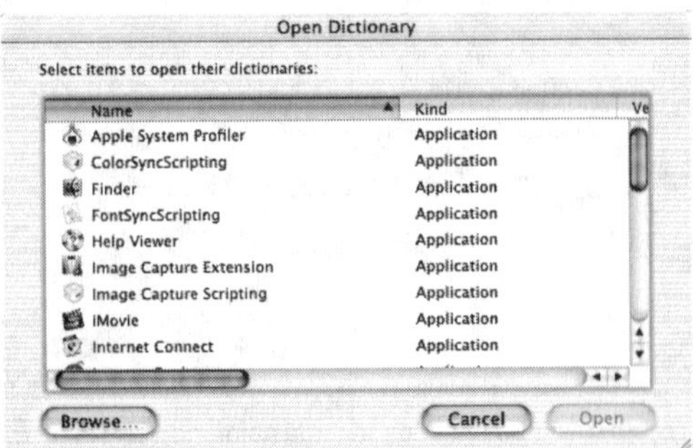

Figure 13 The Open Dictionary dialog.

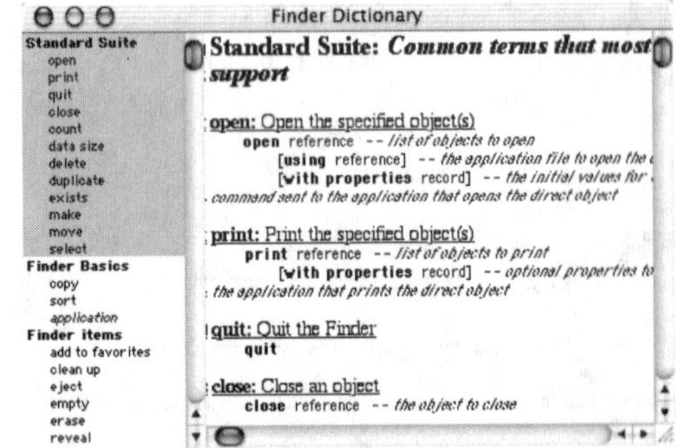

Figures 14 & 15 The AppleScript Dictionaries for Finder (above) and TextEdit (below).

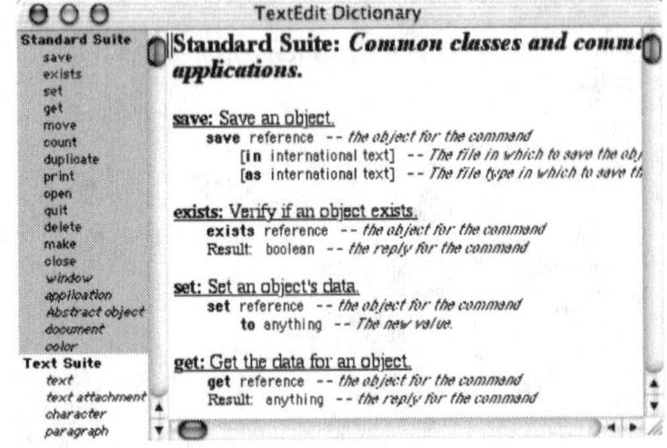

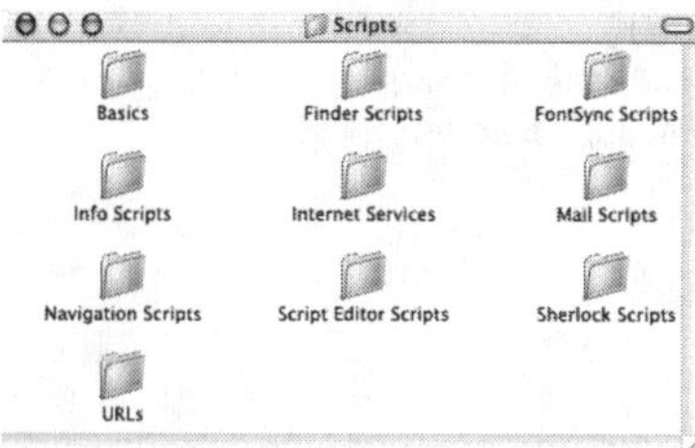

Figure 16 Double-clicking the Example Scripts alias icon opens the Scripts folder.

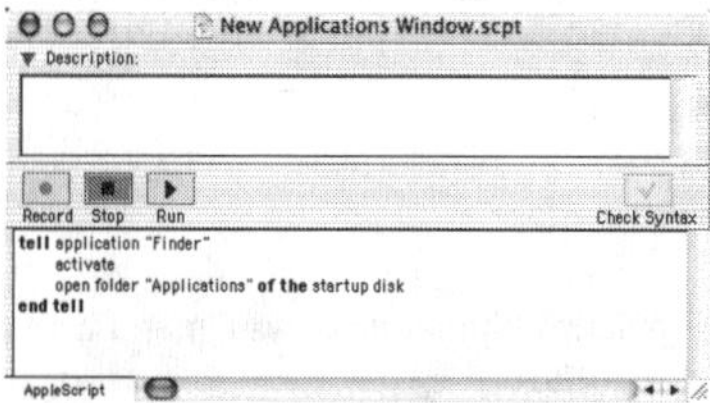

Figure 17 Some scripts can be simple, like this one to open a folder, ...

Figure 18 ...while others can be complex, like this one, which accesses the Internet to get the current temperature at your location. (A thermometer outside your window would be simpler.)

Example Scripts

The AppleScript folder within your Applications folder (**Figure 2**) includes an alias called Example Scripts. Double-clicking this alias opens the Scripts folder (**Figure 16**) inside the Library folder. This is where you can find example scripts that you can explore to learn more about scripting. You can also use many of these scripts as they are or modify them for your own use.

To examine an example script

Double-click the example script file's icon to open it in Script Editor (**Figures 17** and **18**).

✔ Tips

- You can modify and experiment with these example scripts as desired.
- If you make changes to an example script, I highly recommend that you use the Save As command to save the revised script with a different name or in a different location. Doing so will keep the original example intact, in case you want to consult it again.
- You can download additional sample scripts from Apple's AppleScript Web site, `www.apple.com/applescript/`.

Script Runner

Script Runner is an application that puts a tiny Script Runner button in a floating palette on your desktop (**Figure 19**). Click the button to display a menu with submenus of compiled scripts (**Figure 20**). This makes it easy to run compiled scripts without launching Script Editor.

Figure 19 Script Runner appears as a floating palette.

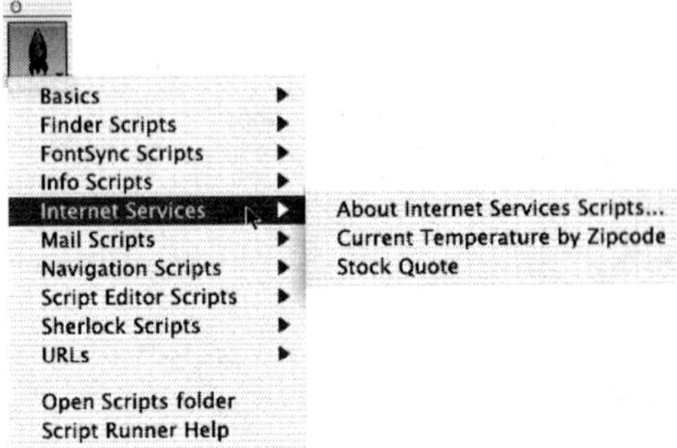

Figure 20 Clicking Script Runner displays a menu with submenus full of scripts.

✔ Tip

- Do the submenu names in Script Runner's menu (**Figure 20**) look familiar? They should. They correspond to the folder names in the Scripts folder (**Figure 16**). And the scripts on each submenu correspond to the scripts within each folder.

To launch Script Runner

Open the Script Runner icon in the AppleScript folder in your Applications folder (**Figure 2**). The Script Runner palette appears (**Figure 19**).

To run a script from Script Runner

Choose the name of the script you want to run from the appropriate submenu on Script Runner's menu (**Figure 20**).

To add a script to Script Runner

Move or copy the file icon for a compiled script into the appropriate folder within the Scripts folder (**Figure 16**) in the Library folder.

✔ Tips

- You can quickly open the Scripts folder by choosing Open Scripts Folder from Script Runner's menu (**Figure 20**).
- You can create submenus within Script Runners menu by adding folders to the Scripts folder (**Figure 16**).

To quit Script Runner

Click Script Runner's close button (**Figure 19**). Script Runner disappears.

Getting Help

Getting Help

Mac OS offers two basic ways to get additional information and answers to questions as you work with your computer:

- **Help Tags** identify screen items as you point to them. This help feature is supported by many (but not all) applications.
- **Apple Help** uses the Help Viewer application to provide information about using Mac OS and Mac OS X applications. This Help feature, which is accessible through commands on the Help menu, is searchable and includes clickable links to information.

This chapter explains how to get help when you need it.

✔ Tip

- Balloon Help and Guide Help, which were available in Mac OS 9.x and earlier, are no longer available in Mac OS X. You can still find them in applications running in the Classic environment.

Help Tags

Help Tags identify screen elements that you point to by providing information in small yellow boxes (**Figures 1, 2,** and **3**).

✔ Tips

- Help Tags replace the Balloon Help feature available in Mac OS 9.x and earlier versions of Mac OS.
- Help tags are especially useful when first starting out with a new software application.

To use Help Tags

Point to an item for which you want more information. If a Help Tag is available for the item, it appears after a moment (**Figures 1, 2,** and **3**).

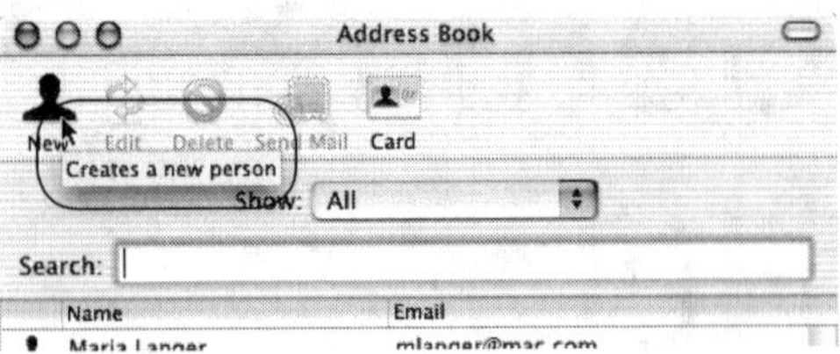

Figure 1 A Help Tag in the Address book main window, ...

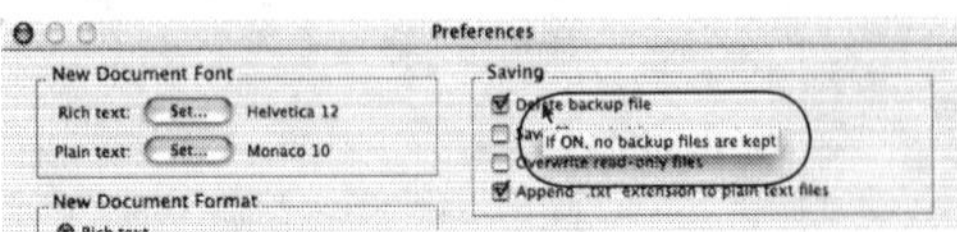

Figure 2 ...in the TextEdit Preferences window, ...

Figure 3 ...and in the Mac Help window.

Apple Help

Apple Help uses the Help Viewer application to display information about Mac OS or a specific application. It includes several features that enable you to find information—and use it—quickly:

- **Quick Clicks** (**Figures 6a** and **6b**) offers links to answers for frequently asked questions.
- **Search feature** enables you to search for topics containing specific words or phrases.
- **Links to related information** enable you to move from one topic to a related topic.
- **Links to applications** enable you to open an application referenced by a help topic.
- **Links to online information** enable you to get the latest information from Apple's Web site.

✔ Tips

- Although this feature's generic name is Apple Help, help windows may display the name of the application that help is displayed for.
- You can find additional support for Mac OS, as well as Apple hardware and software, on Apple's Support Web site, `www.apple.com/support/`.

To open Apple Help

Choose Help > *Application Name* Help (**Figures 4a**, **4b**, and **4c**), or press ⌘?.

or

Choose Help from a contextual menu (**Figure 5**).

or

Click the Help button in a window or dialog in which it appears (**Figure 6a**).

The main Help window (**Figures 6a** and **6b**) or help topic (**Figure 6c**) appears.

✔ Tip

- Using contextual menus is covered in **Chapter 2**.

Figures 4a, 4b, & 4c The Help command on Help menus for the Finder (top), Address Book (middle), and TextEdit (bottom).

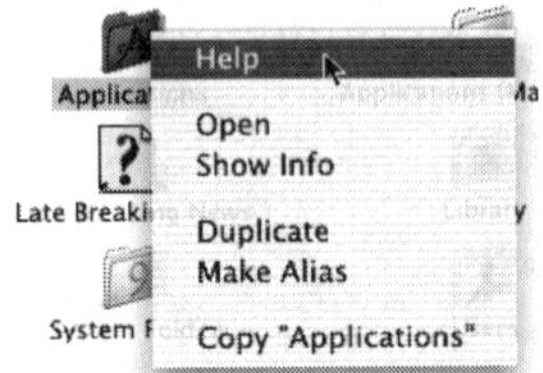

Figure 5 The Help command can also be found on some contextual menus.

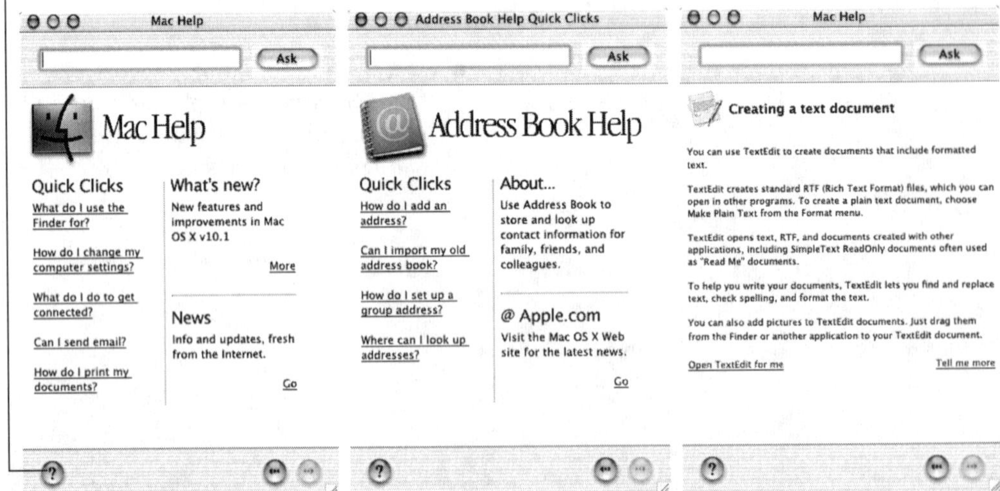

Figures 6a, 6b, & 6c These are the main Help windows for the Finder (left) and Address Book (middle). TextEdit's main Help window (right) is also a help topic, providing information in addition to links.

Figure 7 Enter a search word or phrase in the field at the top of the Help window.

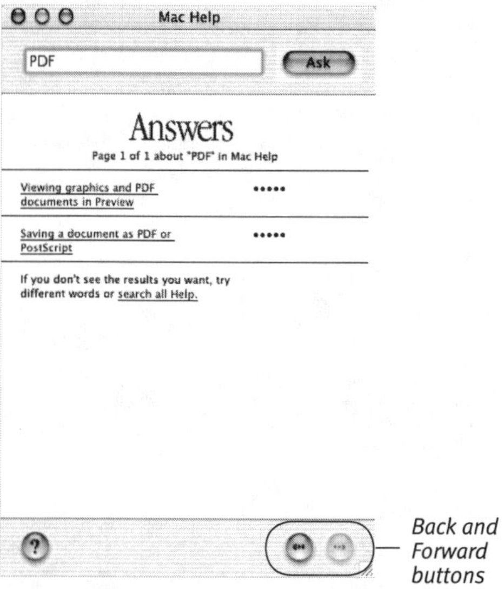

Figure 8 When you click Ask, a list of topics matching the search criteria appears.

Figure 9 Clicking a link displays information as a Help topic.

To search Help

1. Enter a search word or phrase in the entry field at the top of the Help window (**Figure 7**).
2. Click Ask.
3. After a moment, the Help window fills with a list of search results (**Figure 8**). Click an underlined link to display information about the topic in a window (**Figure 9**).

✔ Tips

- The asterisks to the right of a topic name in the Search Results list indicate how well the topic matches your search criteria. The more asterisks, the more relevant the item.
- You can click the Back and Forward buttons to move backward and forward through Help windows (**Figure 8**).
- The search results window may include a link to automatically search all Help files for your search criteria (**Figure 8**). Clicking this link may display more search results.
- The Help topic window may include links for opening one or more applications (**Figure 9**).

Application Help

Many applications include extensive online help. The help features of various applications may look and work differently, so it's impossible to cover them in detail here. Most online help features, however, are easy to use.

Help
Search Word Help
Word Help Contents
Additional Help Resources
Use the Office Assistant
Downloads and Updates
Visit the Mactopia Web Site
Send Feedback on Word

Figure 10
The Help menu in Microsoft Word X offers a number of commands for getting onscreen help from within Microsoft Office or on the Microsoft Web site.

✔ Tips

- Some applications, such as the Microsoft Office suite of products, include an entire online manual that is searchable and printable.
- Not all applications include online help. If you can't locate an online help feature for an application, check the documentation that came with the application to see if it has one and how you can access it.

To access an application's online help

Choose a command from the Help menu within that application (**Figure 10**).

or

Click a Help button within a dialog.

Help & Troubleshooting Advice

Here's some advice for getting help with and troubleshooting problems.

- **Join a Macintosh user group.** Joining a user group and attending meetings is probably the most cost-effective way to learn about your computer and get help. You can find a users' group near you by consulting the Apple User Group Web site, www.apple.com/usergroups/ or by calling 1-800-538-9696 (in the US only).
- **Visit Apple's Web site.** If you have access to the Web, you can find a wealth of information about your computer online. Start at www.apple.com/support/ and search for the information you need.
- **Visit the Web sites for the companies that develop the applications you use most.** A regular visit to these sites can keep you up to date on updates and upgrades to keep your software running smoothly. These sites can also provide technical support for problems you encounter while using the software. Learn the URLs for these sites by consulting the documentation that came with the software.
- **Visit Web sites that offer troubleshooting information.** Ted Landau's MaxFixIt (www.macfixit.com) and Ric Ford's MacInTouch (www.macintouch.com) are two excellent resources.
- **Read Macintosh magazines.** A number of magazines, each geared toward a different level of user, can help you learn about your computer: *Macworld, Mac Addict,* and *Mac Home Journal* are the most popular. Stay away from PC-centric magazines; the majority of the information they provide will not apply to your Macintosh and may confuse you.

Menus & Keyboard Equivalents

A

Menus & Keyboard Equivalents

This appendix illustrates all of Mac OS X's Finder menus and provides a list of corresponding keyboard equivalents.

To use a keyboard equivalent, hold down the modifier key (usually ⌘) while pressing the keyboard key for the command.

Menus and keyboard commands are discussed in detail in **Chapter 2**.

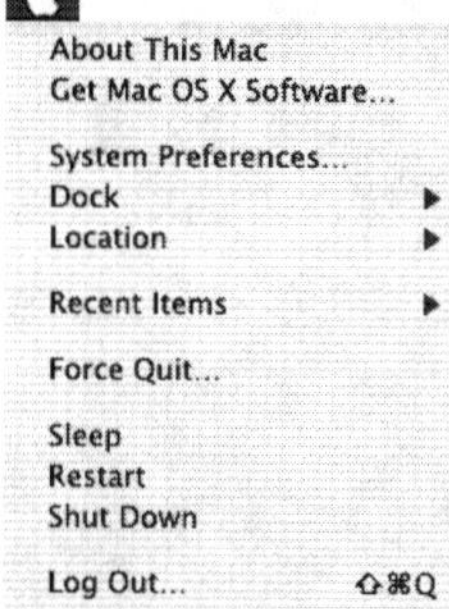

Apple Menu

Shift ⌘ Q	Log Out
Option ⌘ D	Dock > Turn Hiding On/Off

Finder
About the Finder
Preferences...
Empty Trash ⇧⌘⌫
Services
Hide Finder ⌘H
Hide Others
Show All

Finder Menu

Shift ⌘ Delete	Empty Trash
⌘ H	Hide Finder

File Menu

Shortcut	Command
⌘ N	New Finder Window
Shift ⌘ N	New Folder
⌘ O	Open
⌘ W	Close Window
Option ⌘ W	Close All
⌘ I	Show Info
⌘ D	Duplicate
⌘ L	Make Alias
⌘ R	Show Original
⌘ T	Add To Favorites
⌘ D	Move To Trash
⌘ E	Eject
⌘ F	Find

File	
New Finder Window	⌘N
New Folder	⇧⌘N
Open	⌘O
Close Window	⌘W
Show Info	⌘I
Duplicate	⌘D
Make Alias	⌘L
Show Original	⌘R
Add to Favorites	⌘T
Move to Trash	⌘⌫
Eject	⌘E
Burn Disc...	
Find...	⌘F

Edit Menu

Shortcut	Command
⌘ Z	Undo
⌘ X	Cut
⌘ C	Copy
⌘ V	Paste
⌘ A	Select All

Edit	
Can't Undo	⌘Z
Cut	⌘X
Copy	⌘C
Paste	⌘V
Select All	⌘A
Show Clipboard	

View Menu

Shortcut	Command
⌘ B	Show/Hide Toolbar
⌘ J	Show/Hide View Options

View	
✓ as Icons	
as List	
as Columns	
Clean Up	
Arrange by Name	
Hide Toolbar	⌘B
Customize Toolbar...	
Show Status Bar	
Show View Options	⌘J

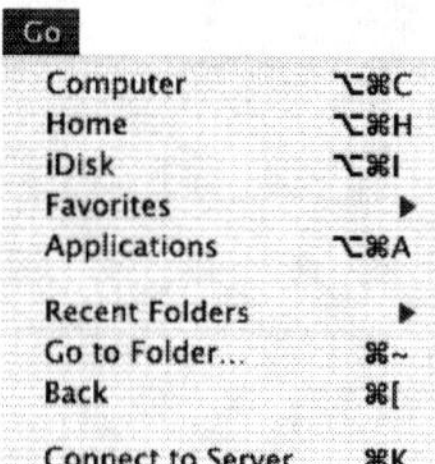

Go Menu

Option ⌘ C	Computer
Option ⌘ H	Home
Option ⌘ I	iDisk
Option ⌘ F	Favorites > Go To Favorites
Option ⌘ A	Applications
⌘ ~	Go To Folder
⌘ [	Back
⌘ K	Connect To Server

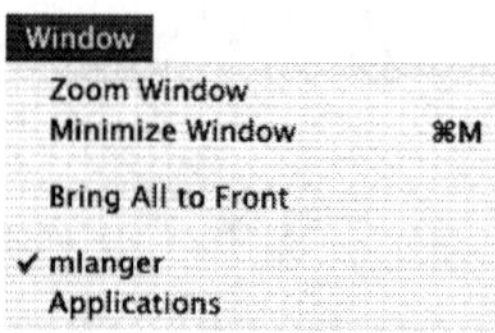

Window Menu

⌘ M	Minimize Window

Help Menu

⌘ ?	Mac Help

iTools

Figure 1 This version of the iTools Home Page appears if you are not logged in to iTools.

iTools

Although this book concentrates on the software that comes with Mac OS X, it wouldn't be complete without at least a brief mention of iTools.

iTools is a group of free Internet-based services offered by Apple Computer, Inc. to Mac OS 9.x and Mac OS X users:

- **iCards** enables you to send greeting cards to anyone with an e-mail address.
- **Email** gives you an e-mail address ending with @mac.com.
- **HomePage** lets you create and publish a custom Web site hosted on Apple's Web server.
- **iDisk** gives you 20 MB of hard disk space on Apple's server for saving or sharing files.

The next two pages explain how to sign up for and log in to iTools.

✔ Tips

- The Internet is covered in detail in **Chapter 9**.
- You can learn more about iTools at `itools.mac.com` (**Figure 1**).
- iTools features are relatively easy to use, with step-by-step instructions and lots of online help.
- iDisk is discussed in detail in *Mac OS X Advanced: Visual QuickPro Guide*.

To sign up for iTools

1. Launch your Web browser and use it to view `itools.mac.com` (**Figure 1**).
2. Click the Sign Up button.
3. Enter the requested information in the iTools Provide your information window that appears (**Figure 2**).
4. Click the Continue button at the bottom of the page.
5. Write down (or print) the information in the iTools Save for your records window that appears (**Figure 3**). It includes your member name and password, along with information you'll need to set up your e-mail software for using mac.com for e-mail.
6. Click Continue.
7. The iTools Announce your new email address window appears next (**Figure 4**). You can use this window to send iCards to your friends to tell them about your mac.com e-mail address.
   - ▲ To send an iCard with your mac.com e-mail address to friends, enter a friend's e-mail address in the Recipient's e-mail field and click Add to list. Repeat this process for each person you want to add to the list. Then click Send iCard.
   - ▲ To skip sending an iCard with your mac.com e-mail address, click No Thanks.
8. A Congratulations window appears next (**Figure 5**). It tells you that you have been successfully set up for iTools. Click Start using iTools.

Figure 2 Fill in this form to sign up for an iTools account.

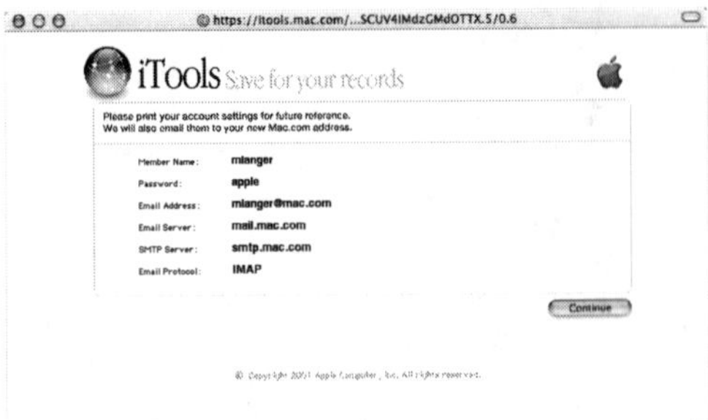

Figure 3 You'll need this information to log in to iTools and to set up your e-mail program to access your mac.com e-mail account.

Figure 4 You can use this handy form to send an iCard to friends to tell them about your new e-mail address.

Figure 5 This window appears when the sign-up process is complete.

To log in to iTools

1. Launch your Web browser and use it to view `itools.mac.com` (**Figure 1**).
2. Click the Login button.

   or

   Click a link for any of the iTools members only features.
3. The iTools Login window appears (**Figure 6**). Enter your User Name and Password in the appropriate fields, and click Enter.

   or

   If you do not have an account, click the Sign Up button and follow steps 3 through 8 on the previous page to sign up for iTools.

   The main iTools window appears (**Figure 7**) or the main window for the feature you clicked a link for appears (**Figure 8**).

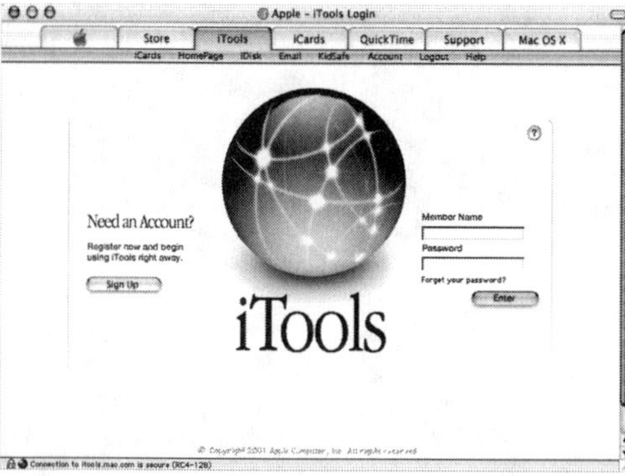

Figure 6 The iTools Login window.

Figure 7 The iTools Home page looks like this when you're logged in.

Figure 8 The Email main window.

Index

D

E

F

G

H

INDEX

P

Q

R

S

T